Frameworks for International Co-operation

Frameworks for International Co-operation

Edited by
A.J.R. Groom and Paul Taylor

Pinter Publishers, London

© The Editors and Contributors 1990

First published in Great Britain in 1990 by
Pinter Publishers Limited
25 Floral Street, London WC2E 9DS

Paperback edition first published in 1994

British Library Cataloguing in Publication Data

A CIP catalogue record for this book is available from the
British Library
ISBN 0 86187 537 0
ISBN 185567 240 5 Pb

Typeset by Witwell Ltd, Southport
Printed and bound in Great Britain by SRP Ltd., Exeter

For Helen and Esther

Contents

Tables

Contributors

George A. Codding, Jr, is a Professor in the Department of Political Science and Director of the International Affairs Program at the University of Colorado in the United States. Professor Codding has written extensively in the fields of international organization, international telecommunications policy, and the politics of Western Europe.

A.J.R. Groom is Professor of International Relations and Director of the Centre for Conflict Analysis at the University of Kent at Canterbury. He has written widely on strategic and conflict studies, international organization and international relations theory. His most recent book is *The Study of International Relations: Then and Now* with William C. Olson.

R.J. Harrison taught International Politics at Victoria University of Wellington from 1957 to 1967, and was a well-known broadcaster and television commentator on international affairs in New Zealand. He was Senior Lecturer at Lancaster University until 1989, and Professor of Politics at Mercyhurst College, Pennsylvania from 1988 to 1989. In 1990 he is Adjunct Professor of International Relations at Limerick University. He has published widely on European government, European Community politics, and integration theory.

Alexis Heraclides is currently research scholar at the Mediterranean Studies Foundation, Athens and attached to the Greek Foreign Ministry as an expert on humanitarian affairs. He has participated in several intergovernmental organizations and conferences dealing with issues of human rights and minorities, and has written about a dozen articles on various aspects of national minorities and separatism as well as on specific ethnic antagonisms and conflict resolution, notably on the Arab-Israeli conflict. He is author of *The Self-Determination of Minorities in International Politics,* London, Frank Cass, 1989.

John Kinnas has taught as Associate Professor, International Relations, with the Athens Pantios University. He is currently with the Greek Foreign Service in Geneva (Mission to the United Nations). His academic interests centre on international organization and the analysis of foreign policy. He has published extensively in Greece and abroad. His latest publication in Greek (1987) covers the subject of *Nuclear Power and Global Responsibility.*

Stuart Mungall graduated from Lancaster University, and took a postgraduate degree at Manchester University. He later entered the Civil Service, and is currently an investment consultant with a leading City firm.

Gunnar P. Nielsson was born in Denmark and is presently Assistant Professor of International Relations at the University of Southern California. He specializes in European international politics and international organizations with special focus on the United Nations, the European Community and Scandinavian regional co-operation. He is co-editor (with Randolph C. Kent) of *The Study and Teaching of International Relations,* London, Frances Pinter, 1980, and has contributed several book chapters on the sociology of nationalism. He is presently working on a case study of United Nations' mediation in the 1982 Falklands/Malvinas crisis and a book on the role of nationalism and state-formation in contemporary world politics.

Mihály Simai became Director of the Institute of World Economy of the Hungarian Academy of Sciences in 1988. He has also worked for the United Nations, and for the Hungarian Investment Bank. His most recent books are *Power, Technology and Global Co-operation,* 1985, and *The U.N. Today and Tomorrow, 1985.*

Paul Taylor is Senior Lecturer in International Relations at the London School of Economics. He has written on the European Community, international organization and integration theory. He has edited five other books with A.J.R. Groom, and his book on *The Limits of European Integration* was published in 1983.

Roger Tooze is Principal Lecturer in International Relations at Staffordshire Polytechnic. He has also taught at the London School of Economics, the University of Southern California and the University of Keele. His publications are mainly in the field of international political economy and he is the Editor (with Craig Murphy) of the forthcoming *The New International Political Economy.*

Peter Willetts is a Senior Lecturer in International Relations at City University. He has written on a variety of aspects of international organizations and international relations theory. He has published two books on the Non-Aligned Movement, one on non-governmental organizations and several chapters on the United Nations in books edited by others. He also edited, with R.J.B. Jones, a book on interdependence.

Foreword

In 1988 we published a volume of essays on *International Institutions at Work*. As its title suggests, this is essentially an empirical work. *Frameworks for International Co-operation* is intended to complement our previous work by providing a survey of theoretical approaches to international co-operation. We have identified three different, but not necessarily contradictory, thrusts in the theoretical literature: that which entails an adjustment within the existing state system; attempts to rebuild the existing state system in a more appropriate form; and an expansion beyond the bounds of any existing or refurbished state system. In this framework we draw upon a book of essays published over a decade ago. However, we, and our contributors, many of whom are the same, have been surprised and delighted to observe the degree to which there has been theoretical innovation and progress in recent years. We see more clearly now, if still not enough, than before.

Any collective enterprise such as this owes much to the goodwill, the experience and the intellect of the contributors. We have been fortunate on all three counts and for this, as editors, we are exceedingly grateful. And we are also dependent upon the skill and professionalism, not to mention the hard work, of our secretarial colleagues Elizabeth Dorling and the Rutherford College office in Canterbury, and Elizabeth Leslie in London.

To all our academic and secretarial colleagues we offer our thanks. We have learned a great deal because of their work and it is our hope and expectation that, through them, our readers too will be able to do so.

A.J.R. Groom
Paul Taylor
December 1989

Part I

Introduction

1 The setting in world society

A.J.R. Groom

Frameworks for International Co-operation is a book of political recipes. We are exploring various ways in which scholars can conceptualize and practitioners can undertake international co-operation in the broadest sense of those terms. By 'international' we mean far more than inter-state or inter-government, and by 'co-operation' we mean relationships that are not overtly or structurally coercive. Put more positively, our concern is with legitimized relationships between different actors in world society. What are the techniques that may be used and the frameworks that are appropriate for taking advantage of opportunities or overcoming difficulties in contemporary world society? While we range far beyond the traditional ambit of diplomacy, no book of recipes is ever complete. Nevertheless, our threefold categorization of adjustment processes within the existing state system, approaches to rebuilding the state system, and conceptions that go beyond the state system, provide ample ingredients for practitioners and scholars to exercise their political imagination.

We wish to show the central thrust of different approaches rather than to draw up detailed blueprints. We highlight their distinctive features in order to make a point. But obviously it is our judgement that some approaches share common elements so that they form three broad categories focusing upon 'within', 'rebuilding' and 'going beyond' the existing state system. However, this can result in some rough justice. Concepts and practice do not fall neatly into an academic typology and we acknowledge that ours is not the only way of approaching this range of theories, and that some may be placed in more than one category.

Our conceptualization does, however, give a context to the activities of practitioners and provides them with an opportunity of learning from the experience of others. Theory is an intellectual mapping exercise which tells us where we are now, from where we have come and to where we might go. The scale of the map can vary from the detail of local Ordnance Survey maps to the very small scale of a child's globe. And different projections show us different worlds so that we may find what we are looking for in the sense that we impose meaning on 'facts' rather than their speaking for themselves. There is a sense in which one can be pragmatic, but behind every 'pragmatic' approach lies a theory or a conceptualization — no matter how inchoate. All social activity requires choice and that choice cannot be exercised without some criteria for judgement — in short, a theory, a conception, a framework. Conceptual thought therefore provides a context for practitioners so that they might have a better knowledge of themselves and what they are about. We hope that this volume contributes to this discovery.

The development of international organization

Europe, and more especially what is now called Western Europe, began to impose itself upon the rest of the world in the fifteenth century with the voyages of Portuguese, Spanish, Dutch, French and British explorers. They created an incipient world system which required a degree of organization. Some of this was provided coercively in the form of empires and it was a process that was not completed until after the 'scramble for Africa' and the Berlin Congress of 1885, or perhaps even the attribution of mandates by the League of Nations following the dismemberment of the German and Ottoman Empires. This degree of organization was neither international nor co-operative in any substantive sense. There was an often formal recognition of the activities of others, but this did not constitute much more than a division of spheres of coercive and imperial influence rather than a genuine international enterprise on the basis of co-operative behaviour freely undertaken in full knowledge of the facts. Moreover, it did not necessitate international institutions.

It was the Industrial Revolution that speeded up the process, thereby giving rise not only to international organization but also to international institutions. By international organization we mean the growth of a structure that enables world transactions to take place, be they economic, political, social or cultural. Such a structure must be able to fulfil four functions, at least to a minimal level. It must have the means to receive and impart communications both endogenously and exogenously; it must be able to integrate its subunits; it must have some conception of loyalty to the whole — a notion of what constitutes 'we'; and, finally, it must have enough self-knowledge, and therefore some form of collective memory about shared values and common interpretation of experiences, to be able to set goals. Without these it will not be able to sustain itself. Whether it should be sustained is a separate question. How it can sustain itself varies over time and is a function of the particular context. The context we are examining is that of the growth of a Eurocentric world system during the last half-millennium. One of the means of doing this has been through international institutions. This is particularly the case if we are concerned with co-operative ventures.

International institutions are worthy of study in themselves since they may have an independent or autonomous impact on the processes which they facilitate. This is especially the case if they are service organizations actively performing functions rather than forum organizations in which norms, principles and policies are discussed. Institutions are also important in that they are the visible sign of a process at work in which there is the transmission of goods, services, ideas or people. They may not be the most important part of this process, like the tip of the iceberg, but they are an indicator of a process and a starting-point for its discovery and analysis, indeed, for its manipulation.

Such institutions began to grow in both number and variety in the nineteenth century as a world economy came into being and with it a world social space. While some institutions, such as the Concert system, reflected an attempt to manage the balance of power in an acceptable and bearable manner, others had as their goal the promotion of a more positive peace in the form of international co-operation. Their *modus operandi* was functional in that there was a task to be performed on a free, fully knowledgeable and largely acceptable basis. Their rationale was not simply to reflect the balance of coercive forces. An early example was the Rhine River Commission which brought together the riparian states of that river so that the river could be utilized to the benefit of all as a single unit. The growth of trade from the Agrarian and Industrial Revolutions meant that international standards were necessary to facilitate international intercourse — weights, measures, time, distance. Economic institutions in the form of international markets and the concomitant financial instruments likewise became necessary. Professional bodies, as well as interest groups, began to emerge on an international basis. The Anti-Slavery League is a case in point, first seeking to abolish the slave trade and then the institution itself. Parallel to the development of political institutions for the management of power politics, other frameworks for international co-operation emerged. Both were a reflection of a new attitude of mind.

This attitude emerged in Europe as both cause and effect of the breakup of the feudal system. It is exemplified by the Renaissance, the Reformation, the growth of capitalism, the voyages of exploration, the Enlightenment and the French Revolution. It is the growth, first, of the idea that the physical and social environment is amenable to analysis, not just as a reflection of divine law or natural law, but as a precondition for the manipulation of that environment. If the 'laws' of nature and society could be understood, then they could be used to harness nature and to change society. The application of rationality and scientific method to natural and social phenomena would enable us, if not to change the world, at least to influence it. Thus we became more competent, and with competence came a sense of confidence that as our ability to understand grew, so, *pari passu,* would our ability to influence others. The notion of social engineering became widespread, in particular in the outlook and practice of Europeans.

Social engineering on a world scale for co-operative purposes emerged as an important factor in the late nineteenth century. It was the philosophical starting-point of working men in the socialist internationals and of the liberal bourgeoisie in Britain, France, the United States, Latin America and elsewhere, who joined together to promote the idea of a league of nations. Their notions were liberal, internationalist, progressive and radical. Working class and bourgeoisie alike wanted to change the world for the better, as they respectively conceived 'better', and they thought that they could do so by the creation and use of international institutions to build a new form of international structure or organization.

The growing momentum for organization and institutions reached a climax after the First World War. The war itself was proof enough that change was necessary if the liberal, bourgeois, internationalist world was to survive. The League of Nations was not just an institution for the management of political disputes, disarmament and collective security, in which by the 1930s it had failed; it was also to be a framework for 'positive' peace. This was to be accomplished in a variety of ways.

First, the founding fathers had a clear conception that both conflict and change were endemic in social life. While collective security and the like were to manage conflict so as to limit or eliminate its dysfunctionalities, peaceful change was to be promoted by bringing together the democratic representatives of the newly-freed nations of the world in open discourse to take advantage of opportunities to build a better world. This was a conscious attempt to promote political co-operation for change. However, functional ties were not neglected either.

The second strand of a policy of 'positive' peace had several elements. There were already in existence a number of international public unions which the League sought, rather unsuccessfully, to bring under its aegis. Bureaucratic rivalries, historical precedence and the need for functional specificity were among the reasons for the reluctance of such unions to 'join the League'. However, the League was not inhibited in creating new functional agencies. Most notable among the new agencies was the International Labour Organisation (ILO) in terms both of its role and of its membership. Its most obvious role was to set standards for the protection of working people and to collect and circulate information about the conditions of labour world-wide. But it also had a further role — that of binding the working class to a reformed capitalist system so that they would not be seduced by the Bolshevik revolution. One way of achieving this goal was to be found in the tripartite structure of the organization. Although states were members of the ILO, they were represented by three separate delegations: government, employers and unions (now management and labour). It was a major and successful experiment in functional representation but one that has not been followed in other institutions. Besides the ILO, the League developed bodies to promote intellectual co-operation, to protect refugees and women, to control drugs and to organize programmes of technical assistance and aid. In short, the foundations were laid for the UN system of Specialized Agencies and programmes.

The third way in which the League was to contribute to a working peace system was through the cultivation of a sense of international community. The purpose of the League was not to bring about world government or supranational integration — rather it was to be a 'league' or 'association' of 'nations'. By the word 'nation' was implied not only governments but peoples. However, apart from the ILO it was governments rather than peoples that ruled the roost in the League. Nevertheless, 'public opinion' in some countries did play an important role as the activities of the League of Nations Union in Britain attest.

In the dismissal of the League for its failure to provide effective collective security, there is often a lack of due recognition of the success of its functional aspects. Yet even as the war clouds gathered over Europe in 1938 and 1939, the Bruce Report on the League acknowledged the major contribution to international life of the functional institutions of the League, and there was no doubt that when the United Nations Organization was founded it would have a strong functional arm. Indeed, the Specialized Agencies each have their own membership, constitution, budget and secretariat. The League had not succeeded in establishing a system of positive peace or in forestalling the Second World War, but the functionalist strategy for creating a working peace system had received a vindication in the League experience as recognized in the Bruce Report and this was the starting-point for the UN system of agencies. But the League system and the UN agencies are only part of the story.

The twentieth century has seen a phenomenal growth of international institutions of all kinds: governmental and non-governmental, universal and regional, general and specific, service and forum, profit-making and non-profit-making as well as a myriad of 'hybrids'. They have increased at a rapid pace in number, membership and diversity. They constitute the basis for a network or a psychosocial community. To be sure, such a range of institutions can be used for the pursuit of coercive politics, but the network has great potential as a framework for co-operation. This potential is not used for such ends to the extent that it might be because institutions of all types frequently develop institutional needs which make networking difficult. These needs arise out of the growth of an institutional self-image, standard operating procedures and an institutional philosophy, together with a bureaucracy and clientele to defend them. Institutional hierarchies and hierarchies of institutions are vertical in philosophy and practice and thus not conducive to the more egalitarian ties of networks. Networks are not systems of command or decision, but of information, persuasion and facilitation. They bring an element of diversity and flexibility since they can grow and wither quickly because the linkage is essentially a consensual and a mental one — the psychology of belonging to the same community and being part of a network. It is not reinforced or preserved by hierarchy, bureaucracy, budgets or commands. Networks are a complement to more formal institutions; indeed, they are often part of such institutions, and they constitute an essential part of global organization.

Global organization is a recent phenomenon. A benchmark was reached in the 1960s when global problems began to supplement world problems (and opportunities). A global question is one in which all members and parts of the globe are necessarily affected, at least to some extent, whereas world issues, while of a widespread and general nature, do not necessarily penetrate to all corners of the globe. The Second World War is a typical example. It affected every continent, but South America to a lesser extent and with regard to a lesser range of issues. A nuclear war, on the other hand, would affect everyone whether a belligerent or not, for example, through nuclear winter. Moreover, the reach of modern weapons systems is global and immediate. Similarly the global economy must in effect be managed as a whole or we shall all be the worse off. The General Agreement on Tariffs and Trade (GATT), the International Monetary Fund (IMF), the International Bank for Reconstruction and Development (IBRD), the Organization for Economic Co-operation and Development (OECD) and the Group of Seven (g7) are all moving in this direction as non-members seek to become associated with these bodies. Smallpox had to be eradicated globally and AIDS will have to be treated in a like manner. World Weather Watch may tell us what we do not like, but it does so accurately because it is global. Communications, too, are global. Companies may be global. Social movements and fashions are becoming global. But above all, ecopolitics are necessarily global, whether they be about the greenhouse effect, the ozone layer, resource depletion, the destruction of the rainforest, or the population explosion. This gives a global aspect to politics that hard-nosed and hard-faced politicians have been forced to recognize. But it is more than this: there is also a globalization of personal politics. Notions of equity and justice, demands for identity and participation, concerns for security — both physical and economic — the need for economic development and the self-development of individuals and groups, and more, are ubiquitous in global society. Ecopolitics concerns far more than the environmental agenda: it is also about individuals, groups, processes and structures. The organizational needs are thus global and they involve far more than governments.They have gone beyond the state system.

International organization and international relations

The evolution of organization and institutions is very relevant to the study of international relations. And it has always been so. Indeed, international relations (IR) as a discipline has two direct forebears — international law and diplomatic history — which combined to give a prominence to international organization (IO) in the early days of the field. After some years in the doldrums there is now a significant resurgence of interest in IO.

The starting point of IR as a discipline can conveniently be taken as the establishment of a Chair at Aberystwyth immediately after the First World War. The naming of the Chair in honour of Woodrow Wilson illustrates the spirit of the times and the dominant influence on the new field. Although later castigated as 'Utopian' or 'idealist', the central intellectual thrust was, as we have seen, internationalist, progressive, rationalist, radical and activist. It was to change the world, not people, so that people could realize their full potential. This meant social engineering on a world scale with international institutions as major vehicles for social, economic and political transformation. Although in practice such endeavours were, in essence, state-centric, in aspiration they were not. The purpose was, through governments, to create conditions in which peoples might have a greater opportunity to participate, build and prosper in an international community. The means which were used can best be classified as adjustment theories since they involved changes in the inter-state structure, although not such as to undermine its essential nature. Sovereignty was attenuated, but not, ultimately, subverted, and the existing state system was deemed to be a satisfactory vehicle through which to conduct social relations.

As the world political climate changed with the rise of ultra-nationalist, fascist governments in Europe and elsewhere in the 1930s, and the active pursuit of power politics, so did the academic climate. Realism became the dominant approach until the 1960s. It stressed the state as actor, power politics in the ruthless pursuit of interest defined in terms of power, a hierarchy of states, competition for the survival of the fittest through war or coercive politics, *raison d'état,* while dismissing co-operative politics as power politics in disguise. It was predicated on the notions that life was essentially zero-sum in nature and that there was no underlying harmony of interests. However, neither international institutions nor ideas of social engineering were excluded thereby. Power politics could be managed and the balance of power made more secure while international institutions had a role in this process. However, such institutions were either a vehicle through which the dominant powers could impose their will or a battlefield in which the principal rivals would confront each other. The United Nations Organization, and especially the Security Council, were conceived in the context of the former function, but in fact came to serve the latter. The Specialized Agencies, where they were important, served the interests of the dominant powers, as in the case of the Bretton Woods institutions, or they were left in a somnolent and starved condition because they were inconsequential. International co-operation took place within the parameters of power politics and was a function of those parameters. The theories to explain such activity either lie beyond the compass of this volume in theories of imperialism or dominance or, to the extent that they involve co-operation, they have no substantive implications for the existing state-centric system beyond that of minor adjustment.

By the early 1960s the bipolar post-war world was seriously in question in all its aspects. Japan and Western Europe had established their economic independence. Britain, France and later China became nuclear-weapon powers, colonial empires were dismantled and a 'Third World' had come into being with its own leading powers and a philosophy and policy of non-alignment. Moreover, a basic schism had occurred in the socialist world sufficient to lead to armed clashes between the Soviet Union and China. Social democracy had become dominant in Western Europe. But as we have seen, a globalization of world politics was also becoming evident.

Intellectually, an anomaly in the realist paradigm was staring scholars in the face. It was the reconciliation of France and Germany in the Schuman Plan and the efforts to create ever closer economic, political and social ties in Western Europe. The experience of the Second World War and the post-war hegemony of the superpowers, together with the economic depression of the 1930s, had convinced many politicians, and not a small proportion of their electorates, that the European nation-state was an outmoded concept as a security unit, an economic unit and, increasingly, as a psychosocial unit. It was, therefore, necessary to build 'bigger and better', not immediately, but through a process which has yet to be completed. In particular a 'neo-functionalist' strategy was pursued by practitioners, or rather, recognized as such by academics. The process of going beyond adjustment to a rebuilding of the state system has been neither easy nor uncontroversial, but it is real in that the sovereignty of the units has been fundamentally adjusted, both affectively and instrumentally, although not in such a way as to go altogether beyond the notion of a state system. It is, in effect, a rebuilding of the state system into what are deemed to be more viable units.

With the growth of global issues, global problems and, let it not be forgotten, global opportunities since the mid-1960s, other conceptual frameworks began to seem more appropriate than hitherto. This explains the resurgence of interest in Mitrany's functionalist approach, John Burton's development of the notion of world society, complex interdependence as a phenomenon worthy of investigation, world order models, and ecopolitics. The agenda was changing with a move away from state-centricity and power politics. Indeed, for some the starting-point was the interaction between the individual and world society with the interplay of different actors, including state actors, in diverse domains, including power politics. The 'green agenda' of environment, human needs, justice, equity, sustainable development and legitimized politics requires, in many instances, going beyond the state system. It points to different forms of international organization and international institutions which enfranchise a kaleidoscope of political actors. In this conception social engineering is again in full flood. The UN system has been augmented by global conferences in which non-governmental organizations (NGOs) play an increasingly influential role. Multinational banks and corporations interact with governments and international financial institutions to manage, in so far as they are able, the global economy. A wide range of NGOs, in the Western world alone, whether Amnesty International, the International Olympic Committee, the World Council of Churches, Friends of the Earth, or Oxfam, captures the hearts and minds of millions and moves them to political activity. Elsewhere Islam sustains the lives of a substantial proportion of the world's population. The world is changing, and so must our conceptualization of it. Realism is no longer able to explain much human activity. Institutionalization goes beyond the state system.

If there is now no conceptual consensus for the study of IR on the basis of realism, and world society approaches have a relevance for international co-operation and a new phase of institution-building, what of the third dominant approach in Western IR, namely structuralism? We can identify at least three broad tracks within the structuralist approach: the economic, the political and the ecological. The economic school has little relevance for a volume on international co-operation because it concentrates on modern forms of imperialism and dominance structures. Our concern, in this instance, is not with the institutional forms of exploitation and injustice, important though they are. With political conceptions of the long cycle in world politics we can have more truck, since such governance, while predominantly coercive, is not seen by its adherents as necessarily so.

Indeed, one prominent writer in the field, George Modelski, while noting that political leadership has usually changed as the result of a general war, suggests that the next change may be an evolutionary one in which several actors will share responsibility for global political leadership. Moreover, he notes that for a substantial part of a long cycle, political leadership and management of a lead economy can be a fairly legitimized function. The institutionalization of this function is likely to be associative in form.

The structuralist tradition that has the greatest relevance for the theme of this volume is that of ecological structure interpreted in a broad sense to include elements of environmental factors, geopolitical relationships and the green agenda. While the world society approaches discussed previously were much concerned with process, here the emphasis is put on structure — its creation, reform and its management. It is the least developed of structural approaches and it presents the greatest challenge to those interested in the international organization and institutionalization of international co-operation.

We have been living in a global society for at least three decades, but we are only just beginning to take cognizance of that fact. However, time is not an abundant resource since the process of change is increasing to an almost exponential rate. Clearly there are many potentialities, indeed imperatives, for international co-operation in this framework, whether through adjustment, rebuilding or going beyond the state system. Yet it is not at all certain that we will realize enough of them to create a world likely to avoid the drift to abdication and thence to catastrophe. Present decision-making procedures, international organization and institutions are not conducive to the successful management of global politics. Our book of recipes reflects this in that the recipes are the accumulated experience of the past. But with imagination, and a growing realization of our peril as well as the opportunities for our improvement, they may provide a starting-point for a better organized world.

Selected reading

Archer, Clive: *International Organizations,* London, Allen and Unwin, 1983.

Armstrong, David: *The Rise of the International Organization,* London, Macmillan, 1982.

Finkelstein, Lawrence S. (ed.): *Politics in the United Nations System,* London, Duke University Press, 1988.

Northedge, F.S.: *The League of Nations,* Leicester, Leicester University Press, 1986.

Olson, William C. and Groom, A.J.R. (eds): *The Study of International Relations: Then and Now,* London, Unwin Hyman, 1990.

Taylor, Paul and Groom A.J.R. (eds): *International Institutions at Work,* London, Pinter, 1988.

Taylor, Paul and Groom, A.J.R. (eds): *Global Issues in the United Nations' Framework,* London, Macmillan, 1989.

2 A conceptual typology of international organization

Paul Taylor

The theoretical literature on international organization in the 1980s could be roughly classified under three rubrics which give a feeling for the coherence of the subject. The word 'theory' is used in this context in a number of rather different ways. It refers to any organized set of propositions about the present or future of international organization, and not exclusively to a set of verifiable or falsifiable descriptive, explanatory or predictive hypotheses as would be required by a strict 'scientific' use of the term. The word 'theory' is used throughout, though some might label the more prescriptive writings as 'speculation'.[1]

The three conceptual rubrics under which theories are grouped are adjustment theories, theories which look to a refashioning of the state system, referred to here as integration theories, and those theories which go beyond a state system, which might also be called constitutional theories.

A. Adjustment theories

Adjustment theories are concerned with the response of national governments to demands made upon them as a result of changes in their environment. Governments are continually faced with the need to carry out new tasks, which may arise from political circumstances in the international system, or from technological change or other features of modernization, or economic development, or from new demands made upon them by their own citizens. The tasks may also include the settlement of international disputes or the maintenance of international order. The essential point is that adjustment theories are about the ways in which existing governments cope with demands made upon them by working through international institutions and carrying through appropriate adjustments in their position. They do not see governments, or other levels of the state, as being fundamentally changed, and, accordingly, they stress the range of intergovernmental arrangements in international organization. Governments are seen as the dominant actors, using international organization to the extent that it serves their interests in the context of a changing environment.

Adjustment theories may be conveniently subdivided into five major styles of intergovernmental co-operation in international organization. The classification helps to overcome the rather naive prejudice — surprisingly widely held — that intergovernmental co-operation is a single kind of procedure. It has, in fact, several distinctive styles. The styles of intergovernmental co-operation may be conveniently labelled co-ordination, co-operation, harmonization, association, parallel national action, and supra-nationalism. They represent a preliminary framework for classification.

Co-ordination involves the adjustment of government policies by a process of intensive consultation within an international institution in order to establish and maintain a programme which is designed to obtain goals generally regarded as being overwhelmingly important. In brief, there is a goal which it is believed can only be obtained through a common programme. The international institution has the task of deciding the programme with the advice and consent of member states. The international institution produces what might be regarded as an ideal package of approaches to the problem on the basis of its own experience and data, and on that of the advice of the specialists which it consults. Frequently, of course, the institution is the main collector of data for the group of states which it serves taken as a whole. It is, therefore, in a good position to develop what could be considered an ideal solution. Subsequently this ideal is modified as a result of consultations with the representatives of governments in the process known as the 'confrontation of policy'.[2] In co-ordination, however, it is the state which retains powers and responsibility for executing the common task. States are pushed towards the adjustment of policy in the common interest — by a process identified originally in the Organization for European Economic Co-operation (OEEC) as the confrontation of policy — but their status is confirmed in decision-making procedures based on the principle of unanimity in the international institutions' controlling committees of governmental representatives.[3] The realization of the programme depends upon a process of co-ordination which extends through a period of time; it involves adjustment of technical arrangements which demand a precision of control in relation to each other in order to facilitate the obtaining of the common goal.

Co-ordination has been detected in a wide variety of international institutions, but it was particularly clear in the case of the OEEC's drawing-up of its Annual Programme, in NATO's procedure for drawing up the Force Plan, and in policy-making in the European Communities. In the Organization for Economic Co-operation and Development (OECD) and other agencies, it has been detected in the mechanisms for the co-ordination of aid programmes to the developing world. In the European Community it seemed to become more readily identifiable, as the scope of the community widened and as the aspiration to supra-nationalism was lost in the mid-1960s.[4] It was found, however, in the making of policy in the field of competence of the Treaty of Rome, that is, in the economic and social areas, and not in the field of foreign policy which is better characterized as a process of harmonization as understood in this volume. In that context there is little sense of an ideal but a strong sense of the need to reconcile the distinctive interests of the separate states. The emergence into a position of importance in policy-making in the Community of the Committee of Permanent Representatives illustrates the growth of co-ordination as the dominant style of the Community. That Committee contains the permanent representatives of member states in Brussels and has become the main forum of the confrontation of policy between member states and between them and the Commission of the European Community, the main representative of the interest of the Community as a whole.[5]

The dominant style of intergovernmental co-operative action in the classical balance of power system, in so far as it succeeds in preserving peace, is co-operation. Co-operation is defined here as a limited involvement of states in a joint enterprise, limited both in scope and duration, and focused upon a specific predetermined objective. Obviously, in matters of security in a balance of power system, co-operation will involve the techniques of negotiation, mediation, arbitration, conciliation or good offices, and the role of the international institution is to service such procedures between member states.[6] It may provide a framework, informal advice, or secretarial facilities but is not itself an element in the stability of the system (in preventive diplomacy, if it is successful, it is such an element of stability as an essential actor in the Concert system). The stability of the balance of power system depends essentially upon the ability of member states to maintain a fluid system of arrangements between themselves, in which alliances are limited and capable of adjustment. The system stands or falls on the ability of the participant states to undertake specific acts of co-operation on their own behalf: in that system the international institution's role is a rather minor, incidental one.

Co-operation, as defined here, obviously takes place in the framework of a large number of international institutions and may be involved in political, economic, social or cultural questions. It has been argued that it is the dominant mode in relations between member states of COMECON in which the sovereign equal states of Eastern Europe co-operate on specific limited projects which they separately regard as beneficial.[7] Co-operative arrangements may also be made, through an international institution, between two or more member states to further the interests of one state, as an exchange for future co-operative arrangements which further the interests of the others. It is essential, though, that the objectives on these various occasions relate to matters which are not connected directly with each other.

Harmonization can be illustrated, first, by reference to the work of the Council of Europe, and by reference to techniques of preventive diplomacy in the United Nations. The work of the Security Council reflects the ability of an international institution to identify and exploit existing compatibilities between the states, and their reluctance to assert distinctive positions to the point where there will be an escalation of conflict. The international institution is allowed an area of operation which depends upon two interrelated factors: the existence of actual compatibility of interests (or structures) which are to be harmonized, and the reluctance of states to act so as to endanger these compatibilities.

In the case of the Council of Europe, the actions of the institution in preparing for further harmonization are not dramatic, but it is evident that part of its role must be to try to steer states around danger zones in which competitiveness and discord could originate. The Council of Europe's work in specifying particular areas for harmonization is especially concerned with technical, economic, social or cultural questions. The normal pattern of the Council's work is for similarities, in principle or practice, to be identified in the various states, for conventions embodying these similarities to be drawn up, and on this basis, for existing barriers to be dismantled and common structures or procedures established.[8] The conventions usually take the form of what have been called 'partial agreements'; a minimum of signatures ensures the activation of the agreement between assenting states while non-members are expected, and reminded, to join at a later date.[9] The list of the Council's partial agreements is impressive: it ranges from the European Convention of Human Rights and its associated Commission of Human Rights, and the Court, to a European students' cultural card, which allows rebates to students in member countries. In all these instances, it should be stressed, harmonization involves chiefly identifying existing compatibilities on the basis of which common elements could be built with very little amendment. No major changes in existing practices or principles of the various states are expected: belief in the success of the process, as Harrison points out below, depends on the assumption of a natural convergence among the interests of states. At the least it establishes a ratchet mechanism which discourages future divergences and discords.

Preventive diplomacy also contains an element of harmonization. It is a product of the post-Second World War bipolar international system in which the dominant security system, incorporated in the United Nations Organization, is the Concert system. This is reflected in the primary responsibility of the Security Council for matters of security, and the introduction of the veto into that institution: action in security questions depends, according to the Charter, primarily upon the agreement of the permanent members of the Security Council, that is, the leading powers of 1945. The ideas of Dag Hammarskjold on the use of 'quiet' diplomacy, 'conference' diplomacy, and peace-keeping forces illustrate preventive diplomacy in action: a minimum permissive consensus between the permanent members of the Security Council, particularly, of course, the two superpowers, is the essential foundation for the action of the institution.[10] The institution then acts to restrain the use of violence between non-members of the Concert (preventive diplomacy cannot be between the permanent members of the Security Council), by negotiation, in which it seeks to represent the common interest, or, if this fails, by the use of peace-keeping forces taken from non-permanent member states which are interposed between the warring parties. In the late 1980s the Concert arrangement was expressed in a new form which was initiated by the British Ambassador to the United Nations at the time, Sir John Thomson. What emerged was in effect a caucus of the five permanent members of the Security Council, who would meet to concert their positions before meetings of the full Security Council. Despite some misgivings on the part of those who were excluded, this new arrangement seemed to work very well and certainly contributed to the settlement of the Iran–Iraq war and the dispute about Namibia. The more positive attitude of the Soviet Union towards the United Nations was, of course, a precondition of the introduction of the procedure.[11] It is fundamental to the idea of preventive diplomacy that the international institution is able to act because the major states recognize a compatibility of interest (a harmony), and are anxious not to jeopardize this by involvement in issues which could increase the level of discord, and that they expect that further compatibilities will be identified in future. The institution does not act directly in this case to modify policy in order to facilitate co-operation as it would in the process of co-ordination.

Harmonization may, however, be detected in a very wide range of contexts in international organizations. It is arguably the common form of decision-making in institutions which deal with questions of human rights, such as in the machinery of the United Nations or in the International Labour Organization.[12] Governments in these cases are brought to accept that there are similarities in their interests, or in their ways of doing things which they are prepared to enshrine in formal agreements and thereby further entrench. What often happens, of course, is that governments are prepared to subscribe to principles which they know, and their partners know, are frequently ignored in the practice of their own states. That they feel it necessary to make even token gestures must however be regarded as an indication of pressure to recognize international standards, and it provides an opportunity for monitoring and judging performance. That there is a process of harmonization lends credence, of course, to the view that there is a natural underlying harmony of interests.

The fourth style of adjustment theory, association, is to be found in relations between countries such as Greece, before accession in 1981, and Turkey, with the European Community, and between members of the Commonwealth or the Non-Aligned Movement. It has a tendency to concentrate on practical, functional arrangements and to postpone or avoid associated questions of political commitment. Sometimes of course the avoidance of political commitment may be a rather one-sided affair, as with relations between Turkey and the European Communities in the late 1980s; Turkey would have preferred a much closer relationship!

Nevertheless, an association framework has the great advantage of allowing consultations between members on a regular basis, as in the biennial meetings of Heads of State and Government in the Commonwealth, without any necessary obligation to agree about specifics.[13] In fact association encompasses a propensity to agree in the long term whilst permitting major disagreements in the short term. There is a great stress on the value of the relationship in itself whilst allowing questions to be asked about any particular aspect of it. This characteristic may be the result of a common belief in the special quality of a past experience, as in the Commonwealth, or a belief in a similar position in the global ideological and political constellation, as in the Non-Aligned Movement. In all cases the closer the approach to specifics, the greater is the probability of revealing disagreements.

Adjustment theories in this volume also include what has been called parallel national action, which is discussed more fully in Chapter 7. The essential feature of this approach is that a number of governments agree to co-ordinate their legislation in their separate decision-making procedures with regard to a wide range of business with the help of common institutions and arrangements. As is stressed below, there is no move towards setting up a new regional government but a determination to run the affairs of a number of sovereign entities in parallel. The best example of this is the Nordic Council between the Scandinavian countries but the arrangement was also to be found between the states before the establishment of the United States of America in the late eighteenth century.[14] It has the advantage of combining relative freedom for the constituent parts, especially in the areas of politics and defence, with a degree of harmonization of the social and economic arrangements sufficient to create a single economic and social space. People can move freely in this space, whilst the different countries are permitted a degree of latitude as regards their defence, in reflection of their different strategic positions.

The next and final form of adjustment theory is supranationalism, which may be regarded as a form of intergovernmental arrangement by which governments allow an international institution to manage an area of common interest on the basis of decisions taken either by majority voting, or by committees of independent civil servants. This unusual power is often exercised by the international institution in an area of narrow scope, and it may be judged as doing so in the interest of existing governments both in terms of their perceptions of self-interest and in terms of individual, collective and institutional views of the common interest. Supranationalism is a modern technique used by governments to assist them to survive, and satisfy new demands in the modern world. It may be viewed as a kind of partial federalism: powers are transferred to a centre, but they are to be exercised in an area, the scope of which is narrowly circumscribed by participating governments. As its scope increases, so the range of independent power in the hands of the institution tends to decrease. Writings which consider this style of supranationalism include those on the High Authority of the European Coal and Steel Community such as Ernst Haas's *Uniting of Europe*,[15] and those which argue for compulsory international jurisdiction in disputes between states.[16]

B. Integration theories: refashioning the state system

These are theories which describe and explain a qualitative change in the context of decision-making: integration theories are about a fundamental change in the international state system which is expected to be persistent at one or more of four levels of the state. These levels are:

1. The people or citizens (the popular level).
2. Organized groups (the level of the competing, non-governmental institutions in the state).

3. The bureaucrats: élites in 'key institutional settings' (the level of administration).
4. The political leaders (the level of the executive).

The discussion of integration theory begins conveniently with theories which concentrate at the popular level on changes in mass attitudes and values. Such theories generally see such changes as the test or major dynamic of integration although they may be concerned with consequent or associated changes at other levels too. Generally, they are concerned with the development of community, or *Gemeinschaft,* at the popular level and see developments at that level as the main determinant of stability, be it in the states involved in the integration process, or in the emerging integrated system.[17] Among the theorists who stress this view is Karl Deutsch, whose ideas on the development of amalgamated and pluralistic security communities put great stress upon changes in popular attitudes.[18] He is concerned clearly with developments at three levels of the state: the changes in patterns of transactions (hence, he is sometimes called a transactionalist), the development of a community of attitudes and values, and the development of political amalgamation (patterns of institutional unity). But the critical development, the one of which changes in transactions are used as an indicator, and on which the persistence of political amalgamation rests, is seen as being the development of a community of values and attitudes. It should be stressed here that Deutsch does not regard development in transactions as *equivalent* to developing community. It is also important to point out that it is the range and quality of changes in transactions that constitutes an indicator of community: too frequently Deutsch's ideas are criticized on the mistaken assumption that he sees *particular* transactions developments as indicators of community. The RA index is one way of summarizing transactions changes in a form which provides, in Deutsch's view, an indicator of community.[19]

The functionalism of David Mitrany is also concerned primarily with attitude changes at the popular level. They provide the test and the dynamic of integration. International institutions which concentrate upon specific tasks are seen as generating supportive popular attitudes, thus modifying loyalties to the state which are thought to sustain the more dangerously competitive aspects of international society. Once the process of transnational community-building begins, it generates new demands for international institutions to satisfy felt needs, which in turn consolidate the emerging community. Eventually international co-operation is seen to be sustained by the interdependencies and cross-cutting ties of international society which impose restraints upon the disruptive ambitions of governments, and by the existence of supportive attitudes.[20] Unlike Deutsch, Mitrany places much more stress on the causal links between the various levels of the integration process: the processes of co-operation, which may be linked with transactions, are seen to modify attitudes.

At this point, however, it must be admitted that Mitrany's functionalism could be placed in either part two or part three of this typology (Parts III or

IV of the volume): in this account, what has been stressed is its character as a theory which contains dynamic elements tending towards the creation of a new community amongst two or more peoples. It may also be understood as allowing a compromise with the state in that the latter is to be left as a residual category, retaining all those functions which are not now to be managed in areas which cut across national frontiers according to the requirements of 'form follows function'. Indeed Mitrany explicitly made this point.[21] The theory may also be applied to the regional level, although Mitrany objected to this, in which case it would be seen as a way of creating larger states within regions. If these elements are stressed, it should be placed in the company of other theories of integration. On the other hand the logic of the functionalist argument that form should follow function is that the state would eventually be transcended in a world system of cross-cutting functions: in this sense it can be seen as being fundamentally hostile to the continuation of the present state system. If this argument is stressed, then the theory logically finds a place in the next section of this typology. It is, however, useful for the student to be aware that ambiguities such as this will arise when the attempt is made to classify social phenomena.

While the functionalists and Karl Deutsch believe that stability in society is dependent upon consensus, the neo-functionalists accept a pluralist model which assumes the dominance of competitiveness in society and sees stability in a general acceptance of the rules of the game. In their view of integration the pressures produced by interest group demands upon decision-making élites, amongst which bureaucrats occupy a key position, are stressed. Interest groups' demands are seen as stimulating decision-makers to apply the experience of successful integration to new areas: once integration begins further integrative decisions, which are seen as rewarding by interest groups, become more likely. Bureaucrats are also faced with problems caused by previous integration in areas which are functionally connected and try to solve them by steps for further integration. They are also seen as being able to relate the political interests of politicians to demands of interest groups as they respond to such problems. They occupy a central position in integration, and it is their work and changes in their behaviour (for instance, in establishing closer links with colleagues in the international civil service, and in other governments), which provide the key test and condition of integration. They are instrumental in creating a new transnational political system, the modalities of which come to be accepted by organized groups as they pursue their various competing interests. As a result of this process, responsibility for performance of crucial tasks is transferred from national governments to new centres in international institutions.

The range of neo-functionalist writings and criticisms and developments of their ideas is very extensive, if now not recent. The work of Ernst Haas on the European Coal and Steel Community (ECSC), and on the International Labour Organisation (ILO),[22] is of central importance, as is the volume of *International Organization* on regional integration theory in the autumn of 1970.[23] This should be compared with Haas's own reassessment of his theories in 1976.[24] There are also a number of summaries and critiques of neo-functionalist ideas contained in larger books on integration theory. Despite the fact that neo-functionalism has been out of fashion since the mid-1970s, and the major writings predate that period, it is opportune to reconsider them in the late 1980s. The recent experience of the European Communities suggests that they will return to centre-stage.[25]

Another approach to the refashioning of the international state system which primarily affects governments should however also be discussed: this is the approach known as regionalism. The question should be put in the context of whether the member states of the international system are becoming more involved in regional international organizations, a condition defined in this context as local sectoralism, as it is not seen at this stage as raising questions about the sovereignty of member states or about collective regional management. Like other integration theories, however, there are dynamic elements to which governments respond, even in this rather modest form of regionalism. These include pressures towards the emulation of developments elsewhere (e.g. establishing common markets in imitation of the European Economic Community), incentives to change the milieu of government action (milieu goals), and to establish a regional role.[26] Regionalism would, however, be revealed in the pattern of decision-making, first, in that it would affect the formation of coalitions in local and universal organizations, and second, in that it would tend to encourage the development of regional transactions and transnational arrangements. The development of regionalism in this rather limited sense in the 1980s is, therefore, considered in chapter 11 below. In chapter 16, however, the potential for going beyond this to systems of regional management is evaluated and the implications of this for the future of international society are discussed. These two chapters should ideally be read consecutively.

In this volume a discussion is included of the implications for regional integration of a relatively recent theory developed in the context of the discipline of comparative government, namely consociationalism.[27] What is stressed in this approach is the way in which integration may respond to and influence the interests of the élite cartel which manages the process and creates disincentives to the development of community at the more popular level. The assumptions upon which this theory is based are pluralist: however, unlike neo-functionalism, it purports to explain the way in which the competitiveness of the interests of actors may be actively reinforced by the process of integration. On the other hand, the incentives towards managing that tendency are also accentuated: the system becomes one which may be described as confined dissent.

This relatively new approach may be conveniently set beside the traditional federalist approach to integration, though this is not discussed at length here. It does have in common with consociationalism, however, a concern with the behaviour and interests of élites and a preparedness to find ways of reconciling differences between participating groups within a common system of government. Federalism assumes that diversities have a clear geographical distribution, whilst consociationalism accepts that these may not be so neatly distributed. Consociationalism implies a process of integration over a period of years, whereas federalism implies a rapid move towards a high level of integration, characteristically by agreeing among political élites a constitution through which diversities may be reconciled. However federalism assumes that once the union is achieved these diversities will be reduced.

This then is the range of theories about the refashioning of the international state system in this volume. A final chapter discusses briefly the reversing of the process. This concerns ways of coping with various pressures towards separation, which may include allowing a measure of local autonomy or indeed independence. There are, however, pressures in *both* directions: smaller units may emerge in larger frameworks. It is useful to organize the various accounts according to the level of the state with which they are primarily concerned. Each may be understood as describing or explaining a process whereby elements in various separate states are brought more closely together. The assumption is, however, allowed that the integration process does not necessarily lead to a fusion of such entities, or that states are subsumed as a result of the process in some new arrangement, though it is possible that a new state may emerge as the result of the integration of a number of older ones. The international state system is refashioned but not fundamentally altered.

It has been stated, however, that these assumptions do not always exclude other assumptions about particular theories which would lead to their being reclassified as 'Group C' and placed in the fourth section of this volume. Attention is now focused upon these different theories.

C. Theories of an emergent world system

These theories may in principle be identified as those which imply or explicitly predict the radical alteration of the international state system, so that it might be said to have been transcended, by-passed or even subverted. Sometimes the prescriptive element in such theories is very evident: on other occasions it may claim to be descriptive and explanatory about existing arrangements, and the prescriptive element in this case is implicit. As with some of those theories in the previous section, it also happens that changing the stress among the assumptions behind these theories may lead to a different classification. At the level of governments there are a number of ideas about changes in behaviour and context which may be judged as forming a part of integration theory in the broader sense but which may also be judged as theories about emergent world systems.

One set of ideas of this kind which emerged mainly in the 1980s has been given the general title of regime theory. This concerns, in the terms of John Ruggie a 'set of mutual expectations, rules and regulations, plans, organizational energies and financial commitments, which have been accepted by a group of states'.[28] There have been a large number of reinterpretations of this definition, in particular the much quoted one by Stephen Krasner

(see chapter 14 below), but broadly speaking they all claim that governments become subject to unstated conventions of behaviour which
frequently emerge under the tutelage of a hegemonic power such as the
United States after the Second World War or Britain before the First World
War. A great deal has also been written about the reasons for the growth of
such regimes — and their growth is of particular interest to integration
theorists — about the factors which may or may not sustain them in the
absence of a hegemonic state, and about the reasons for their decline.[29] It is
not suggested here that regimes are held to be necessarily a modern
phenomenon: they may always have existed between states. But in recent
years they have been identified as constituting significant pressures towards
the refashioning of the international state system. They cannot be ignored
by students of international organization.

But regime theory is also ambiguous in its view of the existing state
system. There is, as has been indicated, a good case for viewing it as
integration theory in the broadest sense. But there is also a case for viewing
it as a theory about an emerging world system which would transcend states.
This is the implication of freeing the regime of the assumption that it
depends upon a hegemon, but may come to rely instead upon the view of
self-interest of a rational egoist as in Keohane's arguments. But the question
then arises of how the interests of the rational egoist are shaped, if they are
not in some sense confined and directed by the hegemon. Keohane and
others have attempted to answer this question by suggesting that regimes
may themselves play a part in shaping the interests of participating actors,[30]
and this possibility is reinforced with assumptions about the tendency for
those who make the decisions in modern states to seek to *satisfice*, rather
than maximize returns from their activities.

These arguments together have major implications. The possibility is
opened up of completely inverting the usual assumptions that are made by
realists about international society: that the sources of the interests of the
primary actors, the governments, are found primarily within the state.
Pressures from beyond the state, suggested by the regime, could prevail; the
stronger the regime the more likely this is to happen. It is for this reason that
regime theory in this volume is placed with theories of an emergent world
system.

There are, however, a range of longer-standing ideas about the way in
which the behaviour of governments may be limited by emerging conventions which may be identified in earlier writings. Regime theory is heir to
this tradition. One example is what might be called process federalism as in
the thinking of Dag Hammarskjold about an emerging constitution in
international society which has governments and states as its primary
members. Hammarskjold detected a process of entrenching in international
society the practice of resorting to procedures which involved international
institutions in order to settle disputes and achieve common interests. He
described the process of moving from a phase of 'primitive institutionalism'
to a phase of 'sophisticated constitutionalism' among states, in which
conventions of behaviour, increasingly adhered to as norms of the society of

governments, were identified and followed.[31] The process was sustained by the experience over a period of years of 'quiet diplomacy' in the corridors of the United Nations and other international institutions, and by 'conference diplomacy' in assemblies of statesmen, such as the General Assembly of the United Nations or the Consultative Assembly of the Council of Europe. The accumulated wisdom and perspective of the institution itself, contained particularly in the international secretariat, would become an element in international diplomacy, continually encouraging states to adjust their positions and attitudes so that peace could be maintained and order consolidated. These ideas, developed by Hammarskjold in a number of his writings and speeches, constitute an approach towards international federalism: governments are expected to merge gradually in an international constitution, to be fixed by entrenched conventions in a co-ordinated global system.

Hammarskjold's ideas contained a strong prescriptive element and because of this they moved towards the style of theorizing which is explained more clearly in the fourth part of this volume, especially chapter 15 by George Codding. They see a constitutional evolution being driven by an increasing realization on the part of governments of what is necessary to preserve their security. In chapter 16, a comparable realization on the part of political élites is predicted, namely that the achievement of an adequate management of their functional activities demands greater co-ordination at the regional level. Compared with Hammarskjold's ideas a technical goal is substituted for the attainment of security. There is a prospect of the development of new regional integrated units which could fundamentally alter the structure of the international system. Such units are seen as going beyond the pattern of increased governmental involvement in local sectoralism, which is the focus of chapter 11, and emerge as frameworks for the management and control of the systems of state activity. Indeed the prospect is presented of tasks, which have been traditionally handled by states, and which hitherto have been the functional concomitants of national self-determination, being carried out increasingly at the regional level. This is an image of a future world which rests on the assumption that in some ways international society will be less rather than more integrated. Its implications for the 'core' theory of integration, namely functionalism, therefore need to be discussed.

Another image of the future system is, however, almost the opposite of this: it is one of an increasing degree of interconnectedness through transactions, systems and networks. This prospect is evaluated in chapter 17. The chapter also discusses emerging world systems and conventions of behaviour, though not just at the governmental level, and explicitly rejects the state. That is regarded as just one of a number of levels at which transnational constraints upon the other levels might develop. It also presents a very sophisticated description of the developments studied. Its inclusion in this section of the volume is justified, however, on the basis of an implied prescription.

Much more episodic and self-consciously prescriptive are the theories of

Clarence Streit and other federalists, radical and otherwise, which are discussed in chapter 15. These are, however, rather more recent representatives of a tradition of thinking about world society which is as old as the state itself.[32] When a realization of the flawed character of inter-state relations dawned, so attempts to discover ways to improve the situation were made. Another rather more recent example was the writing of Clark and Sohn, as reflected in their work on *World Peace through World Law,* which was to be obtained by drastic modification of the Charter of the United Nations, by world disarmament, and by the setting up of an international army.[33] These ideas have the one major disadvantage that it is difficult to see how they could be realized in present circumstances.

These then are the three broad types of theory in international organization. It is possible to fit a wide range of concepts into this typology and to relate a wide range of empirical references to them in a coherent way. There are, of course, some omissions, such as interdependence theory, which would, however, find a place in part two of the typology.[34] Some of the theories may also be placed in different parts of the typology. There are a number of themes in contemporary international organization which might yet escape the typology and need to be considered separately. These include some aspects of the international institution as an actor, particularly those which are conveniently explained by reference to organization theory.

In the following chapters a range of contributions have concentrated on particular stages of the typology. The editors have not covered every step in the typology — this would have led to an unmanageable volume — but rather have encouraged consideration of particularly interesting aspects and perspectives. It is hoped that the merits of the approach will in this way become apparent.

Notes

1. For an examination of the implications of different theoretical approaches for prescribing for the improvement of international organization, see Paul Taylor, 'Prescribing for the reform of international organization: the logic of arguments for change', in *Review of International Studies,* Vol. 13, 1987, pp. 19–38.
2. See M. Palmer *et al., European Unity: a survey of European organizations,* London, Allen & Unwin, 1968.
3. See M.A.G. van Meerhaeghe, *International Economic Institutions,* 5th edn. Dordrecht and Boston, Kluwer, 1987.
4. Paul Taylor, 'The politics of the European Communities', *World Politics,* April 1975.
5. Juliet Lodge, 'EC policymaking: institutional considerations', in Juliet Lodge (ed.), *The European Community and the Future of Europe,* London, Pinter Publishers, 1989.
6. For an account of the procedures of the United Nations regarding the maintenance of international peace and security as they had emerged by the mid-1980s, see G.R. Berridge and A. Jennings (eds), *Diplomacy at the UN,* London, Macmillan, 1985.

7. See chapter 4 below.
8. See A.H. Robertson, *The Council of Europe,* 2nd edn. London, Stevens, 1962. See also chapter 5 below.
9. See A. Glenn Mower, Jr, 'The official pressure group of the Council of Europe's Consultative Assembly', *International Organization,* Boston, Spring 1964, pp. 292–306.
10. See A.J.R. Groom, 'The question of peace and security', in Paul Taylor and A.J.R. Groom (eds), *International Institutions at Work,* London, Pinter Publishers, 1988; and I.J. Rikhye, *Theory and Practice of Peace Keeping,* London, Hurst, 1984.
11. See Mikhail Gorbachev, *Realities and Guarantees for a Secure World,* Moscow, Novosti Press Agency Publishing House, 1987.
12. See Andrew Williams, 'The United Nations and human rights', and George Foggon, 'The origin and development of the ILO and international labour organizations', in Paul Taylor and A.J.R. Groom (eds), *International Institutions at Work,* London, Pinter Publishers, 1988.
13. A.J.R. Groom and Paul Taylor (eds), *The Commonwealth in the 1980s: challenges and opportunities,* London, Macmillan, 1984.
14. Frantz Wendt, *Cooperation in the Nordic Countries,* Stockholm, Almqvist and Wiksell International for the Nordic Council, 1981.
15. Ernst Haas, *The Uniting of Europe,* 2nd edn, Stanford, Stanford University Press, 1968. See also chapter 10 below.
16. See L.S. Woolf, *Framework of a Lasting Peace,* London, Allen & Unwin, 1917. See also Grenville Clark and Louis B. Sohn, *World Peace through World Law,* 3rd edn, Cambridge, Mass., Harvard University Press, 1966. See also Ian Clark, *Reform and Resistance in the International Order,* Cambridge, Cambridge University Press, 1980.
17. For an account of *Gemeinschaft* and *Gesellschaft,* see Paul Taylor, 'The concept of community and the European integration process', *Journal of Common Market Studies,* Oxford, Blackwell, December 1968, Vol. VII, No. 2, pp. 83–101.
18. See Karl W. Deutsch *et al., Political Community and the North Atlantic Area,* Princeton, Princeton University Press, 1957.
19. See the exposition and application of Deutsch's ideas by Donald Puchala in his 'International transactions and regional integration', *International Organization,* Boston, Vol. XXIV, No. 4, Autumn 1970, pp. 732–63.
20. See the interpretation of Mitrany's approach in Harold K. Jacobson, *Networks of Interdependence: international organizations and the global system,* 2nd edn. New York, Alfred Knopf, 1985.
21. See David Mitrany, *A Working Peace System,* Chicago, Quadrangle Books, 1966, for example, in the discussion pp. 61–8, and *passim,* the argument assumes the continuation of the state in some form: 'the functional approach . . . would help the expansion of . . . positive and constructive common work . . . making frontier lines meaningless by overlaying them with a natural growth of common activities and common administrative agencies' (p. 63). 'Meaningless' is a strong term, but note 'overlaying them' i.e. they survive. More clearly stated: 'in other words that most disruptive and intractable of international principles, the principle of state equality, may well be tamed by specific functional arrangements which would not steal the crown of sovereignty while they would promise something for the purse of necessity' (p. 66). In several places Mitrany's argument suggests that a core of social, cultural and local policing functions

would be retained under the exclusive control of the state, and he frequently referred to governments as the participants in common arrangements.

22. Ernst B. Haas, *The Uniting of Europe,* op. cit., and *Beyond the Nation State,* Stanford, Stanford University Press, 1964.

23. *International Organization,* Vol. XXIV, No. 4, Autumn 1970, op. cit. See also: Roger D. Hansen, 'Regional integration: reflections on a decade of theoretical efforts', *World Politics,* Princeton, January 1969, pp. 242–71; Ronn D. Kaiser, 'Toward the Copernican phase of regional integration theory', *Journal of Common Market Studies,* Oxford, Blackwell, March 1972, pp. 207–32; and A.J.R.Groom 'Neofunctionalism: A case of mistaken identity', *Political Science,* Vol. 30, No. 1, 1978.

24. E.B. Haas, *The Obsolescence of Regional Integration Theory,* Berkeley, University of California, Institute of International Studies, 1976.

25. Paul Taylor, 'The new dynamics of EC integration in the 1980s', in Juliet Lodge (ed.), op. cit.

26. J.S. Nye, 'Regional institutions', in Cyril E. Black and Richard Falk, *The Structure of the International Environment,* Princeton, Princeton University Press, 1972.

27. Arend Lijphart, 'Consociation and federation: conceptual and empirical links', *Canadian Journal of Political Science,* Vol. XXII, No. 3, 1979.

28. John Gerard Ruggie, 'International responses to technology: concepts and trends,' *International Organization,* Vol. XXIX, No. 3, Summer 1975, pp. 557–84.

29. Robert O. Keohane, *After Hegemony,* Princeton, New Jersey, Princeton University Press, 1984.

30. Ibid.

31. See Dag Hammarskjold, Speech at the University of Chicago, 1 May 1960, in Wilder Foote (ed.), *Dag Hammarskjold: Servant of Peace,* London, The Bodley Head, 1962, p. 252.

32. See Ian Clark, op. cit.; Hidemi Suganami, *The Domestic Analogy and World Order Proposals,* Cambridge, Cambridge University Press, 1989; and S.J. Hembleben, *Plans for World Peace through Six Centuries,* Chicago, University of Chicago Press, 1943.

33. See L.S. Woolf, *Framework of a Lasting Peace,* London, Allen & Unwin, 1917. See also Grenville Clark and Louis B. Sohn, op. cit.

34. R.O. Keohane and J.S. Nye, *Power and Interdependence: World Politics in Transition,* Boston, Little, Brown, 1977.

Selected reading

Archer, Clive *International Organizations,* London, Allen & Unwin, 1983.

Claude, Inis L. Jr, *Swords into Plowshares,* 4th edn, New York, Random House, 1971.

Harrison, R.J., *Europe in Question,* London, Allen & Unwin, 1974.

Jacobson, Harold K., *Networks of Interdependence: International Organizations and the Global Political System,* 2nd edn, New York, Alfred Knopf, 1984.

Taylor, Paul, *International Cooperation Today,* London, Elek, 1971.

Taylor, Paul and Groom, A.J.R. (eds), *International Institutions at Work* London, Pinter Publishers, 1988.

Part II

International organization and the practice of
diplomacy: adjustment theories

3 Co-ordination in international organization
Paul Taylor

Co-ordination is a way of producing common policies among actors which have legal, or formal competence in particular policy areas. It involves adjustments in the initial positions of the actors in line with the agreed policy and it assumes the acceptance of the overriding importance of common objectives as reflected in a programme of action which is to run over a determined or open period of time. These three elements, then, are the major elements in co-ordination: the actors have an area of discretion; policies are adjusted by them in an agreed direction; and policies are fitted into a programme which is seen to be of mutual advantage.

Although this procedure may be followed at any level of society, it is particularly interesting and complex at the level of international society in international institutions because of the principle of the sovereignty and equality of the principal actors, i.e. the states. In the following discussion, examples will be taken mainly from the experience of the North Atlantic Treaty Organization in producing its annual reviews and, more recently, the Force Plan, and from the institutions of the European Communities in their role as co-ordinator of Community policy. Some examples are also taken from the experience of the Organization for European Economic Co-operation (OEEC), which in 1961 became the Organization for Economic Co-operation and Development (OECD),[1] in working out its Annual Programme. Other examples of co-ordination may be found, however, in the practice of a wide range of international institutions.

The freedom of the actors to reject policies which are the object of co-ordination is reflected in the use of techniques of influence or persuasion to change their position in the agreed direction, and not those of power or coercion. Influence involves the changing of the actors' preferences among policies, from one which was originally preferred more, to one which was originally preferred less, by the promise of rewards such as economic or political gain by other states or by an international institution. It should be stressed that movement is between policies which are more or less preferred, and which are each conceivable ways to the same general end, and not from one which was preferred to one which was definitely opposed. (This would follow from the use of power or force.)[2] The rewards of the co-ordination programme are seen by the participating states as outweighing the costs of such adjustments in policy: there is a superordinate goal.

The process is greatly assisted by the recognition by the actor of the high skills of the staff of the international institution, a circumstance which is likely to be encouraged by the exchange of highly rated staff, possibly on a short-term secondment basis, between the home civil services and the international civil service. This occurs between national administrations and the international civil services of NATO and of the OECD, and to some extent between them and the Commission of the European Communities. (In the latter case national governments have a considerable direct representation through the permanent delegations and the officials linked with the Council and the Committee of Permanent Representatives.) The important point, however, is that there should develop a sense of collegiality among national and international civil servants. The role of the institution is also greatly enhanced by the availability to it of a wide range of accurate and comparable information in the area of its competence. Among the basic tasks which faced the OEEC in its early period, and NATO, was the introduction of techniques for collecting and organizing information, such as economic statistics in various states, which allowed effective collation and comparison at the international level; the EEC also devoted considerable effort to this task; it was not until 1 January 1966 that a harmonized nomenclature for the foreign trade statistics of the EEC countries came into operation; this contained some 4,828 headings.[3]

The acceptance of the high status of the staff of the international institution by national officials may greatly assist the process of gathering comparable information, and of maintaining the confidence of states in its reliability. Indeed, it has been argued that national bureaucracies are sometimes more prepared to allow to international officials the right of inspection in sensitive areas, than they are to members of their own country's elected assemblies: scrutiny by fellow specialists, even international ones, can be more acceptable than scrutiny by nationals who may have a political interest.[4] One reason for this is that it increases the chance of being informed about comparable restricted matter by other states. Comprehensive information about the common programmes should, however, also be available to actors on an individual basis. They are more likely to respond to influence if they are placed in the position of feeling that they too have acquired an accurate oversight of the proposed arrangements. It should also be stressed that this linking of the functions of a mediator of high status with the availability of a wide range of information, adequate to the formulation of a convincing oversight on the common programme, is more likely to be achieved through a formal institution: 'informal exchange among donors is not likely to provide the sustained and intensive informational flows and discussion that effective co-ordination requires'.[5] International institutions have an important role in the construction of a co-ordinated programme.

In most schemes of co-ordination a transfer of resources or skills from one country to another is involved; this is true of the NATO force programmes, of the OECD annual programmes, of the co-ordinated aid programmes, and, of course, of the operations of the EC. But in conducting these transfers it is important that participating donor states should feel that outflows of resources are proportional to their capacity and to the inflows of political or material values which follow from the programme; some states will certainly contribute more than others because of inequalities in circumstances, and others will receive more. The idea of proportionality requires, however, that inflows should be felt to be in scale with outflows and the level of available resources. This is called, in the terminology of EC politics, the idea of the *juste retour*, which was stressed by the British during the 1974-5 renegotiation of the conditions of their membership in the European Communities and which increasingly became a feature of the Communities. Indeed British anxiety about the balancing of contributions to, and receipts from, the EEC was a feature of the politics of the Community through into the late 1980s.[6] It did not mean, of course, that there should be an immediate balancing of accounts, but rather that accounts should be felt to be balanced over the period of the programme, or over a fairly limited period such as one or two years. Some items in this account are difficult to quantify — hence the reference to a feeling of balance, or equity.

There is a tendency for the policies and actions of the state to diverge in the area of the programme, despite the wish for an alignment of policies and activities, because of the technical complexity of the programme concerned, and the existence of competing interests in related areas. The international machinery has the task of continually correcting the divergences in policy among the participating actors. The latter task is a predictable aspect of co-ordination, particularly where it is attempted in areas of policy which are more highly salient, such as security, or the restoration of domestic economies. The programme which emerges from the co-ordinating process is, therefore, inevitably in part a declaration of intent, which may be honestly pursued by the sovereign national actors, but which they cannot be compelled to follow. The co-ordinating machinery generally includes steering procedures — which may even include scholarly reports — which attempt to alter the course of governments within the programme so that they stay in convoy. The value of the objective to be obtained by participating states provides one dynamic of the steering mechanism. But the continuing tug-of-war between the centrifugal forces inherent in the decision-making procedures of sovereign states and the centripetal forces of the programme is very much a part of the character of co-ordination. In areas of lower salience, however, though the centrifugal force may be considerably weaker, the values to be gained are also much smaller.

One of the central processes for co-ordinating policy may be summarized under the heading of the 'confrontation of policy', a term that was coined to describe a technique which was first identified in the OEEC.[7] It refers to the close examination of the policies of each actor by other actors and by the international institutions. The state which bears the examination is made to defend its departures from the proposed programme, which the international institution explains and defends. The sense is conveyed during the confrontation process that the availability of the benefits of the programme is conditional upon successful co-ordination. In this way the policy of each participating state is confronted with the policy of every other participating state in the context of the overall view of the institution: it is a two-way juxtaposition, international institution with each state, and states with each other.

These points may now be illustrated and developed with reference, first, to the experience of NATO in constructing the Force Plan; some points may be illustrated further by reference to the earlier Annual Review procedure, particularly that of 1958. The First Force Plan was constructed in NATO in 1966 for the period 1966–7. They are now designed to plan for a five-year period, though the planning cycle is repeated every two years, with states being formally committed to the Plan only for the first year.[8] It is important to stress at the outset that the machinery involves a continuing and carefully organized dialogue between the various parties concerned in order to achieve the maximum contributions of member states to the agreed common plans by which the NATO area is to be defended jointly against attack from the outside. But the operation of the machinery cannot be understood until it is realized that the actors are not homogeneous entities: different elements of each state actor build relations with comparable elements in other state actors, and the international institutioh, and establish common cause with them against elements in their own state at various points in the co-ordination process. It will be helpful to describe the major institutional elements involved, in order to illustrate this point. This ambiguity of roles is a recurrent feature of co-ordination procedures.

First, there are at the headquarters of NATO in Brussels two groups of civil servants which have rather different functions but which are nevertheless largely interchangeable. There are the civil servant representatives of state administrations which make up the national delegations, containing senior personnel from defence and foreign ministries in the main; and there are civil servants of the international staff, many of whom have transferred from positions in national civil services, either for a short-term or a long-term period. Members of permanent delegations usually make up the Defence Review Committee (DRC) (together with main military commanders and representatives of the Military Committee), which is chaired by a member of the International Staff (the Assistant Secretary-General for Defence Planning and Policy); the Defence Planning Committee, which is a committee which has senior status (parallel with the Council) in military/strategic questions, may meet at the political level (National Defence Ministers), but may equally meet at the level of permanent delegations. (The Secretary-General, Head of the International Staff, is Chairman of the DPC.) Links between national administrations and international staff are close; they meet in a number of working committees and have a natural sympathy with each other. It is not surprising that in working on NATO policies, such as the Force Plan, there is a tendency for national delegations in Brussels, at some stages in the co-ordination process, to veer in their nuancing of policy towards the position of the international staff.

The second element is the political representatives of the states who come to Brussels from time to time to take part in the meetings of senior committees, such as the Defence Planning Committee, or the Council (also chaired by the Secretary-General). These individuals are usually elected politicians and are accompanied by advisors from their national ministries. They are inevitably more in touch with the variety of demands upon scarce resources in national capitals, and the interests of rival departmental chiefs, than are members of the permanent delegations or the international staff.

The third element is the military one. In the co-ordination process this is represented in three main institutions: the Military Committee which consists of the Chiefs-of-Staff of the member states; the offices of the major military commanders, who are Commanders-in-Chief of the various NATO regional command areas with international responsibilities (who naturally have a particularly strong interest in the states which are involved in their regions); and the Defence Review Committee, which includes, as already stated, the major military commanders, together with state representatives, and members of the Military Committee. It is likely that the national military representatives will have a sympathy with the problems and intentions of the commanders. This tendency is likely to be strengthened by the interactions between NATO military staffs in the various command administrative headquarters, such as SHAPE, at Mons, near Brussels. The military element, together with the administrative/bureaucratic elements at the national delegation and international level in Brussels, are groups within which there is a continuing potential for the convergence of interests, which, in turn is potentially in opposition to the political interests of national ministers of the various states. These alignments inevitably affect the way in which disagreements between the participating states are reconciled during the co-ordination process.

The co-ordination process may be divided into three major phases. In the first phase is the formulation of the Force Goals: this is the NATO plan for arranging and improving the common defensive effort in the light of the perceived threat. The Military Committee first assesses the military challenge as it may face the alliance for the five years of the planning period (national military element). This is augmented by the so-called Ministerial Guidance which adds the political and economic factors (national political representatives). In the light of this advice the major commanders then put forward their force proposals on a country-by-country basis (international military commanders). These proposals are probably the most international elements in the co-ordination process, because the military commanders are close to the day-to-day working deficiencies of the alliance and are particularly immersed in alliance planning. The force proposals are then co-ordinated by the Military Committee before being sent to the Defence Planning Committee (usually delegations), which in turn sends it to the Defence Review Committee (national delegations plus commanders plus Military Committee representatives). The Defence Review Committee consults the Military Committee, and refers to the Ministerial Guidance, and on this basis constructs its account of Force Goals in the light of what appears to be desirable because of foreseeable contingencies, and the practical requirement of asking states to attempt to achieve what they judge can be attained. The Force Goals are, finally, approved by the Defence Planning Committee.

In the second phase, Force Plans are produced by the various member countries in response to the account of Force Goals, and in a series of meetings between international military and civilian staffs and the national delegations, and between the national representatives themselves, the attempt is made to iron out any incompatibilities between goals and plans. To initiate this process Force Goals are sent to the various national governments who respond in their plans with an account of their achievements in specified areas, their intentions as regards future deployments, and equipment and force levels, and the available finance: they are intended to cover a five-year period.

The question arises, of course, of why it is, after such protracted efforts to produce a statement of goals, a process which included contributions from national delegations at various points, that country plans should now come to represent different views and intentions. The answer is that country plans represent the input into the co-ordinating process of the political interests of the collectivity of the national ministers, in their own capitals, who compete for scarce resources of the states, whereas the Force Goals largely measure the extent of the national delegation (administration) and international staff alignment, together with the views of the national and international military personnel. The country plans, therefore, generally take a rather more pessimistic view of the extent of available finance, and tend to reflect a greater preparedness to take risks in the military/strategic area, or to discount military/strategic expert opinion. The alignment of goals and plans is attempted first, at the level of military/international staff/delegations and officials, together with commanders' representatives. Success or lack of it is reported to the DRC, which, if necessary, then organizes a series of multilateral examinations, by delegations, of the 'difficult' countries' position.

The multilateral stage of this process can sometimes be quite complex. G.L. Goodwin, who studied the comparable process, the Annual Review, in 1958, reported that the scrutiny of a country's position started with the preparation of a list of questions by the international staff and the NATO military.[9] About two weeks were allowed between notification to the designated delegation and the examining session. It was interesting that not all delegations participated in each examining session: seven states studied the position of the United Kingdom, only four studied that of France and the United States, and six studied Italy and West Germany.[10] On the other hand the United States was designated to study all fourteen other members, while France studied nine, the United Kingdom seven, and Italy and Germany four each. In this is to be found evidence of a wish to achieve proportionality on the part of the largest donor, that is, to ensure that others gave in proportion to capacity as much as itself. As Goodwin points out, the process also allowed the United States to assess the necessary level of mutual aid required for each state, in a form which avoided some of the embarrassment which might arise if the necessary investigation were conducted on a bi-lateral basis.[11] In this way processes may sometimes provide the opportunity for upgrading general standards on the instigation of a leading member of the process in a fashion which does not challenge the susceptibilities of the various national governments.

The third and final phase of the co-ordination of the NATO Force Plan occurs when the DRC with the advice of the Military Committee reports to the Defence Planning Committee. The military Committee assesses the degree of risk inherent in what the DRC has been able to achieve. Eventually the Plan is approved by the Defence Planning Committee, and its adaptation by the Ministers meeting in the Council is recommended.[12]

As in any process of co-ordination between sovereign states, three kinds of achievement result from the adaptation of the NATO Force Plan. First, there is the achievement of establishing standards and laying down guidelines which are generally believed to be closely attuned to the common task. The ministerial guidance is one aspect of this: for instance, standards and guidelines are to include measures for 'rationalising tasks and functions as between nations', to increase the 'flexibility and optimum deployment of all forces available', to standardize equipment and increase interoperability, and to improve co-operation in the 'development and production of military equipment'.[13] Strategic elements were added by the Military Committee and specific force adjustments by the military commanders. Second, departure from the ideal standards and guidelines were measured through the information-collecting process, and the extent to which the actual achievement added up to this ideal was evaluated. Third, a series of pressures on states to fit into the desired framework, to measure up to required standards and follow appropriate guidelines, was set up. These derived in the case of NATO from the pressures upon government of opinion among their peers and from the entrenchment of accepted practice. More detailed requirements were then added to these broad stipulations.

There are of course a host of examples of failure to live up to these standards in NATO, and of failures in member states to make stipulated changes. They cannot be compelled to do so, but the co-ordination process establishes a minimum standard, a point of reference, or a pole of attraction in national defence decision-making, and it helps to define an area within which co-operative defence ventures, such as joint research and production and infrastructure programmes, are acceptable.

Goodwin concluded: 'the impact of the Annual Review [later, biennial] on governmental attitudes and policies is very difficult to measure, and will naturally vary from country to country, but on some issues, or on some occasions, a country may be open to suggestions while remaining adamant on others.'[14] However, 'it can help to focus minds on the collective needs of the Alliance, and, in the process, not only to smooth off the rough edges of national policies but also to induce a frame of mind not rooted exclusively in narrowly conceived national interests. The pressure it exercises may be gradually accumulative.' This judgement applies equally to the Force Plans of NATO in the 1980s.

Policy-making in the European Communities reveals, perhaps surprisingly, the same elements of co-ordination that were discovered in NATO, although many of them take a rather more complex form. Programmes exist at three levels. There are those programmes which are associated with a particular area such as Commercial Policy, the Common Market, the Common Agricultural Policy and Regional Policy. There is the programme of programmes, the common framework into which the particular programmes are to be fitted, which could be called the co-ordinated economic system of the European Communities, such as the 1992 programme. Finally, there are the focused programmes within the area programmes, which are intended to achieve specific objectives in the arrangements of the member states, such as the protection under stated conditions of the right of individuals to remain in the territory of another state, or the removal of specific trade barriers. There are many examples of the working-out of an operational programme at the first and third levels but the scope and nature of the second level is still the subject of debate and argument, and it is by no means certain that it will ever be attained. A further complicating feature in the EEC compared with NATO is that it was for some time a forum of contending concepts. In the period after its foundation in 1958 until the mid-1960s it was expected by many supporters of European integration that the supranational elements would prevail and that there would be a steady increment of powers and authority to the centre, in the shape of the Commission, at the expense of the participating states. There was also the expectation that there would be a transition as was required by the Treaty of Rome, to a majority voting system in the Council of Ministers. The ascendancy of this concept of the potential of European integration, which was sustained by the style of the Hallstein Commission, and by the theories of the neo-functionalists, was challenged fiercely by the French government in the crisis in the Communities in 1965.[15] The concept declined in its relevance fairly rapidly with the confirming of the continuation of the system of voting on the basis of unanimity in the Council of Ministers in the Luxembourg agreement of 1966, and was clearly replaced by the concept of confederal or intergovernmental Europe after the assertion of West German diplomatic strength in the late 1960s, particularly at the Summit Conference at The Hague in December 1969, and the accession of Britain, Denmark and Ireland in January 1973.[16] It was only in the mid-1980s that it appeared that European integration could go beyond mere intergovernmentalism. The process of the co-ordination of policy in the setting-up and managing of the programmes of the European Communities is, however, very much a feature of the later confederal and intergovernmental phases.

As in the NATO setting, the key element in co-ordination is a process which it is useful to identify as the confrontation of policy. The central importance of this process in the Community system is probably immediately attributable to the confirmation of the system by which national governments had a veto on decisions of the Council of Ministers, the main decision-making body on which governments are represented. This veto remained a possibility even after the Single European Act of 1986, which appealed for the greater use of majority voting.[17] In the Treaty of Rome a qualified majority voting system should have applied to an increasing range of areas in the second and third (final) phases of the transitional stage. The use of majority voting would have discouraged the appearance of several of the procedural and institutional devices which became familiar features in the confederal phase in the 1970s. It would have encouraged the Commission, which is the main initiating body in the Community system, to concentrate, in its relations with the Council of Ministers, upon a single policy, or a very closely related cluster of policies, and to introduce into that policy a much stronger European element. It would have had a lesser incentive to employ the existing technique of linking a wide range of areas together in what has been called a package deal,[18] which involves the trading-off of the interests of one state against those of another in relation to various elements of the package.

The Commission would have been encouraged by majority voting to try to build coalitions of support in the Council for more European solutions, and to risk offending a disapproving minority. Furthermore, the need for unity on any important issue is the foundation upon which the very complicated system of consultations among participating actors was developed: the Commission had to work for consensus among the actors by using extensive consultation and amendment and confrontation before the decision was taken. The stress upon these procedures led directly to the development of an institution which has now come to rival the Commission in the co-ordination process, the Committee of Permanent Representatives. This is a committee of permanent delegations based full-time in Brussels, which meets every week, and attempts to establish agreement between delegations and between them and the Commission.[19]

Policy-making in the European Communities has become crucially dependent upon the co-ordination of the position of national actors through their permanent delegations in Brussels.[20] The importance of the issues involved for member states is illustrated by the high status of permanent delegations' officials, and by their number and the range of home departments which they represent. Heads of permanent delegations are of ambassadorial rank and normally come from the Foreign Offices of member states (in 1989 the UK Ambassador to the Communities was David Hannay). Other officials may be transferred from senior positions in a wide range of national ministries. Delegations vary in size: the number of senior staff in the British delegation above the level of Second Secretary in 1988 was around forty. The convention has emerged that the Committee of Permanent Representatives may itself take decisions on the less controversial issues after due consultation, but the more controversial political issues are forwarded for decision to the Council of Ministers. The Committee is, of course, responsible to the Council, and in a sense stands in for the Council when it is not in session. Since the Hague Conference of December 1969, a further layer of decision-making has, however, emerged in the Communities, which also demonstrates the assertion of the separateness and sovereignty of the states in the co-ordination process in the Communities in recent years. Increasingly, crucial decisions on Community policy are left for Summit meetings of Heads of State or Government (after

1974 called European Councils), which used to meet three times a year, reduced to twice in 1986. In the opinion of some commentators, the introduction of this third level has slowed down the work of the Community. It certainly reflects a further step away from the supranational model supported by pro-Europeans in the early 1960s, which envisaged the development of the role of the Commission together with the introduction of majority voting into the Council of Ministers.

The process of co-ordinating policy in the European Communities may be considered under the same three headings that seemed appropriate in the case of the NATO Force Plan. It is indeed possible to find equivalent elements at each stage, and these will be indicated. Some are functional equivalents, rather than precisely parallel institutions, and in the EEC some stages of the process are rather more complicated.

The first phase is equivalent to the production of force goals in NATO; in the EEC the equivalent of force goals is the draft proposals of the appropriate Directorate-General of the Commission. It begins with the statement of general objectives and intentions in the particular area of policy, which may be contained in the Rome Treaty, or in statements made in the communiqués of European Councils (for example, in the Single European Act of 1986, on the completion of the Common Market),[21] or in sessions of the Councils of Ministers, or in generally approved Grand Designs such as the Commission's White Paper of 1985 which outlined ways of completing the Common Market by 1992.[22] Such statements are generally about the first level of programmes and refer to policy areas, rather than the focused programmes of the third level: they refer to expectations in the area of policy on the common market, rather than intentions in specific areas of policy such as anti-dumping. Commitment at this stage is likely to be expressed more forcibly where the area is felt to be less salient, and where it is less specific; the more salient the area, and the more specific it is, the greater the level of caution indicated at this stage. The views of Ministers or Heads of Government, even when codified in the shape of the Rome Treaty, may be seen as the equivalent of ministerial guidance in NATO, and the rather wide-ranging, non-specific advice and evaluation of government specialists, such as economists, may be seen as the functional equivalent of the preliminary statement of the Military Committee. Long-term goals, strategies and problems, such as changes in the position of the 'enemy', in the shape of such factors as inflation, or international monetary crises, or the cost of raw materials, are evaluated.

The next step is the Commission's response to the advice, requests and initiatives of the Ministers. An initiative is now taken at the third level of the focused programmes in the appropriate Directorate-General of the Commission. (Directorate-Generals 5 and 2 in the case of the 1992 process.)[23]

The completion of the internal market, the central feature of the 1992 process, included the establishment of a customs union, the elimination of discriminatory internal taxation, and the elimination of quantitative restrictions and measures having equivalent effect. Each of these items had subcategories referred to in the Single European Act, and for which specific instruments and actions were foreseen.[24]

In producing its draft proposal, the Commission staff consult with representatives of organized European interest groups, with experts, and with the members of the permanent delegations of member states. At this stage it is attempting to inform itself about the kind of arrangements which would be ideal in, for instance, safety aspects of particular products, and the kind of arrangements which might prove acceptable to member states. At this point the advisers from state delegations are not necessarily in close touch with home ministries about the specific topics under discussion, and the chances are therefore greater of a convergence of interest between delegations and the Commission sustained by a shared expertise. It is not, of course, that delegates will now support advanced schemes for European integration, but rather that they are more 'expert', 'rational', individual and less restricted by political directives. The discussion at this stage is analogous with the discussion in the first phase of the Defence Review Committee in NATO, with the Directorate-General roughly in the position of the military commanders, and the national delegations adopting rather a similar general stance in relation to the international staff. At the conclusion of this process the draft proposal (cf. Force Goal), in the form of a Commission initiative, will have emerged.

The second phase of the co-ordination of policy in the EEC is dominated by the confrontation of policy between national positions and between them and the views of the international institution. It begins when the Commission itself (now seventeen members), following the so-called collegiate principle,[25] decides to accept the proposal and send it to the Council of Ministers for decision: any General Report of the Communities contains an account of the wide-ranging proposals which are sent by the Commission, in its role as initiator of Community legislation, to the Council, the main decision-making body and law-maker in the Community (it makes around 400 regulations per annum). The Commission proposal is then forwarded to the Committee of Permanent Representatives, which now, in its formal deliberations, begins the process of evaluating the acceptability of the proposal for its members. This is a second style of work of the Representatives, quite different from the first co-operative, informal style: they are now in the position of obtaining politically informed reactions from home governments, in response to the Commission's proposal, which are analogous with the country force plans of the members of NATO. In addition delegations submit them to their own experts and consult relevant interest groups: they may also seek clarification and possibly modification from the Commission. In its formal meetings the Committee, and supporting subcommittees, will attempt to reconcile national views on the proposal, and, if successful, the agreed draft will be approved without reference to the Council. If agreement cannot be established, the confrontation, in the presence of Commission representatives, will be transferred to a meeting of full Council. At both Committee and Council levels national ministries are fully engaged; as with country force plans the political element is now very evident. It reflects the co-ordinated positions of the ministries in national capitals. The dual role of the delegations which focus upon the Committee of Permanent Representatives as informal advisers to the Commission and as participants in the confrontation of policy is a crucial mechanism in reconciling the international goals of the international organization and the interests of member states. Bodies which face both ways, sometimes supporting the international organization, and sometimes the member governments, are a common feature of the decision-making of international institutions and form a crucial link in the co-ordination process.

The third stage of co-ordination follows the making of a regulation in the Council, which is analogous with the acceptance of the NATO Force Plan by the Defence Policy Planning Committee and the Council. Other forms of decision in the Council of Ministers are also possible. These are, however, weaker in their effects than are regulations. For instance, the Council may agree upon a directive which is binding upon those to whom it is addressed regarding its ends but not its means. Directives addressed to states leave the way of achieving a particular goal to the national authorities. It has been argued that such decisions allow greater latitude to member states and may indeed lead to procrastination and evasion. There are, however, important differences between the consequences of having passed a regulation and having adopted the Force Plan, although there are a number of interesting 'functional equivalents'.

An EC regulation has a legal status, in that it is directly binding on members, and on individuals and groups within the state, whereas the NATO Force Plan is not so binding. As was discovered, the latter is a useful pressure in the agreed direction and keeps states very aware of common goals and the problems of others, but there is no way of enforcing its conclusion. A regulation, on the other hand, requires changes in the behaviour of the actors to whom it is addressed, which are reinforced by the law of the Community: disobedience may lead to the instigation of proceedings against the offender and the use of legal sanctions. The practical results of a successful act of co-ordination are, therefore, very obvious.

The lack of compulsion behind the Force Plan finds a functional equivalent in the EEC, however, in a range of so-called safeguard procedures. The states often include in the co-ordinated programme a statement on the circumstances in which they might avoid implications or consequences which they judge to be undesirable. Although the immediate pressures to co-ordinate are certainly stronger in the EC than in NATO, states generally retain the right in both contexts to protect themselves from changes which they might come to dislike.

There is a wide range of safeguard procedures in the Treaty of Rome and in regulations, by means of which states seek to protect their status as separate actors in the co-ordinated system. These refer largely to courses of action which are open to states in emergencies such as a severe adverse balance of payments.[26] The reader would need to ascertain the relevant safeguard procedures in each individual regulation. There are, however, general reservations and exclusions: for instance, all the Community's regulations which allow employees and self-employed persons to reside in another member's territory, to work there, and to receive social welfare benefits equivalent to those received by nationals are subject to the terms of Article 48, paragraph 3, which allows states to exclude individuals on 'grounds of public policy, public security or public health'. Article 9 of the Council's Directive of 17 December 1974, which greatly strengthened the rights of 'nationals of a member state to remain in the territory of another member state after having pursued therein an activity in a self-employed capacity', repeated the term of Article 48 in stating that 'member states may not derogate from the provisions of this directive save on the grounds of public policy, public security or public health'.[27] States also refused in the Rome Treaty to allow nationals the right to take employment in 'reserved' occupations, such as the civil service[28]: in Germany, university teachers are civil servants: in France, teachers, nurses and even postmen are counted as civil servants, and hence, these are occupations in which foreigners cannot be employed. Another exclusion from the terms of the rules of the Community, perhaps less surprisingly, are goods or information deemed essential to national security[29]; a list of products which were judged relevant to national security was drawn up by the Council in 1959, as required by Article 223 (para. 3), but it has not been published.[30] These various exclusions, limitations and safeguards do, however, together constitute a formidable legal defence of the interests of national actors against unacceptable inroads from the Communities.

The position of the states in relation to a co-ordinated programme in the EEC is, therefore, not as unlike that in NATO as appears at first sight. Indeed, there are a number of similarities at various stages of the co-ordination process, and quite a number of functional equivalents. In both cases, however, co-ordination emerges as a distinctive style of intergovernmental co-operation. This helps to establish the wide variety of forms of the latter. It is not just of a single type, to be contrasted sharply with supranationalism, but rather, as is suggested by the approach of this volume, is part of a wide spectrum of styles of co-operation between governments.

It is striking, though, that co-ordination arises when a mechanism exists for defining a general interest, an optimal solution to a problem, or a common programme. Harmonization, in contrast, exists when the common policy emerges from different policies of equal validity, amongst which a common denominator may nevertheless be identified.

Notes

1. For a further account of the work of the OEEC see William Diebold, Jr, *Trade and Payments in Western Europe,* New York, Harper, 1952; see also chapter 5 on harmonization below.
2. See Peter Bachrach and Morton Baratz, *Power and Poverty: Theory and Practice,* London, Oxford University Press, 1974, pp. 17–30.

3. See William Wallace (Rapporteur), 'The administration implications of economic and monetary union within the European Community', in *Journal of Common Market Studies,* Vol. XII, No. 4, 1974, p. 431.

4. See Hugo Young, *The Sunday Times,* London, 26 September 1976, p. 16, for a comparison of the British Department of Education and Science's differing reaction to scrutiny by a team from the House of Commons, and by a visiting delegation from OECD.

5. Milton Esman and Daniel S. Cheever, *The Common Aid Effort,* Columbus, Ohio State University Press, 1967, p. 252.

6. For an account of the Britain–EC Budget dispute, see Paul Taylor, 'The new dynamics of EC integration in the 1980s', in Juliet Lodge (ed.), *The European Community and the challenge of the Future,* London, Pinter Publishers, 1989, pp. 3–25.

7. See M. Palmer, John Lambert *et al., European Unity: a survey of the European organizations,* London, Allen & Unwin, 1968, pp. 88–9.

8. The following section on the NATO Force Plan is based mainly on informal interviews conducted during two visits to NATO Headquarters in March 1976. A brief account will be found in NATO Information Service, *The North Atlantic Treaty Organization,* Brussels, 1984, pp. 148–50.

9. G.L. Goodwin, NATO, The Functional Approach to the Problem of Community Building, unpublished memorandum, p. 14.

10. Ibid., p. 16.

11. Ibid., p. 26.

12. *The North Atlantic Treaty Organization,* op. cit., 1984, p. 149.

13. *Introduction to Ministerial Guidance 1975,* Annex to M-DPC-1(75)11, Brussels, 1975, p. 5.

14. G.L.Goodwin, op. cit., p. 28.

15. See Leon N. Lindberg, 'Integration as a source of stress on the European Community system', *International Organization,* Vol. XX, No. 2, Boston, Spring 1966, pp. 233–65.

16. See D.J. Puchala 'Of blindmen, elephants and international integration', *Journal of Common Market Studies,* Vol. X, No. 3, 1972.

17. See note 6 above.

18. See Roy Pryce, *The Politics of the European Community,* London, Butterworth, 1973, p. 67. See also Juliet Lodge, 'EC policymaking: institutional considerations', in Juliet Lodge, op. cit., pp. 26–57.

19. Neill Nugent, *The Government and Politics of the European Community,* London, Macmillan, 1989.

20. The following section is based in part on interviews conducted in the Commission, and in the Office of the British Delegation, in March and April 1976 and subsequently.

21. See John Pinder, in Juliet Lodge (ed.), op. cit., 1989.

22. Commission of the European Communities, *Completing the Internal Market: White Paper from the Commission to the European Council,* Luxembourg, Office for Official Publications, June 1985.

23. The Commissioner in charge from January 1989 is Martin Bangemann.

24. See Scott Davidson, 'Free movement of goods, workers, services and capital', in Juliet Lodge (ed.), op. cit.

25. See E. Noel, *How the European Community's Institutions Work,* Community Topic, 39 Brussels, 1974, pp. 7–9; Nugent, op. cit.

26. See Article 73. *Treaty Establishing the European Economic Community.*

27. *Official Journal of the European Communities,* 20 January 1975 (75/34/EC), No. L. 14, p. 12.
28. Article 48, para. 4.
29. Article 223.
30. According to advice given to the author by the Legal Section of the European Communities, October 1975.

Selected reading

Beer, Francis A., *Integration and Disintegration in NATO: processes of alliance cohesion and prospects for Atlantic Community,* Columbus, Ohio State Press, 1969.
Cox, Robert W. (ed.), *The Politics of International Organization Studies in Multilateral Social and Economic Agencies,* New York, Praeger, 1970.
Cox, Robert W. and Jacobson, Harold K. *The Anatomy of Influence: decision-making in international organization,* New Haven and London, Yale University Press, 1974.
Jordan, Robert S. (ed.), *Multinational Cooperation: economic, social and scientific development,* London and New York, Oxford University Press, 1972.
Lodge, Juliet (ed.), *The European Community and the Challenge of the Future,* London, Pinter Publishers, 1989.
NATO Information Service, *The North Atlantic Treaty Organization,* Brussels, 1988.
Taylor, Paul, *The Limits of European Integration,* London, Croom Helm, 1983.
Wallace, Helen, Wallace, William and Webb, Carole, (eds), *Policy Making in The European Communities,* 2nd edn, London, Wiley, 1983.

4 Co-operation: the CMEA experience*

Mihály Simai

Theory and history

There are different possible approaches in studying international organizations. The approach and the motivation of the various disciplines may also
differ. The theory of international intergovernmental organizations from
the point of view of economic science is based on the process of internationalization and its approach is simultaneously functional and structural.
Internationalization is a fundamental process of the world economy. Its
advance is based on the development of production and consumption
patterns in science and technology, transport and telecommunications and
on the advance of the international division of labour. The process assumes
a medium which is able to transmit effects between states, and to transfer
them from one state to another. The results of the process are twofold: on
the one hand, new problems and conflicts are emerging in international
relations, on the other hand, interdependence — the result of internationalization — creates common interests and joint efforts for managing and
deliberately promoting co-operation, and trying to resolve together the old
and emerging new conflicts. This could be achieved in the global system,
through the global intergovernmental organizations and, in the regional
framework, with the participation of the member countries of a given
region. The aims of regional economic co-operation organizations could
also differ. The intensity and the instruments of regional co-operation may
also vary according to the nature of the regional structures. The regional
economic commissions of the United Nations represent, for example, a less
intensive form of co-operation than the regional integration organizations.

What constitutes a region? From the geographical point of view a region
is a community of physical, biotic and societal features that are functionally
associated with man's occupancy of an area. In the present world economic
system, however, the term 'region' is used in more than one sense. The geo-
economic region is conceived as one which possesses certain globe-influenc-

*Editors' Note
This essay was written before the 1989 upheavals in Eastern Europe, and their implications for the future of
COMECON are unclear. Nevertheless, the difficulties of moving beyond co-operation to integration — even
in the rather special sense discussed in the early section — in a system of 'directed' national economics,
emerge clearly. It is hard to sustain an integrated programme in such a context except on the basis of
national political commitment, and integration cannot be driven by economic pressures since these are
shaped by political considerations. We therefore feel justified in categorizing this contribution as 'co-
operation' between states.

ing characteristics and reflects interrelationships in a large part of the world based on common characteristics, interests, economic orientation and ideological bonds. The socialist countries as such constitute a region in the systemic sense. They do not represent a cohesive economic region in the world economy. They are sometimes characterized as centrally planned economies, but an economic region cannot be defined in these terms. The central planning itself, of course, has been the consequence and also a source of certain similarities in the working mechanism of the system, but at this stage the meaning and the scope of central planning varies from country to country. From the economic point of view, most of the socialist countries belong to the framework of the Council for Mutual Economic Assistance.

The Council for Mutual Economic Assistance (CMEA) was founded in 1949. The representatives of Bulgaria, Czechoslovakia, Hungary, Poland, Romania and the Soviet Union agreed to establish an organization for economic co-operation. The founding countries were of differing levels of economic development, varying territorial and population sizes and unequal resource endowment, but with similar socio-political characteristics.

CMEA was originally conceived as a 'defensive economic organization' with the aim of providing the necessary international support for the economic development of the new socialist-type countries. At the beginning of the Cold War which — from the economic point of view — was the beginning of discrimination and embargo policies against the socialist countries, the increase of economic security became an important condition for the implementation of long-term development programmes. Since the development programmes were inward looking with the intentions of creating rather closed economic complexes, at that stage of development they did not make any efforts for the establishment of a planned division of labour among the countries, which could have been based on comparative advantages. The political conditions also created major obstacles for such development. Co-operation was confined to the supply of energy and raw materials for the newly established industries, the supply of technology and expertise in exchange for the products which these countries could offer as compensation. The German Democratic Republic and Albania were admitted (the latter discontinued its participation for political reasons in the 1960s), and later Mongolia, Cuba and Vietnam joined CMEA as full members.

Having started with the promotion of the post-war economic recovery, since the late 1950s CMEA member countries have gradually turned to a more diversified form of co-operation, and its original institutional mechanism evolved step by step. The first comprehensive programme of co-operation with the title 'Comprehensive Programme for the Further Extension and Improvement of Co-operation and the Development of Socialist Integration by the CMEA Countries' was adopted in 1971. This was the very first long-term document characterizing the CMEA as an integration organization. Earlier the word 'cooperation' was used to describe the goal in the CMEA documents. The change in the declared aims was not just a terminological one. It was a result of the achieved level of co-operation and of the intentions of the member countries. The change also represented a new approach to the theory of integration. In the interpretation of the economic sciences in the CMEA countries, integration — as a process — is a more advanced stage of internationalization. As regards its character and definition (and the interpretation and measurement of the process), it is necessary to make certain qualifications. Integration can be the result of the internationalization which may take place in a comprehensive way, that is, simultaneously throughout all major fields of economic activity, and also by sectors. It can emerge at a given stage, when relations are already intensive and multiple. Integration, however, may emerge as the goal of deliberately promoting economic co-operation among states in such a way that the production, consumption, infrastructure, etc. of several countries within a given region became international. In both interpretations, its function is elimination of the contradiction between the internationalizing productive forces and the survival of national boundaries. The conditions and specifics of its development are determined by the socio-economic set-up, the level of economic development and the prevailing concrete world of economic and international political relations.

In interpreting the economic integration of states, economic literature usually examines the removal of obstacles to different flows (commodities, capital, manpower), and often regards it as a sufficient criterion for integration. At the same time, some Western authors emphasize that besides removing barriers (that is, in addition to dismantling some negative elements), positive factors are also needed for integration to evolve, e.g. the harmonization of national (state) economic policies, followed by the elaboration of a common, uniform economic policy.[1]

The distinction between 'market integration' and 'production and development integration' was first introduced into economic literature by Imre Vajda, a Hungarian economist. The former means the possibility of unhindered sales flows on the markets of the member countries, and the latter the raising to an international level of the planning of production in those branches of industry which cannot be developed to an optimum size within national boundaries.[2]

In Marxist economic literature, the Soviet economist, M.M. Maksimova, defines integration as follows:

economic integration . . . is the objective process of deep and persistent relations and of the international division of labour between national economies, the process of the formation of international economic complexes within the framework of groups of countries belonging to the same social and economic system. The process is regulated consciously according to the interests of the ruling classes of the states.[3]

Maksimova stresses five specific features of integration. First, integration is the development of deep and durable relations among national economies on the basis of the growing international division of labour, which implies that lasting and close ties are established among individual countries or industries and companies with the agents making appropriate adjustment to these relations. Second, integration is a flexible and adaptable process, in which the state organs of the member countries have an important role to play. Third, integration is predominantly of a regional nature. Fourth, as a result of integration, profound structural changes take place in the economies of the member countries, and, fifth, integration is closely associated with the socio-economic relations and struggles inherent in the framework of the participating states.[4]

Integration presupposes that the states may have considerable common interests, and therefore may be ready to renounce sovereignty in certain areas by internationalizing their national economic policy decisions. However, the process is contradictory. In the more developed parts of the world, the process of integration is the result of the internationalization achieved, while in the less developed regions, the objective of promoting economic development in the age of internationalization in an efficient way could be the main motive force. On this level integration is also a method of providing a regional pool of scarce human and material resources and an instrument to use the limited capacity of the regional market for the benefit of the producers from the region. The differences in the level of development determine to a great extent the propensity for establishing supranational institutions and for renouncing the right of nation-states to decision-making. These attitudes are not identical even in the individual member countries of the European Community, which is regarded as the most advanced form of international integration in the West.

The community of interests may also develop on the basis of different, often conflicting economic and political factors resulting from specific problems which the member countries try to resolve, and their position may change. Moreover, economic development is not even, consequently the benefits are not constant either, and the conditions of realization are subject to alteration. Compromises and agreements based on them are bound to break down. If the economic and political ties established by the community of interests are not strong enough, and there is no conscious and constant pressure and determination to settle the emerging problems, then the conflicts necessarily arising in the course of development may paralyse the integrational organizations and programmes, while steadily reproducing the disintegrating forces.

In principle, economic integration under certain conditions may be reduced to a smaller scale. Even within the framework of the EC, while it is improbable but not impossible as yet for the individual countries to withdraw, to restore their national customs frontiers and other means of economic protectionism, certain circumstances, for example, different economic interests, political problems, or the slowing-down of economic development may retard the advance of integration and the establishment of the single internal market by 1992. A similar effect may also be exerted on integration if the development of the member countries is extremely uneven. Development could also be slowed down if the present-day framework were extended too much, if such countries were to join the Community whose interests differed to a great extent from those of the other member countries.

The question of when, if at all, any integration group arrives at the point of no return, that is, at the point from which there is no return to the earlier national markets, to national economic policies, cannot be answered definitely. It depends mainly on the effect of economic political and institutional development taking place in its framework, the transformation of the production and consumption patterns of the member countries, the merger of the big corporations, state organs, and the like. Thus we cannot speak yet of a fully integrated European Community, and what is typical of the participating countries is rather complex interdependence. Integration is only a common aim yet to be attained. The other existing regional economic groups are at a much lower stage of the process.

The CMEA member countries' common objectives have called for the promotion of integration only since the end of the 1960s. Detailed objectives were embodied in the Comprehensive Programme of 1971. This programme has been implemented only in a few areas. CMEA member countries by 1989 represented 10 per cent of the population of the globe. About 15–16 per cent of the world product, 21 per cent of the global industrial output, 14 per cent of the agricultural production and 8.6 per cent of world trade came from those countries.

By the 1980s the CMEA countries were conducting about 60 per cent of their overall foreign trade with each other and there has been a fluctuation around this level since then. (There are, of course, differences among the countries concerning the proportion of intra-CMEA trade.) The bulk of the CMEA raw material, fuel and energy requirements are met within the framework of their community. (The proportion is declining since the late 1970s.) There were about 700 specialization agreements valid in 1985 and 40 per cent of the total trade in engineering products was based on those agreements. The link-up of their electric power grids, the common railway carriage pool, and a system of specialization agreements and special target programmes in key sectors represent the most important areas of co-operation. The settlements system is based on the principle of multilateral clearing and the accounting unit of their mutual trade is the transferable rouble. The prices in most cases are modified versions of the world market prices. (For about ten years, for example, the Soviet Union sold oil to the other members of the CMEA at a price which was the average of the world market price during the preceding five-year period.) The forms and content of co-operation have changed in many areas during the past thirty-five years. The organizational structure of the CMEA is also a result of continual changes which were connected with the new tasks and with the introduction of new elements in the co-operation of the member countries.

The structure of CMEA includes such organs as The Session of the Council, which functions as the Assembly; the Executive Committee, which is the main executive organ of the CMEA; the Committees of the Council, which work in special particularly important areas of co-operation; the Standing Commissions, which are the main organs of the CMEA for sectoral co-operation; and the secretariat of the CMEA which is an executive and administrative organ of the Council.

According to the Charter, the member countries enjoy rights of equal representation in the Council and in all its organs. Resolutions come into effect after being adopted by all the member countries. There are two basic types of resolutions: recommendations and decisions. Decisions are taken only in procedural and organizational matters. The resolutions do not apply to countries which declare their lack of interest in the matter concerned. The implementation of the resolutions takes place only after the approval and the necessary action of the member governments. CMEA is not a supra-national body with automatic legally binding decisions.

Bilateral intergovernmental commissions are also very important orga-nizations for co-operation within the framework of the CMEA. Multilateral and bilateral co-operation are closely linked in the CMEA framework. The whole system is basically a special combination of bilateral and multilateral forms of co-operation. The recommendations of the Council or of other different organs, for example, are implemented through bilateral agree-ments concluded by the member countries. This form of co-operation has certain advantages, especially in the field of protecting economic sover-eignty and safeguarding the equality of the member states. At the same time it slows down the implementation of the resolutions and it is a permanent source of different frictions. There are more than forty intergovernmental bilateral commissions, whose practice varies greatly.

The bilateral commissions play an especially important role in the co-ordination of the plans.

The procedure of plan co-ordination

Efforts for the harmonization of economic development with the help of plan co-ordination have been the most important features and basic methods of co-operation within the framework of the CMEA up to the end of the 1980s. This method was based on the centrally planned character of their economies. Since the economies were guided by the mandatory plan targets, it was considered that the mutually agreed obligations should become part of the national central plans. Since the late 1970s the central research organs of the CMEA have been preparing joint economic projec-tions for longer periods, in order to co-ordinate the main longer-term economic targets (ten to fifteen years) for the most important branches. There is a detailed system of plan co-ordination (with the original aims of joint planning in some areas) within the five-year plans, which constitute the most important medium-term development programme for the countries with centrally planned economies. The co-ordination plan includes the following elements:

1. Co-ordination of targets for the most important branches of the

    economy and product groups in industry, which are vital from the point
of view of technological economic progress.
2. A thorough and systematic co-ordination of the development of products, in which the individual countries specialize, within the framework
   of the CMEA, including the co-ordination of shipments of raw materials, ·
   machinery and equipment, foodstuffs and industrial consumer goods.
3. Co-ordination of co-operation and development in special branches and
   projects (including mutual contribution to the financing of certain
   projects), which play a key role in the satisfaction of future needs within
   the region.
4. Co-ordination in the field of regional development of the economy and in
   transport.

    The mechanism of the co-ordination plan went through several stages. At
the first stage, between 1949 and 1954, the member countries, after the
preparation of their national plans, co-ordinated their foreign trade plans.
The result of these activities was a set of mutual obligations for sales and
purchases. The second stage of the co-ordination plan (1955–62) was
characterized by the efforts to harmonize the needs and the possibilities of
the countries in physical terms. This was supposed to take place in two steps.
At first they prepared the preliminary outline of their national plans, which
facilitated the confrontation and the co-ordination of intentions. Then they
prepared balances in physical terms for the region: these balances were the
sums of the requirements and the expected sources of their satisfaction. The
third stage (1963–1975–77) had two distinct characteristics. At the beginning
of the period, ideas were raised to establish a system of joint planning for the
region as a whole, which would have been, if implemented, a modified
version of the national central planning system on the level of the CMEA.
The programme for joint planning as such, however, has never been carried
out. The suggested measures for international allocation of investments were
rejected by certain member countries which felt that it might lead to the
conservation of advantages by the more developed countries. Thus the whole
period was marked in fact by the continuation of the earlier methods with
some improvements of the co-ordination plan.

    Efforts for further steps in harmonization led to the elaboration of a new
programme, the above-mentioned 'Comprehensive Programme' adopted in
1971. This programme envisaged far-reaching developments in the mechanism of the co-ordination plan, also direct contacts between the economic
agents of the countries (firms, ministries, etc.), and the convertibility of the
national currencies. These ideas have not yet been implemented. Neither the
domestic nor the international conditions developed favourably from the
point of view of furthering CMEA integration. The shortcomings in
economic policies and the increasing problems with the inefficient working
of the existing system of planning and management also hindered the
implementation of the Programme.

    The co-ordination of plans for 1986–90 was still a basically bilateral
practice, which took place on the basis of long preparatory work both in the

multilateral commissions and other organs and in the national planning agencies of the respective countries.

The process of co-ordination was carried out along the following lines. Within the framework of the council, CMEA countries agreed on the length of the five-year plans and on co-ordination within the CMEA organs. They put special emphasis on certain issues like technological development. A separate long-term programme was adopted for that purpose. The special target programmes receive in general priority in the co-ordination process (energy, food, microelectronics, etc.). These programmes represent areas which greatly influence the economic development of the whole region. In accordance with those arrangements, a co-ordination programme was elaborated and approved by bilateral intergovernmental commissions. This included the methods, forms and terms of the work. The co-ordination plan was carried out in three stages. The first stage started between twenty-four and thirty months before the end of the previous five-year period in the national planning agencies. They, jointly with the ministries and other agencies, elaborated the main lines of their own national plans, with the help of projections and different calculations, and based on priorities determined by the economic policies. On the basis of this work the national planning agencies of the countries discussed bilaterally those targets, determined and agreed the principal areas of co-operation and envisaged the possible form of acceptable solutions (including tentative proposals for the delivery of goods, specialization, etc.). The targets of the national plans were formulated on the basis of these activities. In the second stage, the same organizations worked out specific terms and conditions of international co-operation for the five-year period. In accordance with the draft five-year plans, targets were tentatively established for the production of export items. The results of the co-ordination plan were formalized also in a bilateral framework by the heads of the central planning agencies, on the basis of which the foreign trade organizations concluded trade agreements for the given period. The results of the co-ordination plan at the third stage were structured in a system of agreements on different levels (firms, ministries, etc.). In the process of implementation there were regular consultations on economic policy issues between the countries covering a wide range of problems.

Earlier, the process of the co-ordination plan contributed to the solution of many difficult supply problems and increased the economic security of the member countries. In the second half of the 1980s the economic crisis of the CMEA region seriously hampered the mutual shipments. The co-ordination plan did not result in a smooth, harmonized economic development even in the earlier decades for the region as a whole. Especially under the difficult conditions of the 1970s and 1980s, it could not give sufficient support to countries in the adjustment process and in technological development. In the very difficult economic environment of the 1980s the cumulative impact of the earlier and the more recent problems of CMEA co-operation reduced its already limited relevance as an integration organization. The changing model of planning and management in certain countries and the continuity of the traditional structure in others became an important source of problems. Some of the very serious constraints are connected with the internal political and economic difficulties of the countries which contributed to the survival or revival of nationalistic trends, and influenced adversely the propensity for co-operation.

The model of a highly centralized inward-looking system of planning based on directives laid the economic foundation of nationalism in the past decades. Instead of creating complementary national economic complexes, it has created and maintained parallel economic structures. The system (mechanism) of planning and management neglected or disregarded, both nationally and internationally, such important categories as realistic prices (reflecting real costs and world market trends) and eliminated or limited the role of market forces (the real supply and demand trends could correct the shortcomings of central decisions and competition could squeeze out the inefficient producers). They did not make proper use of money and credit relations, with the help of which compensatory mechanisms could have been established for the sharing of the gains and losses of co-operation, thereby promoting a more rational and efficient international allocation of resources.

The mechanism of CMEA is still regarded as another very important source of difficulties in co-operation. While important decisions were made in several stages to improve the mechanism of co-operation, in practice, little or no progress was made in many important areas. It has become clearer by the second half of the 1980s that radical reforms are needed in co-operation policies, in the mechanism of capital and trade flows and in institutions in order to facilitate a smoother and more efficient functioning of the CMEA as an integration organization, or a qualitatively new co-operation structure must be established. This recognition was reflected during the summit conferences of the CMEA countries in 1988. Virtually every member country presented a reform programme. Important changes were envisaged, especially at the level of firms, facilitating direct inter-firm co-operation and joint ventures also between the member countries.

The new strategy and relations with the rest of the world

The CMEA summit in June 1984 adopted the guidelines for economic co-operation until the turn of the century. The substantial improvement of the mechanism of co-operation was also envisaged as part of the longer-term strategy. New principles were put forward for the improvement of co-operation with other non-CMEA countries.

Inter-CMEA co-operation has, of course, never been isolated from the political and economic relations of the member countries with the rest of the world. Since the late 1960s there has been an increasing reintegration of the CMEA countries with the other parts of the world economy. This process was facilitated by the *détente* process and by the mutual economic interests of the different partners.

The CMEA countries emphasized in the last ten to fifteen years their intention to include long-term agreements with other non-member countries in their five-year plans similar to the co-ordination plan process. In many cases, industrial and other co-operation agreements were concluded with Western firms or with developing countries and they became structural parts of the national plans. CMEA co-operation, unlike co-operation in the framework of the European Community, does not regulate relations with the rest of the world on a multilateral basis. Relations with non-CMEA member countries were raised in the resolutions of the 1984 CMEA summit as very important issues for all the countries. While it was emphasized that CMEA relations must be strong and efficient enough to defend the member countries from external pressures of different kinds, like discrimination or embargo policies, they should also facilitate co-operation with other countries and regions.

One of the areas where the 1984 principles were partially realized has been the mutual recognition and the agreement between CMEA and the European Communities. After a long period of mutual attacks, a tentative negotiation was initiated between the two integration groups in the 1970s, which was successfully concluded in 1988. Beyond the mutual recognition, it opened the way for direct negotiations and agreements between the Communities and the individual CMEA members.

The future of CMEA co-operation (including its future mechanisms), like any other form of international co-operation, is exposed to the impact of different factors:

- The interests of the member countries are influencing CMEA co-operation in many ways. This in itself is a complex, difficult and changing set of interactions. In the second half of the 1980s the CMEA countries had strong incentives to increase the efficiency of their co-operation, but the concrete expression of these incentives in programme proposals reflected many diverging factors.
- The changing needs and possibilities of the countries dictate the search for new partners. (Technological progress became a vital issue everywhere. Energy and raw material supplies from the USSR cannot be increased in the future at the past rates and conditions.)
- The internal economic difficulties of countries and their ability to overcome their problems are also a very important factor. All the CMEA countries are in the process of introducing changes in their economic policies and in the system of planning and management in order to improve the efficiency of their economies. The scope and the direction of these changes are not identical, but there are certain similarities. In economic policies the acceleration of technological development and the increase in productivity are occupying a central role. In the system of planning and management the autonomy of firms is increasing. The aim of improving the system of central planning by the use of different incentives is also emphasized everywhere. All these changes require more meaningful and flexible international co-operation within the CMEA and on a broader scale.

Conclusions

With over forty years of experience the CMEA has, through its achievements and failures, proved that successful harmonization of economic development on a regional scale through a co-ordination plan cannot be achieved without the presence and optimal combination of several important factors, for example:

- A high level of common interest in achieving similar political and economic goals.
- A genuine political determination by the member countries to carry out co-operation policies which take into account the interests of their partners and to fulfil their obligations.
- A certain degree of similarity of the national economic institutions, including those which are the instruments of international economic co-operation.
- Realistic prices and exchange rates which could be used to compare national input and output, also costs and benefits, in an international framework.
- Such a degree of factor mobility which is necessary at any given level of international co-operation, in order to facilitate smooth relations to balance the possible gains and losses of individual countries and promote the rational allocation of resources within the countries and on an international scale.
- Such a system of central planning in the member countries which can realize the long-term goals and obligations in a co-ordinated way and which is flexible enough to make the necessary adjustments in time in implementing co-ordinated policies.
- A degree of autonomy for economic organizations which provides flexibility in decisions and in their implementation, and allows different forms of co-operation among the economic organizations on various levels (firms, banks, ministries, etc.) on a bilateral and multilateral scale.
- An economic environment within countries and in the international framework allowing the required degree of competition to squeeze out inefficient structures and help to correct supply and demand imbalances.
- A set of regional international institutions, including special international funds for projects and adjustment assistance corresponding to the needs of co-operation.
- Agreements and practices which facilitate active participation in global economic co-operation and contribute to the increase of the bargaining power of the member countries in the global economy.
- A favourable experience (mutual gains) and correspondingly favourable attitudes of public opinion in member countries towards co-operation in the regional framework.

All the above factors must be supported by a favourable global economic and political environment which does not interfere adversely in the system of co-operation within the region.

The necessary supportive factors do not emerge at once and automatically. They must often be created by deliberate actions. They must be changed according to the changing interests and conditions. The less the countries are able to create those factors, the more limited the achievements will be in harmonizing economic development within the region.

Notes

1. *Economic Integration, Worldwide, Regional, Sectoral: Proceedings of the Fourth Congress of I.E.A.,* London, Macmillan, 1976.
2. Vajda, I. and M. Simai, *Foreign Trade in a Planned Economy,* Cambridge, Cambridge University Press, 1971, p. 35.
3. *Economic Integration, Worldwide, Regional, Sectoral,* op. cit., p. 33.
4. Ibid., pp. 32–3.

Selected reading

Machlup, Fritz (ed.), *Economic Integration Worldwide, Regional, Sectoral,* London, Macmillan, 1976.

Mihály, Simai, *Interdependence and Conflicts in the World Economy,* Alpen aan den Rijn, The Netherlands, Siijthoff & Noordhoff, 1981.

——, 'The role of the socialist countries of Eastern Europe in the world economy', *Trade and Development,* No. 5, UNCTAD 1984, pp. 331–48.

5 Harmonization

R.J. Harrison and *Stuart Mungall*

Scope of the activity

A contemporary phenomenon of international behaviour, evident at various levels, is the attempt to ensure that the separate policies of a number of states are in concordant alignment with each other. The label harmonization readily suggests the nature of this activity. In musical use it connotes the contemporaneous pursuit of separate themes within a conventional framework, avoiding discord. International 'harmonization', in this metaphor requires a 'score' of common information, common interpretation, and agreement on relevant values in pursuing separate policies. In practice, the attempt to compose this commonality and agreement usually involves some kind of international organization but, essentially in our conception, the functional activities themselves remain the responsibility of the separate states.

The term is further 'refined' in the present work, beyond popular usage, to distinguish this level of activity from 'co-operation', a term reserved here for the piecemeal working-out of specific agreements to adjust a nationally conducted policy for a specific purpose.[1] There is no attempt to define an overall framework of policy guidelines. Co-operation is therefore more limited in scope than harmonization. We distinguish also 'co-ordination' which denotes policy adjustment by international prescription, laying down a specific policy obligation for states rather than a principle to which their individually shaped policies must conform.[2] In our stipulation then, harmonization is wider in potential scope than 'co-operation' and less specific in its policy implications than 'co-ordination'. Characteristically it results in Conventions expressing principles in a number of fields, under the aegis of one international organization.

Relevant assumptive framework

Such harmonization stands in no explicit, or obviously implicit, relationship to any coherent philosophy of, or approach to, international politics. The closest thing to a coincidental rationalization of it, perhaps, may be found in Benthamite utilitarianism. While Bentham is emphatic that there is no natural harmony of interest between individuals so that 'on every occasion, the happiness of every individual is liable to come into competition with the happiness of every other',[3] he takes a different view of the interests of states or nations. 'Between the interests of nations, there is nowhere any real conflict: if they appear repugnant anywhere, it is only in proportion as they are misunderstood.'[4] This assertion (heavily qualified in the development of Bentham's argument) depends on two basic assumptions: the first is that a state or nation is an artificial construct, not to be considered as a person. It has its property, its honour, its condition, but other things being equal it may be attacked 'in all these particulars without the individuals who compose it being affected'.[5] Private ownership and public sovereignty are all too easily confused.[6] Bentham's second assumption is that there is a natural economic harmony of interests which makes attempts to secure trading preferences and overseas territories pointless and wasteful. Blood and treasure must be expended on securing and maintaining them. And any attempt to encourage a particular trade, or direction of trade, necessarily and *pro tanto* discourages some other, which might have been more profitable[7] — a classical free-trade argument.

Bentham recognizes that these two abstracted deducible realities are very much obscured in international behaviour by prejudice and confusion — a social artifice of habit and convention which results in unnecessary and damaging wars between states who genuinely believe they are defending the 'right'.[8] There are, of course, wars *mala fides,* undertaken for the perfectly rational objective of despoiling another state. The wars of antiquity are examples. So too, Bentham suggests were the wars of the New Zealanders (Maoris) — for while the conquered fry, the conquerors fatten.[9] And it may be quite proper, on calculation, to resist such predatory aggressors and form alliances against them in war. But for the nations of today, who act for the most part, Bentham thought, *bona fides,* a different course recommends itself.

For the individual state, the object of its behaviour should be the general utility, avoiding injury to, and promoting the good of, other nations, saving the regard proper to its own well-being. For all such states, the mutual objective would be to work out a code of written and unwritten agreements in matters where the interests of states are capable of collision; to reduce the possible area of dispute by instituting general liberty of commerce, and to reach previous agreement on such matters as boundaries, new discoveries and the rules which should apply. In sum, the individual states would follow the line of least resistance in the pursuit of their own interests,[10] but would co-operate in the elaboration of a code which would reduce the possibilities of encountering resistance in areas of interdependence. Bentham suggested that a common international court of judicature, without coercive powers, might well play a useful role in interpreting such rules and agreements.[11]

Unlike the functionalist, David Mitrany, Bentham did not contemplate the possibility that internationally performed functional services would reduce the role of national governments and make them 'meaningless'. He shared the functionalist view of the illusory and artificial nature of the nation-state system and its arbitrary and often detrimental relationship to man's welfare interests, but he was too much of a realist to suppose that the system could be fundamentally changed by direction.

Operational experience

Contemporary harmonization conforms with the Benthamite model in that it depends operationally on the possibility that states will at least act in good faith to achieve what are presumed to be generally compatible though not identical interests. Harmonization suggests itself where discussion between national policy-makers may discover an existing value consensus which can be the ground for a wide range of agreements.

Still in line with Bentham's model, the prescriptive implications produce only a limited structural impact on international society. The relevant international institutions may be equated with so called 'forum' organizations as distinct from the more highly developed 'service' organizations.[12] That is to say that their role is limited to facilitating the development of a common framework of principles according to which member states will regulate their own activities. The discussions and agreement serve to legitimize national activities both domestically and internationally, characteristically, by the formulation of open conventions like the International Labour Conventions and the Convention on Human Rights of the Council of Europe. A secretariat may exist for the collection, analysis and dissemination of information relevant to discussion by governments.

The International Labour Organization (ILO)

In its early years, after its foundation in 1919, the ILO, for example, was primarily concerned with framing international labour standards. It brought together, in a tripartite Labour Conference, representatives of governments, employers and workers. All three sections met separately to prepare their positions for plenary sessions. This was a design which exploited the distinction between the citizen and the government of the sovereign state; it might very well have been approved by Bentham. It exploited, too, the potential commonality of interest of like sections of different national communities. This commonality was, to a considerable degree, realized in practice by the two non-governmental groups in expanding the role of the Organization. The International Federation of Trade Unions (Amsterdam International), which co-ordinates union action in the ILO, provided very considerable support for the first Director, Albert Thomas, a French Socialist, enabling him to take initiatives both in the negotiation of Labour standards and in proposals for social policy. This was archetypically 'harmonization' — creating standards implemented as policy by the individual states in their own ways.[13]

The Council of Europe

The Council of Europe is another obvious agency of harmonization. It is a 'forum' rather than a service organization, though, in the intention of some of its creators, it was to be an agency of integration which would produce a United States of Europe rather than merely a device to maintain harmony between separate member states.

For the first two years of its existence the Assembly of the Council of Europe attempted to act as if it were the legislature of a supranational authority. However, it lacked effective support amongst the peoples and interests of Western Europe. It therefore resorted to a less ambitious goal — that of providing some of the conditions upon which a union might in future be built. This involved the mundane task of identifying and giving expression to common interests and values, and, through recommendations and resolutions, urging the Committee of Ministers to establish Conventions and Agreements in an effort to harmonize elements of national policies. The list of conventions and agreements that are the outcome of these pressures is large, wide in scope and somewhat recondite. By 1974, some twenty-five years after the setting-up of the Council, the list had eighty-four items. Apart from the well-known Convention of Human Rights, the conventions and agreements cover a large variety of subjects: social (e.g. European Agreement on 'au pair' placement (1969)); cultural (e.g. European Cultural Convention (1954)); patents (e.g. European Convention on the Formalities required for Patent Application (1953)); broadcasting and television (e.g. European Agreement for the Protection of Television Broadcasts transmitted from stations outside National Territories (1965)); legal (e.g. European Convention on the International Validity of Criminal Judgments (1970)); public health (e.g. European Agreement on the Exchange of Blood-grouping Reagents (1962)); international travel (e.g. European Agreement on Travel by Young Persons on Collective Passports between the Member Countries of the Council of Europe (1961)); environment (e.g. European Agreement on the restriction of the use of certain detergents in washing and cleaning products (1968)).

While the setting of standards and principles is the most characteristic method of harmonization, it is by no means the only method. Of considerable importance are activities designed to socialize significant national actors towards common international objectives, and to encourage the development of an international identity from which policy alignments may follow. The Council of Europe has encouraged such activities by sponsoring specialized conferences. At the instigation of the Assembly, and with the eventual support of the Committee of Ministers, a European Conference of Local and Regional Authorities has been sponsored. Further examples include the European Parliamentary and Scientific Conference, the Conference of Ministers of Education and the Conference of European Ministers of Justice. In an attempt to increase public awareness of the activity of the Council of Europe in 1975, it sponsored European Architectural Heritage Year.

In distinct contrast to the albeit ambiguous goals of the Council of Europe, the purposes ascribed to the Organisation of Economic Co-operation and Development (OECD) by its founders eschew supranational pretensions. The executive body of the OECD, the Council, cannot pass binding decisions. All decisions have to be ratified by due constitutional process before they are so regarded. At its origin the OECD was well prepared for all the limitations and possibilities of a harmonizing role amongst its member states. Its purposes were explicitly economic and non-contentious, avoiding intrusion on sensitive areas of national sovereignty. Moreover, until the latter years of the 1960s, global economic conditions generally sustained the goals of economic growth and development, financial stability and trade expansion. Understandably in these favourable circumstances, the OECD's role as a harmonizing agent was relatively easy.

Four techniques have been available to the organization for harmonization. The first technique is research: that is the investigation, collation and distribution of information against which national policies may be judged or from which national policy-makers may be able to create or modify their own policies. Furthermore, research involves examining the implications of national policies, whether proposed or actual, against the interests of the other OECD members, against other policy areas and indeed, against the needs of the national actor concerned. In order that such research may be useful to governments it must cover important areas of policy, it must be constantly alive to the shifting concerns of government and it must be presented in a fashion that reflects fairly accurately the complex interrelations of issues facing governments.

The second technique for harmonization is that of reviewing periodically the national policies of member states in specific areas of activity.[14] Normally this is carried out annually and it is a technique employed by many of the specialist committees of the OECD. The most important review is that carried out by the Economic and Development Review Committee which results in the publication of Annual Economic Surveys of member states. The technique is also employed, for example, by the Development Assistance Committee and more recently by the International Energy Agency, where the concern is to review energy conservation measures. Officials of the OECD conduct the review in co-operation with national officials in the relevant ministries. A comparison is made between the principles and methodological or statistical assumptions employed by the OECD in its analysis of the issues and those employed by the national officials. Deficiencies and disagreements in the respective analyses can thus be isolated and the reviews allow rational policies to be judged against the interests of the OECD as a whole. Moreover, officials of other member states are able to comment upon the policies of the member under review and thus impart their preferences.

An interesting extension of the review technique both in itself and as an illumination of limits and possibilities of harmonization, is the system of notification and consultation activated by the OECD Council in 1971 in the field of environment policy.[15] Voluntarily and without legal restraint member countries have agreed to notify the OECD whenever they propose or pursue policies which introduce pernicious materials into the environment. Consultation follows, in which the action can be assessed against the principles already evolved by the OECD in dealing with environmental matters (e.g. the Polluter Pays Principle) and the consequences for other countries can be aired. The important points to be noted are the voluntary nature of the notification, the lack of legal sanctions and the reliance upon persuasion and consultation as a means of exercising influence. The aim is to achieve a concern for the consequences of an action by one member state for conditions in other member states. The transfrontier nature of some pollution is thus exploited as a means of attaining harmony: this is another example of interdependence between members aiding the purposes of the organisation. Attempts to impose policies from the international centre are avoided and the issue of national sovereignty is sidestepped.

The third technique is the mutual cross-examination between high national officials responsible for particular areas of national policy. This technique evolved from confrontation in the OEEC but the term no longer seems to be in general use in the OECD. In the opinion of a former Secretary-General:

The impact of the action of the organisation derives to a very large extent from the fact that high level policy-makers from the capitals meet in Paris (the Head-quarters of the OECD) and are able to compare and collate their views directly and to keep each other in touch with policies pursued in various countries.[16]

The technique involves the periodic (normally annual) examination, country by country, of some aspect of life of member states held to be of interest to all members. Such aspects are the economy, social welfare system and energy resources. Each state presents a report to the relevant OECD committee, outlining the situation with regard to this aspect of national life and explaining the policies used to attain certain ends and the assumptions underlying these policies. This process does, of course, get very close to that of co-ordination. The main difference lies in the stress, in this case placed upon mutual information and advice, rather than on amending policies and structures in the interest of a common programme. The scrutiny and debate are carried out in secret and the confidentiality allows a frankness about politically sensitive issues which a public forum would preclude. Since officials rather than politicians are involved a greater degree of detachment is also possible.

Clearly the technique will, on the one hand, heighten the awareness of the international consequences of national actions and provide an opportunity for informed comment on the desirability of the action even from the member's own parochial perspective. On the other hand, it allows other members to acquire an understanding of the premises upon which policies are based and on the political pressures that impinge upon the government of the examined country. Finally, it increases the distribution of knowledge of how other countries have handled similar problems and may thus assist useful innovation. The most important application of the technique is in the field of economic policy where it is operated under the aegis of the Economic Policy Committee. Economic Reports are, however, approved by the states involved before publication. It is also employed by the Development Assistance Committee and, as we saw earlier, the Environment Committee.

Clearly the technique of mutual cross-examination is markedly different in style and even substance from the conventional forum, which, we have argued, is associated with harmonization. It does not conform to the defining criterion of setting standards on the basis of common values. Rather, it assumes these common values, and stresses instead the interdependence of member states and the mutual dangers of pursuing divergent policies. And here policies stand to values in much the same way as ends to means. The scope of the technique can be as extensive as the awareness of transfrontier consequences of national actions. Finally, it conforms to the criterion that functional responsibility should be retained within the member state. Binding agreements are not an outcome of this technique: the examined official is not a plenipotentiary.

The final technique to consider now is the conventional one we have ascribed to harmonization: the forum. Forum activities of the OECD take place within the executive organ, the Council, the various specialist committees, and within the working parties and *ad hoc* groups set up to consider areas of activity or particular issues. From the research activities undertaken in these various organs and from the discussions conducted therein, declarations of principle or guidelines for future behaviour may emerge. The research upon which these discussions are based is carried out by the Secretariat of the OECD. Those involved in the resulting discussions may be Ministers of the member states, in the case of the Council; permanent representatives of the members; national officials drawn from their own capitals on a temporary basis, and finally, in the case of some *ad hoc* groups, experts drawn from various walks of life. What tends to emerge from the forum is a Declaration of Principle in very general terms on such matters as trade practices, pollution and immigration.

These four techniques for harmonization — research, review, mutual cross-examination between high officials and conferences — clearly overlap and it is consequently difficult and perhaps pointless to attempt to weigh them. The general picture, however, is of an organization struggling to achieve harmonization by raising the awareness of its member states of their own interdependence, to the similarity of the problems they face and to the compatibility of related assumptions and principles. The OECD is manifesting some latent transformation potential which, as we noted with the ILO may be inherent in successful harmonization. The extension of the scope of the OECDs activities following the attachment of the International Energy Agency, the Nuclear Energy Agency and the Development Centre are responses to world economic and political developments.

Appraisal

These three examples of major organizational manifestations of harmonization suggest the circumstances that are conducive to this type of approach to international organization. These were already alluded to in the assumptive framework outlined at the start of this chapter but can be briefly restated here. First, a common set of values and a common store of information and interpretation is required. Second, an awareness of interdependence, and an acceptance of the view that transfrontier consequences of national actions ought to be a matter of concern for the national actors, has to exist or to develop. Third, a presumption in favour of the retention of sovereignty within the nation-state is an imperative. Any aspiration for supranationalism threatens the national political actors who alone possess the political resources from which to undertake actions in the interest of the international collectivity.

Of course national actors need not be governmental actors. We have already noticed this in the case of the ILO but numerous less ambiguous examples exist. For example, in January 1976 an international maritime industry forum met in London. It discussed ways of dealing with the oil tanker problem and considered ways of planning the flow of new tankers. We can see that common values, information and its interpretation operated to stimulate action as did an awareness of interdependence and a respect for actor sovereignty.

In such cases the forum established need not be permanent. It may be an *ad hoc* response to specific problems. The Montreal International Conference on highjacking which produced a Convention[17] on the problem seems to fall into this category. Special United Nations conferences can also be included such as the 1974 Conferences on Food and Population problems[18] and the 1976 Conference on the Law of the Sea. The International Conference on Economic Co-operation held in Paris in December 1975 is a further example, although, from this, four specialist committees have been set up to continue research into particular problems.

The major advantage of harmonization in achieving policy congruence amongst various national actors is that it explicitly avoids intruding on national sovereignty. Individual members have been 'maintaining' rather than 'transforming' objectives. The organizations that manifest this approach do not claim or seek supranational authority. They are servants rather than aspirant masters, and while their influence is not thereby negligible, the techniques open to them for the exertion of influence are inevitably undramatic. Pressure has to be applied through the language of national interest and not through the rhetoric of idealistic, collectivist goals. A comparison between the EEC Commission and the OECD illuminates the difference between an organization with a formally dynamic, co-ordinating role and one which eschews supranational goals. The former has been an object of acute political controversy for it has been perceived by some member states as using its mandate for uniting Europe against their interests. On the other hand the history of the latter is marked by the absence of controversy about its operations, its legitimacy or its organizational aspirations. Such controversy as there has been, say, over alternative assessments of national economic prospects is likely to be seen in the long run as a potentially productive technical disagreement rather than a matter

for highly coloured political debate employing all the symbols of nationalism or supranationalism.

While harmonization may be an eminently suitable strategy for an
international organization in a world of nation states, what can be said
regarding its utility as a device for achieving policy congruence while
retaining functional responsibility with the national actors? It is tempting to
rush to a conclusion based upon examination of the declared goals of the
organization, the principles and guidelines it has established, and the
declarations of intent that have been made. Have the goals been attained?
Are the guidelines adhered to? Has the intent been matched by action? In
some cases of standard setting, it is possible to establish a relationship
between the action of the organization and the behaviour of national actors.
A survey by Yemin,[19] for example, suggested that following the adoption by
the ILO of the Termination of Employment Recommendation in 1963, the
principle embraced in the recommendation that 'a worker should not lose
his job without a valid reason', was more rapidly adopted by member
countries than would have been predicted from past trends.[20]

But the important point about harmonization is not whether a specific
outcome weighs more or less heavily with a government facing a particular
decision. Rather it derives from the fact that officials of that government
participate in the process from which the guideline or principle evolves. The
real test of the utility of harmonization is whether, *over time,* organisations
manifesting this characteristic can extend the area over which national
actors find it useful to interact with their fellows. By a rather crude rule of
thumb, that of whether the organization has evolved, or has had attached to
itself, a widening number of interests, the OECD stands out as the most
successful of the harmonizing organizations we have considered. While the
International Labour Organization has evolved a substantial set of service
rather than forum activities it has lacked the organizing principle, such as
economic growth in the OECD, around which novel interests can be woven.
The Council of Europe is limited by the static nature of the values it
embodies: they are declarations of identity rather than dynamic, constantly
evolving commitments. Economic growth and development, financial
stability, trade and aid expansion are concrete goals of government amongst
the member states of the OECD. Attaining or maintaining these goals is a
substantial validation of political regimes at least in the eyes of the political
élites. It is for this reason — that political élites are interested in the same
questions as those examined by the OECD — that the organization stands
out as important compared to the others we have considered.

Evidently changing political objectives on the part of member states could
alter the relative status of these organizations. Socialist states may be more
impressed by the work of the ILO if working conditions come to be
perceived as a basis for their domestic political support. If popular support
for European union suddenly emerged, the weightiness of the statements
and actions of the Council of Europe would undoubtedly be enhanced. The
ideological implications of the Conference on Security and Co-operation in
Europe and the democratic developments in Greece, Portugal and Spain

have undoubtedly allowed the Council to enhance its status, however marginally, by calling for actions to be made in accordance with the values enshrined in its Statute.

A further aspect of the problem of utility is the extent to which international organizations overlap each other in terms of functional interests. This overlap is often deliberate. For example, Working Party No. 3 of the OECD's Economic Policy Committee is composed of the same members as the 'Group of Ten', indeed, they are the same people. The Group of Ten is, in fact, serviced by the OECD, the IMF and the Bank of International Settlement in Basle. As Working Party No. 3 in the OECD the group of Ten 'is concerned with the impact of economic policies on the international payments situation, the adjustment and financing of payments imbalances and with the likely evolution of payments patterns over the longer term'.[21] The location of this Group within the OECD is an appreciation of the fact that an adequate picture of the world's monetary problems was not given within the IMF. It was necessary to deal with the underlying economic problems and the OECD seemed the more appropriate institution for this approach.

Such a potentially creative overlap is by no means invariably the case. Other overlaps are simply the product of separate organizational development and although a creative competition may be one consequence, another may be duplication of effort and the squandering of scarce resources. Such cases of overlap abound: EEC's Euratom and the OECD's Nuclear Energy Agency; the environment protection work of the EEC and the OECD; efforts of the Council of Europe and the European Council to harmonize foreign policies.

The vital factor determining the utility of a harmonizing international organization in terms of its functional scope is the level of awareness amongst member states of their interdependence. Interdependence, the situation in which the action of one affects the environment or conditions or the behaviour of one or several others, provides conditions in which the national interest can be seen to coincide with a collective, international interest. The issue of sovereignty is sidestepped. What this seems to suggest is that harmonizing international organizations can work most effectively in areas where actors operate in a self-interested manner and these are not only areas where values are congruent but where the operational goals of governments coincide. Interdependence is thus both an asset of such organizations and a condition of which they must make member states aware.

Increasing levels of economic specialization, world-shrinking communications, and a widening perception of global resource depletion and environmental pollution together suggest that both the awareness and actuality of interdependence are expanding phenomena. In such circumstances, the scope for harmonization will increase.

It is important to stress once again that this likely development reflects the continued supremacy of the states — whether national or otherwise. Harmonization may well reflect a desire to conduct affairs between states more rationally, it may even spur on this development. But it will not lead, in itself, to the supercession of the nation-state. This is because the sources of political support, the legitimacy of major actors upon the international stage — the national political élites — lie within the confines of each individual state. This is why supranationalist organizations with an élite rather than a mass following normally have insubstantial effects upon national political systems.

But within the marginal structural impact achieved by such organizations a problem does arise. To the extent that such organizations impinge upon specific national policies do they thereby undermine national political processes? There are probably two extreme answers which can be given to this question. The first is that the question is irrelevant because in a context of value congruence, and operational goal coincidence, harmonizing efforts are more likely to lead to the better or faster achievement of national goals and thus reinforce the national political process. In effect, harmonization provides mechanisms for expert cross-examination and diffusion of knowledge. The negative answer would be that through processes of actor socialization, bureaucratic interpretation and such like, valid alternatives open to national actors are perceived to be progressively closed. Moreover, in the context of the problem of partisan control of administration, contracts between high-level national officials may well result in implicit agreements or dispositions which bias the presentation of evidence and options by the official to his political master.

In stating the problem we have probably given more importance to the answers than they are worth, at least within the context of the influence of harmonizing organizations upon their members. However the opinions and pressures generated by the organization are only one factor in determining specific national policy decisions and where the goal set by the organization is couched in terms of an ideal rather than from an awareness of practical politics, the influence of the organization may well be marginal. For example, the Development Assistance Committee of the OECD has struggled to raise the level of aid given by the wealthier OECD members to 1 per cent of their GNP. This is in line with a UN figure. Countries such as Sweden and West Germany are responsive to such appeals while others such as Austria are almost indifferent. But these different responses do not reflect a greater or lesser degree of influence by the OECD because elements within these countries already support such goals, or oppose them as the case may be. As with all international organizations, the relative standing of the organization in the eyes of each national community is a vital determinant of the comparative degree of success of their decisions or declarations or guidelines. In the case above, Sweden and West Germany attribute a higher degree of worth to the decisions and declarations of international organizations than does Austria.

As a corollary to the previous comments, the degree to which such decisions or declarations reflect political realities, will enhance the prospects that the organization's output will be accepted and adhered to. Harmonization by its nature involves a humble approach in terms of achieving structural transformation. It operates within the actual political realities by eschewing supranationalism and appealing to the self-interest of each actor in achieving mutual resolution of the problems of interdependence.

Notes

1. See chapters 2 and 4 on this concept.
2. See chapters 2 and 3.
3. *The Works of Jeremy Bentham, Published under the Supervision of his Executor, John Bowring* (11 Vols, 1843), Vol. ix, p. 6.
4. *Ibid*, Vol. ii, p. 559.
5. *Ibid*, Vol. ii, p. 539.
6. *Ibid*, Vol. ii, p. 554.
7. *Ibid*, Vol. ii, pp. 557-9.
8. *Ibid*, Vol. ii, pp. 539-40.
9. *Ibid*, Vol. ii, p. 557.
10. *Ibid*, Vol. ii, p. 535.
11. *Ibid*, Vol. ii, p. 552.
12. The distinction is made in these terms by R.W. Cox and H.K. Jacobson in their *The Anatomy of Influence: decision-making in international organization*, New Haven, Yale University Press, 1973, p. 5.
13. See E.J. Phelan, *Yes and Albert Thomas*, London, Crescent Press, 1949.
14. See 'Industrial policy developments in OECD countries', *Annual Review 1988*, Paris, OECD, 1989.
15. See for a summary account of this activity, *O.E.C.D. at Work for Environment*, 2nd edn, Paris, OECD July 1973.
16. Emile van Lennep, Secretary-General OECD *Activities of the O.E.C.D. in 1970*, Paris, OECD, 1971, p. 12.
17. Convention for the Suppression of Unlawful Acts against the Safety of Civil Aviation.
18. A permanent World Food Council was set up at the behest of the Conference. For a discussion of such phenomena, see Paul Taylor and A.J.R. Groom (eds.), *Global Issues of the United Nations' Framework*, London, Macmillan, 1989.
19. E. Yemin, 'Job Security: Influence of I.L.O. Standards and Recent Trends', *International Labour Review*, January–February, 1976.
20. Note also the possible link between the Trade Pledge, against protectionist measures, taken by OECD members at a Council meeting in May 1974, (and renewed in May 1975) and the, largely successful, resistance by governments to pressures for such restrictions in the face of balance of payments deficits.
21. OECD Department of Economics and Statistics, Paris, OECD, 1975, p.9.

Selected reading

Cox, Robert W. and Jacobson, Harold K., *The Anatomy of Influence*, New York, Yale University Press, 1973.

Lennep, Emile van, Secretary General OECD, *Activities of the O.E.C.D. in 1970*, Paris, OECD 1971.

Phelan, E.J. *Yes and Albert Thomas*, London, Crescent Press, 1949.

Robertson, A.H., *European Institutions,* 3rd edn, London, Stevens & Sons, 1973.
Taylor, P. and Groom A.J.R. (eds), *International Institutions at Work,* London, Pinter, 1988.
Yemin, E., 'Job security: influence of I.L.O. standards and recent trends', *International Labour Review,* January/February 1976.

6 Association

John Kinnas and *A.J.R. Groom*

Association is not a term that has an immediate and salient meaning in the political lexicon, although it is of considerable, if uncertain, lineage. In some regards the leagues of European history, such as the Hanseatic League, are a recognizable antecedent but the contemporary phenomenon has no direct and clear historical precedent on which to draw. Contemporary thought on the subject reflects some of the qualities of the phenomenon itself — it is of a practical rather than a conceptual bent. Such practice coalesces around two different but complementary forms of association — an association of states and association of a state with an international governmental organization (IGO). While associations of states have links, however tenuous, with a distant past, association with an IGO is a relatively recent phenomenon since IGOs themselves have become thick on the ground only in this century. This form of association has become particularly noteworthy as a by-product of supranational integration projects, and most especially in Europe.

The relevance of an association of states

In contemplating alternative paths to world order, Hedley Bull called attention to a new medievalism:

It is . . . conceivable that sovereign states might disappear and be replaced not by a world government but by a modern and secular equivalent of the kind of universal political organization that existed in Western Christendom in the Middle Ages. In that system no ruler or state was sovereign in the sense of being supreme over a given territory and a given segment of the Christian population; each had to share authority with vassals beneath, and with the Pope and (in Germany and Italy) the Holy Roman Emperor above. The universal political order of Western Christendom represents an alternative to the system of states which does not yet [or no longer] embody universal government. . . .
It is familiar that sovereign states today share the stage of world politics with 'other actors' just as in mediaeval times the state had to share the stage with 'other associations' (to use the mediaevalists' phrase). If modern states were to come to share their authority over their citizens, and their ability to command their loyalties, on the one hand with regional and world authorities, and on the other hand with sub-state or sub-national [or transnational] authorities, to such an extent that the concept of sovereignty has ceased to be applicable, then a neo-mediaeval form of universal political order might be said to have emerged.[1]

Bull held that such a system was not a very good description of contemporary world society and that the 'ubiquitous and continuous violence and insecurity' of Western Christendom was not a very hopeful precedent.[2] Yet his suggestion should not be so easily dismissed.

The extent to which the contemporary world is state-centric is a matter of considerable theoretical dispute and empirical obfuscation. There are those that hold, like Bull, that sovereignty is still a dominating feature of world society while others deny its continuing validity.[3] Some, like Arnold Wolfers, imagine the world in terms of billiards balls — separate, internally coherent and hierarchically organized, able to act as a unit with a hard exterior (or state boundary) — while others, such as John Burton, conceptualize the world as a cobweb where different dimensions have different boundaries, be they economic, security, health or education, each superimposed on the other, so that it makes more sense to think in terms of systems of transactions between a variety of actors across a range of functional dimensions rather than a world in which governments are, or can be, in some sense in charge.[4] What are we to make of thousands of IGOs, INGOs and BINGOs? Of the Mafia, the International Olympic Committee, ICI or of the Association of Commonwealth Universities, not to mention the IMF or the Warsaw Treaty Organization? Moreover, is the government itself coherent? The classic question is no longer 'who governs?', but rather 'is government possible?', in a world in which government departments, agencies and parastatals seemingly have their own foreign policy, each hardly co-ordinated and sometimes contradictory with that of others.

Association has a place in both these worlds, state-centric and non-statecentric. Indeed, it facilitates that great trick of being able to have the cake and eat it. In the real world state-centricity waxes and wanes in different functional dimensions, but not necessarily in the same direction and to the same extent in different dimensions. Flexibility and institutional diversity are thus necessary to accommodate such movements, for to deny movements between state-centricity and transnationalism is to run the risk of irrelevance or conflict. Association can be an important part of the repertoire of institutional forms for obviating such dangers. It can allow a loose grouping of states within which transnational ties can flourish or extend such a grouping in certain dimensions through association agreements between IGOs and third parties, thus enabling form better to follow function.

In such circumstances the plenitude and panoply of sovereignty is not seriously prejudiced, but it is no longer pristine pure. In so far as an association of states is concerned, there are many variations both historical and actual. Association may, of course, be a way-stage on the road to full sovereignty as in the historical examples of the German Empire until 1871 which was in a process of sovereignty through integration, or the British Commonwealth of the inter-war period which was characterized by the *inter se* doctrine,[5] in a process of disintegration to separate sovereign states. Association can now respond to the needs of putative sovereign states by allowing the PLO to act in some regards as the representative of a future

Palestine in respect of other states and international institutions. But association can be an end-state in its own right and there are numerous and important contemporary examples of associations of states. The Commonwealth, the Non-Aligned Movement, the Initiative of Six Presidents and Prime Ministers, and the Contadoro Group all fall into this category. The Commonwealth is sometimes considered to be *sui generis,* however it can more properly be seen not as an anomaly among international institutions but as an exemplar of a particular form of association.[6]

The Commonwealth as an association of nations

The contemporary Commonwealth reached its present form in the early 1970s. It then began to play its new, modest but efficient role in world affairs — economic, political, technical and social — buttressed, as ever, by its network of non-governmental ties. Despite its nebulous character which defies adequate definition, the Commonwealth is real, significant and relevant. It encompasses a network of ties, governmental and non-governmental, in virtually every domain known to humankind: it has grown out of and facilitates an impressive movement of goods, services, ideas and people in a remarkably non-coercive framework. This informality and diversity of relationships is facilitated by the lack of a Constitution, but it is, nevertheless, guided and moulded by a set of formal principles and the evolution of habits rooted in established and acceptable practice.[7]

The Commonwealth is a voluntary association of governments and NGOs sharing an historic British connection who wish to work together to further their individual and common interests. They have a surprising but real sense of fraternity which comes through in the behaviour of even the most hard-nosed participants and which has survived many buffetings of considerable political import. This sense of fraternity, which is characteristic of associations in general, has two elements: the first is a 'distant cousin syndrome' and the second is a sense of common interest. The distant cousin analogy suggests that Commonwealth governments and peoples react to each other in new circumstances in a different way from non-Commonwealth governments and peoples. Just as on meeting a distant cousin for the first time a person will observe the rules of family ties and behaviour by sharing information and affording help in an open relationship in a manner that would not be accorded to a total stranger, so Commonwealth 'distant cousins' do not approach each other negatively, but positively, and in a co-operative and friendly manner. There is a sense of 'we-feeling' pervading Commonwealth relations that includes a notion of Commonwealth interest, and even international community interest, beyond the pursuit of self-interest. Even where disputes arise between Commonwealth members, the aim is, at the very least, to discuss issues in an independent and catalytic manner if this will help and if it is desired. It is to be supportive of the parties rather than to be partisan.

The generally supportive nature of the Commonwealth is illustrated by the decision-making process. The Commonwealth can only recommend: it cannot command or coerce. Its informality in negotiation is exemplified by the seminar-like Heads of Government meetings with their frequent interjections, the general avoidance of set speeches and the usually friendly, even 'matey' atmosphere which, although sometimes interrupted by tension, nevertheless permits the frank discussion of delicate issues. Heads of Government can let themselves go with a peer group without fear that advantage will be taken. This is a situation rare in their experience to which they therefore attach importance. Any decisions, if decisions are required and desired, will be taken by consensus and in private. And they usually return home having found the meeting fertile in ideas. Indeed, the Commonwealth is not only about the business that it does, but also about the way in which it does business.

Yet to participate in this process is in no sense to deny participation in other organizations. Indeed, one of the Commonwealth's virtues is its diversity, and practically all Commonwealth countries also have strong regional or other extra-Commonwealth ties. Indeed, the Commonwealth is not one thing: it is different things in different areas and for different members. Its diversity and flexibility, but continued relevance, allow all to join in to the extent of where and how they wish to do so. It is used by all its members, but it is held dearest by those who have few other avenues into the world. Moreover, as its Secretary-General, Mr Ramphal, has suggested, 'the Commonwealth cannot negotiate for the world; but it can help the world to negotiate.'[8] It is not, therefore, particularly salient but it usually manages to be a haven of relative sanity in a difficult and dangerous world. The world could survive without it, but not as well. It leads to a modest exchange of people, ideas, goods and services transregionally as well as between North and South on a basis more acceptable to the participants than many other institutions. In short, it is an unusual, but legitimized and useful part of the institutional structure of contemporary world society. It is a bond that has changed but it is also one that has held. It is a genuine association of governments and peoples.

Characteristics and properties of associations of nations

The Commonwealth, which calls itself an association of nations, has many characteristics of the *genre* as well as some unique qualities such as the important role played by the 'unofficial', that is non-governmental, organizations. The most outstanding quality of any association of states is its unusually high degree of fraternity among its members, which is an important compensatory factor for the frequent lack of any elaborate constitutional framework. This fraternity is based on understandings and shared values which permit diversity and flexibility but which are firmly rooted in a solidarity based on value consensus. Associations as different as the Non-Aligned Movement, the Contadoro Group and the Group of Six

Presidents and Prime Ministers nevertheless share a desire for a loose consultative association of a non-binding character without wishing to form a bloc or embark upon supranational integration. They act in concert and as a concert. Their members endeavour to maintain an independent stance in regard to world issues but are willing to intervene in them generally in a supportive rather than a partisan manner. They do not cultivate exclusive relationships. They seek to make themselves relevant and available and to present a network of ties among themselves which they will put at the service of others. They cultivate transregional ties that cut across conventional world political, economic, cultural and regional cleavages, ties which complement other universal, regional or issue-related ties since they are of a non-exclusive character.

Associations of this sort are part of the nervous system of the world. They embrace the notion of 'concerned independence'. Independence in this context is a far cry from isolation or autarky — it means an open society with a diversity of ties, be they political, economic, social or cultural, such that there is no exclusivity in relations and there is an element of balance in external relationships overall. Concern signifies a realistic assessment that self-interest has a component of community interest. It acknowledges that no actors escape from some dependence on the international community and therefore it is in the interests of each actor that the community should continue to prosper. Whereas the theory of collective goods highlights the problem of the 'free rider', not all community goods are collective goods. Thus if a small actor does not pay its community 'dues' it may be excluded from community benefits, whereas if a major actor evades its responsibilities then the community may collapse for want of adequate resources — to the detriment of all. Concerned independence therefore involves independent action to ensure not only self-interest in the short term but self-interest in the long term, which is tied to the well-being of the community as a whole. Associations do this routinely among themselves and try to foster such notions among others, especially in conflicts. They do this not in the sense of an alliance against a third party in a partisan manner, but to offer what Nehru once called a 'healing hand'.

To achieve this an association must be without serious rifts between and within its members, for a group that is not at peace with itself is unlikely to be able to foster concord in the world. But assuming the element of fraternity that is the hallmark of association, then the network of ties within and beyond the association are available for such a healing purpose. The selection of which networks and which actors form the ensemble is a function of the issue at hand and the parties concerned. But the association generally strives to develop cross-cutting transregional ties, as with the six Presidents and Prime Ministers, and to break down existing institutional barriers, be they governmental/non-governmental, North/South, East/West, national/transnational, always with a view to enfranchising those excluded, whatever their status and respectability, if they are a necessary party to resolving the issue. It is an approach which stresses not force of arms but the power of ideas and it seeks to create a network of ties on the basis of legitimized transactions which constitute a working peace system through association. Moreover, the ideas can receive their due if they come from a source that is not threatening, as, for example, in the Franco-Mexican initiative in Central America in the early 1980s.

Associations, then, as a fraternal 'family of nations' — both governments and peoples — have both an internal dimension in the pursuit of a wide range of goals by a variety of actors at and across different levels within the ambit of the association. They also have an external dimension in offering a helping and healing hand to others beyond the confines of the association. The Commonwealth stresses the former function and the Contadoro Group the latter. But the second major form of association, that of a government with an IGO, which although in form stresses the external link, nevertheless does so in a manner calculated to enhance the element of co-operation in the wider area in which free play is now possible.

The association of states with IGOs

The association of states with IGOs has been particularly marked since the Second World War. Association[9] in this sense, too, is a general rubric which covers a variety of institutional and practical arrangements, whereby flexibility and diversity are their *raison d'être*. At the same time, this makes the task of classification difficult. It would be overly simplistic to consider that every international association system is essentially the result of the expansion of an international system already in operation, with the addition of new units. In general, association systems are new subsystems of the international system which differ in purpose and institutional arrangements compared to their component units.

Association is a flexible instrument which responds to various needs and demands, according to time, space, political status, level of development and the like. It can have a variety of motivations. It may be a limited denial of the functional imperative. In such circumstances a state may wish to join an IGO for some purposes yet it is not prepared, or able, to become a full member of the IGO because it does not wish to take part in certain activities of the IGO and to be embroiled in a general integration. A case in point is some of the European neutrals and the European Community (EC). On the other hand, an association agreement may simply be an interim stage on the way to full membership of an IGO as is the case of Turkey and the EC. However, where otherwise disparate states have one important shared phenomenon, then association may constitute a useful framework, such as is the case of the EC–African Caribbean Pacific (ACP) country relationship over trade. In all of these cases association promotes that happy situation of both being able to have the cake and to eat it. The main purpose, in other words, is to promote the mutual interests of the associated parties by the creation of favourable circumstances in cases in which full membership of the IGO is not desired.

In terms of classificatory schemes, association of a state with an IGO can be grouped under various rubrics of which the permanent–transitional, monofunctional–polyfunctional and *de facto*–formal dimensions are important. Permanent association schemes are usually the result of political criteria such as those associated with Yugoslavia's non-aligned status and its links at less than full member status with a variety of bodies including CMEA, OECD, EFTA and the EC. The transitional or interim association status is one in which the principle of membership by a state in the IGO is accepted, but not the practice, since either or both parties are not yet ready or able to accept the full panoply of rights and duties associated with membership. Turkey and the EC is an example, whereas Greece and the EC successfully negotiated the transitional period of association. The monofunctional association scheme was exemplified by Britain's former association with the ECSC, whereas the association agreements of the European neutrals with the EC have a polyfunctional character. It is usual to formalize association agreements in the shape of a treaty, particularly where the associate state is keen that it should be seen that its sovereignty has been fully preserved, but informal association is also a technique that may be used in situations of potential political embarrassment, such as the pre-1989 economic links between the GDR and the EC.

Association is a flexible, open, decentralized and collaborative system which enables governments and peoples, states and IGOs to work together to the extent and in the form which suits them best individually. It is a useful tool in a world in which identity is a key value, but one in which complex interdependence accounts for a substantial part of the general well-being. The need to establish a sense of identity as well as political criteria, such as those associated with neutrality or non-alignment, may find expression in the assertion of sovereignty, but economic well-being and a contribution to the community are also elements in self-interest and they may be frustrated by standing completely aside. Association helps to reconcile, in a fructuous manner, such trends since its flexibility enables it to adjust to various and complex situations, its openness enables access to otherwise disparate actors, its decentralized nature minimizes fear of domination, and its generally collaborative nature promotes a climate in which advantages can be realized and problems broached in a constructive manner. A case in point is the association 'bridge' or 'corridor' in Europe.

To paraphrase Churchill's 'iron curtain' speech, from Finland in the north to Greece in the south an association corridor or bridge has been established in Europe. Finland, Sweden, the GDR (through the EC), Austria, Switzerland, Yugoslavia and Greece have all evolved a special role in a divided Europe. Austria and Switzerland are traditional neutrals with rights and duties *vis-à-vis* the great or guarantor powers stemming from the State Treaty and the Congress of Vienna. Sweden is permanently neutral without such systemic obligations and has much in common in its foreign policy stance with non-aligned Yugoslavia. Finland has a special relationship with the USSR, which gives its neutrality an unusual twist arising out of events before, during and after the Second World War and the subsequent peace treaty. The GDR has special economic links with the EC due to the claims of the FRG and its Hallstein Doctrine which were operative at the time of and accepted by the signatories of the Treaty of Rome. Almost every Greek government from that of the colonels to Mr Papandreou has harboured some ambition to develop a Balkans dimension to its foreign policy involving non-aligned, NATO and WTO countries. For differing reasons, and to a varied extent, all these states have nurtured ties with both parts of Europe. But until the 1970s they did so for the most part on an *ad hoc,* individualistic basis. However, the Helsinki process, starting with the negotiations leading to the Final Act and the subsequent 'follow-up' conferences in Belgrade, Madrid and now Vienna, initiated a degree of co-operation between those states associated in one form or another with both parts of Europe. Their motive was clearly in part self-interest, since if tension grew in Europe they would suffer as 'pig in the middle', but they also became more cognizant that there was, and remains, a collective community role for them to play. This was particularly evident in the Madrid Review Conference when, at the height of the second Cold War, the 'associates' acted in concert in both a damage limitation and a bridge-building role. Even the Swiss took initiatives!

It would, of course, be taking matters out of all proportion to suggest that there is an association of 'associables' in Europe, but the existence of a number of states with an association status, either formal or informal but certainly practical, with both parts of Europe (and ties beyond) does suggest that there is a possibility that such an association of 'associables' might emerge. If it were to do so, it would fuse the two modes of association with the cross-cutting ties engendered by overlapping association status of a number of states with a number of IGOs, giving rise to an association of 'non-aligned', concerned, but independent states within the loose framework of the Helsinki process of security and co-operation in Europe. Thus the prime values of fraternity, openness and non-exclusivity which characterizes associations may again demonstrate their utility.

Notes

1. Hedley Bull, *The Anarchical Society,* London, Macmillan, 1977, pp. 254–5.
2. Ibid., p. 255.
3. See the exchange between James Rosenau and Fred Northedge in *Millennium,* Spring 1976.
4. See A. Wolfers, *Discord and Collaboration,* Baltimore, Johns Hopkins Press, 1966; and J.W. Burton. *World Society,* London, Cambridge University Press, 1972.
5. See Alfred Kamanda in A.J.R. Groom and Paul Taylor (eds), *The Commonwealth in the 1980s,* London, Macmillan, 1984.
6. On the Commonwealth see A.J.R. Groom and Paul Taylor (eds.), *The Commonwealth in the 1980s,* op. cit.; and for a comparison with the non-aligned movement, see A.J.R. Groom, 'The Commonwealth and the NAM: back to the source', *Non-Aligned World,* April 1984.
7. See the 1971 CHOGM in Singapore's Declaration of Commonwealth Principles,

the 1977 Gleneagles statement of Apartheid in Sport, and the 1979 Lusaka Declaration of the Commonwealth on Racism and Racial Prejudice.
8. Shridath Ramphal: *One World to Share,* London, Hutchinson, 1979, p. 123.
9. For a detailed study of the application of association in Europe, see J. Kinnas, *The Politics of Association in Europe,* Frankfurt/New York, Campus Verlag, 1979; and J. Matthews, *Association System of the European Community,* New York, Praeger, 1977.

Selected reading

Groom, A.J.R. and Taylor, Paul (eds). *The Commonwealth in the 1980s,* London, Macmillan, 1984.

Kinnas, John, *The Politics of Association in Europe,* Frankfurt, Campus Verlag, 1979.

Matthews, J., *The Association System of the European Community,* New York, Praeger, 1977.

Groom, A.J.R., 'The Commonwealth and the Non-Aligned Movement', *Non-Aligned World,* April 1984.

7 The parallel national action process

Gunnar P. Nielsson

Introduction

The parallel national action process differs from harmonization, co-ordination and co-operation in the sense that, while it involves all of those processes, it goes beyond them in the degree to which it develops continuously expanding integrative behavioural codes of conduct among the participating states and thereby expands the scope and intensity of common activities into an integrative network. The maintenance of autonomous state authority is a basic premise of the parallel national action approach. Consequently, there is no expectation that it may lead to regional political unification. However, the parallel national action process could lead to political integration in the behavioural sense that the states adopt identical or highly similar domestic and foreign policies as a result of continuous consultation, joint investigation and common deliberation which become constant factors in the national decision-making processes. For the analyst of parallel national action, therefore, the focus must be on the behavioural manifestations of identical and co-ordinated actions performed by national actors without the use of supranational decision-making authorities.

The more detailed elaboration of the parallel national action process presented in this chapter is based on experiences among the five Nordic States of Denmark, Finland, Iceland, Norway and Sweden.[1] Previous scholarly work on Scandinavian co-operation has concentrated on the Nordic Council as a regional intergovernmental organization comparable to the Council of Europe.[2] It is our contention that the analysis of the competence, procedures, and participants in the brief annual sessions of the Nordic Council's Plenary Assembly is an insufficient basis for gaining an understanding of the operating characteristics of the Nordic integrative network. It deals only with the tip of the iceberg, as it were, and gives the impression of the discontinuity which characterizes the harmonization and co-ordination processes discussed elsewhere in this volume.

When Scandinavian relations are analysed in the parallel national action perspective, the Nordic Council organizations can be viewed as instruments which assist in providing continuity to the interaction process among different types of actors. That is to say, integrative behaviour, involving Nordic transnational groups, parliamentarians, members of political executives and civil service administrators from the five states is facilitated by the Nordic Council organizations, but it is *not fundamentally dependent upon the regional institutions*.

Such an intensive co-operative network among the Scandinavian states evolved into a parallel national action approach to integration. For historical reasons this was based, first, upon the principle of the avoidance of constitutional fusion, second, upon the expectation that the political structure of the five autonomous states would remain the unalterable basis for regional integration in low politics issue areas, and third, upon the exclusion of the high politics issue area of national security policies from regional integration processes. Scandinavian integration is characterized by a consensus-building process. The use of force or non-violent coercion is an unacceptable practice. Reliance on close majority voting in formal decision-making institutions is eschewed. Persuasion is the dominant instrument. Following the dictum of 'building co-operation from below', it starts with involving the parties most directly affected by the intended co-operative action, then working informally from the level of the individual through the level of secondary, socio-economic groupings to the level of formalized governmental agreements.

The Scandinavian integration process is dominated by pragmatism. Contrasted with the so-called Benelux Procedure,[3] which involved a high-level élite decision on far-reaching principles that served as a mandate on the basis of which investigations could be undertaken and implementing institutions could be established, the Scandinavian approach starts without fixed, long-range political goals by initiating investigations and consultations from which it proceeds to deliberation and recommendations. If strong opposition develops to a proposed Nordic co-operative scheme, based on nationalistic emotions, violation of perceived national interests, fear of socio-economic disadvantage or pressure from outside the Scandinavian region, then the proponents try to meet it and overcome it by new rounds of investigations and consultations until well-founded expert documentation and argumentation demonstrate mutual advantages for all parties concerned.

The primary, if not exclusive, tasks of the Nordic institutions are those of initiating, investigating, deliberating and recommending proposals for co-operative actions. These tasks are carried out through calling conferences which include interest group representatives, parliamentarians, governmental ministers, and national administration experts; setting up *ad hoc* committees of investigation; deliberating in standing committees; and making recommendations to the five national political executives either by expert senior civil servants to inter-Nordic meetings of government ministers or by the Nordic Council's Plenary Assembly during its brief annual Plenary Session.

Nordic co-operation agreements are implemented through the process of parallel national action which takes the form of adopting identical laws and regulations by the five national political systems. There are no regional law-making institutions with supranational authority. The legal or constitutional bases of Nordic integration practices are based on highly similar or identical national laws. In issue areas concerning joint action in extra-Scandinavian relations, implementation occurs through close co-ordination of policy positions and strategies of negotiation or through one state representing Scandinavian interests in executive organs of wider European or global-scope international institutions.

In considering the structural characteristics of the parallel national action approach, to focus exclusively on the formal Nordic Council organizations as the key to understanding the approach is to miss major components in the dynamics of the extensive network. The pattern of interactions involved includes four basic types of actors:

1. National interest groups and their Nordic transnational institutions.
2. Political parties and their national and Nordic parliamentary institutions.
3. The political executives[4] acting in their national ministerial roles and their Nordic roles, formally through the new Nordic Council of Ministers and informally through their regularized inter-Scandinavian meetings.
4. The National Civil Administrations with their Nordic Contact Man System. It is the behavioural code of conduct adopted in the patterns of interaction among these four types of actors which constitute the structure of the Nordic co-operative network.

In a developmental perspective, formal institutionalization of the Nordic co-operative network during the past twenty-five years represents efforts to consolidate systematically already existing co-operative behavioural codes of conduct which have developed incrementally, informally and in an *ad hoc* manner. It has truly been a case of the classical functionalist axiom that 'form follows (or should follow) function'.

In order to provide some impression of a time perspective, the Nordic co-operative network will be described according to the role of transnational institutions, *ad hoc* co-operative practices by both political executive and parliamentary actors, and the administrative Nordic Contact Man System before the Nordic Council organizations are discussed.

The Nordic transnational infrastructure

Contrary to the experiences in the European Communities where Community-wide interest groups and associations have developed *in response to* the establishment of 'supranational' decision-making institutions, the dynamic of Scandinavian integration is dominated by interest groups and parliamentarian groups acting as initiators and co-ordinators of proposals for Scandinavian-wide actions.

Since the late nineteenth century, a transnational infrastructure has developed based on the voluntary formation of Scandinavian-wide organizations — federations, congresses, associations, and unions — at the level of economic interest groups, professional associations, and social groupings. It is impossible within the format of this short chapter to provide a more detailed description of the present transnational institutional network.

To give an impressionistic profile of the early phase of their development, a list of some of the main inter-Nordic organizations, arranged in chronological order, is provided.

Partial overview of the development of a Scandinavian transnational institutional network

1860s: Nordic Schoolteachers' Congresses
1870s: Nordic Congress of Economists
1872: Nordic Assembly of Jurists
1876: Association of Nordic Railwaymen
1886: Nordic Congress of Trade Unions
1888: Nordic Shipping Companies' Association
1888: Nordic Agricultural Congress
1907: Nordic Employers' Association
1916: Nordic Trade and Commerce Association
1917: Nordic Council of Craftsmen
1918: Nordic Association of Consumers Co-operative Societies
1918: Nordic Civil Servants' Federation
1919: Norden Association
1922: Nordic Tourist Industry Committee
1925: Nordic Telecommunication Congresses
1925: Nordic Journalists' and Broadcasters' Association
1931: Nordic Organization of Savings and Loan Association
1935: Nordic Union of Road Techniques

This partial list shows only the establishment of Scandinavian institutions at a 'peak-association' level. In many cases, inter-Scandinavian congresses, federations, associations and unions are established on lower geographical or narrower functional levels such as specific branches of industries or professions. A group of researchers at Gothenburg University in Sweden conducted a representative survey of 300 Swedish organizations. Of the 180 organizations which responded, 75 per cent had had at least one meeting with their Nordic 'sister organizations' during the previous five years and nearly two-thirds of them participated continuous in permanently established Scandinavian institutions.[5]

The result has been that a very intensive and extensive institutional network exists which developed roots prior to the institutionalization of Scandinavian integration at the governmental level. The Nordic non-state actors co-operate by means of regular congresses for representatives of the national branches, continual consultation and co-ordination through committees and active participation in the investigations and planning phases of Nordic integrative activities. The interest groups focus predominantly on objectives which are narrow in scope such as standardization of nomenclature and technical specifications; equalization of working conditions; exchange of personnel and information; identical or similar Scandinavian legislation in the areas of the right of establishment (for commercial activity), trust laws, social welfare, insurance, industrial safety rules, patents, navigation; co-ordination of timetables and schedules for tourist travel; harmonization of school systems and joint Nordic textbooks in various subject areas; and joint radio and television broadcasts. The trade union and employers' associations were more politicized in the early phases with establishment of joint strike funds, agreements on sympathy strikes, agreements not to hire workers striking in another country and not to ship commodities involved in industrial disputes into the country where it was taking place. But by the 1930s, the industrial interest groups had become predominantly technical and more narrow-scope occupational in orientation.

None of the Nordic transnational organizations promote a Pan-Scandinavian ideology striving for political unification. The only organization which deliberately promotes a general Nordic co-operation line is the 'Norden' Association. Formed in 1919, it has developed 500 branches in the five Scandinavian states with a membership of 120,000 in 1959.[6] It has worked most actively in the area of cultural co-operation and has promoted such projects as a friendship cities programme and more general people-to-people exchanges, Scandinavian literature, and jointly authored texts on Scandinavian history to eliminate national prejudice. It has also been a consistent supporter of initiatives in Nordic co-operation in every sphere of activity. The absence of a commitment to use supranational authority in Scandinavian integration is indicated by the fact that the national Norden Associations did not establish a common Nordic Federation with a secretariat until 1965.

In general, the transnational institutional network has been dominated by a focus on 'practical Scandinavianism' which is characterized by acceptance of the existing five state structures, concentration on the least politically controversial issue areas, and operating through the parallel national action approach to integration. As such, the non-state actors have been crucially important as participants in expanding Scandinavian integration.

Ad hoc intergovernmental co-operation

Intergovernmental co-operation developed on an *ad hoc* basis during the first half of this century. It can be viewed as a response to the development of transnational infrastructure activity and to general European international political pressure. At the level of infrastructure activity, the Nordic Assembly of Jurists was instrumental in establishing, in 1901, the Joint Nordic Legal Commission which was the first Scandinavian intergovernmental body with the task of investigating the extent to which laws could be made identical or very similar throughout Scandinavia. In 1906, the Nordic Inter-Parliamentarian Union was established for the purpose of assuring participation by parliamentarians in the planning and deliberative phases of harmonizing legislation. It also reflected the rise of inter-Scandinavian contacts and conferences among the political parties in the

Nordic states. Although no thorough research has yet been published on the role of political parties as transnational actors, most analysts of Scandinavian co-operation point to their significance as an instrument in forging the Scandinavian integrative network. While practically all the political parties in Scandinavia have participated actively, the 'Scandinavianism' of the Nordic Labour/Social-Democratic parties has been especially important in raising co-operation to the political executive level during the 1930s and 1940s. The Nordic Inter-Parliamentarian Union provided a forum for the evolution of continual discussion of Nordic co-operative proposals and for caucusing within the wider European Parliamentarian Union which was formed in 1899.

Regular meetings at the political executive level began with the Nordic Ministers for Social Policy in 1926. However, it was not until after the Second World War that such behaviour patterns became institutionalized. In 1946 regular meetings were begun by the five Scandinavian Ministers of Justice, Culture and Education. At that time, special standing commissions composed of senior civil servants, ministers and, in some cases, parliamentarians, were established in Legal Affairs, Cultural Affairs, and Social Policy Affairs. Since the late 1940s, regular meetings among members of the Scandinavian political executives have become an established behavioural code of conduct. Such meetings have been most extensively practised by the ministers of Foreign Affairs, Justice, Culture and Education, Social Policy, Transportation and Communication, and Trade, Economy, and Commerce.

In the early 1950s, members of committees in the five national parliaments also began to meet on an *ad hoc* basis to deal with specific issue areas in Nordic co-operation. In May 1950 the Danish, Norwegian and Swedish Parliamentary Committees on the Judiciary met in Copenhagen to discuss the proposal for a uniform citizenship law and in 1951 the respective parliaments agreed to establish a Joint Nordic Parliamentary Committee for Traffic Freedom which laid the groundwork for the Nordic Passport Union established in the mid-1950s. Parallel national action at the Parliamentary Committee level was also used in 1960 to consider the proposal for uniform Nordic copyright laws.

High-level intergovernmental co-operation also developed in the area of general foreign policy, but that was a response to European international political pressure, not a result of an intra-regional integrative dynamic. The primary purpose of co-operation in foreign policy was to defend and give enhanced political credibility to the Scandinavian states' neutrality postures in European balance of power politics. In response to the outbreak of the First World War, the three Scandinavian monarchs and their Foreign Ministers met in Sweden in December 1914 to issue a joint declaration of neutrality. It represented a case of parallel national action in which the three states co-ordinated their diplomatic behaviour as a basis for a 'Neutrality Entente' in northern Europe. Throughout the First World War, both the Prime Ministers and Foreign Ministers met regularly to issue joint protest notes concerning violation of neutrality rights as well as to reach agreement to abstain from a mediatory role in the war (1916). Due to the effectiveness of the naval blockade, Scandinavian economic co-operation increased very dramatically and intra-Nordic trade rose from 10 per cent in 1914 to 30 per cent in 1919, but declined to 12 per cent in 1922 when more normal trading patterns were resumed.[7]

Regular Prime Minister and Foreign Minister meetings were discontinued in 1922, but resumed in 1933 (the Finnish Foreign Minister began to participate in 1934). Throughout the 1930s, the Nordic states attempted, by parallel national action, to repeat their joint neutrality policies in response to the increasing international crises in Europe. The 1934 Nordic Foreign Ministers meeting declared that the Scandinavian states would not be divided by large state rivalries in Europe and a renewal of a joint neutrality declaration was issued in 1938 and in September 1939. In 1937 special Nordic Neighbour Country Boards were established to prepare for the stockpiling of strategic economic materials based on a quota system and to promote intensified intra-Nordic economic co-operation in response to the increasing threat of war. With the failure of the Nordic Defence Pact in 1948–9, a joint Nordic Economic Co-operation Committee was formed in 1948 to investigate the prospect for a Nordic customs union. That was a response to United States pressure to form regional groupings as a prerequisite for qualifying for Marshall Aid.[8]

The purpose of this brief review has been to show that Nordic integrative patterns of behaviour developed to a considerable extent by the early 1950s. Although the Scandinavian states had failed to agree on the key issue areas of security policy and foreign economic policy, a considerable number of integrative schemes and interactions had developed both at the transnational and the intergovernmental levels.

Transnational governmental bureaucratic interaction: The Contact Man system

As Nordic integrative practices have expanded at the intergovernmental level, senior civil servants in the five national administrations have become increasingly involved in the work of Nordic standing commissions, *ad hoc* committees and the regular ministerial meetings. They provide the staff services in the investigative and consultative phases of proposals for Nordic integrative schemes as well as monitoring and administrating Nordic integrative activity.

A Nordic Contact Man system was instituted by the five Ministries of Justice in 1959–60 as a response to the growing involvement by the five national administrations. While the Nordic Contact Man system has been adopted in most of the ministries, we shall use the system established in the Ministries of Justice — where it is most developed — as our illustrative description of how the system works.[9] Within each of the national ministries, a senior civil servant, usually at the level of Under-Secretary of State, is designated as the Nordic Contact Man. His responsibility is to co-ordinate Nordic legal co-operation within the home country and to maintain contact with his counterpart in the other four states. He must keep himself informed continually about proposed new laws and legislative revision work being planned or acted upon in other ministries in his home country which might be relevant in a Nordic perspective. The initiative for new laws or revision of existing laws with possible Nordic ramifications can come from the various national ministries, the Nordic Ministers of Justice meetings, the national parliaments or from the Nordic Council. After an initiative with Scandinavia-wide relevance is taken, the Minister or the Nordic Contact Man can decide to establish committees within each of the five national ministries involved. These committees work in parallel and hold periodic joint Nordic meetings or exchange views by correspondence or by telephone. The committees present reports which are dealt with, first, by each country's administration, including preparation of each special administrative department's position on the proposal, followed by the Nordic Contact Men meeting as a group. The joint position reached is then presented to each national Minister of Justice for political executive action. If further deliberation is needed, it takes place at the next Nordic Ministers of Justice meeting. After the planning phase is completed, the proposal is submitted in identical or highly similar texts to the five national legislatures for deliberation and possible enactment. Before legislative action is com-pleted, the final version of a bill is presented to the Nordic Contact Men for comments and recommendations. Hence, Nordic co-operation is very intensive and extensive *within* the national administrations. As a Swedish Nordic Contact Man has commented: '. . . it is no exaggeration to state that during the law-making (or revision) process, I discuss the issues with my Nordic colleagues almost as often as with my colleagues in other depart-ments of the Swedish administration.'[10] As an indication of the scope of Nordic co-operation at the administrative level, the Swedish Contact Man estimated that about half of the sixty committees working on proposals for new laws or revision of existing laws in the Swedish Ministry of Justice are involved in subject areas of relevance for Nordic co-operation.

The Nordic Contact Man in a ministry is usually assisted by a more junior civil servant who co-ordinates the subject areas involving Nordic integrative processes in the various sections within the ministry. For example, the assistant to the Nordic Contact Man in the Swedish Ministry of Education co-ordinates proposals in the area of schools, higher educational institu-tions, and research, dealt with in various sections of the ministry. Additional-ly, he maintains close liaison with the Minister of Culture since all these issue areas are dealt with as one issue area of Nordic cultural co-operation. The organization of the Contact Man System varies from ministry to ministry because of the difference in tasks and civil administration structures in the five states. In some ministries, Nordic co-operation involves parallel national action in regard to monitoring and administering existing Nordic integrative programmes.

Some difficulties have been experienced when the Contact Men's activi-ties involve different ministries; for example, the Swedish Ministry of

Justice co-operating with the Danish Ministry of Commerce, but satisfactory procedures develop over time. Some of the Scandinavian states have institutionalized the co-ordination of Nordic Contact Man activity at the national level. In Finland a single person has been given the task of co-ordinating all Finnish Nordic Contact Man activity. In Sweden the Ministry of Justice provides central co-ordination of all Nordic co-operation issues through a special section of the Ministry. In Norway the national co-ordination is done within the Prime Minister's Office where a State Secretary is responsible for co-ordinating both Nordic Contact Man activities and Nordic Council activities.

A recent development has been the extension of the Nordic Contact Man system into the international sections of the various functional service ministries. Their task is to investigate, plan and deliberate about adopting identical positions in negotiations in international institutions and jointly prepare for international conferences. For example, the five Nordic Health Departments have prepared joint positions on activities in the World Health Organization, and the Ministries of Education have prepared joint positions in activities in UNESCO. Hence, in addition to the national vertical co-ordination between the individual functional service ministries and the Ministry of Foreign Affairs, there is Nordic horizontal co-ordination among the five Nordic Ministries of Foreign Affairs about a subject matter to be dealt with in a general international institution or conference.

The Nordic Contact Man System is an indication of the degree to which Scandinavian integration through parallel national action has penetrated nearly all components and aspects of the decision-making processes in the five Scandinavian political systems.

The Nordic Council organizations

The Nordic Council organizations represent a further institutionalization in the incremental growth of the parallel national action process. They are the only joint bodies within the wide integrative network comprising the national interest groups, transnational institutions, parliaments, political executives and civil administrations of the five national political systems. They serve as a source of initiative in proposals for Nordic integrative action and in promoting support for them among the general public, as instruments of continuity by monitoring and co-ordinating the development of such proposals into parallel national action (in that respect, they can be viewed as a Scandinavian regional pressure group), and they provide a forum for consultation and deliberation in which the Scandinavian perspective can be maintained.

The development of the Nordic Council organizations has been characterized by an aversion to bureaucracy-creating measures which would involve Nordic supranational authority. The organizations have evolved because of a combination of responses to extra-Nordic international developments and recognition of the need for more efficient organizational practices as a result of the expanding scope and magnitude of Scandinavian integrative activities. While the formation of the Nordic Council in 1952 can be viewed as an extension of the Nordic Inter-Parliamentary Union and the evolving practice of inter-Scandinavian meetings of parliamentary committees, the impetus came from the failure to form a Nordic Defence Pact and a Nordic Customs Union both of which demonstrated a new political division among the Scandinavian states.[11]

It is indicative of the caution with which the Scandinavian states approach institution-building that the subject areas of co-operation and the formal role of the Nordic Council organizations were not identified and expressed in treaty form until the 1962 Helsinki Treaty of Co-operation — a decade after the Nordic Council was established. The decision to elevate the behavioural code of conduct into treaty status was a response to external developments in Europe. With the decision of the Danish and Norwegian governments to apply for membership of the European Communities in 1961 and 1962 respectively, it was felt necessary to demonstrate to the other European states that an integrative network existed.

The Helsinki Treaty was also to serve as a basis from which, during negotiations with the European Communities, the Scandinavian states could gain recognition of their claims to protect and maintain Scandinavian integration. The amendment of the Helsinki Treaty in February 1971, involved a significant reorganization of the Nordic Council which enhanced the role of the Presidium, established permanent secretariats and a Nordic Council of Ministers. The changes reflected the need to make the Nordic Council organizations more effective and efficient as well as the need to integrate the governing institutions of the proposed Nordic Economic Union (Nordek — which failed) with the existing organizations.[12] The descriptive overview of the Nordic Council organizations which follows is based upon the revised 1971 Helsinki Treaty.

The Nordic Council organizations consist of the Plenary Assembly, the Standing Committees, the Presidium, the Secretariat and the Nordic Council of Ministers.

The Plenary Assembly consists of seventy-eight members elected from the five national parliaments and about fifty members of the five political executives. Sweden and Norway each have eighteen elected members, Finland seventeen, Denmark sixteen, and Iceland six. The semi-autonomous territories of the Faeroes and Åland Islands have two and one elected members respectively. The national delegations are apportioned according to the distribution of political party representation in the national parliaments. The five national political executives are usually represented by the Prime Ministers, Foreign Ministers and the Ministers of Justice, Education, Culture, Social Affairs, Transportation and Communications, and Commerce, Economics and Finance. The Plenary Assembly meets annually for a week-long session although it can be called into extra-ordinary sessions. The annual session is conducted according to general parliamentary procedures. Both individual members and government representatives can initiate a proposal which, in turn, goes through a first reading, committee investigation and reporting, a second reading with debate and finally a vote.[13] The Nordic Council is an advisory body and it can pass only recommendations for action to be taken by national governments. While the governmental representatives participate in both general debate and committee stages of proposals, only the elected members can vote on recommendations. During the first decade of its operation, i.e. from 1953 to 1962, the Plenary Assembly passed 241 recommendations. Of these, 125 recommendations (or 52 per cent) were completely or partially implemented, sixty-one (or 25 per cent) were either in the process of being implemented or under investigation, while fifty-five recommendations (or 23 per cent) were rejected by the national governments.[14]

The Standing Committees of the Nordic Council consist of the Legal Committee with thirteen members, the Cultural Committee with seventeen members, the Social Policy Committee with thirteen members, the Traffic Committee with thirteen members and the Economic Committee with twenty-two members. The Standing Committee members are usually senior members of the corresponding national parliamentary committees. During the annual Plenary Assembly meetings, the Standing Committee meetings are attended by the five national ministers concerned with the particular subject matter designated to each of the committees. When the Standing Committees meet outside the ordinary annual session, the minister of the host country attends as a representative of the Nordic Ministers Meeting.

The Presidium of the Nordic Council is composed of five members — a President and four Vice-Presidents plus their deputies. Presidium members are usually the chairmen of the national delegations of the elected members to the Plenary Assembly. The Presidium represents the entire Nordic Council between sessions. It can convene extraordinary sessions of the Plenary Assembly, as well as make representations to the Nordic Council of Ministers and to the national governments on behalf of the Nordic Council. Presidium statements of representation now have the same status as recommendations by the Plenary Assembly. It can also receive reports on the status of recommendations from the national governments and it is usually represented in Nordic Council committee meetings.

A Nordic Council Secretariat was established in 1971 to supplement the previous practice of separate national secretariats. The Board of Secretaries is composed of the Secretary of the Presidium and the five national General Secretaries and has its office in Stockholm. The tasks of the Secretariat are to prepare the meetings of the Presidium and conduct the day-to-day affairs of the Council.

The establishment of the Nordic Council of Ministers was the most significant innovation in the 1971 reorganization. It was formed because of the recognition that the governments had no organization which could provide continuity and overview at a level corresponding to the parliamentarians' organizations. It was decided that each state would appoint one of its ministers responsible for Nordic Co-operation Affairs, and these five ministers comprise the Nordic Council of Ministers, different ministers can also act as the Council of Ministers if an important decision is to be made. In fact, while the Nordic Council of Ministers was given competence to deal with the whole area of Scandinavian co-operation, it was stipulated in the 1971 Helsinki Treaty that the regular ministerial meetings by heads of functional service ministries would continue parallel to the Council of Ministers. Typical of the Scandinavian approach to integration, the decision on what format a meeting would take, whether formalized as a Nordic Council of Ministers meeting or kept informal as a regular meeting of ministers, should depend on the matter in question and should be decided on the merit of each case. Hence, the regular ministerial meeting could, in the same session, move to become a Council of Ministers meeting and back to the informal setting of a regular meeting.

The Council of Ministers operates by unanimity in substantive decision-taking and its decisions are binding on the individual member states except where parliamentary approval is needed.

The main task of the Ministers for Nordic Affairs, acting as the Council of Ministers, is to provide co-ordination of policies at the highest level of the political executive in the five member states. It must assure continuity in the relationship with the other Nordic Council organizations as well as monitor the development of Plenary Assembly recommendations in favour of adopting Nordic integrative schemes by parallel national action. The Council of Ministers gives an annual account of current Nordic integrative activity, including the status of government action on Nordic Council recommendations, by issuing a report which becomes the basis for the opening general debate in the Plenary Assembly sessions. A very significant institutional development was the establishment of a Permanent Secretariat for the Nordic Council of Ministers in July 1973 with offices in Oslo.[15] The Secretariat is staffed by senior civil servants who are not responsible to the national governments. Cultural co-operation has also become further institutionalized by the 1971 Treaty of Nordic Cultural Co-operation. The Scandinavian Ministers of Education and Culture will now act as the Nordic Council of Ministers for Cultural Co-operation. The Council is assisted by a Senior Civil Servants' Committee on Cultural Co-operation. A Permanent Secretariat for Cultural Co-operation with a Director was established in January 1972 with its office located in Copenhagen.[16]

The recent institutionalization of the Nordic integrative network is a responsive development through which the five Nordic political systems have adopted the parallel national action process due to a combination of, on the one hand, intra-regional pressures for more effective and efficient methods of integration than the *ad hoc* behavioural practices which emerged in the post-Second World War years, and on the other hand, the extra-regional pressures created by the growing institutionalization of Western European integration.

The structure of the Nordic integrative network is based on the continual interaction among the four types of actors:

1. National interest groups acting individually or through their Nordic transnational institutions.

2. National political parties acting through national as well as Nordic parliamentary institutions.
3. The national political executives acting through the Nordic Council's Plenary Assembly, the Nordic Council of Ministers and regular, informal Nordic ministerial meetings.
4. The national civil administrators acting through the Contact Man System and Nordic Standing Commissions and Committees of Senior Civil Servants.

The extensive diffusion of channels of direct interaction among the five states' governmental organizations was given formal legal recognition in the 1962 Helsinki Treaty of Co-operation. Article 38 permits direct interaction through bypassing the Ministries of Foreign Affairs except in subject areas which '. . . by their nature or for other reasons . . . ' are still to be handled through the traditional established diplomatic channels.[17]

The major task of the Nordic Council organizations is to facilitate interaction among the four types of actors. They perform that task by initiating contacts and proposals for integrative action, by providing impetus and continuity through the investigatory and deliberative stages, and by monitoring developments until parallel national actions are implemented.

Scandinavian parallel national action involves the continual communication and consultation processes among national, transnational and Scandinavian regional actors. A Norwegian Nordic Council official described the integrative interaction processes as follows:

There are always many, many channels which can be used. Private sector, political, and governmental officials have multiple options for communicating, and multiple options for attempting to gain support for their position. One may choose a national strategy, a Nordic one, one emphasizing governmental channels or non-governmental ones; one emphasizing governmental sectoral counterparts or complementing interests. Governmental officials may lead directly, through diplomatic channels, through political party linkages, through Nordic Council machinery, through international bodies, or through counterpart administrative machinery.[18]

While implementation of policies occurs through parallel national action by the five political systems, the increasing institutionalization of the policy-formulating process demonstrates that the Nordic dimension has penetrated the national political system in every issue area except national security and military alliance policies.

Achievements in Nordic integration

The outcomes of the parallel national action process in Scandinavia have been extensive and impressive. They can be dealt with only in a brief summary manner here. The discussion of the achievements has been organized in three categories. In the first place, we will provide an 'inventory-overview' of Scandinavian integration which has resulted in removing those barriers to interaction which were manifestations of previous intense national exclusivity and in equalizing societal conditions in a large number of issue areas. Second, integrative activity involving the pooling of resources and skills will be discussed. Finally, co-operation in the conduct of diplomacy outside of Scandinavia is briefly considered.

Removal of barriers to interaction and equalization of societal conditions

It is in the area of public law that equalization of conditions has progressed most. Uniform laws have been enacted by parallel national action in practically every aspect of the five states' legal systems. Identical or very similar laws exist in citizenship law, family law, inheritance law, property laws, bankruptcy laws, laws on purchases, commercial practices, stocks, bonds, insurance, patents, brand names, copyright, maritime law, air travel law, law on nuclear energy installations, and penal law. In some areas of the legal systems, Scandinavian conventions have been adopted. This is the case, for example, in regard to family law, child support, bankruptcy, inheritance and in penal law where court decisions are mutually enforceable. Uniform legal procedures have been established leading to Scandinavia-wide equalization of judgments. Since 1959 a joint collection of legal cases entitled *The Nordic Collection of Judgments* has been published annually. As shown in Table 7.1,[19] between 1880 and 1965 there have been seventy-eight cases of parallel national action in the legal subject areas listed above. Denmark, Sweden and Norway have been the most active (they participated in between 88 and 92 per cent of the cases), and these three states set the pattern of legal co-operation into which Finland and Iceland have been drawn during the past forty years (Finland participated in 50 per cent and Iceland in 41 per cent of the cases). In sixty-two of the seventy-eight cases (79 per cent) parallel national action involved at least three states while nineteen cases (24 per cent) involved all five states. It is important to point out that these subject areas do not include Scandinavian participation in general international legal agreements and conventions which set global or European-wide standards. They involve subject areas normally considered as exclusively 'within-state' jurisdiction.

Uniformity in social security and social welfare conditions has been achieved through the establishment of a Nordic Convention on Social Security. The Convention came into effect in November 1956 and integration in this subject area has been expanded by amendments of the Convention in 1962, 1967 and 1969. It creates equality of eligibility for all Nordic citizens for unemployment insurance, industrial accident insurance, partial disability insurance, health insurance, old-age pension, widow and widower pensions, invalid pension, public assistance during pregnancy and childbirth, and child support. As a consequence, a Scandinavian citizen moving from one Nordic state to another can claim the same social security and social welfare benefits in the new country of residence as in the 'home country'. A mutual reimbursement system was adopted in the early years of

Table 7.1   Parallel national action in legal affairs among the Nordic states, 1880–1965

	1880–1913	1914–1945	1946–1965	Total
Involving all five states	1	11	7	19
Involving four states	5	10	7	22
Involving three states	5	8	14	27
Involving two states	0	5	5	10
Total	11	34	33	78

Source: 'Oversikt over lagar tillkomma genom nordiskt samarbejde', Stockholm, Nordiska Raadet, Nordisk Udredningsserie, 1965:2.

the Convention, but it was dropped after a few years. In the cases of old-age, invalids', widows' and widowers' pensions, three years' residence in the new country is required, but the 'home' country continues payments during the transition period.

Extensive Nordic integration exists in the areas of travel and transportation. A Nordic Passport Union was established in 1955 which allows for completely free travel by Scandinavians in the Nordic region. Furthermore, only one inspection is required for non-Scandinavians entering or leaving the region. Uniform rates for railway transportation of goods have been established as well as an agreement of uniform 'through-goods' rates. Domestic rates on mail services exist for the whole Scandinavian region arranged through the Nordic Postal Association which has been in existence since 1946.

Achievements in the area of economic integration have been more modest and closely linked to the general development of economic co-operation in Western Europe. The free movement of people was expanded beyond the Passport Union when a Common Labour Market for the Danish, Finnish, Norwegian and Swedish industrial work-force was established by a Nordic Convention in 1954. Workers can seek employment in the Nordic region without work permits. The four national governmental agencies co-operate in providing information on employment opportunities as well as providing statistical analyses of employment trends and co-ordinating employment policies. The Common Labour Market Convention has been expanded since 1966 to include doctors, dentists, nurses, pharmacists and other professions.

The opening of borders has resulted in a significant migration flow. Between 1950 and 1977 slightly more than one million Scandinavians out of a total population of about twenty million moved from one state to another. Since the data is based on the change of registered residences rather than the national origins of the people moving, the migration flow could involve a versatile movement by the same people back and forth over time.

Table 7.2 Migration flows in Scandinavia, 1950–77 and 1986

From:	Finland		Sweden		Denmark		Norway		Total	
To:	1950–77	1986	1950–77	1986	1950–77	1986	1950–77	1986	1950–77	1986
Finland			394,497	5,160	9,792	174	6,737	526	411,026	5,860
Sweden	170,257	6,400			81,708	1,930	53,435	3,180	305,400	11,510
Denmark	7,257	183	104,535	1,833			88,894	3,863	200,586	5,879
Norway	4,919	333	67,460	2,825	87,380	2,772			159,759	5,930
Total	182,433	6,915	566,492	9,818	178,880	4,876	149,066	7,569	1,076,871	29,179

Source: See Note 20.

The dominant pattern is a high level of migration between Finland and Sweden, a bilateral relationship that explains half of the total flow of people. In a more current perspective, of the 72,735 people who emigrated from the four states in 1986, 40 per cent moved to one of the neighbouring Nordic states. Although the Swedish–Finnish migration flow remains the major pattern, the movement of people has become more equalized in the entire Scandinavian region.

Allowing a free movement of goods and services by the removal of barriers to trade and the equalization of production and distribution conditions has not developed on an exclusively Scandinavian basis.This is because the region has been of insufficient significance for the five national economies to make a special arrangement among themselves which involved the risk of retaliatory damage in relations with non-Scandinavian trading partners.

Scandinavia is heavily dependent on foreign trade. However, during the critical stages of their industrialization in the first half of the twentieth century, the Nordic national economies became mutually competitive internationally rather than regionally complementary. Their trade patterns are based on greater interdependence with states outside the region, especially the United Kingdom and the Federal Republic of Germany, than among each other. Until the 1960s, intra-Nordic trade accounted for only 12–15 per cent of the total foreign trade by the five states.

Nevertheless, proposals and plans for a Nordic Customs Union were made as early as 1950 and again in 1957.[21] Plans for an extensive Nordic Economic Union (Nordek) were made in 1969.[22] In each instance, the plans failed because they were overtaken by general European economic integration developments.

The main economic interest groups in each of the five national economies viewed the plans for a Nordic customs union as an imposition on their broader international trade interests. While it would have had few direct economic benefits, it was argued, a Nordic customs union was considered a change which contained an unacceptably high risk of disadvantageous trade diversion caused by retaliatory actions by non-Scandinavian trade partners in response to discriminatory features of a Nordic common market.

Consequently, in the late 1940s and throughout the 1950s, the Nordic states pursued a policy, similar to the British approach, that supported proposals for the widest possible European free trade area and treated the potential of increased Scandinavian economic integration as a secondary 'fallback' position when plans for a wider European free trade arrangement failed.

A partial solution was found with the formation of the European Free Trade Association in 1959. Throughout the 1960s, intra-Nordic trade expanded enormously within the EFTA umbrella which protected their foreign economic relations with the United Kingdom. The division of Western Europe into the European Community and EFTA had provided the impetus for a new commitment by Scandinavian industrial interest groups to develop the growth potential of a Nordic regional market as a compensation for expected economic losses due to trade diversion between the two economic organizations.[23]

The 1969 Nordek plans for a Nordic Economic Union were advanced to consolidate and promote these significant developments in the integration of the Scandinavian economies. In the context of a perceived prolonged stalemate concerning the enlargement of membership of the European Communities, Nordek would have provided a 'fallback' solution through which economic integration in Scandinavia could have continued and a stronger bargaining position vis-à-vis the European Communities could have been developed. When the prospects for the British, Irish, Danish and Norwegian applications for membership in the European Communities improved in late 1969, the Nordek plan was rejected by Finland because of the implication which the Finns perceived such a prospect would have for their precarious neutrality relations with the Soviet Union and the plan was dropped in 1970.[24]

In short, utilizing the Scandinavian market as a basis for remaining competitive internationally was viewed as a compensatory feature which was manifested by a very high increase in commodity exchanges as well as an increased division on labour in production within the region. Hence, while the recent growth in inter-Scandinavian economic interdependence occurred almost inadvertently because of unfavourable conditions for each of the Nordic states' relations with larger non-Scandinavian trading partners, the effect has been that intra-Nordic economic relations have become an important factor.

In general, the 1960s were a period of exponential growth in intra-Nordic trade. While the value of exports in current prices does not control for the effect of inflation, a sixfold increase in Nordic trade clearly demonstrates a significant increase which, except for Iceland, was experienced by each of the Nordic states, and especially by Finland. Between 1960 and 1971, intra-Nordic trade increased as a percentage of total exports by all five states from 17.3 to 26.0 per cent.[25] As another example of the emergence of Scandinavia as a significant trading group, by 1972 the Danes and the Norwegians together bought more industrial goods from Sweden than the original six members of the European Community and Sweden had replaced West Germany as Denmark's second most important customer.

From the mid-1970s intra-Nordic trade levelled off and began to reflect the general fluctuations in international trade among the advanced industrialized countries. Nevertheless, trade among the five Nordic states had more than doubled between 1974 and 1986 and continued to account for about one-quarter of all foreign trade. Scandinavian trade has become especially important for Norway, although the United Kingdom remains its most important trading partner, and Iceland caught up with the other four states in the 1980s. For Sweden and Denmark, Nordic trade has become equal in importance to their combined trade with the United Kingdom and West Germany. Scandinavia is of equal importance to Finland's trade with the Soviet Union.

In spite of the significant increase in Nordic economic interdependence,

Table 7.3 Developments in intra-Nordic trade, 1962–86 (in millions of US dollars at current prices)

Exports to the Other Four Nordic States From:	1962	1968	1974	1980	1986	Percent Increase 1962–74	Percent Increase 1974–84
Sweden	469.5	1,221.3	4,158.3	6,194.9	6,656.4	540	60
Norway	236.8	474.4	1,841.3	4,701.7	6,543.2	678	255
Denmark	286.1	650.1	1,977.7	3,900.6	4,474.0	591	147
Finland	120.0	276.7	1,252.0	2,634.6	3,089.7	943	147
Iceland	15.0	13.8	40.6	260.6	327.2	171	706
Total	1,307.4	2,636.3	9,269.9	17,692.4	21,090.5	609	128

Source: The Nordic Council, *Yearbook of Nordic Statistics*, 1970, 1978 and 1987, Stockholm, 1971; Copenhagen, Nordic Statistical Secretariat, 1978 and 1987.

the Scandinavian national economies remain closely integrated with the rest of Western Europe. The twenty million Scandinavians are consumers of a large proportion of West German exports, and in the 1970s the Scandinavians bought more British industrial goods than Germany and France combined.

Since 1973, the Nordic states have been incorporated into the emerging general Western European common market, but based on different policy positions. Denmark became a member of the European Communities in 1973. Sweden and Norway are included in the general Western European free trade area arrangement in industrial commodities negotiated between the remaining EFTA members and the European Community in 1973, which came into full force in 1980. Iceland and Finland have established special commercial treaties with the European Communities leading to free trade relations as well.

So far, economic relations among the Nordic states have not been seriously affected by the differences in policy positions and intra-Nordic trade continues to expand.[26] The current EC plans for a single integrated market by 1992 will become a crucial challenge for all the Scandinavian states as well as for future Nordic economic integration. It may become a severe test of whether Danish membership of the European Communities will remain compatible with full participation in the Nordic integrative network.[27] It is a development that has made major economic interest groups in Norway and Sweden urge a reconsideration of potential membership in the European Community.

In sum, equalization of economic conditions among the Nordic states has taken place within the wider framework of general European co-operation without, so far, creating impediments to expanded economic interdependence within the Nordic region. However, it is an issue area which clearly demonstrates the limitations of the Scandinavian parallel national action approach. The organization of Scandinavian economic integration, especially when it requires a formal structure, has been turned into a 'high politics' question because it has been seen as possibly detrimental to broader national foreign economic interests. As such, economic integration issues are similar to the approach adopted on national security policies.

Sharing resources and skills within the region

The achievements by parallel national action in sharing resources and skills have developed to the greatest extent in the areas of higher education and research. Scandinavian higher education is becoming a truly integrated system. The universities and academies, and polytechnic institutes recognize the validity of completion of examinations and diploma certification in a single discipline in one Nordic higher educational institution as the complete or partial fulfilment of the equivalent degree programme in the other Nordic institutions. In several academic disciplines, Scandinavia-wide rules for curriculum structures and examination validity have been established.

Table 7.4 Nordic academic, scientific and professional transnational organizations and publications

Field:	Number of organizations	Number of journals	Of which in English
Humanities	7	13	5
Social Sciences	6	18	7
Natural Sciences	6	15	3
Applied Sciences	44(a)	7	2
Agricultural sciences	10	3	—
Medicine	22	25(b)	1
Total	95	81	18

Source: Compiled from *Nordisk Samarbete inom forskningens och den hogre undervisningens omraade:* Stockholm: Nordiska Raadet, Nordisk Udredningsserie, 1967:2.

Notes: (a) Many of these organizations consist of Co-ordinating Committees for specific industries.
(b) In addition, there are fourteen joint Nordic medical textbooks published regularly in updated editions.

Fellowships, grants and loans paid by one state to a student can be used for study in other states' higher educational institutions. An intensive division of labour has occurred in the area of research where specialized Nordic research institutes have been established. An integrated transnational structure in higher education and research has been established. As shown in Table 7.4, there were nearly a hundred Nordic professional academic and research institutions which published eighty-one joint Nordic journals, eighteen of them in English, in the late 1960s.

The integration of higher education and research activities has become highly organized by the establishment of formal regional institutions jointly funded by the five states and many of them with supranational administrative authority. Table 7.5 illustrates this trend of growing institutionalization. There are proposals pending for a consolidation of these new Nordic supranational institutions under the direction of the Nordic Council of Ministers for Cultural Co-operation and its Permanent Secretariat in Copenhagen.

The Nordic Council has been promoting harmonization of the structures of primary and secondary school systems, but so far it has only led to the establishment of co-operation in planning school curricula and research on pedagogy.

Nordic integration in general adult education and promotion of the fine arts has also progressed very significantly. Financial support for Nordic cultural activity — higher education, research, general education and the fine arts amounted to 18 million Danish kroner in 1967–8. That was more than four times the funds spent for comparable purposes by the Council of

Table 7.5 Nordic common administrative institutions

Issue area		Founded	Location
A —	*Higher educational institutions*		
1 —	Nordic Graduate School of Journalism and Press Research	1957	Aarhus, Denmark
2 —	Nordic Institute on African Studies	1964	Uppsala, Sweden
3 —	Nordic Graduate School of Domestic Science	1963	various places
4 —	Nordic Central Institute for Asian Area Research (CINA)	1966	Copenhagen, Denmark
5 —	Nordic Graduate School of Public Health and Welfare	1962	Gothenburg, Sweden
B —	*Research organizations*		
1 —	Nordic Institute for Odontological Material Testing	1971	Oslo, Norway
2 —	Nordic Institute for Theoretical Nuclear Physics (NORDITA)	1971	Copenhagen, Denmark
3 —	Nordic Council for Applied Research (NORDFORSK)	1947	Rotates among Nordic capitals every 3 years
4 —	Nordic Committee for Arctic Medical Research	1969	Uleaaborg, Finland
5 —	Nordic Committee for International Politics Research	1966	Stockholm, Sweden
6 —	Nordic Council on Criminology	—	—
7 —	Nordic Institute for Maritime Law	1963	Oslo, Norway
8 —	Nordic Board for Research on Alcoholism	—	—
9 —	Nordic Institute of Social Planning (NORDPLAN)	1968	Stockholm, Sweden
C —	*General education, fine arts, and information dissemination*		
1 —	Nordic Peoples' Academy	1968	Stockholm, Sweden
2 —	Nordic House in Reykjavik	1968	Reykjavik, Iceland
3 —	Nordic Council Literature Prize	1962	—
4 —	Nordic Institute for Poetry	1959	Aabo, Sweden
5 —	Nordic Cultural Fund	1967	Rotates based on resident country of chairman of Fund
6 —	Nordic Co-ordinating Organization for Scientific and Technological Information and Documentation (NORDOK)	1972	Oslo, Norway
7 —	Nordic Statistical Secretariat	1969	Copenhagen, Denmark

Sources: Faellesinstitutionerne i Norden, Stockholm, Nordiska Raadet, Nordisk Udredningsserie, 1960:2; and *Nordiska institutioner*, Stockholm, Nordiska Raadet, Nordisk Udredningsserie, 1972:5.

Europe and equivalent to 8 per cent of UNESCO's budget for global scope cultural co-operation.[28]

In the area of transportation, the most significant achievement has been the establishment of an integrated airline company. The Scandinavian Airline System is jointly owned and managed by Denmark, Norway and Sweden. Co-operative organizations have been established among Finland, Norway and Sweden for the development of a road system in the northern section of the Scandinavian Peninsula (Nordkalotten) and between Denmark and Sweden for the development of a bridge over the narrow sound separating the two countries.

In the area of communications, joint educational radio programmes are produced and NORDVISION is the organization through which regular education and entertainment television programmes are broadcast. The technical aspects of these co-operative arrangements are administered through the Nordic Telecommunication Council and the Nordic Council for Telesatellites.

External relations

Parallel national action in international politics is based on an informal, unwritten behavioural code of conduct among, in this case, the five Nordic states. It is characterized by continual, extensive consultation, planning, co-ordination and joint policy actions. As a former Danish Foreign Minister once described it,

In our voting in the United Nations, in the Council of Europe, in OECD and elsewhere, we must always bear in mind how our statements, our voting and our actions affect our relations with the other Nordic countries. It is, in fact, one of the permanent factors in the foreign policy of our countries.[29]

The Scandinavian Foreign Ministers meet at least twice a year to consult and co-ordinate foreign policies. At the early autumn meeting, Scandinavian policies are co-ordinated in regard to issues to be dealt with at the forthcoming United Nations session. Consequently, the Scandinavian states have consistently voted identically on nearly all of the issues treated in the General Assembly.[30]

A very high degree of co-ordination among the Nordic states occurs in their participation in international institutions. Jointly planned policy positions are adopted by the Ministries of Justice in negotiations on legal co-operation in the United Nations, the Council of Europe, the Hague Conference and the Rome Institute for Private Law. The Transportation and Communication Ministries co-ordinate their positions within the Universal Postal Union, the International Telecommunication Union and the International Air Transportation Association. The Ministries of Social Welfare and Labour and the Public Health Authorities co-ordinate their policy positions in the International Labour Organizations, the United Nations Economic and Social Council, the UN Social Commission, the

World Health Organization and the Council of Europe's Public Health Committee. In the areas of cultural and educational affairs, Scandinavian co-operation has moved one step further in that it was decided to divide among the states the responsibility for co-ordinating the Nordic position in international institutions. Thus, Denmark co-ordinates the Nordic position on culture and education in the Council of Europe, Finland in UNESCO, Norway in the OECD, and Sweden in CERN. In economic issue areas, the Ministries of Trade, Commerce, Economics and Finance co-ordinate their positions in the International Monetary Fund, the International Bank for Reconstruction and Development, in the OECD, the UN Economic Commission for Europe and EFTA (for the last, without Denmark since 1973).

In international conferences, the Nordic states have often acted as a group or a caucus. In both permanent international institutions and in international conferences, the individual states become spokesmen for a Nordic position on various executive boards and in committees. The greatest success in integrating their foreign policies occurred in 1966-7 when the Nordic states agreed to negotiate as one unit in the GATT Kennedy Round negotiations on tariff liberalization. A single, Chief Negotiator was given authority to act on behalf of the Scandinavian states and he and his four national deputies confronted the key actors of the United States, the European Communities, Japan and Britain with a completely integrated negotiation posture.[31] The aggregate economic capability of the four Nordic states (Iceland was excluded) was of such a magnitude (for example, the Nordic states combined were a larger customer of the European Communities' products than the United States), that it led to the Nordic bloc being treated as the equivalent of a key state throughout the negotiations.

The Nordic Chief Negotiator and his four national deputies formed a steering group which supervised a staff of sixty experts drawn from the four national administrations according to expertise needed throughout the negotiation process in Geneva. Consequently, the Scandinavian states gained concessions on intra-regional economic interests which they would not have received on an individual basis and the Nordic bloc contributed significantly to more liberalized trading policies.

The Nordic states have also shared resources and skills in the conduct of international relations outside the region. Through their Ministries of Defence, Denmark, Finland, Norway and Sweden have co-ordinated a Nordic Stand-by Force available for peace-keeping duties by the United Nations. The five Nordic states jointly fund and manage development projects in Tanzania and Kenya as part of their development assistance policies. The national governments provide joint information services abroad and joint tourist and travel bureaux have been established in many European cities. When abroad, Scandinavians can be assisted by joint consular service; that is, in case the 'home country' of a travelling Scandinavian does not maintain a consulate in a particular location, assistance can be obtained from any Nordic state consulate. This arrangement has been formalized in the Helsinki Treaty on Co-operation.

In sum, the outcome of the parallel national action process has been the establishment of increasingly integrated Nordic societal conditions in most spheres of life. The Scandinavians have complete freedom of movement and transferability of all their social security rights in a region with nearly identical legal systems and mutually enforceable laws. Economic relations are characterized by recently intensifying Nordic economic integration within a larger Western European economic framework, but based on different national policy positions. Resources and skills are shared extensively in education and research where a new network of trans-Nordic institutions with supranational administrations are emerging. Except for the high politics issue areas of national security and military alliance policies, the Scandinavian states have developed a highly integrated pattern of behaviour in international politics.

Summary and conclusion

The central thesis addressed in this chapter is that there is a need to redirect the focus in regional integration studies from a concentration on political structural transformation leading to the replacement of separate states by a larger regional state to a focus on the process of changes in behavioural codes of conduct among existing states. The Scandinavian experiences have been treated as an illustrative empirical model for such a redirection of focus.

The case of Scandinavian integration has been presented by a description and analysis of the governing conditions, the structure and process, and the outcomes of a process characterized as parallel national action. Treated in an historical perspective, the governing conditions consist of: (1) the rejection of the constitutional fusion approach and supranational institutions; (2) the sanctity of maintaining the five autonomous states as the basis for regional integration; and (3) the exclusion from the integration process of the 'high politics' issue areas of national security and military alliance policies.

Scandinavian parallel national action is characterized by a consensus-building process in which an extensive integrative network is maintained and promoted by Nordic regional organizations facilitating interaction among interest groups, political parties, parliaments, political executives and civil administrations of the five national political systems. The outcomes of the parallel national action process have been an extensive equalization of societal conditions in legal, social and economic issue areas and the removal of barriers to interaction by the creation of an open flow of people, goods and services within the region. They have also involved a sharing and pooling of resources and skills in cultural, educational and scientific research issue areas leading to the establishment of new Nordic common administrative institutions. Finally, in the conduct of extra-regional relations, the five Nordic states have developed an integrated behavioural code of conduct involving co-ordinated policy positions in international institutions and joint behaviour in general international bargaining and negotiations.

Among the most significant limitations of the Scandinavian parallel national action approach to regional integration is the exclusion of security policies. It demonstrates the inability to increase the level of integration to a high politics issue area, and that, within the parallel national action framework, such shifts in levels of political integration are more susceptible to the expressed political will of the individual states than is assumed in both classical functionalist and neo-functionalist integration theories. Viewed in a power politics perspective, the conflict among larger European states intruded into the Nordic region and prevented the states' previous parallel national action responses of joint neutrality policies from becoming part of the political integrative behaviour pattern which developed in the low politics issue areas. Similarly, the Nordic states have been unable to institutionalize regional economic integration in the form of an economic union because of the high degree of economic interdependence in a wider European economic network which character- izes the individual Nordic states' economies and because of perceived incompatibilities between national security policies and formation of an economic union.[32]

The use of a case study approach to assess the general development of theoretical frameworks has its limitations. The caveat normally issued that a particular set of experiences may not be a sufficient basis from which to generalize must be heeded. The Nordic case has often been considered unique because of the high degree of cultural homogeneity among the Scandinavian peoples and the extensive similarity in their political systems and in their levels of economic development. In that perspective, it could be argued that the reason for the success of the parallel national action process is the very high degree of mutual confidence which already existed, based on the commonality of attributes among the five political systems. In many respects, these arguments are quite persuasive, but their importance should not be exaggerated. While cultural diversity is greater among the European peoples in general than is the case in Scandinavia, the persistence of strong nationality identification among the Nordic peoples has been as important a factor in the development of separate autonomous nation-states in that region as it has been in the rest of Europe. Furthermore, socio-economic developments during the past thirty years have created a high degree of similarity of societal conditions in many of the political systems of the economically developed states. It is, therefore, not considered pretentious or unrealistic to draw on the Scandinavian experiences as a basis from which to suggest a new conceptual framework.

The Western European integration experiences since the end of the Second World War have been analysed predominantly on the basis of the neo-functionalist analytical framework. It has been assumed that the establishment of regional institutions with supranational authority such as the European Community would be the initial steps in the process of forming a new regional state.

With forty years' hindsight, recent developments suggest the emergence of a regional structure in Western Europe of a number of medium-sized nation states strongly legitimized by the various peoples on the basis of cultural identity, but involved in extensive integration processes in low politics issue areas while changing toward an integrative behavioural code of conduct among the states in high politics issue areas. These changes are indicated by the large number of nationally staffed advisory boards which have been added to the 'supranational' institutions for the purpose of dealing with the economic union issue areas,[33] by the changing style of operation adopted by the Commission with emphasis on the tasks of co-ordinating interests and activities of the member states,[34] and by the setting-up of the European Councils as a forum for consultation and deliberation among the member states' leading political executives, but placed outside the supranational institutional structure.

Conversely, the Scandinavian experiences indicate that what has been considered 'outcome indicators' of socio-economic integration within the European Communities have been achieved in Scandinavia without the use of supranational institutions and the 'community method' of decision-making.

In a different regional context, the Eastern European experiences with co-operative and emerging integrative processes, analysed by Mihály Simai elsewhere in this volume, also suggest the applicability of the parallel national action framework with its focus on behavioural changes in codes of conduct among actors in a firmly fixed structural setting of separate nation states.

Expansion, modification and change of focus in theoretical frameworks are attempts by scholars to adapt to the complexities of empirical events for which previous theories could not account. The trend in regional co-operation and integration suggests that the parallel national action framework, as illustrated by the Scandinavian experiences, might be highly relevant as a model by which to capture an expanding scope of social, economic and political integrative behaviour which is unaccounted for by the neo-functionalist theories with their focus on structural transformation. While the expectations of regional political community formation created by the latter theories lead to pessimistic conclusions of failure, the parallel national action framework could be used as an analytical tool by which to reveal less spectacular, but highly significant increases in co-operative and integrative behaviour patterns within the various regions of the global political system.

Notes

1. The connotation of the terms 'Scandinavia' and 'Nordic' has often been disputed among scholars specializing in the region. Historically, 'Scandinavia' covers the kingdoms of Denmark, Norway and Sweden while 'Nordic' covers the three

kingdoms plus Finland and Iceland. In recent issues of major atlases all five states were identified as Scandinavian. In present-day usage within the region, 'Scandinavia' and 'Nordic' are used interchangeably to encompass all five states, a practice followed throughout the discussion in this chapter.

2. See Stanley V. Anderson, *The Nordic Council: A Study of Scandinavian Regionalism,* Seattle and London, The University of Washington Press, 1967. Amitai Etzioni treats Scandinavian co-operation in a broader perspective, but the focus is on the supranational institutional potential of the Nordic Council organizations, 'The stable union: the Nordic associational web', in *Political Unification: A Comparative Study of Leaders and Forces,* New York, Holt, Rinehart and Winston, 1965. A generally descriptive, historical account of Nordic co-operation is provided by Frantz Wendt, *Co-operation in the Nordic Countries,* Nordic Council, 1981.

3. The concept of a 'Benelux Procedure', which refers to the method used by governmental leaders from Belgium and the Netherlands in deciding to form a customs union, has been used throughout the post-Second World War debate in Scandinavia to convey the basic distinguishing characteristics of the continental European approach to regional integration which has been very different from the Scandinavian approach.

4. We have adopted the term 'political executive' instead of 'government' in order to differentiate between the activities and responsibilities of the high-level elected political élites who constitute the Cabinet in a parliamentary political system, and the civil servants who constitute the permanent staff of the national administration.

5. Bo Anderson, 'The Nordic organization research group', conference paper mimeographed in Clive Archer (ed.), *Conference on Scandinavia and European Integration,* University of Aberdeen, March 1973.

6. Frantz Wendt, op. cit. and *Nordisk Samarbejde Idag,* Copenhagen, Foreningen Norden Udgivelse, 1971.

7. Gunnar P. Nielsson, 'Denmark and European Integration: A Small Country at the Crossroads', Los Angeles, UCLA, Ph.D. Dissertation, 1966, ch. VI.

8. Ibid., chapter VII.

9. The Contact Man System is discussed within a more comprehensive context of transgovernmental integration in Scandinavia by C. Robert Dickerman in 'Transgovernmental challenge and response in Scandinavia and North America', *International Organization,* Vol. 30, No. 2 (Spring 1976).

10. Ove Rainer, 'Det Raettliga omraadet', *Nordisk aembetsmannamoete i Storlien,* Stockholm, Nordiska Raadet, Nordisk Udredningsserie, 1969:9. My translation from page 13. For a brief discussion of the Nordic Contact Man System in English, see Herman Kling, Swedish Minister of Justice, 'Legislative co-operation between the Nordic countries', in *Nordic Co-operation.* Stockholm, Nordiska Raadet, Nordisk Udredningsserie, 1965:9.

11. For a more detailed description and analysis of the Nordic Council, consult Stanley Anderson, op. cit., and Frantz Wendt, op. cit.

12. The Fagerholm Committee on reorganization of the Nordic Council published its report in English as *The Organization of Nordic Co-operation,* Stockholm, Nordiska Raadet, Nordisk Udredningsserie, 1970:13; and as part of the report on the Nordek proposal in *Expanded Nordic Economic Co-operation,* Stockholm, Nordiska Raadet, Nordisk Udredningsserie, 1969:17. The revised Helsinki Treaty has been published in English by the Nordic Council, entitled *Treaty of Co-operation Between Denmark, Finland, Iceland, Norway and*

Sweden, without publishing information. The reorganization is discussed in English by Emil Windsetmo, 'Revision of the Helsinki Treaty of Co-operation and recent developments in Nordic co-operation', *Nordic Co-operation in a European Perspective,* Stockholm, Nordiska Raadet, Nordisk Udredningsserie, 1972:1; and by Gustav Petren, 'The institutions of Nordek', *Nordic Economic and Cultural Co-operation,* Stockholm, Nordiska Raadet, Nordisk Udredningsserie, 1969:21.

13. For a more detailed analysis of Nordic Council procedures, consult Stanley Anderson, op. cit., chapter 4.

14. A complete overview of the status of Nordic Council Plenary Assembly's recommendations and the Presidium's formal statements between 1953 and 1961 is provided in *Nordiska raadets verksamhet, 1952–1961,* Stockholm, Nordiska Raadet, Nordisk Udredningsserie, 1962:8.

15. *Nordiska ministerraadets arbetsformer,* Stockholm, Nordiska Raadet, Nordisk Udredningsserie, 1971:5.

16. *Treaty Between Denmark, Finland, Iceland, Norway and Sweden Concerning Cultural Co-operation,* published by the Nordic Council without publishing information.

17. The full text of Article 38 is: 'The authorities in the Nordic countries may correspond directly with each other in matters other than those which by their nature or for other reasons should be dealt with through the agency of Ministries of Foreign Affairs.' *Treaty of Co-operation . . .,* op. cit., p. 9. A Norwegian official in the Ministry of Foreign Affairs described the development of diffusion of intra-Nordic interaction channels this way:

What happened was roughly this: for a period of time after the war, almost all matters between Scandinavian countries went through the foreign offices and embassies. Then other entities began dealing directly, but consulting closely with the foreign office. Eventually they simply sent us drop copies of correspondence and memoranda. Finally that stopped, too.

(Interview statement quoted by C. Robert Dickerman, op. cit., p. 223.)

18. Interview statement by Emil Windsetmo, quoted in ibid, p. 221.

19. Based on the inventory overview of parallel national action provided in *Oeversikt oever lager tillkomna genom nordiskt samarbete,* Stockholm, Nordiska Raadet, Nordisk Udredningsserie, 1965:2.

20. The migration data for 1950 to 1977 is provided in Nordiska Ministerraadet, *Vaegen till en fri Nordisk arbetsmarknad,* publication 1985:5, p. 63, The 1986 data was obtained in the Nordic Council, *Yearbook of Nordic Statistics, 1987.* Copenhagen, Nordic Statistical Secretariat, 1987.

21. For a more detailed explanation of the Nordic Customs Union proposals in the 1950s, see Nielsson, op. cit., chapters VII and X.

22. The Nordek plans are analysed in Gunnar P. Nielsson, 'The Nordic and the continental European dimension in Scandinavian integration: NORDEK as a case study', *Co-operation and Conflict,* No. 3/4, 1971.

23. Wilhelm Paues, 'Scandinavian and European integration: Scandinavian Experiences in E.F.T.A.', mimeographed in *Conference on Scandinavia and European Integration,* op. cit.

24. Vloyantes, op. cit. and Nielsson, op. cit.

25. Charles G. Nelson, 'European Integration: Trade Data and Measurement Problems', *International Organization,* Vol. 28, No. 3 (Summer 1974), p. 423.

26. *E.F., Danmark og Skandinavien,* Copenhagen, European Communities Information Service, December 1974.
27. The Danish position as a member of both the Nordic integrative network and the European Community is analysed extensively in the PhD dissertation by Roger Selbert entitled, Compatible Two Sphere Integration: the Simultaneous Danish Participation in the European Communities and Scandinavian Co-operation, Los Angeles, University of Southern California, 1980.
28. Nordisk aembetsmannamoete . . . op. cit., p. 15.
29. Per Haekkerup, 'Nordic co-operation and the world around us', *Nordic Co-operation,* op. cit., p. 29. Professor Nils Andren has concluded in his analysis of the subject that '. . . Joint consultation almost assumes the sanctity of an ethical principle in inter-Nordic relations,' 'Nordic integration: aspects and problems', *Co-operation and Conflict,* No. 1, 1967, p. 11.
30. See Bruce Russett, *International Regions and the International System,* Chicago, Rand McNally, 1967. Chapter 4 contains the results of a factor analysis of similarity in UN voting behaviour on various issues.
31. For a detailed account of this experience, see the paper by the Nordic Chief Negotiator, Nils Montan, 'Nordic Co-operation in the Field of International Trade Policy', *Nordic Economic and Cultural Co-operation,* op. cit.
32. Martin Saeter, 'The Nordic area and European integration', *Co-operation and Conflict: Nordic Journal of International Politics,* 1/2, 1975.
33. For a discussion of this institutional development, consult Roger Broad and R.J. Jarrett, *Community Europe Today,* London, Oswald Wolf, 1972.
34. In a study of the changing role of the Commission, Paul Taylor observed:

The Commission of the European Communities — the main independent, active element in the Brussels institutions — has in effect renounced its claim to be a rival center of authority, a putative European government. It has accepted the role of *actor,* like any other in the European *Gesellschaft,* with the specific task of encouraging European arrangements and encouraging alliances to solve particular problems. In other words, it is no longer out to challenge national governments. In helping them to define their interests and to form alliances, it reinforces their right to exist.

'The politics of the European Communities: the confederal phase', *World Politics,* Vol. 27, No. 3 (April 1975), p. 347.

Selected reading

Co-operation and Conflict: Nordic Journal of International Politics, 1/2 1975. Special issue on élite attitudes and Nordic government policies concerning questions of integration and co-operation in Europe in general and in the Nordic area in particular.
Nordic Co-operation in a European Perspective, Stockholm, Nordic Council, Nordisk Udredningsserie, 1972:1.
The Organization of Nordic Co-operation, Nordisk Udredningsserie, 1970:13.
Haskel, Barbara, *The Scandinavian Option,* Oslo, Universitetsforlaget, 1976.
Sundelius, Bengt, *Managing Transnationalism in Northern Europe,* Boulder, Colorado, Westview Press, 1978.

Sundelius, Bengt, ed. *The Foreign Policies of Northern Europe,* Boulder, Colorado, Westview Press, 1982.

Wendt, Frantz, *Co-operation in the Nordic Countries: Achievements and Obstacles,* Stockholm, Almquist & Wiksell International, 1981.

8 Supranationalism: the power and authority of international institutions

Paul Taylor

The concept of supranationalism concerns the interplay between the state and international institutions. It has been most frequently used in discussions of relations between states in the developed world and international institutions which are thought to have interfered in some sense with the traditional pattern of exclusive control by state authorities of their own internal governmental affairs. The concept raises questions about the power and authority of international institutions and about the way in which developments there may have weakened the authority of states and their capacity to survive in their traditional form. The issue arises of whether supranationalism may in some sense have served the interests of the state, by helping it to adapt to the ever-increasing demands and expectations of its citizens and the changing circumstances of international society.

To help the reader, the main components of the argument are set out in schematic form at the end of this chapter. Beloff wrote: 'what supranationalism means is that there is a recognised interest within a political grouping of several nations which is different from, or distinguishable from, the interest of any one of them and which thus claims institutional expression.'[1] Such a recognition is fundamental in the circumstances of supranationalism; it affects the authority of the international institution, the role allowed to it by the states, and its methods of taking decisions. Beloff adds: 'the difficulty lies not in the conception of policy but in its authorisation and execution.'[2] Supranationalism depends upon the states' willingness to allow the international institution a range of powers and an area of independent initiative which are commensurate with the allocated tasks.

Powers are allocated in specific limited areas to a new centre. Decisions are taken there by a majority voting system of some sort, and their execution is supervised by the international institution, rather than by the state. A number of developments in the areas of law, organization, communication and attitudes are found in relations between the states, which both follow from the authority of the international institution and help to sustain it. In sum, supranationalism consists of a pyramid of interrelated elements at the peak of which is majority voting in an international institution, which reflects the dominance of the latter over member states in a limited functional area. In this chapter these elements are considered, and their role in the development of the authority of international institutions is evaluated. Examples are taken mainly from the experience of the European Communities, though, as will become evident, the Communities in their present form are not themselves a supranational organization.[3]

There are three headings under which the following discussion of the main elements of supranationalism are organized. They reflect a convenient way of arranging the materials and ideas in relation to the two main actors involved in the relationship, the international institution and the state. The relationship is seen as having two main components in its impact on the latter. The first heading, therefore, refers to changes in the structure and powers of the international institution; the second refers to challenges to the exclusive competence of the state in its own territory; the third refers to challenges to the separateness or 'integrity' of the decision-making structures in the states. The last two categories should perhaps be explained in greater detail.

They reflect two facets of the sovereignty of states which are affected by supranationalism. The first (the second heading) is the exclusive competence of a government within its territorial frontiers, which is generally understood and widely accepted as essential in sovereignty. In the United Kingdom it means that laws passed by Parliament prevail within the frontiers of that country, and that laws passed by, for instance, the French National Assembly, have no legal standing and will not be upheld by British courts. A discussion of supranationalism should be concerned with the possible effects of the work of international institutions upon this exclusive competence of the state.

The second (the third heading) is the integrity of decision-making structures in the state. It is possible to conceive of circumstances in which the decision-making structures of the state are so affected or controlled by outside forces that the legal effect of exclusive competence disguises a *de facto* subjection to external control. The élites of one state may subscribe to an ideology which disposes them normally to follow detailed instructions from another 'government' or agency outside its frontiers. It is conceivable that the members of one government could be placed in effect in office by another government, and habitually follow the other's instructions because of loyalty, physical dependence or bribery. An example of this would be the Nazi-dominated government of Austria before the invasion by Hitler of 1938. The exclusive competence of the government to make laws for its territory was preserved, but the integrity of the government had been so undermined that the legal forms concealed a *de facto* breach of sovereignty. It is conceivable that a breach of the integrity of national decision-making structures could result from an accumulation of pressures and interventions from international institutions, like the oil companies, or large foreign corporations, like Lockheed. It is, however, extremely difficult to judge the point at which a government's ability to control its own affairs has been so reduced that it could be said that it faced a serious challenge to this aspect of its sovereignty. A situation in which more than 50 per cent of a national budget was allocated according to the wishes of foreign businessmen, who were bribing national officials, might be accepted as constituting such a challenge. But a single intervention, such as the much discussed letters sent to the International Monetary Fund (IMF) by the British Government in

1967 and 1976, which allowed IMF inspection of British Treasury activities, is not enough. An increasing range of interventions in the internal affairs of states could, however, have implications for sovereignty which are similar to those which follow from the placing of personnel by an outside power, or the subjection of the state's own personnel to an ideology through which they could be manipulated. In Keohane and Nye's terms (see chapter 16) this goes beyond vulnerability.

This argument reflects the point that sovereignty has two facets, first an exclusive competence, and, second, the relative independence of law-making entities from outside intervention. A discussion of supranationalism should be concerned with both of these facets in that they represent fronts on which sovereignty may be actually or potentially challenged. In this chapter groups of elements of supranationalism are organized so that they can be related to each in turn. They are concerned respectively with legal questions and with the development of transnational political systems. They are considered after an examination of the supranational elements which have been found in the international institutions themselves.

The governing bodies of international institutions normally have two major elements, a group of international civil servants, and a group of state representatives, where decisions are taken on the basis of either unanimity or majority voting. A third element is sometimes found: an assembly of delegates from national parliaments which usually support one or other of the main bodies, provide additional expertise, and in some cases try to ensure accountability. Distinctive, supranational features, have been found in each of these elements. In this chapter attention is focused on the first two.

In the case of the group of international civil servants, factors conducive towards supranationalism are those which allow the definition and pursuit of policies which reflect the longer-term common interests of member states and which transcend their short-term individual interest. Support for supranationalism is found, first, in the condition of independence of the secretariat. In the case of the European Communities the independence of the members of the High Authority and of the Commission was required by the founding Treaties of Paris and of Rome. The Treaty of Paris includes one of the few instances of the actual use in a treaty of the term 'supranationalism', and it is significant that it is used in the context of discussing the requirement of independence of members of the High Authority: they 'will refrain from any action incompatible with the supra-national character of their duties. Each member state undertakes to respect the supranational character' (Article 9, ECSC). Although the term is not mentioned in the article which replaced Article 9 (ECSC) in the Treaty of Merger of April 1965, under which the High Authority of the ECSC and the Commission of the European Economic Community (EEC) and EUR-ATOM were merged, members were still told that they would 'in the general interest of the Communities be completely independent in the performance of their duties' (Merger Treaty, Article 10, paragraph 2); and that 'they shall neither seek nor take instructions from any government or from any other body', and 'shall refrain from any action incompatible with their duties' (Merger Treaty, Article 10, paragraph 2). As Professor Mathijsen has pointed out, these conditions underline the requirements that the High Authority and the Commission should represent 'the Communities' *general* interest and must be in a position to take a stand against any government which tries to put national interests first.'[4]

A further condition of independence of the Secretariat and one which may be of great importance in allowing it to strive actively for the general interest is a measure of budgetary independence. In the case of the European Coal and Steel Community (ECSC) this independence was established from the beginning by allowing the Community the right to its own finance from a tax directly levied on the coal and steel industries of member states. In the case of the EEC the acquiring of a right to independent finance took many years: the EEC and EURATOM depended upon the contributions of member governments until the mid-1970s. It was only with the Council of Ministers' decision of February 1970 that steps were taken towards the granting to these two institutions of their 'own resources'. The right to decide the scale of revenues was, however, retained by member governments and remained a significant limitation on the supranationalism of the common institutions.

These conditions of independence are only significant in so far as they are exploited by the members of the Secretariat. Less tangible factors such as the quality of leadership in the institution, its energy and even its mood also play a role. The independence of members of the Secretariat from direct instructions from governments is, however, a *sine qua non*. But a Walter Hallstein or a Jean Monnet can be decisive in the definition and pursuit of interests which are separable from those of the states.

Methods of exercising control in international institutions, in committees of intergovernmental representatives or international civil servants, are frequently thought to be good indicators of supranationalism. Reynolds writes:

the word supranational is of relatively recent origin and refers to institutions which have been created for the performance of specific functions, and which have power to take decisions binding on the members whether they have participated in the decision or not.[5]

He refers to the High Authority of ECSC as one example of such decision-making, and also the Committee of Ministers of Western European Union, which could in certain circumstances prevent by majority voting the United Kingdom from reducing the level of her forces in Western Germany below an agreed level. The voting arrangements of the Council of Ministers of the EEC, according to the original form of the Rome Treaty, would also qualify as evidence of that institution's supranationalism. There are, therefore, two situations in which a member could be said — in Reynold's terms — not to have participated in a decision taken by an international institution. The first would be when a binding decision is taken by a group of international civil servants according to rules previously agreed to by member states (as with the High Authority); the second is when the decision is taken by a committee of representatives of national governments according to a system of majority voting. Conversely, member states participate in a decision when it is taken by a committee of governmental representatives on the basis of unanimity or on the basis of a system which gives them the right to say whether they will accept a decision which has been taken by other members. A 'binding' decision is one which is not only taken according to the agreed forms and procedures, and is therefore binding in the legal sense, but is also effective in the sense that it is carried out.

Executive committees of international civil servants and of government representatives may take decisions by majority vote which have two major kinds of effect: either the decision upholds a framework of policies or arrangements already approved by governments, for instance, in a founding treaty, or it initiates new arrangements and policies. The High Authority and the Commission's decision-making role was the quasi-legal one of supporting arrangements already approved by governments rather than of initiating new elements of the framework. The institutions of the European Communities do, however, possess a power which is regarded as supranational, even in the taking of decisions of this kind: governments agreed that the institutions should act directly in relation to individuals and groups within the state without immediate supervision by state authorities (the legal framework and its implications are discussed more fully below). The High Authority acted to impose the rules of the common market in coal, steel and scrap, as agreed by the states which signed the Treaty of Paris. Even in this role, however, the record of the High authority was rather mixed: it failed, for instance, to obtain in the 1950s the rearrangement of West German coal-selling cartels which seemed necessary to the proper working of the common market in coal. The Commission of the European Communities also takes decisions independently only in areas already agreed by member governments: although it is the main initiator of community legislation it does not decide what changes should be accepted. That task is reserved for the intergovernmental Council.

The existence of majority voting in a committee of government representatives may be misleading as an indicator of supranationalism. The committee should not have a permanent majority and an unchanging minority — it should have a fluid majority voting system — and should be backed by communication procedures, attitudes and structures which sustain a general confidence in the majority vote. A majority voting system such as that in the General Assembly of the United Nations could not be said to be supranational; one indication of this is that its decisions are mainly in the form of recommendations; another is the lack of fluidity among majority groups in relation to a wide range of issues. Minorities and majorities tend to solidify and to become either sullen, or over-impressed with the validity of their positions. In addition, of course, the lack of a sufficient consensus among states leads to majority votes being discounted or judged as trivial or irresponsible. It may also, as in Western European Union, lead to a deliberate avoidance of the possibility of majority voting. The British decision to reduce the size of her forces in West Germany in the late 1950s, in order to concentrate on nuclear weapons, was not put to the vote in WEU, although the institution was legally entitled to stop such reductions by qualified majority. The states lacked sufficient confidence in each other: the institution therefore lacked the authority to act in this situation. In the EEC the Council of Ministers has also retained the principle of unanimity, and the Communities lack this critical element of supranationalism.

Although a range of independent powers in administering an agreed framework may be accepted as an element of supranationalism, the ability to take decisions by a fluid majority which initiates new policies and structures is a more convincing indication.

Rigid majority voting systems may indeed help to destroy the foundations on which a more fluid system might be built. They may help to amplify the disagreements of contending groups and discourage the use of the mechanisms for reconciling their interests, the development of linking structures and the softening of hostile attitudes. They lead to mere vote-counting by the majority, rather than consensus-building.

The argument is now concerned with elements of a supranationalism which relate to the facet of the integrity of decision-making structures, and the development of transnational political systems.

The structures which link states with each other and with the international institution are the mechanism through which the common interests are expressed. They reflect and generate interdependence amongst states, particularly among the developed states, which now find that their search for economic stability and for increases in the level of welfare can only be satisfied within a co-operative framework. Andrew Shonfield has picked out some aspects of these structures of interdependence in the context of the European Communities and discusses their implications. He wrote:

dramatic improvement in communications, the greatly increased mobility of people and money, and also the huge concentration of corporate power in the hands of international businesses, taken together, demand the establishment of a new dimension of international public power. At the same time there is a parallel movement, less obvious, but beginning to be significant, among the associations of private and professional persons — farmers, trade unionists, certain scientists, even specialist professional civil servants, who find that the natural links for much of what they wish to accomplish are with their professional colleagues abroad rather than with their own national governments. The transitional lobbies that are thus created look for some international political counterpart. . . . Now I call this amalgam of private groups and agencies transcending national frontiers, together with the official political agencies that have been established in and around the European Community *supranational*.[6]

Shonfield also pointed out that these structures did not stand above governments, but included parts of them.

The structures which have developed across national frontiers in Western Europe are certainly numerous (about 400 examples of one type of structure, interest groups, have been counted in Brussels) but they have not as yet developed their full potential as elements of supranationalism. The reason is that groups which are active in attempting to influence the allocation of values still concentrate their efforts at the national level, and have developed rather weak umbrella organizations at the European level. That they have been able to develop mechanisms for articulating a residual common European interest is an achievement which should not be underestimated but transnational structures are often divided within themselves on national lines about a large number of more salient issues. Their common interest is as yet clearly defined rather infrequently, and rarely exists in a form which could be sought without reservation by various parts of the group at the national and international level. Nevertheless the development of a system of supranational structures depends upon and encourages the process of legitimizing the values of the supranational organization.

Many tests of the emergence of such structures as stronger elements of supranationalism are conceivable. One possibility concerns the attitude of the various subsystems in the structure to the distribution of resources: on the one side the subsystem might be expected to come to rely on obtaining resources from the international level, and to perceive that its activities at that level produced appropriate reward; on the other side the members of the subsystem should be prepared to accept variations in the distribution of resources, sometimes to the obvious greater advantage of members of another subsystem. They should, in other words, not see short-term maldistribution as being contrary to the common interest. The more groups within the state which are encouraged to plan on the basis of the expectation of transnational involvement, the stronger the pressure towards strengthening this element of supranationalism. Planning committees attached to groups and governments within the state which regularly called on regional resources for specific projects are particularly likely to learn to think in regional terms and to choose solutions which are compatible with the general interest. They are likely to be more aware of the problems of creating regional resources, be more convinced of the need to manage them efficiently (not, for instance, to overexploit them in the short term), to be more frequently in touch with the international institution (and hence aware of its preferred solution), and more understanding of the needs and interests of competing groups in other countries. This is, of course, conditional upon the availability of resources at the supranational level.

The legitimization of the goals of Europe in national political processes involves an amendment of concepts about what was previously thought to be reserved to the nation. This has proceeded rather slowly, but it is easy to overlook the remarkable character of this development. For instance, a large number of civil servants and politicians now contact colleagues in corresponding ministries in other states, or in Brussels, as part of the routine processes of decision-making. Even in some of the more cautious member states of the European Communities there is considerable evidence to suggest that those who have been closely involved in its work in the Foreign and Commonwealth Office and other Departments of State have increasingly found themselves at home in the new context and are more sympathetic towards its values.[7] They do not consider they are betraying their country by doing this and are not so regarded by their colleagues. Even in the inter-war period states were far more sensitive about the kind of information which they were prepared to exchange: in 1922, for instance, only four years after the conclusion of the 'war to end wars', negotiations between France and Britain about the possibility of agreeing contingency plans between General Staffs to cope with any new German attack were broken off by the British on the grounds that such plans involved giving too much away to another country. In NATO, West European states now exchange information on security and defence arrangements in a routine way, and similar changes have taken place in the economic area. Conventions in communication have developed between international institutions and member countries, and between member countries themselves, which only a short while ago would have been judged as a betrayal of the sacred interests of the separate nations.

Both the EC and the UN are involved in a legitimization process. But in the United Nations the system of legitimization tends to take the form of individual policies accepted by overwhelming majorities in the General Assembly. The legitimization of anti-colonialism by the overwhelming adoption of a sweeping anti-colonial declaration in 1960, and subsequently, is a good example of this.[8] In the European Communities, however, the Commission's proposals (i.e. those of the institution) are generally legitimized, in the sense that they are usually accepted as constituting an attempt at the general interest, without regard to whether or not they have been approved in the Council. Commission proposals may be regarded as inappropriate, or even just wrong, but they are rarely seen as threatening or partisan. At the same time there is a sense among members of national governments that certain national goals are legitimate whilst some others are out of bounds.[9] The larger number of states with which the UN deals, the nature of the areas within which it is asked to act, and the failure to spell out in the Charter a long-term programme of action for the Secretariat, within which it could exercise a right to initiate, are all difficulties in the way of an incremental extension of the area of legitimate supranational action in the United Nations. In both the EC and the UN there is, however, some evidence of the appearance of limited areas of consensus in relation to which specific supranational powers could develop. This remained true of the EC in the late 1980s, even though the British Prime Minister occasionally appeared to be challenging the Commission's legitimacy as an initiator of European policies.

The argument now turns to the elements of supranationalism which affect the second facet of sovereignty: the exclusive legal competence of the state within its own frontiers. They affect the states' monopoly of law-making within its own territory. In its most obvious form the challenge is in the shape of the development of a rival legal system which has priority over the municipal law of the state within its frontiers. In a second form it consists of changes in attitudes at the popular level which indicate an increasing reluctance on the part of the people of the state to obey the law as handed down to them by their own governments. Where loyalty is undermined, disobedience is the result; where the purpose of the law is changing as supranational goals are legitimized we may find a perfectly loyal citizenry supporting the increasingly supranational ambitions and objectives of its government, or its agents, and other policy-making élites, in a community system.

The one extant example of the setting up of a rival legal system within the state is, of course, that of the European Communities, although lawyers are by no means agreed on how far this constitutes a threat to national sovereignty. It is clear, however, that the member states of the European Communities now accept that law made by the institutions of the European Communities in Brussels is to be followed by domestic courts without the requirement of any special act of approval by national governments or national assemblies. Furthermore, under the terms of the Treaty of Paris (see, for example, Articles 41, 42, 43, 44 and 92) and of the Treaty of Rome (Article 177) it is the Court of the Communities which meets at Luxembourg which is the final court of appeal on Community questions and which acts as interpreter of the Treaty. It is not just that Community laws are to have direct effect within national territories but governments are also to lose their right to decide how that law is to be applied and interpreted. In the event of clashes between domestic law and Community law, furthermore, domestic courts are to give precedence to Community law (in the United Kingdom according to Section 2 (4) of the European Communities Act). In order to ensure compliance with Community law, institutions such as the High Authority and the Commission are given extensive powers under the founding treaties. The High Authority had a particularly wide range of powers to fine firms which broke the rules of the ECSC (see Articles 65 and 66) and 'decisions of the High Authority which impose a pecuniary obligation shall be enforceable . . .. Enforcement may be suspended only by a decision of the Court [of the ECSC]' (Article 92). The Commission may also act directly, without the legal intervention of national governments, in areas such as those covered by Articles 85 and 86 (EEC) on cartels, concentrations and abuse of dominant position. It is this unique character of the law of the Communities, together with the powers of Community institutions to enforce and interpret that law, which some lawyers have considered to be the most important, supranational element of the Communities.

There are, however, various difficulties in the way of evaluating implications for the sovereignty of states of this penetration of national legal systems by the Communities, though the very existence of such difficulties is some measure of the challenge to traditional ideas about sovereignty.[10] That there exists a body external to the member states which makes, enforces and interprets law, which is directly applicable in the states in the areas covered by the founding treaties, cannot be denied; and the conclusion that this represents a challenge to the exclusive competence of the state to make law in its own territory seems to follow in a straightforward fashion. But the difficulties are, first, that it is the Council of Ministers which in effect makes the law by its regulations, directives and decisions, and this institution is made up of representatives of member governments who act on the basis of unanimity. (Member governments do in fact agree to Community laws which are to operate within their frontiers, although when they do so they are acting in a Community institution.) Second, national assemblies, such as the British Parliament, agreed, when they allowed Community law to operate in their states, merely to restrain themselves from challenging that law. 'What has really happened is that Parliament [in the UK] has identified an area within which Community legislative power will operate. Within that area Parliament intends to refrain from exercising its own legislative power.'[11] (The conclusion is that Community law is allowed its status in the United Kingdom by an Act of Parliament, and that Parliament could equally change that status. In some EC states the rejection of Community law would involve the special processes of constitutional amendment.) Third, states could under international law decide unilaterally that they were no longer bound by the Treaties of Rome and Paris, and if they did this, though the political consequences would be serious, there would be little that their partners could do.

The conclusion is that as governments and national assemblies at various points in the establishment of the basic agreements, and in the drawing-up of the detailed day-to-day decisions, agree to be bound, they could equally disagree to be bound — they could take back what they have given and, the argument runs, this does not amount to a breach of sovereignty. The procedures are novel, the Community legal system is indeed unique, and may be justifiably called supranational, but it is still an expression of the states' adjustment to new conditions: it serves them, at their discretion. In this argument, again, the supranational elements help states to survive rather than tend to replace them in new integrated structures.

There is, therefore, a contradiction between the appearance in contemporary Western Europe that the exclusive competence of states has been undermined by the Communities' legal system — and national sovereignty therefore breached — and the various legal safeguards to which states can in theory resort if that legal system displeases them. One way of resolving the contradiction is suggested by the idea of 'entrenchment'[12]: the safeguards remain as possibilities but resort to them becomes increasingly unlikely because of the accumulation of adjustments in national laws and habits of law-making to take account of the Communities' legal system. The latter is therefore 'entrenched' in the national legal system; it becomes increasingly difficult, though legally perfectly possible, to revise the mass of national legislation so that it could be separated from Community law. Entrenchment, though most apposite in the context of Britain's relationship with the EC, is also an important aspect of the relationship between other member states and the Communities. Even in those countries where international treaties, such as the Treaties of Rome and Paris, become a part of the national constitution, there is no certainty of continued adherence to the treaties: withdrawal is made rather more difficult in that it requires special processes.[13] But the practice of assimilating treaty obligations into constitutions should be seen as a way of encouraging the same elements of obligation and commitment which, it is hoped by supporters of European integration, will prevail in the United Kingdom, namely, the process of entrenchment. Continued adherence to the Treaties of the European Communities depends upon that process, regardless of whether the treaties are assimilated into the constitution or not, the major difference being that withdrawal from the treaties would involve the slightly more complicated procedure of constitutional amendment, whereas in the United Kingdom, withdrawal could be effected by the normal process of legislation.

The process of developing international organization envisaged by Hammarskjold is surprisingly similar in some respects, as is the process of maintaining international 'regimes', such as is found in international monetary and financial arrangements. Hammarskjold spoke of the need to build in international society a sophisticated 'constitutionalism', and to move away gradually from the present 'primitive institutionalism'.[14] He saw this sophisticated constitutionalism in the building of conventions about appropriate procedure, for instance, in the event of threats to the peace; he envisaged the construction of an increasingly dense network of accepted practice focused upon the United Nations by which governments would manage international society. Entrenchment is found in this case in the way in which the conventions of international government are gradually built into the processes and structures of national governments, and in the way in which an increasing part of national law, particularly, in the first instance, in public administration and commerce, is made in the light of emerging international practice. Two levels of governmental practice and law are detected, the higher one in international society, being developed and strengthened by involvement and entrenchment in the lower one at the national level. These ideas clearly reflect Hammarskjold's interest in the regulation of relations between the nation-state members of international society, and his acceptance of a Lockean model of man's involvement in society.

Another way of resolving the contradictions between the appearance of a breach of sovereignty, such as is suggested by the penetration of national legal systems by the legal system of the Communities, and the existence of continuing legal safeguards for state governments and assemblies, is the refocusing of popular loyalties away from national governments towards international institutions. In this situation sovereignty could be said to have been lost by the state, and the supranational character of the international institution strengthened as a direct challenge to the state's survival, by the reluctance of citizens to obey national law and their willingness to obey the 'law' of the international institution. The contradiction is thus resolved in favour of the international institution by removing from the state an essential element in its sovereignty: the loyalty of its citizens. The exclusive competence of the state to make laws for its own territory would be challenged not directly by external intervention, but from within by a weakening of its authority.

These then are the major interrelated elements of supranationalism.[15] In this chapter they have been deduced mainly from the experience of the European Communities, but it is apparent that they have not been fully realized, and the Communities could not be said to be supranational. Their central organization in Brussels lacks many of the powers and the background resources of supranationalism. It may be, indeed, that the elements of supranationalism outlined here can only appear when the scope of integration is rather narrow. The wider the scope of the enterprise, the more diluted the elements of supranationalism become. This is because as scope increases, supranationalism gets closer to federalism: while supranationalism, as is partial federalism, serves the existing states — it helps them adapt to new needs and problems — Federalism challenges their existence fundamentally. States might, therefore, be expected to resist any tendency for partial federalism to turn into federalism. In practice even the ECSC was short of several essential features of supranationalism, particularly a body which could take decisions on the basis of a majority voting system which could initiate new structures or principles of policy: it bore the same relationship to supranationalism as was borne by the League of Nations to the idea of collective security — an ideal which was not attained.

The main components of the argument are set out in schematic form below.

Summary of elements of supranationalism

Recognition of a general interest

1. International actor

(a) Independence of international civil servants from instructions of national governments.
(b) Financial independence.
(c) Voting on policy initiatives by 'fluid' majorities.
(d) An effective leadership and buoyant mood in the international secretariat.

2. National actor: integrity of decision-making

(a) Development of extensive procedures for consultation about the general interest linking governmental and non-governmental institutions.
(b) Legitimization of goals of the international institution in the national and collective systems.
(c) Focus upon international institutions in order to obtain 'supranational' resources: acceptance of temporary discrimination in favour of other subsystems.

3. National actor: exclusive competence

(a) Penetration of national legal system by extra-national legal system of the international institution.

(b) Allowing to international institution of decision-making capacity to maintain common legal system within states.

(c) Development of 'entrenchment' of legal system.

(d) Development of habit of obedience to new international actor: 'compliance'.

Notes

1. Max Beloff, in Carol Ann Cosgrove and Kenneth Twitchett (eds.), *The New International Actors,* London, Macmillan, 1970, p. 95.
2. Ibid., p. 95.
3. One of the earliest references to the concept is to be found in the Fabian Society's Draft Treaty, described in L.S. Woolf: *Framework of a Lasting Peace,* London, Allen & Unwin, 1917, although in this case it is 'supernationalism'. The purpose was to construct a supernational authority which would be made up of two components: an International High Court to deal with 'legal' or 'justiciable' disputes, and an International Council, which would help to codify international law and mediate or arbitrate in political disputes. The system was to be supported by a variety of covenants outlawing war, a comprehensive range of economic sanctions, and a permanent Secretariat. The scheme had the objective of achieving the 'superordinate' goal of outlawing war. The Fabian Society insisted that 'what is suggested is no merging of independent national units into a "world state", though to this Utopia future ages may well come. No impairment of sovereignty and no sacrifice of independence are proposed.' (p. 92).
4. P.S.R.F. Mathijsen, *A Guide to European Community Law,* London, Sweet & Maxwell, 1972, pp. 139–40.
5. P.A. Reynolds, *An Introduction to International Relations,* London, Longman, 1971, p. 26.
6. Andrew Shonfield, *Europe: Journey to an Unknown Destination,* Harmondsworth, Penguin Books, 1972, pp. 16–17.
7. Werner J. Feld and John K. Wildgen, 'National administration élites and European integration: saboteurs at work?', *Journal of Common Market Studies,* March 1975, Vol. XIII, No. 3, p. 255.
8. See Inis L. Claude, Jr, 'Collective legitimization as a political function of the United Nations', *International Organization,* Summer 1966.
9. The demand by the British government for a separate seat at the 1976 Paris Conference on basic resources aroused not only political opposition among other EC members but also a feeling that the British demand was in a deeper sense 'wrong': it was in bad taste, a contravention of the emerging conventions of behaviour in the Communities.
10. See J.D.B. Mitchell, 'Community legislation', in M.E. Bathurst, K.R. Simmonds, N. March Hunnings and Jane Welch (eds.), *Legal Problems of the Enlarged Community,* London, Stevens, 1972, pp. 87–103, especially p. 88.
11. Paul Taylor, 'The obligation of membership of the European Communities', *International Affairs,* April, 1981.
12. Geoffrey Howe, 'The European Communities Act 1972', *International Affairs,* Vol. 49, No. 1, January 1973, p. 6.

13. See J.D.B. Mitchell, S.A. Kuipers and B. Gall, 'Constitutional Aspects of the Treaty and Legislation Relating to British Membership', *Common Market Law Review,* London, Stevens, May 1972, Vol. 9, No. 2, pp. 134–50, especially pp. 143 and 145.
14. See Dag Hammarskjold in Wilder Foote (ed.), cited footnote 38, Chapter Two.
15. For a discussion of the light cast upon supranationalism from the perspective of the three paradigms which dominate in the field of international relations, see Paul Taylor, 'Prescribing for the reform of International Organization: the logic of arguments for change', *Review of International Studies,* Vol. 13, 1987, pp. 19–38.

Selected reading

Beloff, Max 'International Integration and the Modern State', in Carol Ann Cosgrove and Kenneth Twitchett (eds), *The New International Actors,* London, Macmillan, 1970, p. 95.

Burrows, Bernard, Denton, Geoffrey and Edwards, Geoffrey, *Federal Solutions to European Issues,* London, Macmillan, 1978.

Etzioni, Amitai, 'The Dialectics of Supranational Unification', *American Political Science Review,* Vol. LVI, No. 4, pp. 927–35.

Haas, Ernst B., *The Uniting of Europe,* 2nd edn, Stanford, Stanford University Press, 1968.

Rosentiel, Francis, 'Reflections on the Notion of Supranationality', *Journal of Common Market Studies,* November 1963, pp. 127–39.

Taylor, Paul, *The Limits of European Integration,* London, Croom Helm, 1983.

Taylor, Paul, 'Prescribing for the Reform of International Organization: The Logic of Argument for Change', *Review of International Studies,* Vol. 13, 1987.

Part III

Refashioning the international state system:
integration theories

9   Functionalism: the approach of David Mitrany

Paul Taylor

David Mitrany's ideas about a functional approach to international organization were of particular importance in the development of thinking about
the role of international organization, and are the starting point of much of
modern integration theory. They should not be confused, however, with
functionalism in other fields such as sociology (as in the structural-
functionalism of Malinowski)[1] or in biology. A group of American scholars,
now generally called neo-functionalists, took Mitrany's ideas as one of the
starting points of their own thinking about integration between states,
particularly in Western Europe.[2] There are also intellectual links between
functionalism and other recently formed islands of theorizing about international organization and international relations. These include
interdependence theory, the world society image of international relations,
linkage politics and indeed, regime theory: functionalism is an intellectual
ancestor of all of these (see chapter 16 below).[3] The existence of these links is
one reason for discussing Mitrany's ideas here. Another is that in being
analysed and reconsidered, his ideas have sometimes been amended so far as
to lose much of their original form and value. Their influence among both
students and servants of international organization, which illustrates a belief
in the continuing relevance of the theory to contemporary problems, is a
further justification.

Mitrany produced his writings mainly in the inter-war period and during
the Second World War. His major contribution appeared in 1943 under the
heading of *A Working Peace System.*[4] Although he produced a number of
essays after the war, including one as late as 1974,[5] his central ideas are from
the earlier period.[6] The timing of their emergence is, indeed, of some
significance, as is the location of their development: although born a
Romanian in Bucharest in 1888, Mitrany worked and lived most of his life
in England and was acquainted there with a number of Fabians and other
Liberal-Left scholars such as G.D.H. Cole, Leonard Woolf, Norman Angel
and Robert Cecil. His theory reflects a number of assumptions which were
also accepted by this group, such as a belief in the desirability of
'engineering' improvements in society by deliberate, rational means; he was
also impressed by the problems and opportunities produced by economic
development. But he reacted strongly against some of the implications of
their arguments, which, he thought, would lead to the isolating of states
more completely from each other, in the attempt to develop better national
welfare schemes, than had previously been the case. Rather, in his vision of
a working peace system, he adapted them to the task of bringing states more

closely together in fruitful partnership, and by these means eventually eliminating war from international society.

In pursuing this task he was sharply critical of the grand theories of the political and social order of the pre-First World War period, which, he believed, were increasingly inappropriate to the understanding and solution of the pressing problems of a new age, both within the state and in international society.[7] Indeed, in linking together national and international problems, he was one of the first to develop the idea of 'world politics'.

Mitrany thought that classical philosophers such as Hume, Burke and Mill had been concerned with the discovery and description of an ideal system of relations between the various elements of state and people; they seemed to believe that there was an ideal order which could be achieved, and, once achieved, maintained. The setting up of arrangements such as Federal or confederal constitutions, was one aspect of this style of approach. Mitrany concluded, in contrast, that the elements of change in society, in the demands and expectations of the people and in the problems posed by the need for the proper management of the economy, were such as to make this prescriptive, overarching approach a futile one. Society was changing so quickly that any attempt to fix the ideal order was doomed to failure, and, indeed, the very attempt to fix an ideal system could itself make the solution of immediate, pressing problems more difficult. In functionalism Mitrany believed he had discovered a real alternative to grand theory, one which could cope with change, and which was orientated towards the more effective solution of immediate problems.

The essential starting point of this new approach, according to Mitrany, was to concentrate in the first instance upon the particular task, problems or function, and to attempt to exclude from this analysis the distorting elements of ideology, dogma or philosophical system. Mitrany was convinced that it was possible to discover a kind of irreducible set of 'relations between things',[8] which were distinguishable from relations suggested by a constitution or a dogma, and which, if left to themselves, would suggest the ideal geographical extent in which the problem could be tackled, and the most appropriate administrative arrangements. Hence the oft-quoted functionalist dictum that 'form follows function': the function, problem or task itself suggests the extent of the area and form of the administration within which it is to be tackled.[9] It followed that the discontinuities in areas and administration were also ideally suggested by the function, though an ideology, such as nationalism, could impose such discontinuities in defiance of the 'relations between things'. Such intervention, it was thought, would inevitably add to the problems and make them more difficult to solve. In sum, functionalism laid great stress on the importance of allowing interrelationships and interdependences to develop according to the requirements of the function. Indeed, the theory was based upon the assumption that to isolate, as with nationalism and its various constitutional appendages, was to reduce, to trap or to limit; while to allow interdependence according to function was to add, to complete, to generate.

Functionalism could cope with change, it was thought, because it worked from the particular problem and the relations suggested by it, rather than from some constitutional system, or idealized set of political or social relationships which were imposed upon it. Mitrany argued further that the irrelevance of traditional theories was particularly clear when it came to welfare problems, or 'service' problems in their broadest sense, which had become more pressing in recent years.

No form of government, no constitutional or traditional claim is now immutably set: in the last resort the form of government and its laws and constitutions are shaped and re-shaped by the restless flux of the communities' social pressures. . . . Government is no longer a guarantor of a set social order, but the servant and instrument of change.[10]

In the manner of most theories in politics which claim a comprehensive relevance, Mitrany did not hesitate to infuse his description with prescriptive elements: he added to the view that these social forces were in fact overwhelming the plea that they should be encouraged to be so. There were advantages in terms of world peace, and a better society, in choosing to work on welfare problems and thus harnessing the pressures which they generated. Man should respond positively to these by developing structures and procedures which allowed 'form' to follow 'function'.

By doing this, long-standing problems could be solved in a new way. Within a state, in Britain, for instance, demands for social welfare had created a new, major social-political problem: that of the lack of effective representation of the people in the government system. The development of the 'community's social pressures' had led to an outdated style of administration and government which defeated attempts to obtain popular control by widening the franchise. There was now more management, and the state was increasingly pervasive, but management escaped the constitutional forms, including those newly established for obtaining popular control, with 'a pragmatical authority of a welfare state which refused to be shackled to any constitutional pillars'.[11]

The result was that the old democratic remedy of widening the electorate has only served to dilute still more the scope of popular initiative and control. All the aims of political democracy were to control government: all the claims of social democracy end in control by government.[12]

The answer to this difficulty, in Mitrany's view, was to develop stronger representative institutions in areas of activity which directly touched upon the lives of the people. We should set up representative assemblies to look after particular sections of our life, such as health, energy or transport, rather in the manner of meetings of shareholders in public companies. These new assemblies would establish control over the crucial areas of government more effectively than old style parliaments (which in some ways had become a positive hindrance to open government) because they would involve people who were directly affected by the work being done, and who would be more knowledgeable about the technical details of the activities involved. Traditional style parliaments, in contrast, tended to lack expertise, and were increasingly remote from the places where the real decisions were made. Mitrany believed that in international institutions, such as the International Labour Organization (ILO), and later in the European Coal and Steel Community (ECSC), the more specialist assemblies recommended by him already existed. In the ILO, for instance, there was an assembly containing representatives of the three major interested groups — labour, management and the government. In this area, at least, international organization was ahead of national government; ECSC also had an advisory, specialist, consultative council of producers and consumers.

Mitrany prescribed that the particular aspect of form should follow from the new functions of the welfare state. Other aspects of the method of obtaining effective control and efficient management should also be adjusted to the nature of the function: some functions needed strong, rapid direction with the possibility of later correction; others needed to be decentralized in relatively strong regional offices, or, conversely, concentrated in more highly centralized ones; the composition and responsibilities of the committee of management would also vary with the function. How much of the detail of this would follow from the function was left rather unclear; as indeed was the more basic question of whether functions needed to be transplanted, as it were, into a society, or whether they would spring up of their own volition.

In developing states, such as India, Mitrany argued 'mass voting and sporadic elections were spurious democratic tools for illiterate, inexperienced populations'.[13] It was much better to build representative systems by functional means, by encouraging participation in the tackling of specific tasks and service industries. In this way an inexperienced people could learn about control over government by acting in areas in which they were immediately involved and therefore more likely to respond. But it may well be that functions would have to be introduced into the society in order to begin the attempt to solve the larger problem of control and representation, i.e. they would not derive from 'felt needs'. In the United States, however, the tasks of the Tennessee Valley Authority (TVA), which was Mitrany's favourite functional model, was seen to be so self-evident and pressing that the problems of the sovereignty of the various states which impinged upon the Valley were set aside in a flood of Federal initiatives.[14] In this case, it seems, form did indeed follow more immediately from the pressing requirements of the function.

Mitrany's advice to concentrate upon function in the interests of greater efficiency in the provision of welfare, and in the attempt to solve a number of linked tasks, such as the obtaining of a better system of representation, and overcoming the barriers of dogma, prescription and constitutionalism, is therefore not quite as straightforward as it would appear at first sight: sometimes function seems to impose itself upon the form (as with the TVA); sometimes the form has to be moulded by man in a positive way, because existing constitutional structures resist change (as with the form of representation in England); and sometimes functions are not at all self-evident and have to be introduced in order to facilitate the obtaining of some linked goals. There is, however, an increasing range of tasks and problems within the state, between the states and transnationally, which have emerged as a result of technological change and development, which demand control and solutions of a specialized, technical kind, and in which it seems a matter of common sense that the role of ideology should be minimized. Such tasks and problems apparently need to be tackled on their own terms and where necessary across national frontiers. The idea that benefits will accrue by concentrating on a particular task, service or function is revealed as indicating a most worthwhile general direction.

In its application to international society functionalism is an extension of the above arguments. As already explained, the theory is conceived as relevant to circumstances within states and among them. Even the theory of the origin of war is implied by Mitrany's view about the value of concentrating upon 'relations between things'. The essential point — one which is very often misunderstood — is that functionalism sees the solution of a problem not in the obtaining of specific, unchanging conditions (to do so would be to move dangerously close to an acceptance of a prescribed fixed order) but in the dynamic 'process' elements between one condition and the next. It is the case that wars may be caused by particular circumstances in the functionalist's conception, as fixed conditions may interrupt the area of administration in which a function might be best tackled. Such circumstances might include physical deficiencies, lack of food, shelter, clothing and also educational facilities which influence national perspectives in favour of war, or persuade national leaders that it might be the least of the range of evils. But the solution to war is not simply a correction of such deficiencies: it is the process of dealing with such deficiencies within organizations which, it is believed, produced the new dynamic of peace. There is, in other words, a lack of symmetry between Mitrany's views on the causes of the problem of war and its solution, which is perfectly consistent with other aspects of functionalist theory. The cause may be a constant or a condition, the solution, however, is a process of involving people in organizations devoted to the improvement of their circumstances and situation.

Critics of functionalism who argue that Mitrany believed that war could be cured by satisfying man's wants have got the stress somewhat wrong. Inis Claude, for instance, quotes Charles Malik with approval: 'The poor, the sick, the dispossessed, must certainly be done justice to. But to suppose that there will be peace when everybody is materially happy and comfortable is absolute nonsense.'[15] Mitrany would agree with this view. His point is rather that it is the *process* of helping the poor, the sick and the dispossessed within an increasing range of organizations which helps to put things right rather than the actual attainment of these goals (they never could be obtained in any absolute sense). He did specify, however, that the participation of the people in the work of the international organization is a *sine qua non;* it should be a response to 'felt needs'. Without such involvement the organization might be judged to be an agent of exploitation, as is the case, sometimes, with multinational business organizations. It is important also to read Mitrany's own views on this question in the context of their related arguments. He wrote in 1944: 'Give people a moderate sufficiency of what they need and ought to have and they will keep the peace: this has been proved time and again nationally but it has not yet been tried internationally.'[16] The context suggests that the stress again is on the process of giving, or trying to fulfil the welfare needs, rather than simply the consequence of their fulfilment.

Two aspects of the process are thought by the functionalists to be particularly promising in their implications for the chances of solving the problem of war. These are, first, the changing attitudes of people involved in the organizations and experiencing the benefits derived from their operation: it is assumed by functionalists that the establishment of a range of mutual contacts in the course of attempting to perform common tasks will change attitudes in the direction of, first, greater amity, or, at least, towards a growing support for co-operation; and second, the development between states in economic, technical or welfare areas of a widening range of interdependencies which are seen to enmesh governments. These interdependencies would be expected to be successful in achieving the enmeshment of governments to the extent that the governments feel that the cost of their severance by war is unacceptably high. The process of functional integration is therefore seen as changing attitudes and creating costs of disruption — the enmeshment process — which make war less likely.

In this century there has developed in international society a wide range of governmental and non-governmental organizations, which is expanding at a remarkable rate. These organizations are paralleled by an increasingly dense range of transactions between states which reflect a growing international, economic, trade and monetary interdependence, the growth of multinational business, and the exchange of ideas and individuals. The functionalist theory illuminates these developments and finds in them a potential for peace; it also prescribes the approach of adding to the level of international organization whenever this is suggested by the task or function.

These two aspects of attitude change and enmeshment are core elements in the functionalist view of international integration. The process starts when international institutions are set up in the area where they might act most efficiently, which is suggested by the nature of the task or function: institutions might also be set up in areas within the state according to the function with which they deal. The immediate initiative for such steps could be either private groups, individuals or national governments. It should be remembered that *A Working Peace System* was published during the Second World War and that it was addressed to national governments as advice on how best to guarantee peace at the conclusion of the war. Mitrany advocated 'a network of international agencies penetrating deep into German economic life'[17] as a way of reducing the threat of any future aggression, a proposal which was very like the European Coal and Steel Community of the early 1950s, and quite unlike the wartime Morgenthau plan. Once established, the international institutions would set in train pressures for further institutions: a number of people would be directly involved, and, it was expected, convinced of the benefits of co-operation, a larger number would realize that their welfare level would be likely to rise as international co-operation increased, and would suffer if it were restricted in favour of autarchic states. There would therefore be set in motion a process of changing popular attitudes gradually as a result of the perceived benefits of international organization, and these would be shaped into an international socio-psychological community reflecting a co-operative ethos which would push for further international organization and help 'form to follow function' across national frontiers. At the same time, fanatical loyalties to the state would be softened as international understanding increased.

The functionalist view of how this process might end is reflected in various dispersed passages of Mitrany's writing. But it is clear that the intention is not to abolish governments though it is expected that their choice of goals for themselves would increasingly come to be predicated upon the survival of the co-operative framework. It has been rightly pointed out that functionalism is an *indirect* approach to the problems of war; it does not seek to confront governments directly or expect that they will undertake commitments of which they disapprove. This indirect approach is illustrated particularly clearly by the rather different concepts of spill-over found in functionalism compared with neo-functionalism. In neo-functionalism the classical style of spill-over — one which has been frequently advocated in Western Europe and criticized as being too mechanical by Dahrendorf[18] — holds that successful integration in an area of lesser salience leads to a series of further linked integration measures which culminate in overwhelming pressure to integrate in the high political areas closest to the heart of sovereignty. Problems resulting from one step in integration can only be solved by further integration: attitudes among élites about the most appropriate ways for obtaining their existing interests increasingly support integration. There is a kind of accumulation of implications of integration which gradually impinge upon decision-makers so that eventually they accept consciously the desirability of integration in areas of high politics — foreign policy and defence — as the best way of furthering their interests. Responsibility for these is transferred to a new common centre, the international institution. In its earliest form this process was thought to have a kind of deterministic quality which led to its being called 'the necessary logic' of neo-functionalism, or the 'functional imperative'.

The functionalist view, in contrast, regards spill-over as involving two stages. The first stage differs from that of the neo-functionalists in that it puts much greater stress upon pressures from, and changes in, popular attitudes. The integration process proceeds from areas which are thought to be less contentious, and which particularly concern questions of welfare, and is pushed on by the 'felt needs' of the citizens. These reflect an increasing concern with welfare issues and a deepening realization of the costs of national frameworks. They suggest functions which are taken up by international institutions and which operate, as has been pointed out, across national frontiers according to the requirements of the particular function. The functionalists, however, believe in the educational effects of successful integration: the hierarchy of tasks from high to low politics is to be ironed out so that the salience of particular functions is changed as the process proceeds. Issues which were thought to be closer to the heart of sovereignty are no longer believed to be so.

The indirectness of the functional approach becomes particularly evident in the second state. This is the stage at which it is thought governments are themselves involved in the education process. The essential point here is not, as in the neo-functionalist approach, that decision-makers have reached the point of integrating what they have always believed to be important, but rather that their views about what is important have changed. They become more involved in questions which relate in the broadest sense to welfare: the question of whether or not to hand over responsibility for defence and foreign policy, for instance, to a new common institution is bypassed because it has become irrelevant. The substantive issues of politics, even high politics, have changed. Governments have been approached indirectly and a new framework created without their full realization of its implication. On the other hand the continued survival of governments, and of identifiable states, within this framework is perfectly compatible with functionalism: the functionalist approach, indeed, allows the view that there is no point at which the state would *necessarily* lose its sovereignty, in the sense that power would now need to be finally transferred, or that the state would lose its legal right to act, if it so wished, against the wishes of the functional agency. It holds, rather, that the issue of sovereignty becomes irrelevant to the important issues in the emerging world society.[19]

As the state is not thought to be necessarily losing its sovereignty, so there is to be no single place in international society which is necessarily gaining it. Functionalism is not, however, either Utopian or teleological in its view of international integration: rather it stresses central principles in the attainment of a more effective 'working peace system'. International society is seen as being made up of an increasing number of international institutions with competence in particular functional areas, the territories of which intersect and overlap with each other. No ideology or political scheme must be allowed to impose a co-extensiveness upon these territories: the function must prevail. It is because of this that Mitrany opposed movements towards regional political unification such as that in Western Europe. There are indeed many functions which should be organized on a regional basis, such as coal and steel in the European Coal and Steel Community. But Mitrany pointed out that there are many others which are best organized on a continental or a universal basis: the nature of the function determines this. The political objective of some supporters of the European Economic Community, in contrast, would lead to the fracturing of the natural overlapping functional areas, and would lead, if successful, to the recreation of all the traditional problems of international society on a bigger scale. The essential task of involving and enmeshing an increasing number of units, and of re-educating people in favour of co-operation, in order to reduce the chances of war, would be completely lost in the interests of yet another regional superstate.

In evaluating the contribution of functionalism to our understanding of international organization, it is appropriate to return to the two aspects of the approach which seemed central to it, namely attitude change and enmeshment.[20] First, a number of critics have focused on points related to the problem of attitude change: is it really possible, they ask, that attitudes can be changed by involvement in international organization or by experiencing the effects of international institutions? On the one hand is the evidence of common sense, and of everyday experience, on which functionalism lays a great deal of stress; what people do together agreeably, if they do enough of it, leads them to greater involvement with each other and to full participation in common institutions. Within the state it seems these methods are one of the steps towards the improvement of relations between groups which are mutually suspicious of each other. It is thought by some to be the most promising way of attempting the solution of the problem in Northern Ireland. At the international level, however, the evidence, which is collected in the face of considerable research problems, is somewhat inconclusive: there is as yet little evidence to suggest that international institutions are capable of becoming the focus of loyalties at the expense of the state.[21] This however depends on the basis on which there is joint endeavour, not the fact of such endeavour. There is evidence of a softening of attitudes towards each other among those who work in international institutions and of an increasing readiness to avoid group criticisms on the basis of in-group out-group distinctions. The worst forms of hostility, usually based on ignorance or prejudice, tend to be less mitigated. There is some evidence of a softening of support for the state in regions such as Western Europe which may be attributable to the work of the international institutions. But the conclusion must be that the evidence about attitude change is as yet not particularly encouraging for those who expect international organization to find its own basis of support in popular loyalties. On the other hand, it is very difficult to refute the functionalist claims in this area, though this may itself be a problem in its formulation as a 'theory' — that it is hard to falsify. The supporter of the functionalist position can always resort to the proposition that enough co-operation over enough time will generate support for integration in the long term, and that a softening of attitudes, and a preparedness to accept involvement, is itself a valuable change in the short term.

A further crucial aspect of attitudes and attitude change is concerned with governments and their expectations. Supporters of the traditional power politics approach to the academic subject of international relations argue that the re-education process which the functionalists stress is a most unlikely development. They argue that governments are bound to retain for themselves ultimate control over their interests and, more importantly, that there can be no gradual process of integration because there are no areas in which international co-operation is likely to have any consequences whatsoever for a governments's primary responsibility for the interests and values of citizens within its territory. There are eternal verities in power politics, it is argued, and it is impossible to transcend these: the primacy of the separate, high political interests of governments cannot be amended.

The absence of any impact upon power politics at the end of the process is matched in the arguments of the critics of functionalism by the view that there is also no easy way in which the process can begin. The argument here is about the so-called separability thesis. Critics of functionalism have argued that Mitrany distinguished between political and non-political areas, which included welfare, and that this is a logical requirement of his gradualist approach.[22] The criticism is offered that such a separation of welfare from politics is entirely unrealistic, and that because of this there can be no easy way into the process of integration: there is, indeed, no possibility that the experience of integration could release a dynamic which made integration in other areas more likely, and eventually modified high politics itself.

It is probably true that functionalists have not been careful enough in their arguments about the relationship between power and welfare or between high and low politics. On the other hand, the criticisms of functionalism in this area have themselves been too blunt and even perversely unsympathetic; there are various ways of relating power and politics to welfare without denying the functionalists their gradualist integration process. Groom has pointed out that any issue can involve either high or low politics: the important distinction is rather between legitimized and non-legitimized relations, and there can be a process of legitimizing relations between actors where they have previously possessed rather low levels of legitimacy.[23] Furthermore, although no area can be essentially or entirely 'non-political', it is possible for there to be more or less contentious issues in the sense that they involve more agreement among specialists or experts, and attract less disagreement among politicians. It is also possible, as Groom implies, for a particular subject to be moved out of the realm of high politics as others may be moved into it. The functionalists might be allowed the possibility of starting their integration process in less contentious areas and of refocusing the object of politics upon welfare issues and upon issues which lay greater stress upon an acceptance of the co-operative framework, without implying that they believe that some areas are essentially matters of high politics and others essentially matters of low politics. Politics in either event is not be to excluded, but rather is to be refocused, as the area of legitimized relations is expanded.

In his treatment of functionalism, Inis Claude has questioned the viability of the functionalist approach in these terms:

Is it in fact possible to segregate a group of problems and subject them to treatment in an international workshop where the nations shed their conflicts at the door and busy themselves only with the co-operative use of the tools of mutual interest?[24]

In defence of functionalism it might be asserted that 'groups of problems' are not to be segregated, but rather identified; the nations are not expected to shed their conflicts at the door, or anywhere else, but rather to attempt to locate less contentious issues and to focus on these to the advantage of the separate states and their societies; and the 'tools of mutual interest' are nothing unless they are recognized and freely accepted by the separate governments.

A second criticism is that the development of systems of transnational transactions, which functionalism recognizes and fits into a strategy of peace, does not trap states in interdependencies or confine them within a co-operative framework. The comment has been made that 'international welfare issues have emerged as high political questions in our time' and that 'in contrast to international politics, partnership, beneficence and threat are all likely to be conceived, perceived, and evaluated economically rather than militarily'. But 'the new politics of international economics seems a major dimension of the substance of international politics in the 1970s'[25] and since. In other words, governments' involvements in the economic affairs of states, i.e. in welfare, and the number of inter-governmental disputes about the international and economic system, seem to some commentators to have increased as a result of increasing co-operation, rather than to have decreased, and their disputes seem to be as intractable as the earlier disagreements about territory or status. Integration has simply increased the range of opportunities for governments to exercise their national muscle and pursue their interests and, within the state, they have involved themselves consistently in more areas of life than before. More issues, within and without the state are, in other words, becoming politicized.

The development of the interdependences has been associated with changes in the kind of objectives which governments normally seek: they are much more likely to stress economic or developmental objectives, and much less likely to stress the acquisition of territory or other symbols of national prestige. This is mainly in response to the rising tide of expectations at the popular level, and it is associated with appearance of a different style of managerial, technocratic politician. These changes themselves tend to strengthen the acceptance of the pre-existing co-operative framework in international society; a system of rules has to be accepted in order to allow the separate national economic interests to be obtained. Despite intense dispute about the details of the economic or monetary systems, it was generally accepted that there should be a system and that it should possess certain broad characteristics. As Professor Morse has pointed out: 'One principal characteristic of foreign policies under modernised conditions is that they approach the pole of co-operation rather than the pole of conflict. Conflictual or political activities, therefore, take place within the context of predominantly co-operative arrangements.'[26]

The costs of breaking interdependence are rising, and the acceptance of the cost depends ultimately upon the priority attached by politicians to alternative values: but the more the enmeshment, the higher the cost of severance, and the more difficult the political choice. It is also evident that a large range of global problems, which demand solutions, on their own terms, has emerged and these have been recognized. These frequently imposed 'functional' adjustments upon the UN Specialized Agencies. On the other hand, if the worst happens, if war breaks out, the functionalist theory probably has little to offer: it may help to build the underlying conditions of peace, but if these prove insubstantial, it has little to offer crisis management.

Any student's knowledge of international organization would be incomplete without being familiar with the writings of the functionalists, particularly the work of David Mitrany as reflected in his *A Working Peace System*. They constitute a starting-point for thinking about the subject and the prospects of international organization. Functionalism reflects a large number of unstated assumptions, mainly of the liberal/rational kind, which cannot be identified in full in this brief chapter, and it is part of a much larger philosophical structure of ideas with implications both within the state and international society.'It is valuable despite its lack of methodology or rigour. But the conventional criticisms of functionalism cannot be ignored although, here too, there is an orthodoxy which should not go unchallenged.

Functionalism is revealed as a useful antidote to the power politics approach to the study of international society. It is, however, essentially modest and pragmatic: it does not claim to eliminate the pursuit of power, but only to consider the circumstances in which it might be limited or redirected, and it accepts that different standpoints might reveal valid insights. It also leads to a concern with practical, short-term steps for improvement, and is not encumbered with a sense of the hopelessness of trying to improve man's condition. That hopelessness lies at the dead heart of power politics.

Notes

1. See Dorothy Emmet, *Function, Purpose and Power,* London, Macmillan, 1958; and B. Malinowski, *A Scientific Theory of Culture,* Chapel Hill, University of North Carolina Press, 1944.
2. See bibliography with chapter 10 below.
3. See Paul Taylor, 'Introduction', in David Mitrany, *The Functional Theory of Politics,* London, London School of Economics and Political Science, and Martin Robertson, 1975.
4. David Mitrany, *A Working Peace System,* London, Royal Institute of International Affairs, 1943.
5. David Mitrany, 'A political theory for a new society', in A.J.R. Groom and Paul Taylor, *Functionalism: Theory and Practice in International Relations,* London, University of London Press, 1975, pp. 25–37.
6. See *inter alia* his *The Road to Security,* Peace News Pamphlet, No. 29, National Press Council, 1944; *The Progress of International Government,* London, Allen & Unwin, 1933; *The Functional Theory of Politics,* London, London School of Economics and Political Science, and Martin Robertson, 1975.

7. David Mitrany, *The Functional Theory of Politics;* 'A political theory for a new society', op. cit., p. 25.
8. 'The making of functional theory: a memoir', in *The Functional Theory of Politics,* op. cit., p. 37.
9. See *A Working Peace System,* op. cit., pp. 72–3.
10. 'A political theory for a new society', op. cit., p. 27.
11. Ibid., p. 28.
12. Ibid., p. 31.
13. 'Memoir', op. cit., p. 33.
14. *A Working Peace System,* Chicago, Quadrangle Books, 1966, pp. 56–7.
15. Inis L. Claude, Jr, *Swords into Plowshares,* 3rd edn, London, University of London Press, 1964, p. 353.
16. *The Road to Security,* op. cit., p. 15.
17. *The Road to Security,* op. cit., p. 13.
18. R. Dahrendorf, *Plädoyer für die Europäische Union,* Piper Verlag, 1973, pp. 78–9 and *passim.*
19. See *A Working Peace System,* op. cit., pp. 30–1, and see especially pp. 65–6. Mitrany spoke of slices of sovereignty being '*transferred* . . . through a function', though he implies that the transfer is to many centres not a single, new centre (p. 31). Elsewhere, however, he speaks of *sharing* sovereignty, and argues that 'specific functional arrangements would not *steal* the crown of sovereignty' (p. 66).
20. For a consideration of the problems of testing functionalism, see R.J. Harrison, 'Testing functionalism', in A.J.R. Groom and Paul Taylor (eds), *Functionalism,* op. cit., pp. 112–38.
21. See Peter Wolf, 'International organization and attitude change: a re-examination of the functionalist approach' *International Organization,* Vol. 27, Summer 1973, pp. 347–71.
22. See Ernst B. Haas, *Beyond the Nation State,* Stanford, Calif., Stanford University Press, 1964, pp. 47–8. It is not intended to suggest here that Haas is linked with supporters of the power politics school in general opposition to functionalism. But he has criticized this particular aspect of the approach.
23. See A.J.R. Groom, in Groom and Taylor (eds), op. cit., pp. 99–100.
24. Inis Claude, Jr, op. cit., pp. 353–4.
25. Donald Puchala and Stuart Fagan 'International politics in the 1970s: the search for perspective', *International Organization,* Spring 1974, Vol. 28, No. 2, p. 263.
26. Edward L. Morse, 'The transformation of foreign politics: modernization, interdependence and externalization', *World Politics,* April 1970, p. 382.

Selected reading

Green, Andrew, Wilson, 'Mitrany re-read with the help of Haas and Sewell', *Journal of Common Market Studies,* September 1969.
Groom, A.J.R. and Taylor, Paul (eds), *Functionalism: theory and practice in international relations,* London, University of London Press, 1975.
Imber, Mark, 'Rereading Mitrany: a pragmatic assessment of sovereignty', *Review of International Studies,* Vol. 10, No. 2, 1984.
Mitrany, David., *A Working Peace System,* Chicago, Quadrangle Books, 1966.
Mitrany, David, *The Functional Theory of Politics,* London, London School of Economics and Political Science, and Martin Robertson, 1975.

Sewell, J.P., *Functionalism and World Politics,* London, Oxford University Press, 1966.

Taylor, Paul and Groom, A.J.R., *Global Issues in the United Nations Framework,* London, Macmillan, 1989.

10 Neo-functionalism
R.J. Harrison

The neo-functionalist conception of international organization finds direct expression in the European Community. The Community in its early stage was the inspiration for the thesis in the form of which it was originally offered by E.B. Haas in his study *The Uniting of Europe*. He examined the European Coal and Steel Community and provided an academic rationalization of the strategy and goals incorporated in the Treaty. In summary form these had been made clear by M. Robert Schuman in his Declaration of 9 May 1950, introducing the proposal for the new Community. He said:

Europe will not be made all at once, or according to a single, general plan. It will be built through concrete achievements, which first create a *de facto* solidarity . . . . The pooling of coal and steel production will immediately provide for the setting-up of common bases for economic development as a first step in the federation of Europe.

In this statement, in concise summary, are some of the most important neo-functionalist tenets. First, the object of the exercise is stated quite clearly to be *federation* (though in elaborations of the neo-functionalist argument and in later political debate, the vaguer term *political union* has often been used). Second, the strategy is basically 'functionalist' in conception. Indeed, Mitrany, the father of 'functionalism', when he refers to the European Community experiment and its underlying theory, calls it 'functional-federalism'. It is clearly, however, functionalism with a difference. Thus, though Schuman talks about the need to create a *de facto* solidarity, and later in the Declaration talks about the importance of building a wider and deeper community between countries, the social-psychological overtones of the term 'community' are not given the weight that they are accorded in Mitrany's argument and in his conception of community. And though the notion of a transfer of loyalties to a new regional centre was visualized by neo-functionalist theorists in their original conception of the dynamic process of integration, this is specifically abandoned by Haas as a necessary component in later reflections on the Community experience and its implication for the theory. In any case what Haas and Schuman stress is the importance of a fusion of *economic* interests and the sector which Schuman chose for the first step in the master plan was seen as one of vital economic importance: coal and steel production and marketing. It was thought to be so important that its integration would make any future war between France and Germany 'not merely unthinkable but materially impossible'.[1] Another vital part of Schuman's strategy and of neo-functionalist theory which differentiates it from that of functionalism is the setting-up of central institutions for the proposed Community — institutions that are supposed to be capable of playing a creative role in the realization of the overall objective, and are distinctly federal in the sense that decisions made by them within their formal powers are binding on the member countries. Ernest Haas's study of the Community a few years after it came into effect is a theoretical vindication of its economic and institutional emphasis.

He saw it as particularly appropriate to the advanced industrial pluralist societies in which it was being tried. Haas was a proponent of the view that the politics of the international arena are not markedly different from domestic politics. 'As a major premiss', he stated in an earlier work,[2]

We assume that the ends of foreign policy are qualitatively similar to ends implicit in any other field of politics. Whatever 'laws' of political behaviour, group conduct and élite leadership can be isolated and identified in the domestic field are therefore considered applicable to the international field as well. In both cases the agent of action is man acting within a group. We doubt that this group is necessarily identical with that called the nation, hence we have attempted to synthesize the study of political behaviour and social action with an analysis of international relations as one manifestation of group aspirations.

This major premiss is a vitally important one in the neo-functionalist thesis. All the original states of the European Coal and Steel Community were advanced industrial pluralist democracies. That is to say, they had highly developed party organizations and activity and there were pressure groups purporting to represent almost every conceivable sphere of activity and interest which might impinge upon government. These, it was argued, were the background conditions most favourable to the strategy of integration by stealth, that is, by incremental, concrete, economic achievements which build up *de facto* 'engrenage' or enmeshment of one national political and economic system with another. Haas recognizes that the policy which emerges from group competition in such societies does not in every single instance represent a common or community interest. But it is critical to this thesis that group activity by its long-term results does engender commitment, at least, to constitutional procedures. With the right strategy, Haas thought, that commitment could conceivably be transferred to the regional level. Pressure groups and political parties are, he says, 'singled out as significant carriers of values and ideologies whose opposition, identity or convergence determines the success or failure of a transnational ideology'.[3]

If anything, in Haas's conception, the interest groups are more important than parties. They are the dynamic element of political process in advanced pluralist democracies, and this is especially true of the groups which operate in the economic sector. Haas says, 'almost universally economic groups seem to be in the forefront of those who clamour for the recognition of common needs.'[4] If groups can be caught up in the integration process, therefore, they could push it forward, overcoming even the resistance of national governments. They would generalize the commitment to integration and promote that solidarity which Schuman thought necessary.

These assumptions about the group basis of politics are fundamental to the neo-functionalist theory. It was best to pick the economic sector for the first measure of integration, because this is where the groups are most active. The possibility of collaboration in other sectors like education, social policy and defence does of course exist, but according to the theory, the most fluid, adaptable area in the advanced, industrial democracies is the economic area, and this is also the area in which the major, organized, interest group activity is concentrated. If the groups active in the economic area are affected by integration it is very likely that they will become involved. To involve groups and parties the initial integrative step must be fairly important and fairly controversial. It must not be so controversial that states feel that their vital interests are affected, since this might very well arouse the opposition of national political élites who feel their power and vested interests are threatened. But strains and distortions should be felt, as a consequence of integration, which will give rise to a need, and consequently a demand, by affected groups, for adjustment. That adjustment could well be by means of further integration. This is most likely if the initial integrative task itself is inherently expansive; that is, if the joint activity is larger than the sum of the original independent activities.

The demands for task-expansion expressed by pressure groups and parties would be felt originally at the national level. However, as regional central institutions are given more power and functions in response to pressures, the theory is that the demands, the expectations and the loyalties of groups and parties will gradually shift to the new centre of decision-making — not entirely, but significantly. Central institutions will respond and become, thereby, the driving force or 'motor' of the process of community development. Thus, in this conception, 'the process of community formation is dominated by nationally constituted groups with specific interests and aims, willing and able to adjust their aspirations by turning to supranational means when this course appears profitable.'[5] Haas, in other words, expects the regional community to be very like the national communities which make it up, only writ larger. He is quite explicit about this: 'Group conflict is a given and expected form of conduct in the nations under study . . . a larger political community . . . may well be expected to display the same traits.'[6] This is the main reason why the advanced industrial democracies whose interest groups, as Haas puts it, 'pulsate with life and vigour',[7] are considered the best, perhaps the only possible candidates for integration.

The building of community then, in the neo-functionalist theory does not depend initially upon mass support. It is directed towards political union, but identical aims on the part of all the participants in the process do not have to be assumed. There may be different advantages in integration for different groups. As Haas points out, 'the European Coal and Steel Community was initially accepted because it offered a multitude of different advantages to different groups'.[8] He argued that this *compatibility* rather than *coincidence* of group interests provides the basis for an expansive logic of integration, which includes what he calls the 'spill-over' effect. Haas defines 'spill-over' as something which occurs when 'policies made pursuant to an initial task and grant of power can be made real only if the task itself is expanded.' Leon Lindberg, who most closely follows in Haas's footsteps, with his study of the European Economic Community, restates the definition so that it denotes the process whereby 'a given action, related to a specific goal, creates a situation in which the original goal can be assured only by taking further actions, which in turn create a further condition and a need for more action, and so forth.'⁹ Now, spill-over according to these definitions could occur in a number of ways. A given step in integration might very well alter the conditions of competition in a manner that calls for new central policy decisions, either to restore something like the original competitive balance of advantage within the sector affected, or to open up new opportunities for all the affected parties. Or, the alterations, strains and distortions resulting from one integrative step may result in pressures by groups for their correction. Their pressures ensure that the spill-over effect works itself out productively for further integration. For example, a transport and road system, relatively unco-ordinated, might continue to impede the flow of goods and services after the elimination of tariffs, so that steps would have to be taken in the transport sector itself. An original agreement say, on tariffs, might be evaded by some of the member states of the nascent community, or by constituent groups, through actions which fell outside the literal scope of the obligations created. An agreement on tariff elimination for example, might be negated by the imposition of differential transport rates, or border health inspections and regulations, and other non-tariff barriers to trade; yet the original agreement though ineffective or only partially effected may have aroused expectations among business and other groups who planned accordingly. These groups are likely to press for agreement on further measures which will make the first step effective, and so vindicate their plans. Spill-over may also occur because an integrative step is redistributive in its effects, *between* states. That is, it benefits some states more than others. The disadvantaged states will look for ways in which they can redress the balance in their favour, possibly in another sector altogether.

This is the essence of what has come to be called package-dealing within the European Community. This involves the reaching of complex agreements in a number of what may well be disparate areas, tied together, as it were, in a package which in one way or another satisfies all the member states of the European Community. It can be argued that, as integration develops from sector to sector, increased scope would exist for a resolution of conflicts over income redistribution by such bargains between sectors. Spill-over may also occur either because the effects of an integrative step, although they produce no clear balance of advantage or disadvantage for states or groups, clearly show the likelihood of benefit from, or the need for, further integration in some way which can be readily agreed, or because the integrative step has automatic integrative implications in other sectors. Haas is emphatic that sector integration . . . begets its own impetus towards extension to the entire economy even in the absence of specific group demands and their attendant ideologies . . . [thus] while not in principle favouring the control of the scrap trade with third countries civil servants in the Council of Ministers decided on supranational administrative measures just the same merely in order to make the common market for steel a reality.[10]

Lindberg offers another example of this impetus at work in the Acceleration agreement of 12 May 1960. He suggests that

business circles, after initial reactions ranging from cautious support to outright hostility, had accepted the Common Market as a *fait accompli* and jumped in with almost breathtaking speed to form a network of agreements within the Six. An acceleration of the realisation of the Common Market, far from exceeding the pace desired by business groups, would only catch up with the pace they had already set . . . it was from business circles that much of the political pressure for acceleration originated.[11]

Another example of this impetus at work was the way in which agreement on agricultural prices in the 1960s immediately had implications for exchange rates among the Six. European officials congratulated themselves on having achieved exchange rates stability without negotiation merely as a by-product of their agreement on agricultural prices.

There are, then, possibilities of spill-over without direct group involvement, but group activity is seen as the most likely and dynamic element in most examples of the process, bringing about an increasing 'politicization' of integrative activity, moving further and further into the areas of traditional concern of political élites.

A distinction which may be drawn between 'negative' and 'positive' integration helps to clarify the notion of politicization. 'Negative' integration connotes policy agreements which remove existing barriers to communications and transactions of all kinds between countries. The removal of tariffs, for example, has this aspect. The effects of negative integration may be far-reaching but the policies do not, singly, detract very much from the powers of national governments to fulfil what has become their primary role in most states, whatever their stage of development — the management of the national economy. As measures of negative integration are multiplied, however, the cumulative effect does begin to touch on government's ability to perform this important role. To remove the tariff weapon, the import quota, and the elaborate fair competition rules which regulate the circumstances in which subsidies and tax concessions can be provided by national governments; to fix prices for agricultural products which, as we have noted, inhibit exchange rate flexibility, is to begin, noticeably, to impair the management capability of governments. It raises the question whether, in the circumstances, the regional community institutions should not assume management responsibility for the regional economy, including such basic problems as sectoral and regional unemployment, demand management and exchange rate stability. In other words, it raises the question of the need for an economic and monetary union — or what may be termed 'positive' integration. Given the pragmatic decision-making style in advanced industrial pluralist societies, the perception of this need by bureaucrats will, it is presumed, lead to proposals for its fulfilment in ways which upgrade community decision-making to higher, increasingly 'political' levels. Policies will be redistributive across national frontiers because they serve the interest of the community as a whole as it is perceived by people in key institutional settings, national and international.

There would be, in fact, according to this thesis, a virtually ineluctable 'interpenetration of élites', national and international, governmental and non-governmental, brought together in the various meetings and institutions of the regional organization. There would be, therefore, a process of 'élite socialization' 'as the immediate participants in the policy-making process, from interest groups to bureaucrats and statesmen, begin to develop new perspectives, loyalties and identifications as a result of their mutual interactions'.[12]

The attempt to build the European Community has proved a concrete test of neo-functionalist theory and it must be conceded in the light of experience that many of the expectations have been disappointed, particularly those relating to the role of groups and of regional institutions. The actual goals laid down in specific terms in all three of the European treaties, the institutions that are created, and the relations between them which are specified, give the Schuman, or neo-functionalist strategy, an operational definition. The goals laid down in the treaties are to be achieved incrementally rather than all at once. Some are immediate and some are remote.

In the 1950s there were a number of presumptions about the role which Community institutions might play. These are apparent in the text of the Treaty in the formal allocation of powers and they provide the inspiration for the neo-functionalist conception of the role of central institutions in an integrative process. At the heart of it all was the provision for what has been called 'the dialogue' between the Commission and the Council of Ministers. To a considerable degree, the expectations which were focused on the dialogue depended on the creative role assigned to the Commission of the Community. In the neo-functionalist conception it was expected that the Commission would become the focus of the informal pressures of the various national groups and of European-wide 'umbrella' organizations for the regional groups, making their demands for integrative measures which would promote their interests, or at least helping the Commission to ensure that its own promotive role was conducted in a way that would maximize the involvement and support of as wide a range of groups as possible within society.

All the devices and powers of the Communities' institutions have, in the neo-functionalist conception, practical power implications. The policy role of administrators, by analogy with national governments, was expected to fall on the Commission, strengthened by the specific Treaty provisions, particularly the initiatory power. It was supposed, second, that the Commission would be able to play and exploit an arbitral, mediatory role stemming from its well-protected Community orientation. It was supposed also to be able to utilize Parliament and the Economic and Social Committees as supports. Together, they were to ensure that the pressures of spill-over worked themselves out productively.

In practice, there have been a number of problems with this conception and they have reflected on the theory. First, the ultimate power of the Council in the institutional structure has made it the dominant institution, reducing the significance of the initiative and amendment monopoly of the Commission. The formal power to decide is the Council's alone. The formal initiatory power enjoyed by the Commission is still important to it, but in a mediatory conciliatory role rather than a creative one. The obligation on the part of the Commission to put forward a Community interest has had to give way, in spite of all the informal assets of the Commission, and the political skills of the individual Commissioners, to the brutal realities of the non-distribution of formal power, and the consequent need to present something that will get through the unit-veto procedures of the Council of Ministers. For the Council of Ministers did not become a majoritarian body at the stages and in the way prescribed by the Treaty, and only in the past few years, since the Dublin summit, has it departed from the unanimity principle. The proposals therefore which the Commission has made to the Council have, for the most part, been a product of the quasi-diplomatic sounding-out of national government attitudes and opinions, and the incorporation into proposals of the appropriate concessions and compromises.

A second problem is that there does seem to be a genuine conflict between administrative tasks and policy leadership. The analogy which was drawn with the influential role of national administrations was incomplete. Bureaucratic competence without the support of political leadership tends to be ineffective, incapable of taking charge of problem situations and giving direction and purpose to their solution. It would seem too that the very qualities that are associated with the bureaucratic ideal — impartiality, expertise, hierarchical structure and anonymity — are inimical to a political leadership role.

It seems clear then that the provisions made by the Treaty for creative leadership were inadequate. The hopes focused on the institutions by neo-functionalists like Haas and Lindberg, by Deutsch and by Etzioni, by Schmitter and others were unrealistic.

A critical weakness of the domestic politics model which they incorporated into their integration process model was that it tended to relegate the formal, legal and coercive powers of the state to a relatively insignificant position. Haas himself characterized the study of regional integration as 'concerned with tasks, transactions, perceptions, and learning', rather than questions of governance and power. Neo-functionalist theory is based on a primarily consensual model of a political community in being an idealized conception of a self-regulating pluralist society whose unity and stability rest on mutual adjustment between groups following accepted norms. No adequate theory is offered, however, of consensus formation mechanisms and their relationship to formal institutions in the international regional setting. But formal powers and questions of sovereignty have proved important in Community experience, and quasi-governmental powers have not proved enough to ensure the realization of task expansion and spill-over through the European 'system-élite'. The Treaty provisions were inadequate because the initiatory role and administrative competence of the Commission was in latent and, it proved, actual conflict with the deciding role of the Council of Ministers. Leadership in the Community is not sustained by an effective, accepted pattern of consensus formation, simplifying choice and legitimizing decision. The consensual support of the Council of Ministers is fragmented among the member countries. Divergent views have to be resolved at the highest level, namely the Council itself. The Council was originally, and has remained, an intergovernmental body, not a regional governmental institution. This has limited the potential for effective action. The absence of any real powers in the Parliament and the Economic and Social Committees has reduced their usefulness. In particular, the interest and involvement of political parties and pressure groups has not been stimulated to any great extent. There is no electorate for the parties to organize. There is no point in pressure groups exerting themselves very energetically at the Community level.

This is also partly because, not surprisingly, the policy achievements of the Community have been relatively low. Schuman's (and Haas's) expectations have not been fulfilled. The agricultural policy was achieved only after exhaustive nationalistic bargaining which very much reduced Community enthusiasm. It is the major achievement of the Community in that it is the policy most like national policies, redistributive in the conceived interests of the whole Community. It is the policy which most closely conforms with Haas's highest category of conflict resolution 'upgrading the common interest' rather than mere 'splitting the difference' or even settling on 'the lowest common denominator' of interests. It has created, however, vested interest among the beneficiaries and resentment among those who pay, rather than solidarity as Schuman would have hoped and as the neo-functionalist thesis with its emphasis on critical tasks as the most productive and expansive would lead one to expect. It made a regional policy, even the very small one which the Community finally did agree upon, very difficult to achieve. Germany quite simply did not want to pay for any more reallocation. In general, those who have to pay can be expected to veto any important redistributive schemes and those who benefit from existing policies have an interest in preventing any changes, so that the French remain the ardent champions of the agricultural policy.

The first and most obvious critical point then, to be made about the neo-functionalist argument is that there is no evidence in the Community experience of the beguiling automaticity of step-by-step economic integration, leading eventually to political integration. What has been achieved within the Community has depended upon political leadership by national élites and by political agreements between national governments. As the then President of Germany, Herr Scheel put it, 'Only political impulses will unite Europe . . . Europe has grown beyond the blind belief that political unity will automatically and inevitably follow communal institutions in the economic field. This conception has unfortunately shown itself to be false.'[13]

However, undue optimism about the potential promotive role of 'quasi-federal' or 'supranational' rather than genuinely federal institutions is not the only weak point in the neo-functionalist argument. The argument too readily glosses over, or ignores, the differences between domestic and international politics, between sovereign government and international organization. This fault in itself results from the tendency on the part of the theorists of pluralist society, as we have seen, to underrate the importance of the formal powers of central government in a political process, and to overemphasize the importance of group activity and informal power relationships. Behavioural studies generally have tended to neglect the importance of constitutional arrangements and formal power as systemic variables affecting behaviour. The ultimate formal power, in fact, of the Council within the range of powers and functions of the Community has proved a decisive factor. The residual and still overwhelmingly dominant powers of member state governments have not only determined the behaviour of the Council, which represents them, but have continued to determine the behaviour of parties and interest groups.

Yet another weakness in the neo-functionalist argument is that interest groups do not really, in fact, anywhere fulfil the role described for them in the pluralist apologia which is so important a part of the neo-functionalist thesis. They fall short of it. First they do not compromise and channel in any society, to any marked degree, the demands of their members. They have become more or less remote oligarchies, and the mass membership is neither much involved, nor committed through them to procedures for conflict resolution. They cannot, therefore, in any significant sense be looked to as possible creators of 'community' or 'significant carriers'[14] of an ideology of integration. Second, the competition between groups in pluralist societies does not ensure that, on the whole and in the long term, a community interest is represented to government as a product of countervailing interests which make themselves felt. Countervalency in most societies does not obtain to any general degree. Some groups are very much more powerful than others. Some interests go virtually unrepresented. Third and finally the institutionalization of pressure group consultation with government accentuates both the tendencies mentioned above. Group leaders, through their association with government develop a different viewpoint from their members. The recognition of one group rather than another for consultation accentuates the disparity of power between groups. It may even effectively shut off the voice of dissent. Group leaders, in other words, are part of a *national* leadership complex. The internationalization of national group leadership is not likely to be any easier than the internationalization of political leadership. To suppose that group leaders will perceive common interests with similar groups in other countries and combine with them to promote policies at a new international regional level is quite unrealistic.

Whether the orthodox model of the pluralist society ever corresponded to an existing reality is open to argument. It does not depict any contemporary reality but it is, unfortunately, a part of the framework of neo-functionalist assumptions.[15]

Some of these weaknesses of the neo-functionalist theory and approach to international organization have been recognized, at least in part, by the early proponents of the thesis. Haas himself has noted the extent to which spill-over, though its logic may be apparent, is checked by what he calls 'the built-in autonomy of functional contexts'[16] (what I have called elsewhere[17] circumscription and counteraction: conservative equilibrium restoring forces in any social system which limit and reduce the impact of any change). Leon Lindberg, faced with the example of General de Gaulle's intransigent opposition to the expansive logic of integration has noted, sorrowing, that 'the evidence indicates that the governments can avoid the logical consequences of integration for an unexpectedly long time'.[18] They act as 'gatekeepers' against expansionist, spill-over pressures. Lindberg was also the first to recognize and point out that a successful integrative step might actually have a negative effect on the prospects for further integration, creating stress rather than solidarity among the participant states, reinforcing the gatekeeper effect. This could happen both because negotiations were protracted and harshly competitive and because the policy in action was redistributive in its effects. The European Community agricultural policy is an obvious example.

There are other respects in which the academic theory of neo-functionalism may be challenged. More relevant for our purposes, however, is the identification of the central problem of the European Community itself, since it was the inspiration for the theory and remains the unique actual example of the strategy. We have pointed out that the architects of the Treaty believed that they had created something new in international relations and organization. What was new, and believed to be unique, was its institutional framework, which was said to be not federal but 'quasi-federal' or 'supranational' — federalism in prospect. Its distinctive feature was the dialogue between a designedly federal body — the European Commission with its autonomous protected powers, and the Council of Ministers — a deliberately intergovernmental body with its unit-veto procedures. The Treaty was, therefore, like the Council of Europe before it, a compromise between federalism and intergovernmentalism. In the Council of Europe it was the Assembly which embodied the federal principle. When that experimental compromise was seen to be a total victory for intergovernmentalism (as it was after the failure of the Assembly's Strasbourg Resolution of 1950 to make any headway in the Council of Ministers) the ECSC was designed with a much stronger federalist component. What is evident, after more than three decades of trial of the new design, is that, in any sort of compromise between intergovernmentalism and federalism, the triumph of the former has a certain logic about it. Unit-veto decision-making procedures impose themselves on any organization in which they play an integral part. They restrict its organic growth and its policy potential and they tend to be self-sustaining.[19]

In neo-functionalist theory the very general conceptualization of central institutions, or what Etzioni calls vaguely 'system-élites', though capable of embracing the ambiguities of the institutions of the Community, is a major weakness. Given the role anticipated for such illustrations there are necessary questions of detail about requisite structures, formal powers, rules, consensus, procedures, which are neither raised nor answered by neo-functionalists.

Notes

1. Quotations from the Schuman Declaration are from U. Kitzinger, *The European Common Market and Community: a selection of contemporary documents,* London, Routledge and Kegan Paul, 1967, pp. 37-9.
2. E.B. Haas and A.S. Whiting, *Dynamics of International Relations,* New York, McGraw-Hill, 1956, p. vii.
3. E.B. Haas, *The Uniting of Europe,* 2nd edn, Stanford, Stanford University Press, 1968, p. 5.
4. E.B. Haas, *Beyond the Nation State,* Stanford, Stanford University Press, 1964, p. 46.
5. *The Uniting of Europe,* p. xxxiv.
6. Ibid., p. 5.
7. *Beyond the Nation State,* p. 37. citing R.C. McCridis, 'Interest Groups in Comparative Analysis', *Journal of Politics,* XXIII, 1961, 45.
8. *The Uniting of Europe,* p. xxxiii.
9. Leon Lindberg, *The Political Dynamics of European Economic Integration,* Stanford, Stanford University Press, 1963, p. 10. Haas's definition is from his 'International integration: the European and the universal process', *International Organization,* XV, 1961, p. 368.
10. *The Uniting of Europe,* p. 297.
11. Leon Lindberg, op. cit., p. 170.
12. See L. Lindberg, and S.A. Scheingold, *Europe's Would-be Polity,* Englewood Cliffs, Prentice Hall, 1970, p. 119; and J. Nye, *Peace in Parts,* Boston, Little, Brown, 1971, pp. 69-71.
13. Address by Herr Scheel to the Annual Congress of the Free Democratic Party, of which he was Chairman, in November 1973. For a balance sheet of supranational versus intergovernmental promotion of integration see Neill Nugent, *The Government and Politics of the European Community,* London, Macmillan, 1989, pp. 321-4.
14. Haas, *The Uniting of Europe,* p. 5.
15. I have described these developments more fully in *Pluralism and Corporatism,* London, Allen & Unwin, 1980, especially pp. 64-98.
16. 'International Integration', op. cit., p. 376.
17. *Europe in Question,* London, Allen & Unwin, 1974, p. 187.
18. 'Decision making and integration in the European Community', *International Political Communities* (an Anthology), New York, Doubleday, 1966, p. 228.
19. The elected European parliament produced a 'federalist' plan to overcome this obstacle to community development. The only problem with the plan was that it had to be approved by the European Council with the unit-veto procedures. The

result was the very modest Single European Act setting goals for 1992 which must themselves be agreed in the Council of Ministers to become effective. On this see Paolo Cecchini, *The European Challenge 1992,* Aldershot, Wildwood House, 1988.

Selected reading

Alundel, Prenden, *Aspects of European Integration* Odense, Odense University Press, 1986.

Groom, A.J.R. and Taylor, Paul (eds), *Functionalism: Theory and Practice in International Relations,* London, University of London Press, 1975.

Haas, Ernst B., *Beyond the Nation State,* Stanford, Stanford University Press, 1964.

Haas, Ernst B., 'The Joys and Agonies of Pretheorising', *International Organization,* XXIV, 4, 1970.

Hanson, R.D., 'Regional Investigation: Reflections on a decade of theoretical efforts', *World Politics,* 21, 2, January 1969.

Harrison, R.J. *Europe in Question,* London, George Allen & Unwin, 1974.

Lindberg, L.N. and Scheingold, S.A., *Europe's Would-Be Polity,* Englewood Cliffs, Prentice Hall, 1970.

11 Regionalism: the thought and the deed

Paul Taylor

In the 1970s and 1980s regionalism became rather unfashionable in the academic community. At the same time it was in practice extended in various parts of the world. The reasons for this incongruence are now examined, and the implications of developing regionalism discussed.

There are, of course, a large number of views about its essential character.[1] A selection has to be made. One recurrent theme, however, is a concern with that particular scale of geographical area which is best fitted to the performance of tasks judged crucial for the welfare of individuals, or for the advantage of governments. That area may extend beyond the boundaries of existing states, or be a part of their territory, or even be coterminous with their frontiers. But what is stressed in this definition of regionalism is a concern with finding that area in which functions might be most efficiently performed and because of this it is a utilitarian concept. Regionalism may therefore be seen as part of a strategy for the focusing of popular loyalties upon the institutions, symbols, or even what have been called the icons of the larger area, but it does not necessarily do so. The territory is also seen as not necessarily being the best for the performance of individual tasks, but rather it reflects a compromise: it is that single space which has been judged suitable for the attainment of a range of tasks, and it may be more or less appropriate for any one of them. In some sense, therefore, there is a general competence within the region as a whole. This means that in this chapter, and in chapter 16, in which the arguments are further developed, regionalism is seen as being necessarily multidimensional.

This definition of regionalism may be sharpened by considering those concepts with which it may usefully be contrasted. First, there are forms of nationalism which insist that the criterion of utility should always come second to the criterion of demarcating and strengthening the nation.[2] In a nation-state which had such an ideology transnational arrangements within regions would be rejected even at considerable cost in terms of the welfare of individuals. This is not to deny that there are occasions when the region can be reasonably judged to coincide with the boundaries of the state, or that nation-states with different ideologies might not find regional arrangements congenial. Second, certain forms of 'one-world' doctrine stand in opposition to regionalism. These are those which involve a view of the organic unity of spaceship earth which, in their implications, are an equivalent at the global level of exclusive nationalism at the level of the state: to allow any intermediate level of competence is seen as permitting an unacceptable compromise with the integrity of the essential whole.[3]

A third option to regionalism is a group of approaches which can be put under the general heading of sectoralism. These are concerned with individual problems and hold that they can be solved in their own terms. In its more explicit forms, as with Mitrany's functionalism, the idea that problems can be isolated or contained in some way is fundamental.[4] It is the individual problem, in this case identified as a function, which suggests the manner of its solution and the geographical area within which this is to be attempted. As Groom, Burton and others have pointed out, the geographical areas of responsibility of the various institutions in the functionalist world are not seen as being co-extensive, though they overlap in the manner of a cobweb, and the approach rejects the idea that they should be adjusted so that they might be tackled together by a single institution with a general competence in a single territory.[5] Regionalism and functionalism are therefore opposing doctrines, which was one of the reasons for Mitrany's opposition to the emergence of the EEC, in contrast to the ECSC.

But sectoralism may be revealed in other approaches. Whenever problem-solving assumes the primacy of the solution of the particular problem above attainment of satisfactory solutions to the range of interrelated problems in a particular territory, it may be judged as being sectoralist. Hence there is a case for saying that in the United Nations system the Specialized Agencies have sometimes taken a sectoral approach in that they have concentrated upon problems in their individual fields of competence at the expense of co-ordinated programmes. As Robert Cox argued, the academic approach known as problem-solving (sometimes called puzzle-solving) has also shown a tendency to be concerned with narrowly defined specific issues at the expense of a concern with the validity of the whole.[6] At one extreme, therefore, are those who seemed to be concerned only with the global 'whole' seen in the longer term — the short-term concerns of the lesser 'wholes' could be sacrificed to this[7]; whilst, at the other extreme, it has sometimes been implied that even the unique individual was better seen, not as a single, but as several actors, which could have varied and inconsistent characters, depending upon the needs or interests being pursued. Even the individual personality could be sectoralized![8] Sectoralism may, therefore, be found in approaches other than functionalism which is, however, one where it is particularly stressed.

Each of these options to regionalism has an extreme form — the exclusive nation state or the organic globe — which are hard to reconcile with the regional approach. Each has, however, a more moderate expression which allows compromise. After all, involvement in regional arrangements has frequently served the interest of the state; and the global community can be interpreted as relying upon a regional substructure. There is a considerable literature upon these themes.[9] As yet, however, sectoralism has made no such compromise and has emerged as the major theoretical and practical alternative to regionalism. It follows that if the sectoral approach could be shown to be flawed, then this would have major implications for regionalism, as sectoralism is its one major alternative. Any defence of the one must also involve an attack on the other. If sectoralism is flawed, however, so is functionalism, as functionalism requires that the economic and social realm be reduced to its individual sectors of interest and activity. The question also arises of whether there is any way in which functionalism can be reconciled with regionalism. In other words can a more moderate version of sectoralism also be found? In chapter 16 the implications of any weaknesses found in sectoralism for functionalism are discussed.

A reconsideration of regionalism must also include a discussion of the reasons for the decline in the frequency of writings on that subject since the mid-1970s. What seems to have happened is that the consideration of regionalism as a general phenomenon or as a political doctrine became unfashionable, and regionalism in this sense was replaced with studies of the operation of particular policies in the various areas of the world. In other words, at the local level there were area studies but little or no regionalism.

It is, however, essential to realize that the literature on regionalism covers a very wide range. At least five categories may be detected. First is writing which focuses upon the development and application of various indicators of regionalism. These may be seen as measures of the consequences of the practice of regionalism as defined earlier in this chapter. The question is asked of the sense in which international regions exist: how far do economic, social, cultural and political dimensions coincide? The classic book which discussed questions of this type was that by Bruce Russett, first published in 1969 and reissued in 1976.[10] He was concerned to discover the degree to which regions showed 'social and cultural homogeneity . . . with respect to several kinds of internal attributes'; how far regions shared political attitudes or external behaviour, for instance, in voting in the United Nations; the degree of political interdependence as revealed by joint membership in supranational or intergovernmental political institutions; and the extent of economic interdepencence, 'as identified by intraregional trade as a proportion of the national income'.[11]

Unfortunately this work, which used a highly sophisticated quantitative methodology, was also one of the reasons for the decline of interest in the subject. Russett concluded that he had been largely correct in his expectation that

the degree of congruence among the clusters produced inductively by the various criteria would be relatively low: that is, the socio-cultural groupings would not closely resemble the political groupings, nor the trade groupings etc.

He added that

there is no region or aggregate of national units that can in the very strict sense of boundary congruence be identified as a subsystem of the international system . . . such a subsystem must be identified empirically by the agreement of several different criteria.[12]

In other words regional groupings showed no particular signs of acting together in the international system. From the point of view of the study of regionalism, it was rather depressing.

A second type of writing on regionalism was concerned with describing the dynamics of integration. In the terms of the definition of regionalism suggested here, the question was put of what factors would tend to increase a propensity to tackle problems at the regional level. Whereas Russett sought to apply measures at particular points, other writers, particularly those who came to be called the neo-functionalists, sought to explain how the measures of regional integration were altered.[13] Hence they developed dynamic variables such as 'spill-over'. It is not necessary to discuss this very considerable literature in this chapter, but it should be pointed out that it also became unfashionable in the 1970s. The main reason for this was probably that it appeared to have failed to predict successfully the development of regional integration in Western Europe. The leading neo functionalist, Ernst B. Haas, somewhat self-consciously signalled the 'obsolescence of regional integration theory' in 1976, though there were many who thought that in this he was somewhat premature.[14] Once again however, there were reasons for the decline of another style of writing about regionalism.

A third style sought to explain regionalism primarily in terms of the motives of the political élites who participated in the process. What in their view were the costs and benefits of regional organization? Involvement could be the result of growing popular support for regional integration. Alternatively it could represent attempts to bring about specific improvements, such as a better economy, or the leaders concern with milieu goals such as improving the channels of communication with other governments in the region or speaking more directly to the peoples of neighbouring countries; or leaders might seek to develop regional institutions because they were a way of enhancing status as a regional power. Such arguments were to be found in a study published in 1972 by Joseph Nye who noted that, despite the ambiguity of Russett's conclusions about the indicators of regionalism, it had been clear from his evidence that regional intergovernmental organizations had continued to increase in number, and nongovernmental organizations had increased even faster.[15] Between 1957 and 1966 international non-governmental organizations of the regional type had increased some five times as rapidly as other non-governmental organizations. These developments needed to be explained.

Nye argued that 'there will continue to be strong incentives for élites to create and use regional organizations.' Moreover,

if the demand for identity should lead to widespread dissatisfaction with existing nation-states and the development of strong regional attitudes, the technological changes that are reducing — but not eliminating — the importance of proximity could lead statesmen to support more effective regional institutions. If identitive demands are not intense at the regional level, it seems more likely that technological changes will lead in the direction of functional type organizations.[16]

On balance, however, the conclusions were that it was unlikely that the level of regional integration would continue to increase, in the sense that there would be a transfer of powers to the regional centre, and that it was more probable that an equilibrium would be found at which the regional attainment would be fairly modest. The main reason for this was that there were costs as well as advantages in further regional involvement: most leaders would not want the limitations on freedom of action which would begin to increase with the strengthening of regional institutions. Hence

under the current structure of international incentives most political decision-makers will find some point of equilibrium at which they would rather tolerate the inconvenience of the existing level of process forces (i.e. instability producing pressures in the more open international system) than incur the greater political costs of full integration or disintegration. . . . a rapid transformation as the result of existing integration processes is unlikely.[17]

Despite his recognition of an increase in the quantity of regional organization, the balance of Nye's argument was, therefore, that it was unlikely that new political actors were in the making. There were good reasons for the ambiguity of Russett's evidence about the increased importance of regional systems. Rather states would balance involvement within the region with continuing high levels of autonomous contact outside it, and the net effect would be to preserve the existing character of the international system. These judgements reinforced arguments developed in 1968 in an article by Oran Young on 'Political discontinuities in the international system'. He pointed to an emerging pattern of links between the various regions of the world, which would focus leaders' attention upon extra-regional interests and activities.[18] But the point should also be stressed that Nye seemed to interpret regional organization as suggesting the conditional involvement by governments in a series of local arrangements with one or more contiguous states. This amounts to local sectoralism rather than regionalism in the sense in which this is understood in this chapter, of englobing most dimensions. His image was not of a world in which there were specific territories in which contiguous states increasingly acted together — a question mark in this regard was even put against the European Community: the question of whether or not states were prepared to accept an increase in the powers of common institutions (federalism) was addressed — and answered in the negative. The conclusion could be drawn from both of these studies that, all in all, there was now not much in the evidence on regionalism to interest students of international society.

A fourth style of writing about regionalism was concerned with prediction and prescription and may be differentiated according to the weight given to each. What should, and what would happen to the level of co-operation? The literature in which the element of prescription predominated was frequently derived from the view that globalism inevitably involved exploitative relations between North and South, and therefore, the various regions in the South should be encouraged to develop stronger relations economically and politically among themselves.[19] Dependency theory was of course one of the main sources of such recommendations. It may also be found, however, in the work of those who were not so self-consciously structuralist, such as Rajni Kothari. The flavour of the product may be indicated in his recommendation that

> there is need for much greater regional co-operation among the various small and weak countries of the world, pooling their economic political and military resources, entering the world power structure on that basis, and ultimately upsetting the system through which a handful of states are able to dominate the world.[20]

The stress here was upon what ought to motivate regional leaders in their own interest and that of their subjects rather than upon what had in fact motivated them.

A somewhat different kind of prescription and a greater concern with prediction was to be found in the 1985 Bertrand Report, which is one exception to the earlier observation that no significant writing about regionalism as a general phenomenon had been produced since the mid-1970s.[21] Being himself a scholarly insider — a member of the United Nations Joint Inspection Unit — Bertrand was probably unaware that regionalism had become unfashionable among the academic community. For all its merits it was unlikely to have been produced in the mid-1980s by a student of international relations in the universities in either Western Europe or the United States, because of the climate of opinion about regionalism among the academic specialists.

Bertrand condemned the existing United Nations development arrangements with their tendency to what he called 'sectoral functionalism', and their 'remote control by staff members living in the greater capitals'[22] in favour of stronger, better-defined regional arrangements. What was needed was the development of a 'third generation of world organisation' which transferred significant responsibility for economic development to the regional level.[23] There should be an attempt to turn the United Nations into a 'centre for negotiations designed to identify and develop zones of convergence', which would be regions in Africa, Latin America and so on. As the sectoral approach, represented in the established division of labour among the Specialized Agencies, had become 'altogether inappropriate for a problem which calls for an integrated approach and organized co-operation by all the parties concerned . . . the only possible structural response lies in the organization of integrated systems of co-operation at the regional level'.[24]

A greater concern with prediction and, indeed, description, when compared with the previous approach, was reflected in Bertrand's awareness of the continued growth of regional arrangements. They had, however, become too numerous — there were around 280 of them — and they were irrationally organized.[25] They needed to be related to new structures which should include an organ representing the governments of the countries of the region, another body on which outside countries contributing to the development of the region would be represented, and finally a joint council or commission to carry out the plans negotiated and adopted.

A fundamental reorganization of the United Nations was necessary in which new regional Development Agencies would take over the 'resources, duties and staff of the present operational agencies, UNDP, WFP, UNFPA, UNICEF, etc.',[26] whilst central institutions would be left with the research and overall supervisory functions. At the same time it was necessary to strengthen the representation of the various new regional groupings in the central institutions of the United Nations such as the Economic and Social Council. The reader will not be surprised to learn that the Bertrand prescriptions were generally greeted with a marked absence of enthusiasm in the community of international civil servants, though his diagnosis of the problems in the economic and social arrangements of the United Nations was widely welcomed. Their reception in the academic community was enthusiastic with regard to the diagnosis but also contentious as regards the practical implications of the proposals.

Bertrand's arguments, though they favoured the radical alteration of the existing arrangements of the United Nations system, were, however, in many ways reminiscent of a train of argument which was very evident when the United Nations was established. This held that regional arrangements regarding defence, economic and social questions should be encouraged, if, in Burton's words, they were associative between those with common interests, and were not dissociative in that they created new divisions in international society. An associative security arrangement would concern the maintenance of security between members whilst a dissociative one would be directed against outsiders. One advantage of this development would be to relieve the central system of a burden of administration and responsibility, in security and other matters, which would otherwise become excessive. Associative arrangements would lessen that burden, whilst dissociative arrangements, such as the two great alliance systems which emerged in the 1940s and 1950s, would have the opposite effect. Burton pointed out, however, that it was unfortunate that the government representatives at San Francisco and Dumbarton Oaks had not clearly asserted the associative version of regionalism.[27]

A fifth category of writing upon regionalism completes the list. Roger Masters' article on a multi-bloc model of the international system may be taken as illustrative of this style.[28] It accepted the possibility that regions might emerge more clearly without examining in much detail the evidence for this, and without specifying any indicators of regionalism; nor was it explicitly prescriptive though it is arguable that such a concern was implicit. Rather it focused upon the implications for the international system if regions were to emerge more clearly, and considered such questions as how far general security and stability would be affected by such developments. Masters drew upon Kaplan's work on 'system and process' in international

politics and also upon the theory of oligopoly, both of which used rigorous a
priori reasoning in the specification of assumptions and in the logical
development of arguments. It is not necessary to discuss these in detail here.
The conclusions were, however, encouraging from the point of view of those
who might support regionalism for other reasons. Masters concluded that a
multi-bloc world, one which in effect contained stronger regions, would
possess significant stability-inducing elements. In other words, there was no
reason to fear such developments, and there were some grounds for
supporting them, as they could make international society more stable and
peaceable. Once again, however, the reader will not be surprised to learn
that Master's outstanding article was not from the academe of the 1980s —
it dates from 1961.

A number of questions emerge from the preceding discussion. That
writing on regionalism entered into a period of decline in the late 1970s has
been established and some of the reasons for this have been discussed. But
academic writing in the field of international relations, as elsewhere in the
social sciences, is capable of setting a mode of thinking which becomes
partly detached from the real world. It sets a fashion on occasions which is
in itself an impediment to an academic response to developments in the
evidence. It is certainly the case that Russett's book attracted such a barrage
of criticism in the academic journals as would be likely to deter for a while
all but the most intrepid or foolhardy of scholars. This was mainly because
of the cumbersome methodology but also because of the negative findings:
that there were no multidimensional regions to be found. Nevertheless, after
a decade it is perhaps time to challenge the fashion and to ask whether the
real world has changed. What is the evidence for the practice of regionalism
at the beginning of the 1990s? Does it still support the judgements of those
who wrote in the early 1970s? If it is found that the world has indeed become
more sharply demarcated in regional terms, how is this to be explained?

On the one hand, regionalism as a general phenomenon had received
relatively little attention after the mid-1970s. On the other hand, however,
evidence from the 1980s suggested that regional organizations were increasing in number at a rapid rate and that governments were becoming relatively
more involved with them than with global organizations (see Table 11.1).
This was true not only of Europe but also of Africa and Asia. The growth of
regional organization is not, however, the same thing as regional integration; the quality of the arrangements and their implications for the scope
and level of integration will be considered later.

A number of aspects of the evidence on the growth of regional organization which was available to the present writer should be pointed out. First,
the main source, which is the highly prestigious *Yearbook of International
Organizations,* has been presenting its quantitative data in a form which
permitted the identification of regional growth only since 1980; such a range
of data was not available to earlier students! Second, the figures are about
the number of organizations of which a country, or groups or individuals
within a country, were members at the times indicated. These are not
numbers of organizations. There is, however, separate information, dis-

Table 11.1: Number of organizations of which a country is a member, added together for each named region

a) *Europe, East and West*

	A Total	B Total NGOs	C Regional Total	D Regional NGOs	Ratio C to A	%
981	31,765		10,965		2.89	34
982	37,229	35,323	15,290	14,539	2.43	
983	38,205	36,201				
984	39,466	37,392	17,104	16,256	2.3	
987	41,885	39,883	18,519	17,819	2.26	44
					Percentage increase	+29%

b) *Africa*

	A Total	B Total NGOs	C Regional Total	D Regional NGOs	E Ratio C to A	%
981	10,662		1,949		5.47	18.2
982	12,943	11,056	3,070	2,351	4.21	
983	13,632	11,602		2,602		
984	14,362	12,292	3,731	2,898	3.84	
987	15,904	13,605	4,476	3,504	3.55	28.1
					Percentage increase	+ 54.39%

c) *Asia*

	A Total	B Regional NGOs	C Regional Total	D Regional NGOs	E Ratio C to A	%
981	11,484		1,839		6.24	16
982	13,687	12,453	2,849	2,516	4.8	
983	14,190	12,892	2,888	2,574	4.91	
984	14,914	13,553	3,199	2,831	4.6	
987	16,592	15,166	3,905	3,829	4.24	23
					Percentage increase	43.75%

Notes: Total = all memberships, regional and non-regional, intergovernmental and non-intergovernmental

IGO: intergovernmental organization

NGO: non-governmental organization

Source: Yearbook of International Organizations, ed. Union of International Associations, Munich, New York, London, Paris, K. G. Saur. 19th edn, 1981, to 25th edn, 1987/8.

cussed later, to suggest that the number of intergovernmental organizations in Africa has increased. Third, the evidence does have the disadvantage that it takes the grouping of countries, which it places together in the region, as a given, and looks at the growth of organizations within that space. It is not possible from this information to plot regions from memberships in the various regional organizations. The evidence may, therefore, fail to reveal the emergence of subregions within the major regions selected, which are Europe, Africa and Asia.

The main feature of the evidence set out in Table 11.1 is a comparison of the total number of memberships in international organization of countries in a region with the number of regional memberships. Except where otherwise stated, these figures are for both intergovernmental and non-governmental organizations. The figures for a series of years indicate a declining ratio of regional memberships to total memberships, so that for Europe the total number of memberships was 2.89 times greater than the number of regional memberships in 1981, but only 2.26 times that number in 1987. Although the strength of regional organization measured in this way may be judged to have increased relatively little in Europe over the period 1981 to 1987 it had nevertheless increased to some degree and the percentage change in the ratio of regional to total memberships was 29 per cent. Nevertheless this somewhat modest increase was to be expected in view of the relatively high level of regional organizations reached before the period of study in an area which was dominated by the European Community. It was also striking that the changing ratio was explicable mainly in terms of increases in the number of memberships in non-governmental organizations. In other words, societal interdependence seemed to have been increasing, although participation by governments in intergovernmental organizations did not increase. Indeed, the total number of memberships in regional intergovernmental organizations reported in the *Yearbook* decreased between 1984 and 1987 from 848 to 700. I am at a loss how to explain this change.

The trend towards regional involvement was, however, more striking in Africa where the ratio of regional to total memberships increased over the seven years from 5.47 to 3.55, an increase of 54.39 per cent. In the same period the total number of memberships had increased 1.49 times whilst the number of regional memberships had increased by 2.29 times. Both the number of non-governmental regional memberships and the number of intergovernmental regional memberships had increased, the latter from 719 in 1982 (figures for 1981 were not included in the *Yearbook*) to 972 in 1987. Regional organization in Africa seemed to be considerably strengthened through the 1980s in terms of these indicators. In Asia, too, participation in regional organization increased as compared with that in global organization during the 1980s. As Table 11.1 (c) indicates the increase in the ratio for governmental and non-governmental memberships together was 43.75 per cent, and the number of memberships in both kinds of organization increased at the regional level. Non-governmental memberships increased

Table 11.2: Increase in total number of intergovernmental and non-governmental organizations, and regional intergovernmental and non-governmental organizations, 1981–6

	1981	1982	1983	1984	1985	1986
All	4,602			4,980	5,054	5,018
Regional	3,246			3,666	3,736	3,667

Source: Yearbook of International Organizations, op. cit., 1987, Vol. 2, Statistical Appendix.

by 40 per cent, while intergovernmental memberships increased by almost 13 per cent.

This evidence suggests that in terms of membership regional organization was increasing faster than organization in general. This interpretation may be reinforced with a selection of data about the numbers of organizations. A source of information about African organizations is another highly respected yearbook called *Africa South of the Sahara*.[29] In its list of international organizations in that region in 1987 were seventy-one which I identified as being intergovernmental, as not having a headquarters outside the region, and as containing at least three members. All organizations which formed a part of the United Nations system were counted as constituting a single organization. The comparable figure for 1988 was seventy-six but that for 1975 was forty-six. In other words, the number of intergovernmental organizations defined in these terms had increased in Africa south of the Sahara by 39.4 per cent in the period 1975–88. The 1987 *Yearbook of International Organizations* also contained some data about the increase in the numbers of regional compared with the total number of organizations in the world from 1981 until 1986. As Table 11.2 shows, the total number of organizations increased by 416 a rate of 9.0 per cent over the six years, whilst the total number of regional organizations, including both governmental and non-governmental organizations in both cases, increased by 421, a percentage increase of 12.9 per cent. When this evidence is added to that about participation, it is hard to resist the conclusion that the 1980s was a period of remarkable growth in regional organization, though perhaps not as rapid as that reported by Nye for the period 1957 to 1963 which was mentioned above. The obvious point should be made, however, that the evidence for the latter period was likely to have been affected by the pace of creation of new states and by the general development in international economic arrangements after the period of economic recovery in the industrialized world in the 1950s. This makes the evidence for the 1980s seem even more remarkable.

The evidence presented so far includes nothing about the quality of the organizations, in terms of the powers of their controlling committees or the salience of their areas of competence. Nor did that used by Nye in his 1962 article. Presumably his excuse for such an omission, with which I sympathize, would have been that in a chapter of acceptable length it is impossible to add much of a systematic character about such a complex subject.

Nevertheless, I can add some qualitative evidence taken from the yearbook *Africa South of the Sahara*.[30] In the 1980s twelve or thirteen organizations attracted attention in that they were judged by the experts to be worth individual accounts. These were the United Nations and its fifteen subsidiary agencies then working in Africa, the African Development Bank, the Arab Bank for Economic Development, the Commonwealth, the Communauté Economique de l'Afrique de l'Ouest (CEAO), the Conseil de l'Entente, the Economic Community of Western Africa (ECAWOS), the Lomé arrangements, the Franc zone, the Islamic Development Bank, the Organization of African Unity, the Organization of the Islamic Conference, and the Southern African Development Community Conference (SADCC). In addition to the central core of organizations, there were in 1975 five further listed organizations working in what could be regarded as areas of high salience under the heading of Trade and Industry, whereas there were fifteen such organizations in 1988. In 1975 there were nine entries under the heading of Government Politics and Economics, whereas in 1988 there were fourteen items under these headings. This evidence at least suggests that the tasks dealt with in the increasing number of regional organizations were not trivial: they were dealing, whether effectively or ineffectively, with issues of great importance from the point of view of the member states. This point does not need to be laboured with regard to European regional organizations, and it will be assumed in this chapter that it is also valid for Asia.

The salience of the issues dealt with by the regional organizations may also be suggested in the motives of decision-makers for creating and joining them. Such motives vary in the degree to which they are recognized explicitly by the leaders and also in the circumstances which lead to their being suggested. It is therefore useful, before discussing them, to construct a typology in terms of which they might be arranged to recognize these possibilities.

Incentives to join the regional organizations might arise, first, from the immediate political circumstances of the state. These might be called contingent incentives. Second, the leaders might be pushed towards regional organizations as a way of solving the pressing specific economic or social problems of the state or of pursuing longer-term social or economic goals. They may, of course, sometimes be steered in that direction by a civil service or other advisers who have not made their intentions explicit: in this sense the leader is not fully aware of the motives for his action, which is more a consequence of continuing pressure, of social and economic propensities, rather than of explicit demands. Third, decision-makers might wish to join because they are responding to the kind of consideration which realists would place under the general heading of the pursuit of the national interest: they wish to expand or consolidate the power of the state which they govern and see in regional arrangements a way of achieving this. Finally, there exist pressures which derive from the perception that there are fundamental deficiencies in the way in which attempts are made to solve problems within the state or in the general character of its relations with others. In other words, there are structural problems which the decision-maker may attempt to rectify by joining regional organizations. For these various reasons decision-makers may seek membership in regional organizations, and they will now be further considered and illustrated in turn.

Among the immediate political circumstances of the states outside the Western capitalist world which have contributed towards their leaders' involvement in regional organizations since the mid-1970s, the central feature must be the failure of the earlier efforts to bring about the alteration of the global system so that their economic interests were better served. The attempt to create a New International Economic Order in 1974 had faded by the early 1980s, mainly because the developed states recovered from the shock of the first oil crisis and became increasingly reluctant to grant the concessions demanded by the Group of 77, such as the setting up of a Common Fund which would be large enough to stabilize commodity prices at an acceptable level, and the creation of a link between inflation and the price of commodities.[31] The work of the Conference on International Economic Co-operation held in Paris in 1976 was largely futile from the point of view of the Group of 77. The rich states refused to accept any significant alteration of the existing arrangements in the international economic system. Hence for the developing states there was a need for an alternative strategy: that was an increasing resort to regional organization in the absence of anything better.

A number of other problems were associated with the failure of the New International Economic Order. Global international institutions, including those which had been set up as a consequence of Third World pressure, proved relatively ineffective. Chief among these was UNCTAD. As the debt crisis worsened in the early 1980s, a number of other organizations began to appear as positively hostile. In particular, of course, the International Monetary Fund, in pursuit of monetary stability, imposed harsh conditions upon the debtor states, which were seen as essential by the lenders if further credit was to be extended.[32] These developments contributed to the growing feeling that global organization was at best only a part of the solution to the various economic problems of the worse-off states. The European Community also encouraged a greater resort to regional arrangements with specific measures to encourage trade between the developing states in the Lomé Three agreements; Lomé One in particular had been criticized for discouraging such intra-Group of 77 links.[33] A further pressure in the same direction came from the Brandt Report which can be seen as announcing an emerging consensus amongst the international development community: that regional arrangements among developing states were to be encouraged as their growth depended mainly upon increases in South–South trade.[34] Although efforts at the global level had to continue, by the mid-1980s there was a feeling among the Group of 77 that, far from radicalizing the global system, they would have to make concessions at that level. By the late 1980s these had come to include the acceptance of the right of the main contributing states to increase their control of economic and social policies in the United Nations.[35] A retreat at that level was accompanied by greater efforts at the regional one.

The second category of pressures upon African governments to participate in organization at the regional level was a range of economic and social
developments within their states. Chief amongst these was the emergence of
a somewhat larger number of people with higher levels of education and
experience of the outside world who expected higher standards of living,
and modernization, and who were prepared to exercise pressure upon their
governments to achieve these goals. Accordingly more people became
involved in non-governmental organizations because they were ways of
expressing the new aspirations and of pursuing them. The large number of
non-governmental groups at the conference on women's rights at Nairobi in
1976 was one illustration of this.[36] It was to be expected that a good number
of these would involve people from a number of contiguous states: regional
non-governmental organizations were therefore in part a consequence of the
rising tide of expectations.

Once such organizations began to appear, there was set in train a self-
sustaining process which had as its main dynamic an inclination to emulate
arrangements which seemed to have been successful in other parts of the
world. The tendency towards emulation should not be underestimated as a
reason for new economic and social developments once a particular stage of
awareness has been reached amongst a people. The European Community
was probably the most powerful role model of the freeing of trade, if only
because it had seemed to provide for economic growth in Western Europe.
Similarly pressures upon governments to create regional development banks
were likely to increase regardless of the arguments about their specific
technical merits: there were equivalents elsewhere, such as the European
Investment Bank, which were more likely to be imitated as the World Bank
was seen more frequently as an instrument of exploitation by the richer
states.

Emulation was a very important political fact. But it was, of course,
encouraged by its association with a very persuasive literature about the
advantages of regional economic activities, in particular of common
markets. The theories of economists, such as James Meade, Jacob Viner
and others do not require extended discussion in this chapter.[37] Suffice it to
say that they argued the benefits of establishing freer trade within a larger
area rather than a smaller one, as this would allow more efficient producers
to prosper at the expense of the less efficient ones. Larger producers would
be able to lower unit costs and would be able to spend more on research.
One implication of this was that there would be trade creation between
members of the market and trade diversion between members and outsiders.
These various factors would boost economic performance in the larger
regional economy.

Kuznets added a further point which was very much in favour of the
creation of regional markets.[38] He argued that, despite trade diversion, as
development proceeded the value of external trade in Gross National
Product (GNP) always increased. This could be interpreted as meaning that
GNP could only increase if external trade increased. But the same theorist
also recognized that although his argument held for all states regardless of

Table 11.3 Countries in which the greatest number of principal secretariats are located (regionally defined membership only)

	1983/84	1985/86	1986/87	1987/88	1988/89
Kenya	32	24	24	29	32
Nigeria	20	25	26	21	28
Senegal	20	24	25	21	25
Egypt	27	19	17	17	19
Côte d'Ivoire	N/A	N/A	15	13	N/A
Ethiopia	16	15	15	17	19
Algeria				7	
Tunisia			13		14
Ghana		15		7	

Source: Yearbook of International Organizations, op. cit., for years shown.

their size, the proportionate value of external trade for larger states was smaller at any particular level of development. Hence regional common markets had two interrelated advantages: they not only helped with the efficiency of businesses within the area, by which means they helped the economy to grow, but they also mean that a lesser amount of external trade had to be created in order to attain a specific level of GNP. The theories of academics are frequently of no great political importance. But, in this case, because of the emergence of a more informed and politically and economically aware public, and because of the temptation to emulate developments elsewhere, these theories were more likely to become part of the stock in trade of those who were in a position to advise leaders. Hence the generation of regional arrangements was further stimulated. Writing in the early 1980s, Sarkesian confirmed the impact of these various practical and intellectual incentives when he noted that in subregions 'plenty of specific accomplishments are evident', but 'the institutionalization of such co-operative efforts may increase their effectiveness'.[39] Such institutionalization proceeded apace, as has been shown, through the 1980s.

A third category of incentive towards the creation of regional organization was that which was particularly stressed in Nye's article, discussed above. The traditional realist ambitions of statesmen were reckoned to have been to do with the acquisition of possessions, especially in the form of territory. In modern times, however, it was more likely that statesmen would pursue what had been called milieu goals, such as those which were intended to change the environment in which a state operated so that it would be found more congenial. For instance, governments might see participation in regional organizations as providing a context in which leadership at that level could be sought. It is also probable — perhaps more so in Africa or Asia than in Europe — that governments would seek to establish such organizations on their own territory in order to facilitate the exercising of influence. It was striking that the headquarters of regional organizations tended to be set up in the capitals of a small number of states — Kenya, Nigeria, Senegal, Egypt, and less frequently in Ethiopia, Algeria

Table 11.4   Total number of secretariats by continent

	1983–4	1985–6	1988–9
Africa	261	288	299
Asia	287	296	348
Europe	2,783	2,739	2,508

Source: Yearbook of International Organizations, op. cit., 1988/9.

and the Côte d'Ivoire (see Table 11.4), though the *Yearbook* figures between 1983 and 1988 showed a marked increase in the total numbers in the lead states. Another factor was that regional organizations could be seen as an element in a local regime, as discussed by Krasner and others, which once in place would make it easier to conduct negotiations about matters of mutual interest with neighbours, and as has been mentioned, would facilitate direct communications between a government and the attentive public in the other member countries.

These general inclinations were, however, also subject to guiding principles. For instance, the evidence about regional organizations discussed above suggests that the traditional associations arising from the experience of colonialism still affected the choice of partners. The Francophone countries tended to do things together — hence the prominence of the Côte d'Ivoire in Table 11.4 — as did the Commonwealth countries, and as Sarkesian mentioned at the continental level, 'it is very difficult to do anything concrete'. Nevertheless, there was some evidence to suggest that organization which cut across the subregions was growing stronger.[40]

Another guiding principle was likely to be the urge to minimize intervention by the superpowers in the affairs of the region. In the 1970s and 1980s United States policy on this went through a long cycle which was not without its ironic aspects. In the early 1970s, precisely when developing countries, spurred on by the success of OPEC and the radicalism of dependency theory, were concentrating upon trying to alter fundamentally the global system, Kissinger and Nixon tried to encourage a higher degree of regional self-reliance in defence and other matters. Conversely — and predictably — when Reagan argued that the Soviet 'evil empire' should be resisted actively wherever it acted in pursuit of its global strategy, and adopted an activist interventionist role, states in Africa and Asia pursued regionalization more vigorously. The prospect of superpower intervention sharpened the appetite for doing it locally. One illustration of this was the Indian action in support of the government of the Maldive Islands after it had been attacked in November 1988 by mercenaries. Mr Gandhi pointed out explicitly that the success of Indian forces on this occasion confirmed the efficacy of regional arrangements. India's involvement in Sri Lanka reflected a similar interest. Superpower involvement would have been undesirable and unnecessary. This is not to say, however, that the idea of alliance with outsiders had now been rejected in Africa and Asia, but rather that there had arisen an inclination to seek security more actively at the regional level.

It is in conformity with the point that states more frequently pursued milieu goals that security was less often seen as being just a question of military capacity and strategy. There was a heightened realization of the need to seek economic defence against possible exploitation by outsiders, and against turbulence in the international economic system,[41] though abject economic circumstances often made the effective pursuit of such goals problematic. More specifically defensive mechanisms were needed to lessen dependence on external suppliers of essential materials, including food; to reduce dependence on a narrow range of exports, which created high sensitivity, even vulnerability, to adverse movements in particular product or commodity markets; to avoid excessive dependence on a particular market, which generated power for the recipient state over the suppliers — the Marks and Spencer syndrome[42]; and to increase the level of. trade dependence upon insiders, thus reducing economic and political risks. One plausible response to this list of economic defence requirements would be to strengthen regional economic arrangements. It is not argued here, however, that such goals always had the highest priority in the thinking of statesmen, but that nevertheless they were a source of continuous pressure to move in the direction of greater economic security wherever possible.

The three categories of incentive towards participation by governments in regional organization which have now been discussed were in support of local sectoralism rather than regionalism as it has been defined in this chapter. Regionalism in the sense of seeking a single space in order to facilitate the performance of a range of interrelated functions may be encouraged by three further kinds of pressure. First is the much discussed one of the appearance of a regional sentiment which persuaded statesmen of the need for a move towards greater regional unity. Second is the appearance of a belief among statesmen that a union would be desirable because it was seen as a grand enterprise, as was the case with the Founding Fathers in the United States. A third kind of pressure may, however, now be added: that regionalization may also result from the continual demonstration not only that specific benefits resulted from its intensification but that, conversely, costs consistently arose from its alternative, the sectoral approach. Of course, in practice a regionalization process will probably be fuelled by a mixture of these elements, but it is useful to identify the third more clearly as it has been underestimated. For instance, in Nye's article, mentioned above, regional sentiment was posed as the only counterweight to sectoralism. The fourth category of incentives towards regional organization is therefore different from the others in that it is also capable of being seen as an incentive towards regionalism as distinct from local sectoralism.

It is, however, unlikely that the fourth set would be found explicitly in the arguments of statesmen. The incentives are generated on the one hand by the failure of the sectoral approach in the organization of programmes for economic development, and on the other by the problems which arise from the way in which international society was structured in the 1980s. The failure of sectoralism may be felt by leaders in the form of a failure to reach particular developmental goals, or in marked inefficiences in the way in which limited resources are used. It may also be noted in the intuitive judgements of observers such as Bertrand, or in the previous practice of development programmes as with the Marshall Aid programme in Western Europe from 1948 to 1952, in which the US Congress specifically rejected a sectoral approach in favour of an integrated regional programme, or in the attempts to introduce regional devolution in France in the late 1960s. The effects of the failure may, therefore, be observed and on this basis alternative development strategies may be chosen which were represented, for instance, in the setting-up of the UNDP or in the appointment of Round Tables of advisers by the World Bank.[43] But the *reasons* for the failure of sectoralism are more difficult to identify, and this necessary task is attempted in chapter 16.

The political élites of developing states must also be aware that pressures towards regionalization are also being created by the long-term evolution of international society. That regional institutions are growing is evident. The question arises, therefore, of whether there are not also systemic pressures in favour of that process. What is the nature of these pressures and to what kind of international system will they tend? These questions, which also relate to the fourth category of incentives towards regional organization, are discussed in chapter 16 below.

It is, however, worth returning briefly in concluding this chapter to the question of the unfashionability of regionalism, even as local sectoralism, in the academic literature in the 1970s and 1980s. It was striking that in much of the later writing on international organizations, such as that on regime theory or on North–South relations, there was little or no reference to regionalism. Part of the explanation for this must be the fashion of the times, or, to put the matter more pretentiously, the emerging patterns of the sociology of knowledge. The development of regime theory was motivated in part by the need to discover factors which would make for international stability as US hegemony declined.[44] For Americans, however, it was easier to see internationalism as the alternative to US hegemony, and more difficult to contemplate a future in which rival centres of power, and more self-contained economic blocs, emerged. For American regime theorists in the 1980s, internationalism, not regionalism, was the ideologically acceptable alternative to American hegemony.

In some cases a different view was presented, which also just missed the case for regionalism. This view was to be noted in the writing of Robert Gilpin who, in his admirable text, described the processes of international capitalism as naturally involving the decline of particular economies and their succession by rival centres.[45] The United States was joined by the European Community and Japan. The assumption here, and it is hard to see why it was necessary, was that the process of development in some part of the global system was necessarily related inversely to the process of decline in some other part of that system. There are strong arguments, as Gilpin explained, in favour of the globalization of capitalism, but its consequences

could as easily be the emergence of islands of more or less equal development on a regional basis as a process of creating new hegemons. Neither the
neo-realists nor the regime theorists, therefore, have been led to notice a
resurgence of regionalism, the first because even when they dealt with the
forces of global capitalism they tended to see these as undermining old
hegemons and creating new ones, whilst the latter were disposed to see
existing hegemons as being merged into a new internationalism sustained —
by implication — by global regimes.

Notes

1. For discussions of the nature of regionalism see Ronald J. Yalem, *Regionalism
   and World Order,* Washington, Public Affairs Press, 1965; and Bruce M.
   Russett, *International Regions and the International System: a study in political
   ecology,* Chicago, Rand McNally, 1967.
2. Ernst B. Haas, *Beyond the Nation State: functionalism and international
   organization,* Stanford, Stanford University Press, 1964, especially chapter 14.
3. Kenneth Boulding, *Ecodynamics: a new theory of societal evolution,* Beverly
   Hills, Sage, 1978.
4. David Mitrany, *A Working Peace System,* Chicago, Quadrangle Books, 1966.
   For an extensive bibliography on functionalism, see Margot Light and A.J.R.
   Groom (eds), *International Relations: a handbook of current theory.* London,
   Frances Pinter, 1985, chapter 12.
5. A.J.R. Groom, 'Functionalism in world society' and John W. Burton, 'Functio-
   nalism and the resolution of conflict', in A.J.R. Groom and Paul Taylor (eds),
   Functionalism: theory and practice in international relations, London,
   University of London Press, 1975.
6. See Robert W. Cox, 'Social Forces, States and World Orders', in Robert O.
   Keohane, *Neorealism and its Critics,* New York, Columbia University Press,
   1986, pp. 204–54, especially pp. 208–9.
   Cox distinguishes between problem-solving theory and critical theory. Problem-
   solving focuses upon the solution of specific problems whilst assuming that
   other things are constant, and it is therefore conservative. Critical theory, 'unlike
   problem-solving theory, does not take institutions and social and power
   relations for granted but calls them into question by concerning itself with their
   origins and how and whether they might be in the process of changing' (p. 208).
   In other words, critical theory is concerned with the wholes rather than the
   parts. The argument in this chapter is in these terms critical theory rather than
   problem-solving.
7. Ian Clark, *Reform and Resistance in the International Order* Cambridge,
   Cambridge University Press, 1980, especially chapter 2, 'Kant and the tradition
   of optimism'.
8. See A.J.R. Groom, op. cit. in note 5 above.
9. Yalem, op. cit., *passim.*
10. Russett, op. cit.
11. Ibid., p. 11.
12. Ibid., p. 168.
13. Leon Lindberg and Stuart Scheingold, *Regional Integration* Cambridge,
    Harvard University Press, Mass., 1971.

14. Ernst B. Haas, *The Obsolescence of Regional Integration Theory* Berkeley, University of California Press, 1976.
15. Joseph S. Nye, 'Regional institutions', in Cyril E. Black and Richard A. Falk, *The Structure of the International Environment* which is Vol. IV of their *The Future of the International Legal Order,* Princeton, Princeton University Press, 1972; reproduced in Richard A. Falk and Saul H. Mendlovitz (eds), *Regional Politics and World Order,* W.H. Freeman and Company, San Francisco, 1973.
16. Ibid., p. 92.
17. Ibid., p. 90.
18. Oran R. Young, 'Political Discontinuities in the International System', *World Politics,* Vol. 20, no. 3, 1968, pp. 369–92.
19. Andre Gunder Frank, 'The Development of Underdevelopment' *Monthly Review,* September 1966, pp. 17–30.
20. Rajni Kothari, *Footsteps Into The Future: Diagnosis of the present World and a Design for an Alternative.* The Free Press, New York, 1974, p. 135.
21. Joint Inspection Unit, *Some Reflections on Reform of the United Nations,* prepared by Maurice Bertrand, JIU/REP/85/9, Geneva, 1985. Henceforth referred to as the Bertrand Report; reproduced in part in Paul Taylor and A.J.R. Groom (Eds), *International Institutions at Work,* Pinter Publishers, London, 1988.
22. Ibid., p. 54.
23. Ibid.
24. Ibid.
25. Ibid., p. 55.
26. Ibid., p. 64.
27. See J.W. Burton, 'Regionalism, Functionalism, and the United Nations', *Australian Outlook* Vol. 15, 1961, pp. 73–87.
28. Roger Masters, 'A Multi-bloc Model of the International System', *American Political Science Review,* Vol. 55, no. 4, Dec. 1961, pp. 780–98.
29. *Africa South of the Sahara,* London, Europa Publications, 1988.
30. Ibid.
31. Joan Edelman Spero, *The Politics of International Economic Relations* 3rd edn, London, Allen & Unwin, 1985, especially chapter 7; Gautam Sen, 'UNCTAD and international economic reform', in Paul Taylor and A.J.R. Groom (eds), *Global Issues in the United Nations Framework* London and Basingstoke, Macmillan, 1989.
32. Robert Gilpin, *The Political Economy of International Relations,* Princeton, Princeton University Press, 1987, especially chapter 8.
33. Carol Cosgrove Twitchet, *A Framework for Development: the EEC and the ACP* London, Allen & Unwin, 1981.
34. The Brandt Commission, *Common Crisis North–South: co-operation for world recovery* London and Sydney, Pan Books, 1983.
35. Paul Taylor, 'Reforming the system: getting the money to talk', in Paul Taylor and A.J.R. Groom (eds), *International Institutions at Work,* London, Frances Pinter, 1988, pp. 220–35.
36. R.J. Harrison, 'Women's rights: 1975–85', in Taylor and Groom, *Global Issues . . . op. cit.*
37. Their ideas are ably discussed in Peter Robson, *The Economics of International Integration,* London, Allen & Unwin, 1980.
38. Simon Kuznets, *Modern Economic Growth: rate, structure and spread,* New Haven, Yale University Press, 1966.

39. Sam C. Sarkesian, 'African Community Building', in Gavin Boyd (ed.), *Regionalism and Global Security,* Lexington, Lexington Books, D.C. Heath, 1984.
40. Sarkesian, op. cit., p. 64.
41. Michael Handel, *Weak States in International Relations* London, Frank Cass, 1981.
42. Marks and Spencer, a major high-street retailer, had a reputation for acquiring power over suppliers by taking most of their product, though this was generally in order to be able to insist upon high standards.
43. Douglas Williams, *The Specialized Agencies and the United Nations: the system in crisis,* London, C. Hurst, 1987.
44. Regionalism is ignored in Robert Keohane's classic text, *After Hegemony* Princeton, Princeton University Press, 1984.
45. Robert Gilpin, *The Political Economy of International Relations* Princeton, New Jersey, Princeton University Press, 1987.

Selected reading

Black, Cyril E. and Falk, Richard, *The Future of the International Legal Order,* Princeton, New Jersey, Princeton University Press, 1969.
Cantori, Louis J. and Spiegel, Steven, 'The International Relations of Regions', *Polity,* Vol. 2, No. 4.
Lindberg, Leon and Scheingold Stuart (eds), *Regional Integration* Cambridge, Mass., Harvard University Press, 1971.
Nye, J.S. *Peace in Parts: integration and conflict in regional organisations* Boston, Little, Brown, 1971.
Russett, B.M., *International Regions and the International System,* London, Greenwood Press, 1976.

12 Consociationalism and federalism as approaches to international integration

Paul Taylor

Students of international organization over the years have frequently shared concepts with those who study comparative government. Most prominent have been the grand theories of constitutional arrangement such as federalism and confederalism, but the list of shared analytical concepts — pluralism, balance, hierarchy and the like — is enormous. Consociationalism is a relatively recent addition to the literature of comparative government: it was developed by Arend Lijphart in his book on *The Politics of Accommodation: Pluralism and Democracy in the Netherlands*,[1] which was published in 1968. A few years later one of the leaders in the field of comparative government, Hans Daalder, concluded: 'The typological coining of the model of consociational democracy constitutes a major contribution to the literature. It widens our understanding of the variegated possibilities of effective democratic rule.'[2] Since then a number of other political scientists, of mainly European background, developed a literature of increasing impressiveness, one of the interesting features of which was a concern with the relevance of the concept to the solution of the problems of societies in which there was interethnic violence, such as in Northern Ireland or Israel.[3] Nor is the concept irrelevant for the theory of international organization.

It is possible to place the theory of consociation in the context of three somewhat overlapping conceptual typologies, defined in terms of the main purpose which the analyst has in mind in its employment. Two of these are evident from the preceding discussion; a third is now added. First is the typology within which it was originally developed, namely that which concerns the range of forms of existing democratic governments. In this case it is essentially an explanatory concept, purporting to enrich our understanding of what exists, namely deeply divided, yet stable democracies. Other concepts in this typology, as Lijphart has pointed out, include the three models of democratic political system distinguished by Gabriel Almond in 1956, namely the Anglo-American, Continental European and Scandinavian–Dutch forms.[4] Lustick contrasted to this list a non-democratic alternative to consociationalism called hegemonic control, such as was found at one time in South Africa between whites and blacks, or in Israel between Israelis and Arabs, though the *intafada* has indicated that the risks of this system degenerating into chaos are considerable.[5] The argument was that the techniques could be used by a dominant superordinate group to control another subordinate group in a stable relationship.

Second is a typology which stresses the use of consociationalism as an instrument, a way of solving the problems of existing deeply divided societies such as Northern Ireland. It is a prescription which is appropriate only in so far as certain general characteristics of a situation, i.e. deep divisions within a polity, resemble instances where it has in fact appeared. The conditions of its success are necessarily lacking, and also need to be introduced. In this context O'Leary has coined the term *coercive consociationalism* to describe a situation in which pressures need to be deployed to push a society into accepting consociationalism.[6] Other concepts in this typology have been identified by O'Leary as integration, partition, hegemonic control, internationalization and arbitration.

Third is a typology, now added to the others, about the range of forms of international integration. As will be argued below, in this case the concept illuminates by analogy ways of strengthening the functional arrangements among states whilst not mitigating antagonisms between the major groups of peoples, i.e. the nations, which they serve, and at the same time creating a framework within which dissenting minorities can be allowed eventually a measure of autonomy. Indeed, when translated to the international level the concept of consociationalism in its various aspects suggests something rather startling: that comprehensive international arrangements may challenge rather than reinforce the process of developing a transnational socio-psychological community. Integration may release pressures that encourage the encapsulating of nations, and the firmer definition of ethnic and cultural minorities. Other concepts in the typology of integration theory include functionalism, neo-functionalism and federalism. Functionalism and neo-functionalism are both different from consociationalism in that they imply the development of a supporting socio-psychological community and of its structural concomitant, namely, in the terms of Seymour Martin Lipset, 'cross-cutting cleavages'.[7] In contrast federalism has in principle in common with consociationalism a capacity to accommodate sharp cleavages in society as long as these are clearly geographically demarcated, but it is also different from consociationalism in various respects which will be examined below.[8]

What are the necessary features of consociation? This question should be distinguished from that of the nature of the conditions in which it might arise or survive. It has been described by Lijphart as having four aspects.[9] First it relates to a number of groups which are in some sense insulated from each other, in that their interests and associations are more inwardly directed than overlapping with those of members of other groups in the same state: there are relatively few cross-cutting cleavages, and authority within that state is segmented in relation to such groups. Second, the state is dominated by what Dahrendorf called a *cartel of élites:*[10] the political élites of the various segments are each involved in some way on a continuous basis in the process of decision-making and decisions are the product of agreements and coalitions among the members of that cartel. None is placed in the ranks of the opposition in decision-making, as, for instance, in the event of defeat in an election, which would be the case with a majority system. The cartel need not necessarily require that all actors be positively involved in the same way on all occasions: variations on the theme would be an arrangement, as in Switzerland, whereby it is agreed that each member of the Federal Council acts in turn as President for a year, or in the Lebanon before the civil war where there was an agreed division of responsibilities between Muslim and Christian leaders.[11]

The third aspect is a logical extension of the cartel principle: it is that all the political élites should have the right of veto over decisions of which they disapproved. In other words the majoritarian principle in the system as a whole, which is characteristic of other forms of democracy, is suspended in favour of the requirement of consensus, though it may apply within the segments, or, on some issues which are less contentious, among the members of the cartel or among the population at large, as is the case with the use of the referendum in Switzerland. Finally is the law of proportionality, which means that the various segments of the population have proportionate representation among the major institutions: the bureaucracy, legal systems, and so on, of the state. In all these various aspects the crucial point is that the rights and interests of the subordinate sections of society, as interpreted through the members of the cartel of élites, are safeguarded in relation to the rights and interests of the majority. Indeed, political arrangements are so ordered that the minority is protected from the dictatorship of the majority.

The central problem of consociation in the context of each of the three typologies is that of the maintenance of stability in a situation of actual or potential mutual tension. Indeed, the problem implies an irony which is more characteristic of international relations than of stable democracies: the need to generate enthusiasm for stability precisely because of the continuing threat of fragmentation. As Lijphart put it, 'The leaders of the rival subcultures may engage in competitive behaviour and thus further aggravate mutual tensions and political instability, but they may also make deliberate efforts to counteract the immobilizing and unstabilizing effects of cultural fragmentation.'[12] The imminence of mutual tensions is revealed in the determination of the segments' leaders to defend the separate interests of the groups in the common forum. In the Anglo-American systems in contrast,

because the political culture tends to be homogeneous and pragmatic, the political process takes on some of the atmosphere of a game. A game is a good game when the outcome is in doubt and when the stakes are not too high. When the stakes are too high the tone changes from excitement to anxiety. But in consociational democracies politics is treated not as a game but as serious business.[13]

The leaders are faced continually with the dilemma of acting to preserve the general system whilst at the same time seeking to protect and further the interests of the groups which they represent.

With regard to their own groups, therefore, élites must be able to rely on a high degree of homogeneity, and be capable of backing this up on occasion with techniques for the maintenance of internal discipline. This explains

Lustick's contention that within segments control may sometimes be so powerful as to challenge the judgement that they are internally democratic. The stability of the whole may require the discipline, even in undemocratic ways, of the segments. With regard to relations between particular élites and other élites in fragmented societies, four interrelated conditions must apply, according to Lijphart, if the dangers of political anxiety are to be mitigated.[14] The élites must have the ability to accommodate the divergent interests and demands of the subcultures. This requires in turn that they have the ability to transcend cleavages and to join in a common effort with the élites of rival subcultures. They must therefore be committed to the maintenance of the system and to the improvement of its cohesion and stability. And finally, 'all of the above requirements are based on the assumption that the élites understand the perils of political fragmentation'.[15] Such is the political conjuring act which the élites of stable consociation systems are expected to perform.

In his discussion of the differences between consociationalism and control in deeply divided societies, Lustick brilliantly highlighted the main characteristics of the former as a process. There were seven such characteristics and I am heavily indebted to Lustick for the following discussion.[16]

First, the criterion that effectively governs the authoritative allocation of resources in the consociational system is the common denominator of the interests of the two segments as perceived and articulated by their respective élites.

Second, linkages between the two subunits or segments in the system take the form of political or material exchanges, negotiations, bargains, trades and compromises. In the control system, however, the segment which has dominance extracts what it needs from the subordinate segment and delivers what it sees fit.

Third, in the consociational system hard bargaining between subunit élites is a necessary fact of political life, and this is a concrete sign that it is operating successfully. In the control system, however, precisely the opposite is the case: hard bargaining signals the failure of the control mechanisms.

Fourth, the role of the official regime, the civil service, law agencies, public education system, armed forces and the like, in the consociational regime is to act as an umpire or interpreter of the bargains which have been reached: but in the control system the official regime is the legal and administrative instrument of the superordinate segments. It is there to act as the instrument of control.

Fifth, the normative justification for the regime adopted by authorities in the consociational regime is likely to be couched in terms of vague and general references to the common welfare of both subunits, whereas in a control regime it is more likely that there will be an elaborate ideology to justify the subordination of one group to another.

Sixth, the central strategic problem that faces élites in the consociational system is symmetrical for each subunit: each must strike bargains which preserve the integrity of the whole system, but which can also be enforced within the respective subunits which they represent. In a control system, however, the superordinate subunit élites strive to devise techniques for manipulating the subgroup, whilst the subordinate group's leadership attempts to minimize concessions to the superordinate group. 'In spite of this asymmetry, however, the strategic concern of élites of both sub-units in the control system is much more externally focused than that of sub-unit élites in the consociational system.'[17]

Finally, the visual metaphor for the interaction between the subunits in the consociational system is that of a set of scales, delicately but securely balanced, while that of the control system is that of a puppeteer manipulating the stringed puppet. 'Though reflective of the basic differences between the two sorts of relationships, both images contain a suggestion of the separateness of subunits, of the specificity of the linkages that join them, and of their overall stability.'[18]

What are the implications of consociationalism for integration between states, as, for instance, in the European Community? The theory is useful in that it presents a conceivable outcome of the integration process which differs from those indicated by other theories and allows the identification of aspects in the current situation which could be seen as tending towards that outcome. The use made of the theory in this essay is a modest one: it is used to highlight and place in a particular perspective what has been happening in the European Community over the last few years. As has already been stated, the implication is that integration in the sense of the strengthening of the regional functional systems may help to sharpen rather than soften the cleavages in the existing society of nations.

One reason for this is seen to be that members of the cartel of élites are likely to be faced with a dilemma: they will have an interest in increasing the size of the cake, and the share obtained by their own segment, whilst at the same time protecting the distinctiveness of their segments in comparison with others, since they serve as each member's individual constituency and power base. The process of increasing the size of the cake, which is the essential condition of larger shares, tends, however, to encourage the development of intersegmental social and cultural links, alongside the economic ones, which may have a cost in terms of the chances of maintaining the segment's viability in the longer term. Integration may, therefore — apart from committing them to enlarging the cake — also generate in the élites an increasing interest in actively resisting any tendency towards the strengthening of the horizontal links between the segments since that would also tend to weaken their constituencies. The status and authority of the members of the cartel are dependent upon their capacity to identify segmental interests and to present themselves as leaders and agents of a distinct clearly defined community. Unlike other theories of integration, consociationalism highlights the politics of the relationship between the leaders and the led, and the way in which the interests of the former may depart from those of the latter during the process. The theory suggests the possibility that élites will become more determined to strengthen controls over their own segments as integration proceeds: there may be cases, indeed, where regional integration helps to reinforce the anti-democratic tendencies of élites. Internal discipline enhances their power in the cartel but also allows them to sell more easily the packages which they have been able to negotiate.

A worse case suggested by the theory is a conspiracy of élites to promote their own interests even when these conflict with those of the segments which they nominally serve. This would be, indeed, the apotheosis of the danger that was advertized by the left wing of the political spectrum in Britain and elsewhere: that European integration was essentially a bourgeois conspiracy of élites and big business — in alliance with governments — against the interests of the mass of the people.[19] In the late 1980s Prime Minister Thatcher's opposition to the Commission's proposal to introduce a social charter into the EC to protect the interests of workers seemed to some commentators to suggest an intention to make the Community a happy hunting-ground for capital.[20] There must be no hindrance in the way of capital's exploiting differences in the cost of labour and the level of welfare provision in the various parts of the EC, even though this also meant keeping social security provisions for British workers at a lower level. The integration process seems to provide an opportunity for the élites to favour their own.

To put the matter more mildly, the theory of consociationalism adds something to our understanding of regional integration when it points to the way in which the process could be reconciled with the existing interests of élites. It could be seen by them as providing a means by which their power base could be consolidated; not only would their capacity for rewarding as far as was necessary the collective interests of the distinct segments be enhanced, but their capacity to influence the definition of such interests would also be increased. This lends support to the view that integration tends to reinforce rather than weaken the nation-state.

The theory is also suggestive, however, about existing élites' attitudes towards minorities in the integrating system and the attitudes of the leaders of those minorities. The appearance of the regional arrangements provides the leaders of dissenting minorities with a forum within which to push for increased specific returns and separate representation. Traditional theories of integration, such as functionalism and neo-functionalism, have no way of coping with this observable political fact. Scots, Welsh, Basque, Irish and even Catalan nationalists have all seen the Community as an opportunity for furthering their cause. The minority seeks to consolidate direct contacts with regional level organization whereas the existing élite cartel members seek to limit such contacts. One test of this hypothesis could be found in the attitudes of governments toward permitting or preventing direct links between local groups and the Community when seeking support from the latter's structural funds. The British government has tended to oppose such contacts, and this certainly has modest implications for the perceptions of people in the non-English areas in Britain of themselves as forming distinct communities.[21] Even more striking in the context of consociation was the strength of the opposition to the free movement of people in the Dutch

Parliament in the late 1980s, despite the traditional support of the Dutch government for European union, and their commitment to going ahead of the others in that direction with the French, West Germans and other Benelux countries. Conversely the British government has also sought to raise the patriotic temperature regarding the EC, whilst denying that this was really a challenge to the latter — a circumstance which also fits with consociationalism.[22] In this context, however, O'Leary has suggested the generation of cross-frontier programmes to be financed by the Community as a way of softening the sectoral tensions in Northern Ireland.[23] The logic of consociationalism in its application to the integration process is, however, that national governments would resist this approach until a late stage. This point is discussed further below.

This logic provides, however, a small further part of the explanation of the observed pattern of behaviour of the minorities in the European Community. The universal habit is for them to see the Community as the context in which they can obtain a greater level of independence and at the same time increase the level of specific returns to their groups. This suggests that contrary to first impression, the tendency might be for successful integration to sharpen divisions between minorities and the dominant segments, rather than lessen them. In that it stresses the propensity of leaders of the dominant segments to increase their countervailing resistance to minority dissent, consociation theory seems to raise the possibility that integration might serve to exacerbate intercommunal tensions.

There is, however, a more optimistic scenario which may be valid in the longer term, which is also suggested by the theory. However, this is — it must be admitted — a rather pale dawn. Leaders may quite suddenly decide that the game of keeping a minority within the dominant segment is not worth the candle. This outcome would arise if the level of tensions within segments rose to an intolerable level. But it would also be encouraged by the integration process in that the latter amplifies the separate expectations of minorities and provides a focus for them, whilst at the same time sharpening the identity of the cartel of élites as a forum to which non-members might aspire. The theory of consociation does not suggest on the other hand that attempts to strengthen cross-frontier functional arrangements between members of the same minority are likely to be acceptable to national governments until the level of tensions within the segments has risen to a very high level. We are therefore faced at best with a two-stage process: a first stage of increasing resistance to change, but then a sudden giving-way to the demands of minorities for autonomy. In the context of this argument the interesting point is that the integration process is itself a variable in such outcomes in two senses: first, in that it sharpens the identity of the cartel of élites, and second, that it encourages the clearer definition of minorities and the articulation of their separate interests.

The process of decision-making at the centre of the system is also illuminated by the theory of consociationalism. The theory suggests that in this context members of the élite cartel will become more inclined to insist that they retain an ultimate veto on decisions of which they disapprove and more resistant to decision-taking on the basis of majorities. Decision-making would become more difficult because of the success of the process. At first sight the Single European Act seems to be evidence against the proposition that this is true of the European Community, but the informed reader will at least entertain a rather cynical view about its terms regarding majority voting.[24] On the whole the states have reserved the right, either explicitly in the Act or in terms of stated intentions, to veto anything which affects their vital interests. Further it appears to have been generally accepted that the Act did not supersede, but only circumscribe, the Luxembourg Accord of 1966 which allowed the veto.

The members of the Council of Ministers do indeed behave like the members of an élite cartel in a consociational multi-party government, with enormously complex consensus-building and a relative immobilism. Its working style is more like that of the Swiss confederation or the government of the Netherlands than of the Anglo-American democracies. Even the British, with their somewhat different tradition of adversary politics, have been forced reluctantly to learn the modalities of this system. It follows that the Council of Ministers is not a place where leadership can be exercised and initiatives taken: it has never increased the pace but has always slowed it down. The great initiatives of the 1980s have invariably begun elsewhere: in the Commission, the European Parliament, or a particular government, or a small group of like-minded governments such as France and West Germany. The consociationalism model of the working of the European Community has precisely the opposite implications for the working assumptions and background conditions of decision-making from those which are suggested by traditional functionalism or even neo-functionalism: these indicate the prospect of greater accord as integration proceeds, the former promotes a more complicated arrangement which might be better described as one of confined dissent.

The implications of this for the central bureaucracy — the Commission — are also worth considering. Consociational theory sees the state apparatus as being an umpire rather than a promoter of any specific ideology. Within an existing consociational state the bureaucracy is an umpire in that it must avoid attaching itself to the ideology of a particular segment. This is also true of the Commission of the European Communities, and this of course is not a particularly original point. But there is a more interesting development of this idea which is suggested by consociationalism. It is that integration has the effect of compelling the central institution to adopt more frequently, and at an earlier stage of the decision-making process, the role of umpire. The task of presenting initiatives which reflect the general community interest is by no means eliminated, but what tends to happen is that the grand designs are more frequently changed out of recognition through compromise and are at continuing risk of being entirely lost to sight as decision-making proceeds. Members of the pro-European lobby hold that this is the consequence of the close involvement of government representatives in decision-making at a very early stage in the formulation of policy by the Commission, as in the Committee of Permanent Representatives. It is hard to see how this can be avoided in view of the way in which the decision-making process has evolved over the years. The theory suggests, however, that pressures to enlarge the role of the Commission as umpire are increased rather than diminished as integration proceeds. As the stakes rise so the members of the élite cartel become more careful to protect their interests and insist that the condition of movement is consensus.

A further insight from consociationalism concerns the staffing of the Commission. Whereas integration theory predicts an increasing prepared-ness to accept appointments to the central bureaucracy on the basis of ability, regardless of geographical or social distribution, the theory of consociationalism suggests an increasing determination to insist upon proportionality in the central institutions, and indeed an increasing ten-dency for particular élites to identify their nationals in those institutions as their representatives. This is a useful theoretical perspective upon the tendency for the collegiate principle in the Commission to become weaker — dissenting members are now much more frequently identified than they were — and for state governments to act as if Commissioners from their states were their representatives. For instance, Leon Brittan has been reported in the United Kingdom as taking particular positions in Commis-sion meetings which reflected British government policy, such as his position on the European Social Charter in 1989. Another indication is Mrs Thatcher's habit of referring to British Commissioners as 'our commissio-ners'. It is widely accepted that the collegiate principle and the Treaty of Rome's requirement that Commissioners should not be instructed by governments have always to some degree been transgressed, but as integ-ration has proceeded there has been in the press and the statements of politicians a more general acceptance of this as routine.

What are the main differences between federalism and consociationalism? Lijphart has pointed to the way in which they may work in rather similar ways within stable democracies, the crucial difference being that federalism requires that the various segments be readily identifiable on a geographical basis whereas consociationalism allows for degrees of overlap in the physical location of the segments.[25] When viewed as integration processes, however, the two emerge as having rather different implications. Federalism is by definition a single-step process relying upon a meeting of political leaders — a constituent assembly — and the agreeing of a constitution which reconciles regional differences. In classical federalism the product of this process, the constitution, is seen as a political solution to the problems of diversity. Consociationalism does not, however, require such a conscious act of political creativity and there is no need to reconcile diversities: it can be a process proceeding beyond the control of specific political actors. Indeed, the dynamics of integration which were identified by the neo-functionalists may proceed alongside the processes of consociationalism. What the latter adds is a view about a set of pressures which shape the political process which derive from its social and cultural setting.

The federalist integration process requires the establishing of two levels of government separate but co-ordinate — being the government of the whole, the federal level, and the government of the parts, the state or local level.[26] Such levels may also arise in a consociation. In the latter, however, the idea of a central government in which there is a habit of identifying and acting upon a common interest is relatively weak. Federalism tends to the upgrading of the common interest in the general system whereas consociationalism tends to the reinforcement of the search for the lowest common denominator at that level. More precisely, the general interest, in so far as it emerges, is more likely to be an interest of élites than of segments. As has been pointed out earlier, consociationalism underlines the potential for divergence between the interests of élites and publics in a political process such as integration. Similarly the assumption behind federalism in its mainstream form is that the system will over time gradually strengthen the perception of the common interest at the general and élite level, whereas the logic of the consociational approach suggests that the sense of intergroup rivalry will be sharpened. Indeed, when the consociational model is applied to the integration process, intergroup rivalry is stressed as one of the dynamics of integration, whereas in the federalist model of integration the opposite is the case, namely the strengthening of the sense of community. It follows that in the consociational model the segments expect their leaders to be activist and politicized in their pursuit of interests in the cartel of élites. As was pointed out above in a consociational system, politics tends to be a serious business as the stakes are seen as being high: there is no tendency towards depoliticization. In the federalist process of integration, however, there is an expectation of depoliticization and of the transmuting of politics into a game.

What keeps the consociational system alive is that the costs of collapse, in terms of the dangers of exacerbating internal tensions and the risks of intervention from outside, are seen to exceed those arising from maintaining the cumbersome internal arrangements, and the range of specific benefits arising from the latter are seen as being sufficient. Indeed, an awareness of the external implications of internal failure is more pressing than with other constitutions: in the case of several of the existing consociational systems in Western Europe, such as Holland and Switzerland, there has been experience of intervention, or undue pressure from outside, at times of internal weakness. An awareness of this danger is part of the political ideology of these countries. It is striking, though, that as international integration in the European Community has evolved, a parallel argument, even a sentiment, has appeared. This is reflected in the strengthening perception that for all the tedious burdens of EC decision-making, and the undignified horse-trading, the breakdown of the Community would be horrendous in its international implications. The fear of vulnerability in international society is a powerful incentive towards maintaining the viability of the cartel of élites as a management coalition. Consociationalism sharpens this point.

One analyst has pointed out that in a consociational system a relatively low level of intergroup contact was helpful from the point of view of encouraging stability, as such contacts and mutual transactions tended, in sharply divided societies, to increase awareness of differences and tensions.[27]

The consociational theory suggests that in an integration process leaders may indeed have an interest in minimizing such contacts. In a Federal system, however, the development of intergroup links is generally seen as desirable on the part of élites as it reinforces the sense of community, reshapes interests so that they are less conflictual, and reduces the load upon the governmental and administrative arrangements. It remains to be seen how far European leaders will permit or encourage this, but, as has been argued above, the theory of consociationalism suggests that any European socio-psychological community is more likely to emerge despite rather than because of the intentions of leaders.

In sum, consociationalism highlights the ways in which existing political élites might pursue international integration for their own selfish reasons at the cost of community solidarity — it is in a sense a dynamic view of intergovernmentalism — whereas federalism and other integration theories expect them to act in the interests of the greater number in the longer term. There are very few instances in which politicians have in fact acted in the interests of the larger number in the longer term, and this might add credence to consociationalism. The theory undoubtedly helps to highlight many aspects of the current integration process in Western Europe, though the tone which it lends is often bleak in the eyes of those who would prefer to see an emerging European federation on the model, perhaps, of Almond's Anglo-American style of government, with decisions increasingly taken by majority vote, an increasing range of cross-cutting cleavages between the segments of the European society, and an emerging socio-psychological community. These things may yet emerge but consociationalism helps to identify some of the roadblocks that are in the way.

On the other hand the theory may be regarded as more optimistic by those who see the good life as involving the freeing of dissenting minorities and the admission of their representatives to the conferences of statesmen. There is a sense indeed in which consociationalism challenges the doctrine of national self-determination: it permits in some circumstances the detachment of national groups from larger segments with which they have been housed, without requiring that the fabric of the technical/functional arrangements of the state are similarly relocated. National detachment — the segmental autonomy which is a building-block of consociationalism — is possible in part because such systems have already become non-terminous with nations: self-determination has fewer implications for what the nation does or can do. If in Birch's terms nationalism is by definition a search for polical autonomy,[28] any list of the purposes to which such autonomy would be put is bound to become shorter and shorter as integration proceeds. This can only be to the advantage of minorities seeking a greater say in their own destiny. The irony of their position, however, is that integration both increases in some ways their chances of achieving autonomy, but also reduces the range of purposes to which it could be put.

Notes

1. Arend Lijphart, *The Politics of Accommodation: pluralism and democracy in the Netherlands,* Berkeley and Los Angeles, University of California Press, 1968.
2. Hans Daalder, 'The consociational democracy theme', *World Politics,* Vol. XXVI, July 1974.
3. See Arend Lijphart, 'Review article: Northern Ireland problem; cases, theories and solutions', *British Journal of Political Science* Vol. 5, 1975; Brendan O'Leary, 'The limits to coercive consociationalism in Northern Ireland', *Political Studies,* Vol. XXXIII No. 4 p. 562–88, 1989. These both contain extensive bibliographies.
4. Arend Lijphart, 'Consociational democracy', *World Politics* Vol. XXI, No. 2, 1969, p. 207.
5. Ian Lustick, 'Stability in deeply divided societies: consociationalism versus control', *World Politics* Vol. XXXI, No. 3, 1979.
6. O'Leary, op. cit.
7. Seymour Martin Lipset, *Political Man: the social bases of politics* Garden City, 1960, pp. 88–9.
8. For an excellent brief account of the theory and practice of federalism in the European Community, see R.J. Harrison, *Europe in Question,* London, Allen & Unwin, 1974.
9. Arend Lijphart, 'Consociation and federation: conceptual and empirical links', *Canadian Journal of Political Science* Vol. XXII, No. 3, 1979, pp. 499–515.
10. R. Dahrendorf, *Society and Democracy in Germany* Garden City, 1967, p. 276.
11. K. McRae (ed), *Consociational Democracy: political accommodation in segmented societies* McLelland and Stewart, Toronto, 1974.
12. Lijphart, 1969, op. cit. p. 211–12.
13. Gabriel A. Almond, 'Comparative political systems', *Journal of Politics,* Vol. XVIII, August 1956, pp. 398–9.
14. Lijphart, 1969, op. cit., p. 216.
15. Ibid.
16. Lustick, 1979, op. cit. pp. 330–2.
17. Ibid., p. 332.
18. Ibid.
19. See Stuart Holland, *UnCommon (sic) Market* London, Macmillan, 1980.
20. Peter Kellner, *The Independent* 22 March, 1989.
21. For instance, the British government was careful to protect its position as overseer of applications to the structural funds of the EC from local authorities and other organizations in Britain, and, indeed, appeared to be using EC disbursements not, as had been intended, to increase the size of available funds (the principle of additionality), but rather as an alternative to what would otherwise have been available from the British Treasury.
22. The rhetoric of the Thatcher administration regarding the EC frequently implied that the motives of the partners were either foolish or dishonourable. Particularly noteworthy — and indicative of an attitude though not directly about the EC — was the Prime Minister's statement when a guest of President Mitterand at the bicentennial celebrations of the French Revolution in Paris in July 1989, that this was not much to celebrate and that in any case the British thought of it first. A distinguished English historian, Christopher Thorne, commented in *The Guardian,* Saturday, 15 July that this had made him ashamed to be British: Thatcher's comments had been impertinent and wrong in fact.

23. O'Leary, 1989, op. cit.
24. Paul Taylor, 'The New Dynamic of EC integration in the 1980s', in Juliet Lodge (ed.), *The European Community and the Challenge of the Future,* London, Pinter Publishers, 1989, pp. 3–25.
25. Lijphart, 1979, op. cit.
26. The classic text on federalism is K.C. Wheare, *Federal Government* 2nd edn, London, Oxford University Press, 1951.
27. David Easton, *A Systems Analysis of Political Life,* New York, Wiley 1965.
28. A.H. Birch, *Nationalism and National Integration* London, Unwin Hyman, 1989. Birch writes on p. 6: 'A nation is best defined as a society which either governs itself today, or has done so in the past, or has a credible claim to do so in the not too distant future.'

Selected reading

Daalder, Hans, 'The consociational democracy theme', *World Politics* Vol. XXVI, July 1974.
Lijphart, Arend, *The Politics of Accommodation: pluralism and democracy in the Netherland,* Berkeley and Los Angeles, University of California Press, 1968.
Lustick, Ian, 'Stability in deeply divided societies: consociationalism versus control', *World Politics,* Vol. XXXI, No. 3, 1979.
O'Leary, Brendan, 'The limits to coercive consociationalism in Northern Ireland' *Political Studies* Vol. XXXVII No. 4, 1989 pp. 562–88, 1989.

13   From autonomy to secession: building down

Alexis Heraclides

Old and new states alike have sought security and consolidation both internationally and domestically by political integration. The first avenue of consolidation manifests itself aggressively as well as peacefully. Aggressive policies include intervention, annexation, irredentist policies, colonialism and generally the utilization and execution of threats. Peaceful policies include co-operation, association, alliances with other states, various con-federal or community schemes and unions with other states. Intra-state integration, the second avenue of consolidation, applies primarily, but by no means exclusively, to the newer states of world society and has come to be known nas 'nation building' and, more appropriately, as 'state-building'. The two avenues of consolidation are complementary and interrelated in several ways. Both tendencies are part of the *modus operandi* of states, they are part of the normal expected behaviour of governments. To put it in the language of a discipline concerned with the behaviour of other less assertive creatures, ethology, such policies are 'species specific' to statehood. This crown of normality for behaviour of this kind is not unrelated to the fact that expansion, creation and preservation through integration of constantly larger wholes is deeply ingrained in conventional wisdom. Radically different solutions to security are considered an aberration. This applies to one approach in particular, the process of forming smaller entities or more loosely knit ones, 'building-down' instead of 'building-up'. Such a process is deemed to be neither 'viable' nor 'progressive'. Indeed, like violence and revolution, it is regarded as the immutable sign of crisis, as the mark of failure, as a very last resort if all else has failed.

However, today's world system comprising of more than 170 'sovereign independent states' raises some doubts about the validity of such assumptions. The vast majority of these states are small or even minuscule. This may be the result of haphazard colonialism, archaic treaties, geography or the fiat of cartographers and other mishaps, but what is more baffling is that sheer size is not a good indicator of economic viability nor indeed of political integration. And several noteworthy attempts at 'nation-building' as well as interstate integration (not to mention the several ludicrous attempts at union) have run aground.

But how serious is the reverse of integration — the process of 'disinte-gration' or separatism? Does it warrant a thorough study as a possible alternative avenue of state security and consolidation? Our submission is that it does. Ethnic and communal politics are ubiquitous. Communal assertiveness that has been stifled by governments tends to reassert itself at

times in more extreme forms, such as separatism. Moreover, there are few
recognizable signs that the phenomenon of disintegration is on the retreat
bereft of vitality and purpose, and will soon vanish from the real world. I
nothing else, the phenomenon appears to have acquired the trappings o
modernity and it can no more be regarded as a simple echo of the past
Separatism and more generally communal assertiveness have become
permanent features of today's world.

In the Third World the well-known cases of separatism included the
secessionist movements of the Eritreans in Ethiopia, the Kurds of Iraq, the
Karens of Burma, the Southern Sudanese, and the Moros of the Philip
pines; and the formal secessions of Iranian Azerbaijan, and the Kurdish
Republic of Mahabad in the 1940s, the South Moluccas and Nagaland in
the 1950s, Katanga and Biafra in the 1960s, and Bangladesh in the 1970s
Moreover, the phenomenon continues unabated as new movements spring
up, such as the Tigrinyas and Oromos in Ethiopia, the Kurds of Iran and
Turkey, the West Papuans in Indonesia's West Irian (West New Guinea)
the Sikhs in India, the Tamils of Sri Lanka and the secession of the Turkish
Republic of Northern Cyprus. But even this list does little justice to the
countless lesser-known separatist insurrections, or to the various attempts at
secession *cum* merger, such as Ogaden, Kashmir, the Pattanis of Thailand
and Arakans of Burma and many others. There are also irredentist
independence movements along the model of the Jews in the 1940s, such a
the Palestinians and the Armenians today and the most obscure of cases, the
pan-irredentist movements, those seeking the creation of a state out of two
or more future secessions such as the creation of a Pashtunistan, or of a
state for the Ewe, the Azande, or the Ba-Kongo.

The First World, the developed Western world, has hardly remained
immune to communal resurgence, even in the content of regional integ
ration. There is communal grievance and even separatist tendencies among
the Basques in Spain, the Quebecois in Canada, the Sardinians and
Southern Tyrolese in Italy, and there is communal unrest in Belgium
Northern Ireland and other parts of Britain. Even archetypical nation-state
such as France appear less nationally integrated than they did before (note
the cases of Brittany and Corsica). Not even that celebrated melting-pot, the
United States, where all ethnic groups were to partake uninhibitedly in the
bliss of the 'American dream', has been absolved from the flurry o
communal assertiveness. The 'unmeltable ethnics' persevere and many are
not even prepared to subscribe to the various recurring American dream
such as Manifest Destiny, the New Frontier, the Great Society and othe
rationalizations. And the phenomenon is hardly confined to the 'unruly
Third World or the 'libertarian' First World. It has also been evident in the
Second World, the socialist world, where the so called 'nationality question'
has shown little sign of 'withering away' and bowing to 'the real engine o
history', the class struggle or submerging into the noble goal of 'proletaria
solidarity' and more tangibly, paying homage to the 'vanguard workers
party! In the West the level of communal violence is markedly reduced for a
variety of reasons. There is a higher degree of political integration, effective

means of channelling grievance and redressing inequality, there is peaceful evolutionary change and a far greater ability to enforce law and order. However, the issue has evoked grave concern among most states, developed as well as less developed.

Furthermore, whatever one chooses to call the phenomenon of separatism, subnationalism, ethnonationalism, tribal nationalism, unsatisfied nationalism, resurgent nationalism, ethnic separatism, aspiring nationhood, non-state nationalism, parochial nationalism or simply communalism, it tends to defy the simple criteria of progressive or conservative. In fact the very same movements have shown both qualities at different periods or even during the same period when represented by rival fronts.

Nevertheless, separatism, and more generally communal assertiveness, still remains obscure. The last ten or fifteen years have seen several seminal attempts to understand the phenomenon with cues from several other disciplines of the social sciences. These attempts have not yet resulted in the question becoming part of the mainstream of comparative politics and international relations, but it is by now clear that the question is much more pervasive, complex and intriguing than it was thought to be. The dimensions of the problem are such that it calls for a reassessment of long-standing approaches on integration and state-building with a view to coming to terms, both intellectually and practically, with the phenomenon.

Separatism, or the more negatively value-laden term disintegration, can be defined as the final stage or process whereby one or more units of a state assert themselves and limit (or attempt to limit) or eliminate the scope of the government in a particular region of a state. Separatism can manifest itself as a search for autonomy, various forms of federation, confederation or independence. The independence of a region which constituted part of the metropolitan territory of a state can be achieved through secession or through partition, and in very rare instances through what could be called 'ejection'. With secession there is the unmistakable opposition of the central government which is not prepared to accept the unilaterial decision of its renegade territory, as seen with the secessions of Hyderabad in 1948, the Kurdish Republic of Mahabad in 1945–6, Katanga, Biafra, Nagaland, Bangladesh and others. Ejection has one post-Second World War case to offer, the ejection of Singapore by the Federal Government of Malaysia in 1965. Among partitions we note Iraq from the Arab Union in 1958 (the union of Iraq and Jordan which lasted only a few months), Bahrain and Qatar from what was then called the Federation of Arab Emirates in 1971, Senegal from the Mali Federation in 1960, Syria from the United Arab Republic (UAR) in 1961 and, in a European case, Norway from Sweden in 1905, Iceland from Denmark in 1918, and Finland from Russia in 1919. The borderline between partition and secession can be blurred when there is no mutual consent in the first instance. Thus the independence of Norway, Syria and Senegal were to begin with secessions but developed into partitions as the central government accepted, however reluctantly, the *fait accompli*.

International law, as it has developed in the years after the Second World

War, in no circumstances tolerates secession, or for that matter ejection, as a creative means of statehood and independence. For an entity to be able to seek independence unilaterally, it must be a so-called 'self-determination unit', that is, a colony, protectorate, or the like.[1] This post-war solution is far from intellectually satisfying. Why afford such a right to arbitrarily carved colonial units and not to entities deeming themselves a nation or groups in a situation of flagrant inequality akin to colonialism? Note that the original concept of self-determination was in fact a right of nations to secede. Today there are few signs of any such development in international law, despite the extended debate triggered by the single post-war secessionist war that led to independence — Bangladesh. The main reasons against extending the principle are the spectre of a Pandora's box, the fear of the infinite divisibility of a state which accepts that part of its territory becomes independent, the problem of stranded minorities in the new state and the question of the viability of the new state and of the rump state.[2]

Constitutional law is almost equally as negative as international law, but the issue regarding federal constitutions has not as yet been completely resolved among constitutional lawyers.[3] In fact, three federal constitutions have recognized secessionist self-determination, those of the Union of Burma, the Soviet Union and Yugoslavia. The Burmese Constitution between the years of 1947 to 1974 afforded two of its states such a right but under particularly strict rules of procedure and, not surprisingly, denied such a right to the two states most likely to seek independence, the Karen and the Kachin states. The Constitution of the USSR under its article 72 gives 'the right freely to secede' to 'each Union Republic,' but this article while, until recently thought never likely to be applied and generally regarded as the product of political expediency,[4] rather than a principled judgement inspired by the Leninist approach to self-determination (the liberal Marxist approach in contradistinction to the most orthodox approach of Rosa Luxembourg), has now assumed a new political relevance. Moreover, it is worth noting that, on paper at least (but for how long?), one superpower accepts the legitimacy of secession, while the other, again a federation, does not, and has fought a civil war to quell secession. This appears to have some practical implications as seen by the Soviet Union's more sympathetic stance towards its own internal secessionist movements. Finally, the Yugoslav Constitution qualifies self-determination as 'including secession' in the very beginning of its preamble but in Article 5, paragraph 3 of the operative part, it states unequivocally that any change in the existing state boundaries is possible only with the consent of all six Republics and the autonomous provinces. In other words secession amounts to partition and not to secession as such, i.e. not to a unilaterial act of independence by a constituent unit of the state.

On the whole orthodox legal science tends to treat secession with a mixture of suspicion and contempt, almost universally ostracizing it. Many a separatism movement, realizing that the legal odds are against it, has shunned away from declaring independence outright and has chosen the route of violent or relatively peaceful attempts at autonomy.

With this empirical setting in mind it is time to examine more closely the existing theories of separatism and communal conflict.

Existing theories of disintegration

Disintegration is still largely regarded as 'a crisis rather than a process that may even be desirable'.[5] Explanatory theories of disintegration are fairly recent, the product of little more than the last decade. Two of the better-known approaches are the theory of internal colonialism and that of ethnicity, the two polar opposite models of separatism. A number of other approaches can be placed under the general rubric of theories of communal conflict or communalism.[6]

The problem of internal colonialism, studied by such figures as Lenin and Gramsci and recently by students of Latin America, black ghettos in the United States, and the Palestinians of Israel, was developed more thoroughly by Michael Hechter. According to Hechter, states that are not culturally integrated tend to split into two cultural groups: the 'core', that is the dominant cultural group extending from the political centre of the society outwards, and the 'periphery', those territories largely occupied by the subordinate or peripheral cultural groups. When the division of labour is cultural and when there are economic inequalities between the cultural core and the periphery, the deprived cultural group resists integration and tilts towards separatism.[7] Along the same lines, Krippendorff argues that the essence of all forms of separatism is social discrimination and class stratification which are the outcome of existing social distances.[8] Similarly, Galtung claims that separatism emerges when there is a relation of dominance directed against a group or groups, when this dominance is linked with a specific distinct territory within a state and with a distinct people living in that territory.[9]

The perspective of the ethnicity approach, which is propounded by a rising number of scholars from several social science strongholds, is markedly different. The basis of separatism is ethnicity, that is ethic identity or national identity. Ethnicity, which emanates from the search for a more inclusive ascriptive identity, constitutes the driving-force for group assertiveness and ultimately separatism.[10] Social and economic differences per se create discontent and may incite revolution, but disaffection founded on ethnic symbols such as language, religion, race, origin and culture can lead to separatism and the threat to the territorial integrity of a state.[11] Today, it is argued, distinct communities prefer to be governed poorly by their ethnic brethren instead of by aliens, however justly or compassionately. The latter is worse than oppressive, it is degrading. To put it in Miltonian terms, 'it is better to reign in our Hell than serve in their Heaven.'[12]

The main thrust of theories of communalism are scarcity, conflict of interest, rising aspirations, modernization and the political power of old and new élites. Common to all theories of communalism, which are of varied intellectual origins, including even Marxist versions, is the thesis that communal politics is essentially a modern phenomenon. It constitutes a strategy within a constantly shrinking civic arena, the strategy of 'retribalization' or 'supertribalization'. And it is a highly potent technique for it can combine 'emotional sustenance with calculated strategy',[13] or 'interest with an affective tie'.[14] Under this approach the roots of separatism are to be found in élite disputes over the direction of change and grievances emanating from the scarcity of resources. Separatist activity is imminent when previously acquired privileges are threatened, or when underprivileged groups realize that the moment has come to redress existing inequalities. Middle levels of economic development are more conducive to communal unrest, for at that stage the institutional structures are still communal in scope and thus unable to cope with social mobilization and the need for political participation. The modern state cannot satisfy the aspirations it generates and the distribution of benefits of growth is likely to be uneven or perceived as such.[15]

The process of separatism

The process of separatism can be seen as starting from the development of communal identity nurtured by deprivation and inequality to group demands for recognition and respect *qua* group and from then on to participation and political effectiveness. This is the classic process applicable in the case of the separatism of the underdog, and thus appears to be *prima facie* less relevant to cases of rich territories or relatively privileged groups, such as the Basques in Spain, the Scots or the French Canadians or the secessions of Katanga, Biafra, or Cabinda in Angola. But many such communities were, to begin with, the victims of discrimination or inequality as seen in particular with the case of the French Canadians. Furthermore, this longer process is useful to present for heuristic reasons. Two phases can be discerned in this process. The first is the emergence of a group apart from the power establishment of a state and the mobilization and politicization of that group. The second is the phase of politicized distinctiveness that can, under certain circumstances, develop into active separatism.

Potentially separatist groups are of different kinds. Such is the variety of potentially separatist groups that it is difficult to pin-point them with any decree of accuracy. One is almost tempted to confine oneself to a tautological answer. That is, that potentially separatist groups are all those which can develop into a fully-fledged separatist organization with a mass following. Or to put it more dramatically, all groups that are willing to go through fire and sword to attain their coveted goal of self-rule. Of course such answers beg the question. To begin with, one thing is clear. Whatever the character of a separatist group within a specific political entity, it must erect a fairly permanent boundary between ingroup and outgroup (the outgroup of course being the established authority). Such a boundary is the outcome of the concrete social-historical setting at any given time. A social category (an other-defined group) can develop into a group as a result of its ultimate self-awareness, and it could originate from having been thrust into a category or class because of the division of labour and the attitude towards it, and its treatment at the hands of the outgroup.[16] A plausible theory of how communal groups emerge has been presented in the literature of social psychology. According to Henri Tajfel the incubation process commences with 'social categorization' which then leads to 'social comparison' and finally to 'psychological group distinctiveness'. The result is either a positive or a negative definition of one's identity as a member of a particular group. A negative social definition creates acute intra-psychic conflict (cognitive dissonance) for all want to have a positive self-definition of themselves and of their group. However, changing a negative definition can be a long process for there are several techniques whereby the psychological imbalance can be suppressed without achieving the desirable 'positive group distinctiveness'.[17] Such techniques range from 'happy slave situations' to various elaborate rationalizations that make the negative definition appear as the natural order of things and as such justified (in this category falls the case of Jewish self-hatred that had intrigued Kurt Lewin and other noted social scientists). But in the world of today it has become increasingly difficult to satisfy one's self with psychological alchemy of this kind.

The negative self-definition can become positive through a number of strategies, some more effective than others. These include individual 'passing' to another group (the group with a positive definition); 'group self-effacement', that is merger with the top-dog group; developing a positive definition by rejecting or arriving at the rejection of the validity of the comparison altogether; enhancing the position of the group as a whole. The first and second strategies may in fact not be available due to the policy of the outgroup, or due to race and other physical characteristics that are immediately discernible. But even without such obstacles these two varieties of assimilation may prove inadequate so long as a sizeable portion of ingroup members choose to remain outside this one-sided integration process. The third strategy, rejection of the comparison, amounts to the development of group pride and ethnocentrism of the type, 'we are what we are because they are not what we are'. The fourth strategy, enhancing the position of the ingroup as a whole, involves a process of mobilization and politicization.[18] At that stage, integration (two-way integration, the creation of a nation) may be sought, or various arrangements proposed whereby the group's distinctiveness and separate identity is retained and not threatened. Goals within the latter option include the following: proportional representation, disproportional representation (the consociational model), dominance reversal (role reversal), non-territorial autonomy, territorial autonomy, multiple or dual federation, confederation, and various as yet unrealized forms of semi-independence and independence. The means to achieve these goals vary from essentially peaceful strategies such as those used by the Sikh party, Akali Dal, the Parti Québecois and the Tamil United Liberation Front of Sri Lanka (until 1983), to various degrees of violent confrontation from sporadic terrorist attacks (the Basque ETA, the

Armenian ASALA, the Front de Libération de Bretagne or the Front de Libération de Québec), to extended guerrilla warfare and civil war (Southern Sudanese, Karens, Nagas, Kurds, Eritreans, Moros of the Philippines).

At the second phase of the building-down process, the goals and means as well as the mass following of separatist movements are determined to a great extent by the central government's policy. At the early stages the government can diffuse or accommodate ingroup assertiveness. But as time goes by, and one goal after another is frustrated by the government, with the separatist organization gaining ingroup support, only a dramatic and genuine *volte face* by the incumbent government can arrest the situation from drifting into overt separatist conflict. This new policy should amount to no less than a radical redefinition of the situation on the part of the established authority and a quest for extended and meaningful autonomy or a federal solution to be reached by involving the separatist group in the negotiation process.

The essential elements of separatism

We will now attempt to piece together the various basic elements of separatism and thus provide a model of the etiology of separatism. To begin with three factors appear indispensable. First of all there should exist a distinct community or a society, that is, a self-defined human collectivity which is a numerical minority within a state.[19] Second, there should be an actual or perceived inequality or disadvantage in continuing within the existing state framework. Finally there must exist a strong territorial base, that is, a distinct and integral territory in which the separatist group is in a clear majority. These three factors are independent and necessary variables. Without all three, separatism is inconceivable, indeed nonsensical.

Communities (collectivities with an ascriptive basis of unity) that have historically sought some form of separatism can be distinguished into four categories. First are ethno-nations, based on ethnic identity in its most restrictive sense of communality of language and culture, such as the French Canadians, the Tamils, the Basques, the Kurds and the Bengalis. There are nations (collectivities with a common culture, social communication and cohesion emanating from a long process of history forged on common sacrifice) where the basis of distinctiveness is not linguistic, either because the language is the same as that of the dominant group as is overwhelmingly the case with the Scots, or because there is no overall common language as with the Nagas and the Karens. The are also groups based on religion such as the Sikhs, the Moros, and the Catholics of Northern Ireland. And there are separatist groups based on race, such as the Southern Sudanese, the West Papuans or the Amerindians.

Societies distinct from the society or community in charge of the central apparatus of a state are based on territory, ideology and a differing societal structure from the remaining state. The majority of such distinct societies are the product of separate colonial administration as with Katanga, Eritrea and Eastern Nigeria (if regarded as an all-Eastern movement and not as exclusively Ibo). Others may consist of societies that come to split a nation-state into two, as with the independence movements of the New World and the Confederate States of America.

Inequality or disadvantage manifests itself in two forms in secessionist situations: as total and cumulative, that is, as inequality in all conceivable spheres; and as marginal and relative. A somewhat inbetween case also exists. This is when a group is the most privileged in a state-nation, with the exception of the most dominant group, as with the Tigrinyas of Ethiopia in the provinces of Tigray and Eritrea. Marginal or relative disadvantage exists when there is preponderance in some spheres and not in others. Potential secessionist groups can be better off economically and educationally, but they do not wield great political power, nor is their culture the state's culture, nor a culture of equal stature as the dominant one, or at least one held in high esteem. To date at least, no absolute top-dogs, not even those in a numerical minority, have developed into active secessionists. However secessionist tendencies may come to the fore when the power of a minority is slipping away as was seen with the Baganda of Uganda in the 1960s and may be the case in the near future with the Maronites in Lebanon, the Alawites in Syria and, most dramatically, the Afrikaaners of South Africa.

At this point one can put forward a tentative hypothesis. The more a group can be characterized as an ethnic group or nation, the more secondary is the role played by the factor of inequality or disadvantage in spurring active separatism, or put differently, the lesser the degree of inequality necessary to spawn secession. Conversely, the more a group lacks the trappings of ethnic or national identity, the more decisive is the role of inequality, and the greater the required degree of inequality. Most but not all, separatist movements conform to either of the two variants of this hypothesis.

A strong territorial base (the existence of territorial contiguity), the appearance of a distinct community or society cognizant of its separateness from the group of the centre, and some degree of disadvantage in the existing or future relationship can all develop and achieve political salience within a number of historical settings. They may come to the fore and achieve prominance after the independence of a state, or when an entity was still a colony or simply a territory of an older state or empire. The historical experience and a series of related factors can, under certain conditions, reinforce identity and disadvantage or the territorial base. These facilitating background factors can be distinguished as political, social, economic, psychological and international facilitating factors, or otherwise into structural and actor-orientated reasons. Background factors include, among others, colonialism and colonization, the rise of state intervention in social and economic affairs, modernization and communication, the alienation generated by the modern state, the fulfilment of non-material needs, the 'shrinking of the political arena', the lack of feasible alternative non-regional forms of group action, the international or regional economic system, the existence of a world system comprised mainly of small states and others.

Mobilization and politicization for separatism takes place as interaction with the central government intensifies. The various events prior to and after politicization (the creation of a separatist leadership or political party that is vertical-sectarian in nature) function as precipitants of separatism and consist mainly of the actions, reactions or inactions of the central authority, or actions attributable to that authority. The actual decision to resort to armed separatism or to secession may be the result of considerations of feasibility, though in practice it has often been the case that regions or groups are left with little choice but to resort to armed violence. As we have noted earlier the process to separatism can be halted only if the central government is prepared to concede extended self-rule and power-sharing to the region or group in question

Political integration, one of the classical modes of security and consolidation is increasingly less of a realizable goal in its narrow sense as 'national' integration, the creation of a nation-state from above. Its more crude version, 'smite to unite', a concept which has its supporters among many an established authority, is becoming impractical and runs counter to the very essence of integration and 'political community'. Few communities today are prepared to lose their cultural identity or regard themselves as denied of culture because many state authorities refuse to recognize them. More and more are prepared to take extreme risks and even resort to an armed struggle to retain and defend their cherished group identity, which is inexorably bound to their sense of worth and dignity. Under this light, disintegration or separatism, the antithesis of integration, can be regarded as a building process, a 'building-down' process as it were, rather than as a disruptive, retrogressive and dysfunctional exercise. It can be seen as the process that pushes regions further apart in order to allow them to survive as distinct communities or societies, whereas integration would have meant for them, as well as for the core group of a state, perennial conflict and mutual destruction. The various forms of separatism, from autonomy to secession (or partition), can in the short run create more harmonious and participatory societies and in the longer term pave the way for increased functional transactions across communities and states, transactions that will overlay psychological boundaries, eroding the seeds of conflict, but not threatening the coveted group identity of each unit. Only then can a lasting legitimized relationship be forged if it is clear that classical integration is unworkable.

Notes

1. Lee C. Buchheit, *Secession: The Legitimacy of Self-Determination*, New Haven, Yale University Press, 1977; James Crawford, *The Creation of States in International Law*, Oxford, Clarendon Press, 1979; Rupert Emerson, 'Self-determination', *American Journal of International Law*, 65 (1971), pp. 459-75; Hector Gross Espiell, *The Right to Self-Determination: implementation of the*

United Nations resolutions, New York, United Nations, 1980; Hakan Wiberg, 'Self-determination as an international issue', in I.M. Lewis (ed.), *Nationalism and Self Determination in the Horn of Africa*, London, Ithaca Press, 1983, pp. 29–51.

2. Buchheit, op. cit., pp. 20–30, 216–49; Charles R. Beitz, *Political Theory and International Relations*, Princeton, Princeton University Press, 1979, pp. 92–105.

3. Paul Taylor, *The Limits of European Integration*, London, Croom Helm, 1983, pp. 269–75.

4. Joseph Silverstein, 'Politics in the Shan State: the question of secession from the Union of Burma', *Journal of Asian Studies*, 18 (1958), pp. 43–57; Buchheit, op. cit., pp. 100–2, 121–7.

5. Johan Galtung, *The True Worlds: a transnational perspective*, New York, The Free Press, 1980, p. 260.

6. Crawford Young in a review of the literature on ethnicity distinguished two main currents, the 'instrumentalist' and the 'primordialist' camps. Under the first he subsumes both internal colonialism and the theories of communalism. See Crawford Young, 'The temple of ethnicity', *World Politics*, 35, No 4 (July 1983), p. 660.

7. Michael Hechter, *Internal Colonialism: the Celtic fringe in the British National Development, 1536–1966*, London, Routledge & Kegan Paul, 1975, pp. 9, 39–43.

8. Ekkehart Krippendorff, 'Minorities, violence, and peace research', *Journal of Peace Research*, 16, No. 1 (1979), pp. 27–40.

9. Johan Galtung, op. cit., pp. 257–63.

10. Nathan Glazer and Daniel P. Moynihan, 'Introduction', in Nathan Glazer and Daniel P. Moynihan (eds), *Ethnicity*, Cambridge, Mass., Harvard University Press, 1975, pp. 1–26; Cynthia H. Enloe, *Ethnic Conflict and Political Development*, Boston, Little, Brown, 1973; pp. 319–55, Walker Connor, 'Ethnonationalism in the First World', in Milton J. Esman (ed.), *Ethnic Conflict in the Western World*, Ithaca, Cornell University Press, 1977, pp. 19–45; Donald L. Horowitz, *Ethnic Groups in Conflict*, Berkeley, University of California Press 1985; Harold R. Isaacs, 'Basic group identity: the idols of the tribe', *Ethnicity*, 1 (April 1974), pp. 15–41; Daniel Bell, 'Ethnicity and social change', in Glazer and Moynihan (eds), op. cit., pp. 141–74; Leo Kuper, *Race, Class and Power*, London, Duckworth, 1974; Pierre L. van den Berghe, 'Ethnic pluralism in industrial societies: a special case?', *Ethnicity*, 3, No. 3 (1976), pp. 242–55; Anthony D. Smith, *The Ethnic Revival*, Cambridge, Cambridge University Press, 1981; Joseph Rothschild, *Ethnopolitics: a conceptual framework*, New York, Columbia University Press, 1981. For further reading consult the bibliography in A.J.R. Groom and Alexis Heraclides, 'Integration and disintegration', in Margot Light and A.J.R. Groom (eds), *International Relations: a handbook of current theory*, London, Frances Pinter, 1985, pp. 183–6; C. Young, op. cit., pp. 652–62.

11. Clifford Geertz, 'The integrative revolution: primordial sentiments and civic politics in the new states', in C.E. Welch (ed.), *Political Modernization*, Belmont, Calif.: Wadsworth, 1967, p. 170.

12. Rothschild, op. cit., pp. 14–15; Buchheit, op. cit., p. 8.

13. Rothschild, op. cit., p. 61.

14. Daniel Bell, op. cit., p. 169.

15. Immanuel Wallerstein, 'Ethnicity and National Integration in West Africa', in

Pierre L.van den Berghe (ed.), *Africa: social problems of change and conflict*, San Francisco, Chandler, 1965, pp. 472–82; Immanuel Wallerstein, 'The two models of ethnic consciousness: Soviet Central Asia in transition', in Edward Allworth (ed.), *The Nationality Question in Soviet Central Asia*, New York, Praeger, 1973, pp. 168–75. Samuel P. Huntington, 'Civil violence and the process of development', *Adelphi Papers*, no. 83 (December 1971), pp. 1–15; Robert Melson and Howard Wolpe (eds), *Nigeria: modernization and the politics of communalism*, East Lansing, Michigan State University Press, 1971, pp. 1–42; Milton J. Esman, 'The management of communal conflict', *Public Policy*, 21, No. 1 (Winter 1973), pp. 49–78; Milton J. Esman, 'Perspectives on ethnic conflict in industrialized societies', in Esman (ed.), op. cit., pp. 371–90.

16. Tamotsu Shibutani and Kian M. Kwan, *Ethnic Stratification: a Comparative Approach*, New York, Macmillan, 1965, p. 223; Muzafer Sherif, *Group Conflict and Cooperation*, London, Routledge & Kegan Paul, 1966, pp. 1, 12; Paul Mercier, 'On the meaning of tribalism in black Africa', in Pierre L. van den Berghe (ed.), *Africa*, op. cit., pp. 483–501; Fredrik Barth, 'Introduction', in Fredrik Barth (ed.), *Ethnic Groups and Boundaries*, Boston, Little, Brown, 1969, pp. 9–38; Wallerstein, 1965, op. cit., pp. 472–7; Wallerstein, 1973, op. cit., pp. 168–72.

17. Henri Tajfel, *The Social Psychology of Minorities*, Minority Rights Group, Report No. 38, 1978; Henri Tajfel, 'Social categorization, social identity and social comparison', in Henri Tajfel (ed.), *Differentiation between Social Groups*, London, Academic Press, 1978, pp. 61–7; J. Turner and R. Brown, 'Social status, cognitive alternatives and intergroup relations', in Tajfel (ed.), op. cit., pp. 203–7.

18. Tajfel, in Minority Rights Group Report, op. cit., pp. 9–14; Horowitz, in Jackson and Stein (eds), op. cit., pp. 169–70.

19. The only exception to this rule is the case of East Pakistan, whose population was somewhat larger than that of West Pakistan. With the one thousand mile distance between the two wings of Pakistan the East Pakistanis would have not been able to control the West. Furthermore a large segment of the Eastern Pakistanis, the sizeable minority of the Biharis, were apparently not separatist.

Selected reading

Banton, Michael, *Racial and Ethnic Competition*, Ithaca, Cornell University Press, 1983.

Esman, Milton J. (ed.), *Ethnic Conflict in the Western World*, Ithaca, Cornell University Press, 1977.

Glazer, Nathan and Daniel P. Moynihan (eds), *Ethnicity: theory and experience*, Cambridge, Mass., Harvard University Press, 1975.

Horowitz, Donald L., *Ethnic Groups in Conflict*, Berkeley, University of California Press, 1985.

Rothschild, Joseph, *Ethnopolitics: a conceptual framework*, New York, Columbia University Press, 1981.

Smith, Anthony D., *The Ethnic Revival*, Cambridge, Cambridge University Press, 1981.

Tajfel, Henri, *The Social Psychology of Minorities*, Minority Rights Group, Report
  no. 38, London, 1978.
Young, Crawford, *The Politics of Cultural Pluralism*, Madison, University of
  Wisconsin Press, 1976.

Part IV

Transcending the State?
Theories of emergent world systems

14 Regimes and international co-operation
Roger Tooze

In the past fifteen years much has been written about the nature and content of 'regimes' in international relations and the importance of 'regimes' for the process of international co-operation in a world characterized by high levels of interdependence. This chapter will explore the nature of the 'regime' concept and look at its implications for the analysis of international co-oeration in its broadest sense. We shall seek to identify and evaluate the strengths and weaknesses of 'regime analysis' as a 'useful' conceptual framework and we shall suggest certain areas of further investigation and development. For this chapter, then, the central question is: what, if anything, does the study of 'regimes' add to our understanding of international co-operation in an interdependent world? Our conclusions on this question will partly reflect the fundamental political question we should direct at the literature on 'regimes': do 'regimes' matter?

As with any concept used to analyse international relations and international co-operation, 'regime' brings with it a range of assumptions about the world and about how we gain understanding of that world. Accordingly, the definition of 'regime' and the extension of the concept into a framework for understanding and explaining international co-operation is not simply a matter of developing (either from the existing literature or in an empirical sense) an 'objective', inclusive definition that reflects a given empirical reality; it must involve an evaluation of the competing theories and approaches that constitute that reality in different ways. This is necessary because 'the way we perceive reality is linked to the way we think about reality through the concepts we use'.[1] Hence, when we use the concept of 'regime' to describe and explain international co-operation 'between states' or 'beyond the state', we contemplate the reality of international relations in a different way.

However, using a 'new' concept such as 'regime' to think about reality does not *necessarily* mean that the reality of international relations has changed in any substantive or material way, and therefore that as a result we need new or different concepts to capture that change. It may be that through using 'regime' we could recast and reinterpret the process of international co-operation throughout history to give an understanding of a feature that may be inherent in the process itself and which has not just 'emerged' in the last few years. Whatever the case, we need to be aware that concepts do not arise and are not developed in a vacuum — they are not pure intellectual responses to pure intellectual deficiencies in existing frameworks. Concepts such as 'regime' have purpose and meaning that go beyond the immediate function of identifying and defining particular aspects of international co-operation, and it is therefore necessary for us to investigate this wider purpose. As Robert Cox has pointed out in a discussion of international relations (IR) theory which is central to the argument used here,

There is . . . no such thing as theory in itself, divorced from a standpoint in time and space. When any theory so represents itself, it is the more important to examine it as ideology, and to lay bare its concealed perspective.[2]

Because of the problematic nature of the meaning of 'regime', and given that we need to start somewhere, let us initially use a simple notion of 'regime' that, although reflecting certain values and interests, can if necessary be modified later in the chapter: regimes are

the rules and procedures that define the limits of acceptable behavior on various issues.. . . [They] often include formal organizations, but are not limited to them. Regimes are institutions in a broader sense: recognized patterns of practice that define the rules of the game.[3]

This notion immediately identifies a focus on rules and norms in explaining outcomes in international co-operation — a focus that is far removed from an analysis of international relations based on concepts of power and anarchy. It also allows the possibility that many different entities can be the subjects of these 'rules and procedures' and not just states. For example, outcomes in 'international' co-operation may be influenced by rules and norms that exist among subnational, transnational or transgovernmental groups.

From a synthesis of the literature, whose authors are mainly American, the initial and central core of the 'regime' argument is reasonably clear, whatever the particular definition we deploy: in conditions of international interdependence characterized by complex relations (multiple channels, multiple issues and the irrelevance of military power) and the consequent breakdown of the traditional distinction between international and domestic politics,[4] the assumption that international relations are characterized by anarchy is no longer appropriate (if it ever was). The traditional exercise of power and diplomacy is for most purposes either irrelevant or counter-productive. What has taken the place of anarchy is some form of international authority. The existence of authority is demonstrated by adherence to 'sets of implicit or explicit principles, norms, rules and decision-making procedures around which actors' expectations converge in a given area of international relations'; that is, adherence to regimes, as identified in this 'consensus' definition by Stephen Krasner.[5] It is claimed that 'the formation and transformation of international regimes may be said to represent a concrete manifestation of the internationalization of political authority.'[6]

In this argument the path of causation, and hence the logic of explanation, is relatively straightforward. High levels of interdependence are assumed to change the nature of the international system and in these changed conditions alternative (i.e. non-anarchical) structures and policy instruments are deemed necessary for groups (including states) to achieve their objectives in the system. 'Managing' interdependence thus requires instruments and structures that go beyond conventional diplomacy and formal international organizations to encompass rule and norm governed 'social' behaviour which legitimizes certain activities and, perhaps more importantly, delegitimizes other activities. (One good example is the regime for international trade which clearly legitimizes certain state practices leading towards 'free' trade but treats trade protection as a 'disease'.) These 'new' structures can be dependent on the power of a dominant state (giving rise to the sometimes simplistic theory of hegemonic stability[7] or be the product of a negotiated consensus among the relevant political entities ('after hegemony'). For regime theorists, whatever the underlying configuration of power, the processes of 'regime' formation, maintenance and change thus become the major features of international co-operation.[8]

The above synthetic argument represents the minimal claim of 'regime' analysis. Many authors may disagree with the precise emphasis in the explanation but, as with most attempts to explain international relations, once we investigate in more detail we find a wide range of definitions and analyses and a variety of assumptions that underpin the explanations offered. As a consequence we find a diverse literature that at times is not always clear and contains a number of competing claims and explanations. This, of course, is in one sense a healthy sign of a disputed concept but it makes the interpretation and use of regime theory more problematic because we need to be clear exactly which of the many varieties of regime theory we are using and upon what assumptions it is based. In addition, our task is made more complex because regime analysis has been developed rapidly (in academic terms) and, *within a particular range of assumptions*, the latest literature is more sophisticated than that produced in the earlier stages of the development of the analysis. Before we can evaluate the claims of regime analysis, we therefore need to review, albeit rather briefly, what these claims are and how they are articulated.

Regime theories and international co-operation

Although all theories of international regimes are based on the concept of regime, this has a number of definitions and the theories use several kinds of explanation. To expedite our review I shall use the analysis of 'theories of international regimes' developed by Stephan Haggard and Beth A. Simmons. This provides a broad overview of the varieties of regime analysis which is useful as an evaluation from within the regime literature itself.[9] As will be suggested later I think a different and broader evaluation is necessary, but this does not invalidate the use of the Haggard and Simmons categories for our purposes here.

First, we can identify three clusters of definitions of regime through a spectrum of the very broad and all-inclusive to the relatively restricted. The broadest 'equates regimes with patterned behavior'. Haggard and Simmons quote Puchala and Hopkins as an example of this comprehensive use: 'a regime exists in every substantive issue-area in international relations. . . Wherever there is regularity in behavior, some kinds of principles, norms or rules must exist to account for it.'[10] They rightly conclude that this use does not take us very far, partly because the existence of patterned behaviour does not necessarily denote a regime and partly because the concept is tautological (all co-operation will be *defined* as regime-based), and note that it has now been largely abandoned. The 'middle ground' definition is that of Stephen Krasner, as used earlier in the chapter: regimes are 'sets of implicit or explicit principles, norms, rules and decision-making procedures around which actors' expectations converge in a given area of international relations'.[11] This definition emphasizes the normative aspects of international co-operation and carefully specifies each component. However, the application of this definition has generated much academic disagreement. 'Norms' and 'principles' are themselves very difficult to define and how can we measure the degree of commitment necessary before a regime is said to exist? Haggard and Simmons clearly show the problems here, particularly with the notion of an 'implicit regime', and their argument implies that this 'middle' definition, although potentially useful, does not in application lead to enhanced understanding. This is a view that seems to me well justified.

The third definition 'treats regimes as multilateral agreements among states which aim to regulate national actions within an issue area'.[12] Haggard and Simmons see this definition as being the most useful at present, partly because in this definition it is clear what regimes do and do not do: they 'define the range of permissible state action by outlining *explicit* injunctions' (emphasis in original).[13] Here, this definition and use of regime may be thought as too formal in that it only focuses on formal international agreements, but Haggard and Simmons do not seem to see this as a problem, principally because of their particular view of international relations (see the next section of the chapter). However, what this definition does allow is a clear understanding of regime in this context, namely 'Regimes are *examples of cooperative behavior, and facilitate* cooperation, but cooperation can take place in the absence of established regimes' (emphasis in original).[14] This distinction is important for us as it establishes 'regimes' as a subset of international co-operation. Further, this conception enables us to distinguish regime from institution, as 'Regimes aid the "institutionalization" of portions of international life by regularizing expectations, but some international institutions such as the balance of power are not bound to explicit rights and rules'.[15] The third definition of regime is clearly more 'usable' in analysis of international co-operation than the first and second, yet it is open to a number of fundamental criticisms. These will be considered in the next section of the chapter.

Second, the three definitions have been used in four 'families' of theory to explain regimes in the processes of international relations and international co-operation. These families are structural, game-theoretic, functional and 'cognitive'. As Haggard and Simmon suggest, these approaches are not mutually exclusive but 'often speak past one another' because of their different assumptions and their different foci. They each have a particular view of the nature and explanation of international co-operation:

1. Structural explanations locate co-operation within international conditions which define possibilities and limits.

2. Game-theoretic explanations focus on the rational preferences of the state actors, emphasizing the 'interstate game' as the constraining and enabling structure.

3. Functional explanations also assume rational actors but allow for greater uncertainty and complexity in the world political economy.

4. 'Cognitive' explanations (as labelled by Haggard and Simmons) take on a very different perspective and focus on the intersubjective meanings and ideological structures that form the basis of international co-operation.

Each of these gives a different explanation and each has strengths and weaknesses, some of which are common. My own view is that regime analysis will not achieve its objectives until the 'cognitive' explanations are developed much further, but this may need a major change in the way that IR and international co-operation are understood in the United States.

Structural explanations cluster around the theory of hegemonic stability which 'links regime creation and maintenance to a dominant power's existence and the weakening of regimes to a waning hegemon'.[16] Specifically, hegemonic stability is claimed to be necessary to maintain the 'liberal' international economic order created after 1945, although Keohane argues that the liberal order is being maintained by a consensual, negotiated regime resulting from self-interests.[17] In this theory the existence, nature and processes of international co-operation must be explained in the broader context of the structure of power for the system as a whole. As such, the theory is open to the evaluation and criticisms to which all structural explanations are subject: what defines the structure, and how is the structure translated into outcomes? Haggard and Simmons offer an excellent detailed review of the pros and cons of hegemonic stability, and indicate that the answers to the two questions posed above are far from clear.

Game-theoretic explanations attempt to 'explain how co-operation can evolve under anarchic conditions which lack supranational authority to enforce compliance'. Here, game theory does not specify regime-based co-operation but any form of international co-operation. What it can do is to 'explain the conditions under which regimes might arise' and also 'suggest the conditions conducive to stable compliance'.[18] However, whilst game theory is attractive because of its clarity and procedures (and the promise of its predictions), it tends to oversimplify the complexity of international co-operation. The preferences of actors, even assuming the validity of the idea of a 'unified state actor', are not easily specified. Moreover the 'international game' is not always the relevant game being played: domestic considerations often have a far greater impact on preferences than the structural factors of anarchy.

Functional explanations of regimes emphasize the effects of regimes: 'If regimes serve to reduce information and transaction costs among their adherents . . . the rewards of compliance will *reinforce* the regime.. . . Similarly, the modification of regimes or their weakening is likely to occur when they become "dysfunctional".' In addition, and importantly, functional theories attempt to explain regime strength, 'particularly the puzzle of why compliance with regimes tends to persist even when the structural conditions that initially gave rise to them change'.[19] Hence these theories would explain the demand for a regime and why some regimes remain, but have a difficult job in going beyond this. As Haggard and Simmons rightly suggest:

The proper test of a functional theory is not the mere existence of a regime, but the demonstration that actors' behavior was motivated by benefits provided uniquely, or at least more efficiently, through the regime, or by reputational concerns connected to the existence of rules.[20]

Here the underlying assumptions of all functional explanations, and not just regime explanations, are exposed: just because a regime exists does not mean that it necessarily fulfils a general need, usually articulated in the notion of global welfare. Regimes can quite easily be used as instruments of hegemony and control and one of the consequences of the use of functional analysis in this way is to legitimize the regime through the assumption of liberal pluralism contained in functional theories of regimes.

Finally, 'cognitive' explanations of regime suggest that 'cooperation cannot be completely explained without reference to ideology, the values of actors, the beliefs they hold about the interdependence of issues, and the knowledge available to them about how they can realize specific goals'.[21] This means that 'cognitive' theories stress learning and experience and hence are dynamic in a way that the other three theories are not. In one sense, the 'cognitive' theory of international co-operation is a direct critique of structural approaches because the structuralists demand that different entities respond similarly to the same opportunities and constraints provided by the structure. 'Cognitive' theory argues that this is a fallacy and that much depends on the past experiences of the entities involved, the levels of knowledge they have and the nature of understanding between them. This approach to regimes makes no claim to predict the occurrence of regimes, principally because prediction itself is regarded as neither possible nor desirable by many of the 'cognitive' theorists. What it does is to identify the important processes of co-operation within regimes, particularly the role of consensual knowledge. However, like the other theories, it has at present fundamental weaknesses: how do power and ideas interact? What consensual knowledge drives international co-operation in what issues?

From our review of the definitions of regime and the categories of regime theory we are now in a position to evaluate the various claims made in this literature. The first step of our evaluation is to locate the literature within its broad political, social and economic context.

The aetiology of regime analysis

The development and application of the concept of regime and theories of regime can be explained in two ways, reflecting different notions of 'how we know what we know'. The first, which is the notion contained within much of the regime literature itself (except for some of the 'cognitive' theories),[22] is that the reality of the world political economy has changed and that the concept of regime accurately and objectively identifies these changes. Here, the process of developing a 'new' analysis based on regime is part of a broader intellectual endeavour which produces an objective explanation of co-operation in the world political economy. Regime theory can thus be tested against the reality of the changes and modified and further developed as and when necessary. This is the process that is carried out in much of the American literature and is explicitly demonstrated in Keohane and Nye's *Power and Interdependence* and later in Keohane's *After Hegemony*.[23] The second notion, which I referred to in the introduction, denies the possibility of such an objective explanation and an objective concept of regime. This second epistemology locates the development of regime analysis (and indeed all 'academic' analysis) within the broad framework of the social production of knowledge. Here, the concept of regime is not divorced from the political and economic context in which it is developed.[24] Hence, even though regime and regime theory may actually reflect a changed reality of international co-operation, the regime concept must be understood in a broader sense which takes into account the interests of those who articulate regime theory and the way that the use of regime theory itself changes and redefines the nature and understanding of international co-operation and international relations.[25] After all, the kind of changes and phenomena that are identified and explained by the concept of regime may more accurately, or just as adequately, be captured by another concept or approach. Here, for example, the 'world society' approach of John Burton and others or Gramsci's core concept of 'hegemony' and the derived notion of 'international civil society' offer rich potential for alternative explanations because each allows for the existence and importance of norm-governed behaviour *as part of a wider explanation of international relations*.[26] We need then also to explain *why* regime analysis is so prevalent in the contemporary literature on international co-operation.

The vast majority of writing on regimes is American in origin and most of the references in this writing are American also. This may be simply a reflection of the fact that most of the literature of IR and international co-operation is produced in the United States. However, the result is that the development of the concept of regime and regime theory and its application is bounded by a strong intellectual and academic ethnocentrism and a particular American conception of the structure of the world. This academic ethnocentrism means that the articulation of regime and regime theory takes place within a relatively narrow, mainly American-based literature with little regard for other forms and sources of analysis (although this may be slowly changing now). This tendency is not confined to regime analysis but is characteristic of much of the American study of international relations.[27] Within the regime literature itself the first analysis of the need for such a concept as regime to understand international co-operation is generally credited to John Ruggie writing in 1975.[28] In the fifteen years since then, regime analysis has proliferated and has produced some interesting work, but generally still seems bounded by an emphatic ethnocentrism and a firm commitment to state-centric analytical frameworks. Perhaps these limitations would not matter if regime analysis had produced from within this framework broadly acceptable explanations of international co-operation, or elements of international co-operation. But it has clearly failed to do this, as evinced by Haggard and Simmons' own discussion and conclusions,[29] and, more importantly, by Susan Strange's still relevant trenchant critique of regime analysis, first published in 1982.[30]

If we consider regime analysis as a purely intellectual response to the growing complexities of the world political economy (that is, we use the first of the epistemologies outlined above), its origins and development appear fairly straightforward. Here, the genesis of regime analysis within the dominant intellectual traditions of realism and idealism comes from two dissatisfactions: one is the inability of realist conceptions to generate understanding of the complexities of interdependence and the other is the inability of studies of formal international organizations to explain 'new' forms of international co-operation. The result is the attempt to focus on the 'institutionalized' international behaviour that lies between the two traditions. This point is summarized by Haggard and Simmons, in the following way:

Regime analysts assumed that patterns of state action are influenced by norms, but that such norm-governed behavior was wholly consistent with the pursuit of national interest. Hence, the regimes literature can be viewed as an *experiment in reconciling the idealist and realist traditions*.[31] (emphasis added)

It is clear from this statement that the reconciliation of the two traditions has been a selective process that, right from the start, has emphasized the state as the key actor and the instrumentality of regimes for state interest. In this sense regimes are extensions of foreign (economic) policy for states. Regimes do indeed take aspects of international society from idealism, particularly the importance of norm-governed behaviour, but tend to do so in a selective way that constructs international society as made up solely of state forms. One of the important elements of idealism as a tradition of thought in IR was that it allowed the possibility of a multiplicity of significant actors in international relations and not just the state.

The combination of the selective 'reconciliation' of the two approaches to international co-operation and the inherent ethnocentrism of the American study of international relations has produced (with notable partial exceptions[32]) a framework for analysis that assumes a state-based process of regime formation and maintenance within a state-based world political economy according to a state-based agenda and a state-based hierarchy of issues. Not only has regime analysis ignored the contribution of non-state based frameworks such as Burton's 'world society' analysis but regime analysts, including Keohane and Nye themselves, have dismissed much of the earlier work done on interdependence and transnationalism. It is salutary to note that the conclusions reached by Haggard and Simmons from their critique of regime theories carries out in 1987 are very similar to those reached by John Burton fifteen years previously:

the study of world society is not one that is separate from the study of different societies that comprise world society. Any separation between municipal politics and international politics is an artificial and probably a misleading one.. . . We can understand world society only by examining all relationships, not just those that take place between governments.[33]

It is precisely the consequence of locating regime analysis within a state-centric framework that Haggard and Simmons attack, but although their critique identifies a major weakness of regime theory for explaining international co-operation, it does not go far enough. Even if regime analysts do now consider 'domestic' levels of politics (as Burton also suggests), the conception of the world political economy that is held is still one that does not reflect the dynamism and complexity of contemporary developments. *If* the concept of regime does indeed reflect the reality of international co-operation today, then why does it have to be based on a state-centred reality? It is not possible to envisage a multiplicity of entities, intra-national, international and transnational, each having an interest in creating new regimes and maintaining or modifying existing regimes? And could these interests not be translated into power within regimes? Moving away from a state-centric view highlights the degree to which regime analysis is prone to exaggerate the extent of regime consensus. As Susan Strange pointed out, 'the reality is that there are more areas and issues of nonagreement and controversy than there are areas of agreement.'[34]

The possible importance of 'domestic' groups in understanding international co-operation through regimes is not limited to these groups having 'regime interests', namely, that they perceive their interests to be linked to or dependent on a particular state-based regime. Once we accept the potential significance of 'non-state actors' within regime theory, then we also of logical necessity need to accept the redefinition of the basis of international co-operation in a world political economy which is structured by a variety of forces and entities, and not just states and state policies. If regimes are to be useful in an analysis of international co-operation, can we not identify transnational and 'private' regimes that establish significant norm-governed behaviour at levels other than the inter-state? The process of international co-operation must reflect the increasing complexity of world structures, and any theory of regimes, as a particular form of international co-operation, must also reflect these developments. One of the central insights that comes from understanding the process of the internationalization of production and services is that sectors of the 'domestic' economy of a state become integrated into the world economy directly, without necessarily having the state as a mediating or intervening structure. Consequently the interests of groups or individuals that are part of the world economy can be different from the interests of those who are still part of a national political economy and may require a different regime or different rules. A clear example of this difference is the question of 'protectionism', where purely nationally based production would argue a different case from that of a national sector of an internationalized business. Hence a regime which would suit the interests of 'national' production would not necessarily suit the interests of 'international' production.

Explaining regime theory in the way we have done in the above paragraphs gives a 'one-dimensional' view and evaluation of the concept. We can explain that the development of regime analysis has been skewed by the adoption of a particular model of world politics and by a particular conception of the use of regimes, both buttressed by a strong resistance to take account of writings from outside of the United States. We can then point out the implications of this for our understanding of international co-operation and can suggest alternative frameworks or more highly specified definitions. These alternatives or wider conceptions will then be 'tested' against the reality of co-operation in the world political economy. However, the testing of our suggested alternatives and 'improvements' will hit the same kind of problems that we have already found in the regimes literature so far, unless we add to our evaluation by explaining the development of regime analysis using the second of our two notions of 'how we know what we know'. This locates regime analysis within its broad political and social context and links theory to interest and ideology.

In an article concerned with analysing the 'social science' of the American study of international relations Stanley Hoffmann considers the range of factors that have influenced the development of international relations in the United States. The factors that he identifies are all relevant to an understanding of the emergence of regime analysis: the peculiarly American 'operational paradigm' of intellectual understanding leading directly to progress; the status of science and technology within American ideology; the desire of scholars to be useful and 'help promote intelligently the embattled [economic] values of [their] country'; the political pre-eminence of the United States which enables its 'scholarly community' to look at global phenomena and a number of specific institutional factors.[35] Each of these factors helps to explain why the concept of regime was seized upon and how it was applied. In addition, Hoffmann discusses the link between the perceived needs of government (for policy advice, for general explanations and for legitimations and justifications) and the 'intellectual production' of scholars. He describes this link in the context of the emergence of international political economy:

the literature on the politics of international economic relations . . . coincides with what could be called the post-Vietnam aversion for force, and with the surge of economic issues to the top of the diplomatic agenda. . . . Once more, the priorities of research and those of policy-making blend.[36]

Extending Hoffmann's argument we can identify a 'coincidence' between the emergence of regime analysis, as part of the understanding of international co-operation in a complex world political economy, and the changed reality and perception of American power in that world political economy. Regime analysis emerges at the time when the world economy is becoming much more difficult to 'manage' through the mechanisms and power structures initially set up after 1945. The changes occur partly because of the changed distribution of political and economic power within the system, particularly the reality and perception of the change in American power, and partly because the world economy has by this time become much more complex in its structures and processes. These developments are further complicated by the actions of President Nixon in 1971, OPEC in 1973, a temporary worsening of relations between the United States and Europe in 1974 and a world economic recession in 1974–5. As a result US policy-makers were forced to rethink the process of international co-operation as the 'old certainties' and mechanisms of American leadership could no longer be relied upon to produce outcomes that were supportive of American interests. The development of the regime concept was, in this interpretation, not just a 'coincidence' but clearly reflected the needs and goals of American policy. This is not to say that 'regime' is a deliberate attempt at intellectual conspiracy or a conscious articulation of interest by regime theorists. Nor is it to say that individual intellectual and personal values are not important in the development of the theory of international co-operation. But it is to say that regime analysis allows for the continued articulation of interest by a dominant political and economic power. In other words, the concept of regime and its widespread adoption not only changes the way that we think about international co-operation, but also enables and legitimizes a continuation of American power within the 'new' regime framework.

This second interpretation enables us to think about the implications of the *use* of regime analysis. If we accept that 'regime' is not politically neutral, then it is possible to see the emphasis on regimes in both academic analysis and actual international negotiation and co-operation as part of 'the process of institutionalization of hegemony'.[37] This process rests upon the continued general acceptance of the values underlying the structure of the world political economy. If these values are accepted, they provide the framework for international co-operation and in effect mean that issues of international co-operation within regimes are considered as 'technical' non-political matters, requiring 'technical' solutions.[38] The evident 'liberal' content of much regime theory, particularly in its emphasis on global or collective welfare, indicates the assumption of a liberal-pluralist framework which denies the existence of any major forms of asymmetry and inequality in the world. If we also accept Susan Strange's criticism that regime analysis is biased towards the maintenance of 'order' as opposed to justice, legitimacy or efficiency, we can conclude that the 'order' being maintained through regimes is one supportive of American interests. The question then becomes: how far do American interests reflect the interests of other groups or the interests of the system as a whole?

'Regimes' as frameworks for international co-operation

From our considerations of theories of regimes we can now come to some conclusions regarding the value of the concept of regime, and the way it has been extended, for an understanding of international co-operation. First, we need to confront the question of whether regimes are or are not the 'institutionalization of hegemony'. If they are, the prime purpose of regimes is to maintain and extend the power of the hegemonic state. Other groups *may* benefit from 'hegemonic' regimes only to the extent that the interests of the hegemon overlap with other group interests. However, even if the 'hegemonic' interpretation is accepted this does not mean that current regimes are always hegemonic, as 'international institutions may also become vehicles for the articulation of a coherent counter-hegemonic set of values' and 'they may become mediators between one world order and another.'[39] Making a decision about this question ultimately goes back to your own way of understanding international co-operation and the philosophical basis of that understanding and there is no 'objective' way of providing either analysis. My view is that we can only understand regimes (and international co-operation) within the context of the prevailing structure of power, and I should initially see all regimes as extensions of that structure.

Second, and assuming a satisfactory resolution of the above question, do 'regimes' add to our understanding of international co-operation in an interdependent world? The answer to this is again dependent upon a wide range of factors. From the argument presented in this chapter it is possible to conclude that yes, regimes *do* add to our understanding, but not by as much as the majority of the regime theorists claim. Generally, the assumptions incorporated into regime theory make some of the broader claims of the theory very questionable and we have to treat them with great caution. But regime analysis *as it is currently articulated* may give us a specific gain in understanding in particular circumstances. One of the best applications of regime analysis is that developed by John Vogler in the latest Open University course in Global Politics.[40] He focuses on the problem of Regimes and the politics of Space Technology and produces a well-argued, thoughtful and sceptical analysis using regime theory. In my view he succinctly demonstrates the most appropriate use of regime analysis and that is to analyse a specific and clearly defined regime. He grapples with the problem of deciding whether or not a regime exists and what conditions give rise to regimes, using a very interesting classification scheme initially developed for the study of human rights.[41] His conclusions are important for this discussion. They are tentative but none the less significant: 'technological change leads to extensive co-operation in terms of the formation of a strong and valued regime in so far as it creates conditions of interdependence defined in terms of mutual vulnerability.'[42] If generally valid this conclusion provides a clearly defined set of conditions for the operation of regimes. However, the conclusion may have to be modified because in this analysis Vogler does not consider the broader problems of 'hegemonic' regimes.

A subsidiary but no less important question is whether regimes do in fact represent international or global authority as regime theory sometimes claims. Again, Vogler is clear on this question: 'regimes at best allow for policy coordination between nation-states and do not represent, at present at least, a decisive shift to new global authority structures.'[43] This conclusion is in line with the functional theory of regimes, but more critical theories would indicate that such a shift is very unlikely given the present configuration of power in the world political economy.

In response to the question: do regimes add anything to our understanding of international co-operation?, we have then a qualified 'yes', but the conditions in which we can successfully use regime theory are narrow and specific. Our conclusion to this question modifies any answer to the question: 'do regimes matter?' According to the view that is taken on the question of regimes as an extension of hegemonic power, different conclusions are possible here. If regimes are extensions of hegemonic power they 'matter' to the extent that they are successful in maintaining power, partly by legitimating their own existence. If regimes are seen as more plural, collective entities, then they also matter to the extent that the policy co-ordination they effect is important and beneficial. What we cannot do, however, is to assume that even if a regime 'exists' in any area it automatically matters for the world political economy.[44]

The above conclusions relate to regime theory as it is currently defined and applied, but much of our criticism in this chapter is aimed at the inadequacies of the current definition. Moving from a state-centred basis of regime theory to a multiplicity of actors would enable the use of the concept of regime in a far wider range of situations where it is already clear that some form of transnational authority is in existence.[45] This would bring an important gain in understanding. Another gain in understanding would come from a revaluation of the basis of understanding regimes and the total process of international co-operation. Again, a start has been made on such a revaluation, principally through moving towards a new philosophical basis for our understanding of international co-operation.[46] However, whatever the future developments of regime and any consequent increase (or decrease) in our understanding of international co-operation, this understanding will only and can only reflect our views of the world political economy as a whole. Until we have a better understanding of the world political economy, our understanding of international co-operation will be limited.

Notes

1. See John Maclean, 'Interdependence — an ideological intervention in IR', in R.J.B. Jones and P. Willets (eds), *Interdependence on Trial* London, Pinter, 1984, p. 147.
2. Robert W. Cox, 'Social forces, states and world orders: beyond international relations theory', *MILLENNIUM: Journal of International Studies*, Vol. 10, No. 2, Summer 1981, p. 128.
3. This preliminary definition is from R.O. Keohane and J.S. Nye, 'Two cheers for multilateralism', *Foreign Policy*, No. 60, Fall 1985, p. 151.
4. See R.O. Keohane and J.S. Nye, *Power and Interdependence* Boston, Little, Brown, 1977, especially ch. 2.
5. Stephen D. Krasner, 'Structural causes and regime consequences: regimes as intervening variables', in Stephen Krasner (ed.), *International Regimes*, Ithaca, Cornell University Press, 1983, p. 2. This volume is regarded by many as the definitive set of studies on 'regime' and is still significant.
6. For this quote and a discussion of authority, see John G. Ruggie, 'International regimes, transactions and change: embedded Liberalism in the postwar economic order', in Krasner, op. cit., 1983.
7. For an assessment and summary of the work done on 'hegemonic stability', see Michael C. Webb and Stephen D. Krasner, 'Hegemonic stability theory: an empirical assessment', *Review of International Studies*, Vol. 15, No. 2, April 1989, pp. 183–98.
8. The literature upon which this synthesis is based is exemplified by Krasner, op. cit., 1983; Keohane and Nye, op. cit., 1977; and Robert O. Keohane, *After Hegemony: co-operation and discord in the world political* economy, Princeton, Princeton University Press, 1984.
9. Stephan Haggard and Beth A. Simmons, 'Theories of international regimes', *International Organization*, Vol. 41, No. 3, Summer 1987, pp. 491–517.
10. Ibid., p. 493.
11. Stephen Krasner, op. cit., 1983, p. 2.
12. Haggard and Simmons, op. cit., p. 495.
13. Ibid., p. 491.
14. Ibid., p. 495.
15. Ibid., p. 497.
16. Ibid., p. 501, and see their footnotes 30 and 32 to 45 for a good guide to the literature on 'hegemonic stability'.
17. See Keohane, op. cit., 1984.
18. Haggard and Simmons, op. cit., p. 504.
19. Ibid., p. 506.
20. Ibid., p. 508.
21. Ibid., p. 509–10.
22. Particularly John Ruggie and Friedrich Kratochwil, 'International organization: a state of the art on the art of the state', *International Organization*, Vol. 40, Autumn 1986, pp. 753–76.
23. Keohane and Nye, op. cit., 1977; Keohane, op. cit., 1984.
24. This argument represents a non-positivist position and is extended in Roger Tooze, 'The unwritten preface: "international political economy" and Epistemology', *MILLENNIUM: Journal of International Studies*, Vol. 17, No. 2, Summer 1988, pp. 285–94.

25. John MacLean has cogently demonstrated this kind of analysis on the concept of 'interdependence', see John MacLean, in Jones and Willets (eds), op. cit., 1984.

26. See, *inter alia*: J.W. Burton, *World Society* London, Cambridge University Press, 1972; J.W. Burton, *Systems, States, Diplomacy and Rules*, London, Cambridge University Press, 1968; Michael H. Banks (ed.), *Conflict in World Society*, Brighton, Wheatsheaf, 1984; and Robert W. Cox, 'Gramsci, hegemony and international relations: an essay in method', *MILLENNIUM: Journal of International Studies*, Vol. 12, No. 2, Summer 1983, pp. 162–75.

27. See Stanley Hoffmann, 'An American social science: international relations', *Daedalus*, 106(3), 1977, pp. 41–60; and F.H. Gareau, 'The discipline of international relations: a multi-national perspective', *Journal of Politics*, Vol. 43, No. 3, August 1981, pp. 779–802.

28. John Gerard Ruggie, 'International responses to technology: concepts and trends', *International Organization*, Vol. 29, Summer 1975.

29. Haggard and Simmons, op. cit., 1987.

30. Susan Strange, 'Cave! hic dragones: a critique of regime analysis', *International Organization*, Vol. 38, No. 2, Spring 1982.

31. Haggard and Simmons, op. cit., p. 492.

32. See in particular Oran Young, 'The politics of international regime formation: managing natural resources and the environment', *International Organization*, Vol. 43, No. 3, Summer 1989.

33. John Burton, op. cit., 1972, p. 35.

34. Susan Strange, 'Cave! hic dragones', reprinted in Krasner, op. cit., 1983.

35. See Hoffman, op. cit., 1977.

36. Ibid, p. 48.

37. For this analysis, see Robert W. Cox, 'The crisis of world order and the problem of international organization in the 1980s', *International Journal*, Vol. XXXV, No. 2, Spring 1980, p. 377.

38. See Cox, op. cit., 1980; and Roger Tooze, 'Liberal international political economy', in R.J. Barry Jones (ed.), *The Worlds of Political Economy*, London, Pinter Publishers, 1988.

39. Cox, op. cit., 1980, p. 377.

40. John Vogler, 'Regimes and the politics of space technology', Paper 10, *Global Politics,* D312, Milton Keynes, Open University, 1989).

41. See J. Donnelly, 'International human rights: a regime analysis', *International Organization*, Vol. 40, No. 3, pp. 599–642.

42. John Vogler, op. cit., p. 52.

43. Ibid.

44. On this question, see Oran Young, 'International regimes: toward a new theory of institutions, *World Politics*, Vol. XXXIX, No. 1, October 1986, pp. 104–22.

45. Some regime theorists are already doing this, see, for example, Oran Young, op. cit., 1989, but the analysis is still limited by the particular methodology employed.

46. See Ruggie and Kratochwil, op. cit., 1986; and Friedrich Kratochwil, *Rules, Norms and Decisions*, Cambridge, Cambridge University Press, 1989.

Selected reading

Haggard, Stephen and Beth A. Simmons, 'Theories of international regimes', *International Organization*, Vol. 41, No. 3, Summer 1987, pp. 491–517.

Keohane, R.O. and J.S. Nye, *Power and Interdependence*, Boston, Little, Brown, 1977.

Krasner, Stephen (ed.), *International Regimes*, Ithaca, Cornell University Press, 1983.

Ruggie, John Gerard, 'International responses to technology: concepts and trends', *International Organization*, Vol. 29, Summer 1975.

Strange, Susan, 'Cave! hic dragones: a critique of regime analysis', *International Organization*, Vol. 38, No. 2, Spring 1982.

15 World federalism: the conceptual setting

George A. Codding Jr

The concept of federalism has always had an important place in international organization literature. Almost from the beginning of the modern nation-state men have put their minds to the problems of expanding the territorial limits of their creation to include more territory and more people. The motives for this expansion have varied from the simple desire for more power, imperialism, to the aspiration to construct an edifice better equipped to meet the evolving needs of mankind. Among the latter are the advocates of the federalist approach to supranational political authority.

Although there is an infinite variety in the details of the various federal plans for international integration, there are certain core elements. The most basic of these is the creation of a supranational government which will share power with member states. The amount of this power, which depends upon the functions to be given to the supranational government, is set forth in a basic treaty, a constitution, which cannot be changed easily by either level of government. As defined by Carl J. Friedrich:

A federal system then is a particular kind of constitutional order. The function it is supposed to serve is to restrain the powers wielded by the inclusive community, *as well as* those of the communities included within it. It is . . . a kind of division or separation of powers, but applied on a spatial basis.[1]

The process of integration is as simple as the concept itself. Through education and propaganda the political élites of the area to be federalized will be made to realize the need for the creation of a supranational federal system. Once the need is realized, the political leaders will sit down together to draft the constitution which will create the new supranational state and the necessary institutions to permit it to carry out those tasks desired by the member states, which will tend to preserve the division of powers between the levels of government. The new world constitution would come into effect upon ratification by the member states.

There are a number of basic assumptions to this somewhat unsophisticated 'future world' model-building, which contain both the theory's strength and its weaknesses. The first is the assumption that the nation-state system, as it is presently constituted, is incapable of carrying out certain tasks which are crucial to the well-being of mankind, such as the control of international violence. The second is that man's creation, government, despite all of its imperfection, can be adapted for use as a supranational authority. Third, the protection of sectional differences, which is inherent in the federalist position, is both healthy and desirable. And fourth, the federalist approach relies heavily on man's rationality in that he will be able to perceive the need for a revolutionarty change in his governance and that he will be willing to make that change.

Historical setting and schools of thought

While the creation of federations of states for various purposes dates back to antiquity,[2] the concept of federalism is a fairly modern invention. Carl J. Freidrich, for instance, traces the beginning of federalist theory to Althusius in the sixteenth century.[3] Other important names in this early period include Grotius and Montesquieu and three of the first architects of a world federal government, Duc de Sully, William Penn, and Abbé de Saint-Pierre.[4] Most of these early schemes for a world federal government, it should be noted, were concerned mainly with the integration of the 'civilized' states of Europe.

The successful American experiment in federalism and its apologia, the *Federalist* papers, set off a spate of federalist theorizing which included some of the greatest names of the time, including Immanuel Kant, Jean-Jacques Rousseau, de Tocqueville, and Proudhon, not all of whom found it a panacea. The Swiss experience in federalism was not long in following and helped to reinforce the proponents of the federal solution.[5]

In this century, the Second World War, the events leading up to it, and its aftermath provided an impetus to federal world order modelling that has not as yet ebbed. Most of these plans were claimed by their proponents to be solutions to the problem of world peace. Among the more prominent of these plans are included the projects of Ely Culbertson, the international bridge expert, which stressed the idea of an international police force; Emery Reves, who wrote *Anatomy of Peace*, where he preached that wars would be ended as soon as sovereignty was transferred to a larger unit; and Cord Meyer, who presented the first plan of the United World Federalists.[6] Of a different nature was the draft constitution of the Federal Republic of the World, inspired by the bombing of Hiroshima, and drafted by a group known as the Committee to Frame a World Constitution, under the leadership of Chancellor Hutchins of the University of Chicago.[7] One of the most important names of the time was Clarence K. Streit, who argued that while world federation should be the ultimate goal, it was absolutely essential to start with a smaller group of nations with something in common and to build from there.[8]

The impact of the federalist movement in the United States was so strong that by 1950 twenty-one states had passed resolutions favourable to a world federation of one type or another and hearings were being held on the subject in the Senate Committee on Foreign Relations.[9]

Although the enthusiasm for the creation of a world federal government on a universal scale has waned somewhat since the Senate Foreign Relations Committee held its hearings, the late 1950s did see the presentation of the comprehensive plan authored by Grenville Clark and Professor Louis B.

Sohn, which has been revised on a number of occasions; and in 1972 the successor to the United World Federation, the World Association of World Federalists under the presidency of Norman Cousins, claimed national World Federalist Associations in thirty-three countries throughout the world.[10]

Post-Second World War institution building in Europe has provided the lodestone for integrationists, non-federal as well as federal. Among the major European groups are the European Federalist Movement, the successor to the European Union of Federalists founded in 1946, and the European Centre for Federalist Action (Centre d'action européenne fédéraliste, or AEF), which dates from 1956 when it broke away from the other group. The names of prominent European federalists include Henri Brugmans, Guy Heraud, Alexandre Marc, Denis de Rougemont, and Altiero Spinelli.[11] The European federalist movement has a slightly different orientation from the universalist or large-scale federalist movements already mentioned. The main thrust of these movements has been the creation of a supranational institution which would eventually eliminate the need for national armies and thus would tend to ensure international peace and order. This element is not a consideration in the European federalist movement, except perhaps for those who see it as a method of keeping Germany under control. The main considerations are economies of scale and the building of Europe into a democratic supranational institution of a size that would permit it to compete on an even footing with the superpowers in any field of national endeavour. In addition, although some see the proposed European federal government including eventually all of Europe, if it is mentioned at all, universalism is only a secondary aim.

The federal plan

The content of any particular federalist plan is limited only by the bounds of the imagination of the particular author, and there are many. Some plans are a page or two in length, some are several hundred pages. Nevertheless, there are two broad areas, at least in most of the older plans, which can be readily identified and grouped for comparative purposes — the extent of powers that should be granted to the supranational authority and the structure of this authority.

Almost without exception, the universalists and quasi-universalists would grant the federal authority the powers necessary to maintain peace and security. For the minimalists, the powers would be restricted to this function. Cord Meyer believed that '. . . only those functions of government that are determined to be indispensable to the prevention of war need to be transferred . . . while the member nations retain their independence of action in all other matters.'[12] Clark and Sohn in *World Peace Through World Law* echoed this sentiment: 'The powers of the world organisation should be restricted to matters directly related to the maintenance of peace. All other powers should be reserved to the nations and their peoples.'[13] These powers 'would *not* include such matters as regulation of international trade, immigration and the like, or any right to interfere in the domestic affairs of the nations'.[14] The purpose of this restriction, on the part of Clark and Sohn, at least, has nothing especially to do with any feeling that the central government should be limited to only those powers, but to the concern that if too much were attempted it might engender a crippling opposition to any supranational plans based upon the fear of interference in the domestic affairs of the nations and, in general, because agreement on anything further might well be beyond the abilities of this generation of mankind.[15]

The exact powers necessary to carry out this basic purpose would, for Clark and Sohn, include:

1. the power to enact and enforce laws and regulations relating to universal and complete national disarmament, including the control of nuclear energy and the use of outer space;
2. the power to enact and enforce laws and regulations to prevent actual or imminent breaches of internationl peace and any serious refusal to comply with the basic treaty;
3. the power to enact and enforce laws and regulations to prevent acts or omissions of individuals and private organizations which violate the basic treaty or which cause damage to the property of the supranational government or to any person in its service while engaged in official duties; and
4. the power to maintain a military force large enough to enforce universal and complete disarmament and for 'the prevention and removal of threats to the peace, for the suppression of acts of aggression and other breaches of the peace, and for ensuring compliance with this revised Charter and the laws and regulations enacted thereunder'.[16]

Clark and Sohn would also confer on the world government the power to raise revenues and to make the jurisdiction of its judicial arm compulsory in certain classes of disputes.

Clarence Streit would widen the scope of the powers of his original supranational government to include such things as the right to grant citizenship, the right to regulate inter-state and foreign trade, to coin and issue money, and the right to control communications.[17] Perhaps the most detailed of the plans is *A Constitution for the World* drafted by the Committee headed by Chancellor Hutchings (see note 7), which provides for: the regulation and operation of means of transportation and commerce which are of federal interest, 'laws concerning emigration and immigration and the movements of peoples; the granting of federal passports; the appropriation, under the right of eminent domain, of such private or public property as may be necessary for federal use', and administration of the federal capital district.[18] In justification of the wider powers, Elisabeth Borgese argues that 'war is not something separate that can be added to or subtracted from the total weave of the social, political, and economic life of peoples.[19]

The powers that the European federalists would grant to their supranational authority differ from the others primarily because of the difference in its basic purpose. As a superpower among superpowers, it must be given authority over foreign affairs and defence policy, powers which would be non-existent in the other plans. The emphasis on economic problems in their model, the EEC, and the wider range of authority over economic and social problems in European states also has had an effect on European conceived proposals as contrasted to those which have come from American authors. Pinder and Pryce point out a number of issues which cut across national boundaries which must be regulated by the supranational authority, including modern industrial production, monetary stability, communications and multinationals. Underlying everything is the need for large-scale social and economic planning.[20]

An interrelated problem to which the federalists have addressed themselves is the structure of the proposed federal world authority. In general, the architects of federal world government have tended to borrow from the familiar. Saint-Simon, writing in 1814, advocated that a federated Europe be governed by a single parliament and a single king which would regulate all questions of common concern including colonial expansion and economic and social affairs of the component states.[21] American writers and those inspired by the American system tend to envisage an organization similar to the American federal system. As stated by Clarence Streit:

Those who would constitute unions can turn now to many time-tested successes. For reasons that will be seen when we study carefully the American Union I believe that we should turn particularly to the American Constitution and experience for guidance.[22]

Streit advocates a two-house legislature, on the American model, with one based on population and the other on member states. The latter, which would have the task of safeguarding the small democracies and decentralization, would be made up of two representatives for each member state.[23] The Streit proposal also provided for an independent Supreme Court. Streit abandoned the American presidency, however, for a five-man executive which would delegate its responsibilities to a Prime Minister and his cabinet.

Clark and Sohn's proposals, as well as a number of the early post-Second World War ones, including that of the United World Federalists, would build on the United Nations. Among the reasons given are that 'it seems logical and reasonable to utilize an existing organization of such scope and experience,'[24] that the primary prupose of the UN is to prevent war, and that the creation of a new world organization adequately equipped to maintain peace would necessarily overshadow the present United Nations.[25] The Clark and Sohn proposal envisages the transformation of the General Assembly of the United Nations into a popularly elected body with final responsibility for disarmament and the maintenance of peace. In the new General Assembly states would be given voting power proportionate to their populations.[26] The present UN Security Council would be replaced by a seventeen-member Executive Council, elected by the General Assembly, which would act as the executive arm of the world government with broad powers to supervise and direct the disarmament process and other aspects of the system for the maintenance of peace. The new authority would have a revamped and strengthened International Court of Justice and Economic and Social Council. Innovations in the Clark and Sohn proposal include a World Peace Force of between 200,000 and 600,000 effectives and between 600,000 and 1,200,000 reserves to police the disarmed world, and a revenue system made up of a specific portion of the taxes of the subordinate units. In the third edition of the plan, Clark and Sohn added another new organ, the World Development Commission, with 'very large sums at its disposal', with the task of aiding 'the underdeveloped areas of the world to the extent necessary to remove the danger to world stability and peace caused by the immense economic disparity between those areas and the industrialized regions of the world.'[27] John Logue suggests that an expanded UN development effort could be financed from revenues obtained in the exploitation of the riches of the ocean floor and Antarctica.[28]

With the Europeans, as would be expected, the institutions of the European Community provide the foundation on which to build the federalist edifice. They have succeeded in bringing about a degree of economic integration between the member states and they have passed the test of time.[29] What would be more logical than to give these institutions political as well as economic power?

John Pinder and Roy Pryce provide us with a multi-phased, long-term plan to accomplish this purpose. The main thrust of this proposal is to place the nation-state dominated Council of Ministers, alongside a Commission and Parliament as part of the federal authority, as the final and unchallenge-able sources of decision-making. There is no strict time limit as regards moving from one stage to the next, the only criterion being the progressive reinforcement of the common institutions so that they would ultimately be capable of assuming the powers which at present are largely in the hands of national authorities.[30] In the first stage, the transitional period, arrange-ments would be made to institute a system of direct financing for the Community along with a new procedure for the approval of the annual budget in which the Commission and Parliament would have a major role. At this stage plans would also be made to introduce, again by stages, direct election of a substantial proportion of the members of the Parliament and to involve the Parliament in the legislative process.[31] The Council would be required to transmit its decisions to the Parliament; Parliament would have to approve these decisions before they had the force of law, and Parliament would be given the power to amend the Council's proposals. In the second stage other existing Community institutions, such as the Economic and Social Committee and the Court of Justice, would be strengthened and a new institution would be created to represent regional authorities. In the final stage the direct election of all the remaining members of Parliament on a uniform system would be introduced as would be a new method for the selection of the Commission which would eliminate the present role of the European governments. Possibilities are a two-stage direct election on the

French model or an indirect election by an electoral college or by Parliament.[32] These two institutions would then assume the ultimate decision-making power of the Community. The final result would be a federal government with three levels, Community, regional, and national, with an independent source of income and based on the democratic process.[33]

One of the most recent attempts to strengthen the European Community is contained in the draft Treaty Establishing the European Union approved by the European Parliament in February 1984. This document, which must be adopted by member governments before it can come into force, would reorganize the existing structure of the European Community and increase the decision-making powers of its various organs, especially the Commission. The sponsors of the draft treaty are quick to admit that one of the major purposes for introducing the draft treaty is to try to prevent the possible collapse of the European integration effort.[34]

If there is disagreement among federalists over the proper structure for the new federal world government, there is just as much disagreement over the proper strategy to achieve it. Probably the most significant division is that between the universalists and those who would accept a federation in a smaller geographical area, either as an end in itself or as one piece of a puzzle to which other pieces will be added as circumstances dictate. Among the former are the World Federalists and Clark and Sohn. Inasmuch as universal disarmament is a prerequisite to world peace, one of the primary aims of the Clark and Sohn proposal, they are forced to argue that virtually the whole world must accept membership. Anyway, since the Clark and Sohn plan would not come into effect until ratified by five-sixths of the world's population and must include each of the twelve largest countries, 'it is possible, and even probable, that there would actually be no nonmember nations whatsoever.'[35] However, in case there are states which refuse to join, they would in effect be under the authority of the world government because they will be bound to refrain from violence and to settle all their disputes by peaceful means.[36]

Clarence Streit is an example of those who would start with a less ambitious number of nation-states, a more homogeneous group. In one of his earlier books he advocated a federal union of the United States and the members of the British Commonwealth. In his 1940 book he proposed to start with 'the North Atlantic or founder democracies' which would include the United States, the British Commonwealth (specifically the United Kingdom, Canada, Australia, New Zealand, South Africa, and the Republic of Ireland), France, Belgium, Netherlands, Switzerland, Denmark, Norway, Sweden and Finland. These states were selected because they include 'the world's greatest, oldest, most homogeneous and closely linked democracies, the peoples most experienced and successful in solving the problems at hand — the peaceful, reasonable establishment of effective interstate democratic world government'. This group did not have too great a linguistic diversity and above all: *'None of these democracies has been at war with any of the others since more than 100 years.'*[37] Later Streit changed his founders of the union to the fifteen-nation membership of NATO (this substituted Iceland, Luxemburg, West Germany, Greece, Italy, Portugal and Turkey for Australia, the Republic of Ireland, Finland, New Zealand, Sweden, Switzerland and South Africa). This new combination of founder states was much less ideal than the original fifteen, but more practical in that they had already made some efforts in common. As the term 'founders' suggests, Streit had no exclusivist tendencies. The founding fifteen would actually be so strong and democratic, according to Streit, that the Union would be a most powerful attraction to other countries and one by one their citizens would turn their governments into democracies and enter the Union until there would be a single peaceful democratic world government.[38] Streit did not rule out the possibility that the Atlantic Union would provide an immense impulse toward federation in other regions of the world which some day would federate with the Atlantic Union.

Europe provides a third approach, with federal theorizers and the federal movement directed primarily at creating a new federal state out of a number of European states and only secondarily or incidentally to serve as a nucleus for a larger federation. The aim, in fact, of some of the schemes is to create a federal union of Western European democracies which would permit it to remain independent of other major powers, including the United States.[39] Others, while starting with the Western European democracies, expect the new federal union eventually to include all of the states of Europe, both East and West.[40]

Perhaps the most important aspect of strategy is the method which is employed to influence governments to give up their power to the supra-national federal government. Some are very simple and direct. Streit, for instance, sees an overwhelming pressure arising from the people. To obtain the Federal Union, 'the first thing those who want it should do is to say so.'[41] The supporters of the Federal Union need not wait on diplomats to obtain it for them; they

need only turn to themselves and their neighbours. . . .. The first necessity then is that Unionists wherever they are should make known their will for The Union and organise their neighborhood, and state and nation, and keep on uniting for The Union, and co-ordinating their work in all the democracies, until they form the majority needed to get The Union.'[42]

Direct pressure on public authorities is important. The federalist 'need' only write, telegraph, telephone his Representative, Senator, Deputy, Member of Parliament, Premier, President'.[43] Eventually these pressures will have the necessary effect. 'The raindrop on the window seems powerless, but the crudest mill-wheel moves if only enough raindrops take the same channel.'[44]

A more sophisticated approach is evident in the European branch of the federalist movement. In fact, according to one authority, the 'theoretical discussion of federalism as a strategy for bringing about political unification arises almost entirely in the context of contemporary European integration.'[45] This same authority divides the European federalists into the moderates and the radicals. The moderates, such as those represented by the AEF, believe in an incremental, evolutionary approach, and will take any opportunity offered to create political institutions. First, the activity of the EC and the Parliament, along with propaganda for the federalists, will draw the attention and the support of various groups in industry, commerce and agriculture to European unity. The second state would be to bring about an agreement to elect the European Parliament by direct suffrage. The final stage would be the drafting of the federal treaty by the Parliament and its ratification by the member states. The federalists at all times would be involved in explaining, interpreting, and working to move the process from step to step.

The radicals in Europe, on the other hand, under the banner of the MFE (European Federal Movement), are for more drastic action. First, the task is to create an intense international campaign of public persuasion to convince individuals as well as leaders and groups that the nation-state as it is known is obsolete and that it is up to the people to help create the alternative. The second would be to rally massive support for calling a constituent assembly which will have the limited task of drafting the federal treaty, which will then be submitted to governments for ratification. An interesting minority of the radicals are those who feel that it would help, perhaps even be necessary, to have a crisis to exploit in addition to the necessary popular force. The main advantage claimed for the radical method is that it would bypass the states by making the constitution drafting a matter between parties with interests at stake and not governments. The moderate method, it is claimed, would demand too much of the goodwill of governments by making them parties to the process of giving up their own power.[46]

Claims and counterclaims

The advantage claimed by the federalists for a federal supranational political authority are numerous. Above all, the division of powers between different levels of government recognizes and accounts for the dual trend toward the need for world-wide solutions to world-wide problems and the contrary trend toward the need for local solutions for local problems. Some problems, such as inter-state violence, obviously demand the highest level of action. According to the World Association of World Federalists, peace requires that the world community substitute the process of law for armed conflicts in settling disputes: 'We believe . . . that world federal government with powers adequate to establish and maintain laws and justice on the world level is the only practicable way to achieve a just and lasting peace.'[47] Clark and Sohn add development to world priorities that only a world federal government would be in a position to attack. Other problems demand purely national solutions, such as freedom to manage domestic affairs and to choose political, economic, and social institutions.[48] Only those close to the problem can provide effective and acceptable solutions.

A federal authority also provides a barrier to central despotism by guaranteeing autonomy of its subunits and their participation in the federal government. The central government will have only that authority which is specifically granted in the constitution while the member states will retain all the rest, and this division of authority is protected by being stated clearly in the founding document which should be incapable of easy change and which is protected in its turn by the institutional framework. Further, and this is a corollary, the federal system is a guarantee of regional diversity, a characteristic which is inherently good. In addition, by keeping a considerable amount of decision-making at the local level, one would be guaranteeing the participation of as many people as possible, the civic participation counselled by Rousseau.

The federalist approach is also claimed to have a number of tactical advantages. First, it will appeal to the weaker nation-states, those which will be more reluctant to enter into a supranational authority, both as regards the retention of local authority and the placing of restrictions on the power of the central authority.[49] It is in effect a method of achieving world order at a minimal cost to national identities, another attraction to the states which are asked to give up some of their sovereignty. Second, it is attractive because of its simplicity and the familiarity of the analogy from which it derives.[50] Finally, it is realistic. It does not rely on the back-door approach to integration that is advocated by the functionalists or the incidental approach of the neo-functionalists, but rather it relies on the direct approach, which recognizes the importance of political will and political settlement.

The critics of the federalist position, and there are many, fall into two categories: those who question the intrinsic value of the federal form of government and those who question the merits of the direct political approach of the federalists to structural change. One of the more vocal of the critics was David Mitrany, the father of the functionalist approach to integration in which the final form of supranational government evolves from function. The heart of the 'federalist fallacy' according to Mitrany, is the belief that a federal form of government is adequate for present-day needs. Mitrany and most other critics question the ability of any federal state to suppress internal armed conflict.[51] In addition, federal states are considered notorious for the difficulties they have encountered in the everyday performance of new tasks that have arisen since the Second World War including such non-political tasks as banking, the building of highways, and provision of health services.[52] The reason for this is a lack of flexibility which is a result of the federal compact, the heart of the federalist solution, the main purpose of which is precisely to delimit the competence of the various organs.[53] Problems are becoming larger and governments, of necessity, are becoming omnipresent and almost omnipotent. The new supranational government cannot be restricted if it is to solve these problems. 'For any new federal experiment, if it is to be free to develop the modern attributes of a welfare society,' according to Mitrany, 'the working prototype is likely to be not the U.S. Constitution of 1787 but rather something nearer to the federal system of the U.S.S.R.'[54]

From a purely European context, the federalist solution is even more unacceptable to its critics. A supranational European government would have to have a free hand in both defence policy and foreign policy. Federal states have had their right to act in the international arena challenged by their subordinate units, an unacceptable action in modern international politics. Even more serious, some federal states have been faced with the threat of secession and in one case there was a bloody civil war.[55] It is interesting to note that Pinder and Pryce, although federalists, when discussing the US experiment in federalism, warn that 'it would be unwise for Europe to copy a system which itself is now considered by many to be outdated.'[56]

R.J. Harrison in his critique of the European federalist movement refutes the concept that federalism will remain a guarantee of local autonomy, individual freedom or even democracy. 'Empirical studies have amply demonstrated,' according to Harrison, 'that the specification of powers in a formal constitution does not mean that there will be an absence of conflict over jurisdictions or that there will be no actual encroachment.'[57] He does concede, however, that a federal constitution and the machinery for its enforcement *tend* in the long run to preserve a balance between centrifugal and centripetal forces. As regards individual freedom, Harrison points to the studies of William H. Riker, who claims that it is not individual freedom that is protected in a federal state, but the special interests of capitalists, landlords, linguistic minorities, and racists.[58] Finally, as regards the argument that to leave meaningful decision-making to the local units encourages civic participation, Harrison points out that there is a much weaker turnout for state elections in the United States than there is for national elections, which has been attributed by some to the fact that people are simply discouraged about the belief that 'state politics are more prone to corruption, more concerned with the spoils of office, more gerrymandered, administratively inefficient, weaker in quality of personnel, and more conservative than central government.'[59]

The second major area of criticism deals with tactics. The opponents of the federalists consider that the direct method of attaining supranational government of the federalists flies in the face of reality.

Federalism continuously reminds politicians of what it is they are being asked to yield: political arrangements are necessary in order to get beyond existing political arrangements. The implication is that the question is so important that it cannot be left to existing politicians.[60]

Some even claim that the federal approach is so antagonistic to the power élites that even the advocacy of the idea itself is a hindrance to any political action.[61]

Neofederalism

The discussion up to this point may give the impression that all the international federalists have definite goals and definite sets of institutions to propose to the world at large. This was probably true in the earlier post-Second World War years for most of the federalists, but more and more are turning away from the somewhat simplistic approach to a more pragmatic approach which has been described as neo-federalism.[62] Basic to this approach is a refusal to be tied down to any specifics in regard to either the division of power or structure, much to the dismay of many of the critics of the more classical federal approach.

Carl J. Friedrich, for instance, has suggested that federalism is not necessarily only a union of states, but also can be a process 'by which a number of separate political organisations, be they states or any other kind of associations, enter into arrangements for doing various things jointly'.[63] Any action of this type is a part of a 'federalizing process'. Even in old federations there is never a constant relationship between unifying and diversifying forces, sometimes one being dominant and sometimes the other. In response, David Mitrany points out that this 'is true of all government; and it is least true of federal government. A new union or association is not conceivable without some formal compact whose main purpose is precisely to delimit the competence of the various organs.'[64] The very purpose of any such written compact, continues David Mitrany, 'is to introduce an element of fixity in the index of power; and no political system is so fixed as a federal constitution'.[65] Such tactical vagueness, according to Mitrany, destroys the meaning of federalism. Denis de Rougemont, long a leader in the European federalist movement, can also be described as a neo-federalist. Addressing the essential question of the division of powers between the various levels of government in the future European federal system, de Rougemont believes that the answer is so complex it is beyond human reason. But he does have a method by which the answer can be reached. The first step in the federalist analysis is to consider 'the nature of the task or of a particular function whose necessity has been agreed upon or recognized. As a second step, it estimates the optimum dimensions of the area of operation required, and does it in terms of the three following factors: the possibilities of *participation* (civic, intellectual, economic), *efficiency* and *economy of means*. The third and final step, once the dimension of the problem and the corresponding unit (communal, regional, national, continental, or world-wide, according to the case) has been determined' de Rougemont suggests, 'is to designate the *level of authority* at which the *decisions* relative to the task will be taken.'[66] De Rougemont concedes that the number of combinations this method would lead to would be staggering, but feels that this problem can be solved by the modern computer. 'For me,' he concludes, 'federalism is the autonomy of regions plus computers, in other words, respect for reality and for its infinite complexities finally made possible by modern technology.'[67]

The neo-federalist approach has also invaded the international federalist movement. In a publication of the World Federalist Education Fund, Donald F. Keys explains the meaning of neo-federalism and how it came to replace federalism for the world federalist movement. The early post-Second World War federalists were under the impression that all that was required was simply a structural change in the United Nations following the pattern set by the thirteen American colonies, and that the main doctrinal difference was one between those who would give a broad range of powers to the new federal United Nations government and those who would grant it only minimal powers. A number of events occurred which chilled the federalist movement, including the Cold War, the nuclear arms race and Vietnam, and caused it to reassess the function and goal of the federalist movement. The federalists found out what the functionalists had already found out:

that the world community is in fact beginning to establish a series of global departments to deal with specific global tasks. Instead of the strictly vertical or hierarchical structure — which has been the presupposition and vision of early Federalists — we see a horizontal proliferation of organs to perform specialized functions.[68]

They also found that the nation-state was a harder obstacle to move than expected. 'There are no more illusions about the case of convincing governments to relinquish national sovereignty.'[69] The new strategy of the neo-federalists, then, is no longer the frontal attack on national sovereignty but the back-door strategy of the functionalists. In essence it is to reinforce these organs wherever they are found, both inside and outside the United Nations, in order to whittle away at national soverignty and to create a firmer base on which to build the future world federal government.[70] As a result, 'Federalists no longer have the luxury of seeking a neat and orderly solution to world government.'[71]

Functionalism and neo-federalism are not the same thing, however, argues Donald F. Keys. The neo-federalists recognize that 'world institutions cannot stand on thin air but must be based upon "community".'[72] The traditional federalists, again according to Keys, (with the exception of Kant), have overlooked the cultural diversity in the world which is a serious obstacle to the necessary community of values and behaviour. The neo-federalist solution is to support a Planetary Citizenship Campaign, which 'attempts to accelerate the development of the world community-minded plasma that will support a fusion reaction of human convergence — a major 'consciousness-raising' exercise.'[73] In sum: 'The new federalism, or, if you like, neo-federalism, is no less idealistic than the old, but the time scales are different and the policies more pragmatic.'[74]

Whether or not the neo-federalists are actually destroying the meaning of federalism by their new-found pragmatism, or are merely taking on the colouration of their arch enemies, the functionalists, is likely to remain a subject of discussion for some time to come among the theorists of international integration. The main problem, of course, is that there is little evidence that political integration is taking place in the world at large, or even within the confines of Europe, so there is no urgent need to solve this question or the numerous other problems that have been raised by the federalists and their critics. There is even the possibility that none of the present theories of integration have any real validity. This it seems is the thesis of some of the more recent writings of Ernst B. Haas.[75]

Nevertheless, the federalist goal remains a valid goal to the many idealists who hope to transform an imperfect world into a better world. Men will continue to be attracted to federalism by its simplicity and the familiarity of the analogy. In Europe the European Communities and their institutions will continue to be considered as adaptable to federal ends and the mere presence of the EC should keep the issue of European unity alive and with it the aspirations of the federalists. The statement of Ernst B. Haas, although directed specifically at the European experience, has a validity for all federalists:

Federalist theories . . . retain relevance whenever a group of actors profess a commitment to the introduction of a specific set of objectives and plans which herald a new order when a deep and abiding consensus on such a new order prevails for some time.[76]

Notes

1. Carl J. Friedrich, *Man and His Government*, New York, McGraw-Hill Book Company, 1963, p. 597.
2. See Adda B. Bozeman, *Politics and Culture in International History*, Princeton, New Jersey, Princeton University Press, 1960, pp. 97-8.
3. See Carl J. Friedrich, op. cit., p. 588.
4. Ibid., pp. 587-90. See also, Louis René Beres, 'Examining the logic of world federal government', *Publius*, Vol. 4, No. 3 Summer 1974, pp. 77-9.
5. Friedrich, op. cit., pp. 589-94. See also his *Trends of Federalism in Theory and Practice*, New York, Frederick A. Praeger, 1968, especially chapter 2.
6. See Ely Culbertson, *Total Peace: what makes wars and how to organize peace*, Garden City, NY, Doubleday, Doran, 1943; Cord Meyer, Jr, *Peace or Anarchy*, Boston, Little, Brown, 1947; and Emery Reves, *The Anatomy of Peace*, New York, Harper & Brothers, 1945.
7. See Center for the Study of Democratic Institutions, *A Constitution for the World*, New York, The Fund for the Republic, 1965, pp. 25-54.
8. See Clarence K. Streit, *Union Now With Britain*, New York, Harper & Brothers, 1941; and *Freedom's Frontier: Atlantic union now*, Washington DC, Freedom & Union Press, 1961.
9. Norman Hill, *International Organization*, New York, Harper & Brothers, 1952, p. 585.
10. See Grenville Clark and Louis B. Sohn, *World Peace Through World Law*, 3rd edn, enlarged, Cambridge, Mass., Harvard University Press, 1966. And, World Association of World Federalists, 'The World Association of World Federalists', Ottawa, circa 1972. A more recent publication claims national World Federalist Associations in twenty countries and individual members in thirty. See United World Federalists, *To Abolish War*, Washington DC, circa 1983.
11. Most of the information on the European federalist movement in this section comes from the excellent book by Reginald J. Harrison, *Europe in Question: theories of regional international integration*, London, Allen & Unwin, 1974.
12. Cord Meyer, Jr, op. cit., p. 151.
13. Clark and Sohn, op. cit., p. xvii.
14. Ibid., p. xix.

15. Ibid., p. xvii.
16. Ibid., p. 36–7. See also pp. 111–12.
17. Streit (1961), op. cit., p. 242.
18. Center for the Study of Democratic Institutions, op. cit., pp. 29 and 30.
19. Ibid., p. 6.
20. John Pinder and Roy Pryce, *Europe after de Gaulle*, Middlesex, England, Penguin Books, 1969, pp. 16–19, 22–4 and 174.
21. See F. H. Hinsley, *Power and the Pursuit of Peace*, London, Cambridge University Press, 1967, p. 102.
22. Streit (1961), *op. cit.*, p. 245.
23. Ibid., pp. 247–9.
24. Clark and Sohn, op. cit., p. xlii.
25. Ibid., p. xlii.
26. In the 1966 edition the states of the world were divided into six categories, the largest of which would have thirty representatives each and the smallest, one; ibid., p. xx.
27. Ibid., p. xxxvii. For another example of a plan to build on the United Nations, see Everett Lee Millard, *Freedom in a Federal World*, 3rd edn, Dobbs Ferry, NY, Oceana Publications, 1964.
28. See John Logue, 'The way to peace and justice: a reformed, restructured and strengthened united nations', *Common Heritage*, No. 39, June 1984, p. 3.
29. For a recent evaluation of the European Community as a federal institution, see Clive Archer, *International Organization*, London, Allen & Unwin, 1983, p. 164.
30. Pinder and Pryce, op. cit., p. 168.
31. The first stage, at least, was accomplished in 1979 when the European Parliament became elected by direct popular vote.
32. Pinder and Pryce, op. cit., pp. 166–77.
33. According to Harrison, 'The [European] federalists, as a movement, have addressed themselves in the seventies to the subordinate objective of providing popular authority for Community institutions and independent financial resources, two of the most important attributes of political power' Harrison, op. cit., p. 59.
34. See the statement of Altiero Spinelli on behalf of the draft treaty in *Official Journal of the European Community*, Debates of the European Parliament, 1983–1984 Session, Report of Proceedings from 13 to 17 February 1984, Doc. No. 1–309, pp. 26–8.
35. Clark and Sohn, op. cit., p. xxvi.
36. Ibid.
37. Clarence K. Streit (1961), op. cit., p. 197.
38. Ibid., p. 199.
39. See for instance, Pinder and Pryce, op. cit., chapters 7 and 8.
40. Denis de Rougemont, 'The campaign of the European congress', *Government and Opposition*, Vol. 2, No. 3, April–July 1967, p. 349.
41. Streit (1961), op. cit., p. 252.
42. Ibid.
43. Ibid., p. 254.
44. Ibid.
45. Harrison, op. cit., p. 46.
46. Ibid., p. 52.
47. World Association of World Federalists, 'Policy Statement', Washington, DC, circa 1975 (mimeo.), p. 1

48. See 'The World Association of World Federalists', published by The World Association of World Federalists, circa 1974.
49. See Friedman, *Man and His Government*, op. cit., p. 597.
50. Charles Pentland is of the opinion that these two qualities are responsible for the fact that federalism continues to dominate the field of integration theory. See his 'Functionalism and theories of international political integration', in A.J.R. Groom and P. Taylor (eds), *Functionalism: theory and practice in international relations*, London, University of London Press, 1975, p. 13.
51. See, for instance, Beres, op. cit., pp. 84–7.
52. See David Mitrany, 'The prospect of integration: federal or Functional?', in Groom and Taylor, op. cit., p. 60.
53. Ibid., p. 61.
54. Ibid., p. 62.
55. Ibid., p. 60.
56. Pinder and Pryce, op. cit., p. 176.
57. Reginald J. Harrison, op. cit., p. 66.
58. Ibid., pp. 62–3.
59. Ibid., p. 70.
60. Paul Taylor, 'Functionalism and strategies for international integration', in Groom and Taylor, op. cit., p. 91.
61. David Mitrany, *A Working Peace System*, Chicago, Quadrangle Books, 1966, p. 170.
62. See Donald F. Keys, 'The new federalists', *New Federalist Reprint Paper 1*, World Federalist Education Fund, Washington, DC, circa 1973, p. 7.
63. From papers presented at an Oxford meeting on Federation in September 1963, and for the Sixth World Congress of the International Political Science Association in Geneva in September 1964, as discussed in David Mitrany, op. cit., pp. 60–1. See also Carl J. Friedrich, *Trends of Federalism in Theory and Practice*, op. cit., p. 7.
64. Mitrany, *The Prospect of Integration*, op. cit., p. 61.
65. Ibid. See also his *A Working Peace System*. op. cit., p. 191.
66. Denis de Rougemont, 'Towards a new definition of federalism', *The Atlantic Community Quarterly*, Vol. 8, No. 2, Summer 1970, p. 231.
67. Ibid.
68. Donald F. Keys, op. cit. See also Lawrence Abbott, *World Federalism: What? Why? How?*, Lawrence, Massachusetts, May 1976 (mimeo.), p. 27.
69. Ibid., p. 12.
70. Among the recent objectives of the new world federalist, in addition to arms control and disarmament and strengthening the United Nations, are a more equitable international economic order, expansion of human rights, a just sharing of ocean resources, a healthier environment, a comprehensive law of the sea treaty, intercultural understanding, and an appropriate international regime for Antarctica. See Jesper Grolin and Ron J. Rutherglen (eds), *World Federalist Reader, 1985*, Amsterdam, World Association of World Federalists, 1985.
71. Keys, op. cit.
72. Ibid., p. 12.
73. Ibid., p. 13.
74. Ibid., p. 1.
75. See, for instance, Ernst B. Haas, 'Turbulent fields and the theory of regional integration', *International Organization*, Vol. 30, No. 2, Spring 1976, pp. 173–212.

76. Ibid., p. 177.

Selected reading

Birch, A.H., 'Approaches to the study of federalism', *Political Studies*, Oxford, Vol. XIV, No. 1, February 1966, pp. 15–33.

Friedrich, Carl J., *Trends of Federalism in Theory and Practice*, New York, Frederick A. Praeger, 1968.

Harrison, R. J., *Europe in Question: theories of regional international integration*, London, Allen & Unwin, 1974.

King, Preston, *Federalism and Federation*, Baltimore, Johns Hopkins University Press, 1982.

MacMahon, Arthur W. (ed.), *Federalism, Mature and Emergent*, New York, Doubleday, 1955.

Riker, William H., *Federalism: origin, operations, significance*, Boston, H.B. Brown, 1964.

Streit, Clarence K., *Union Now with Britain*, New York, Harper, 1941.

16 Regionalism and functionalism reconsidered: a critical theory

Paul Taylor

Functionalism, in Mitrany's conception, is essentially aterritorial and unidimensional, whereas regionalism has of necessity a territorial basis and is usually conceived in multidimensional terms. Thus the two approaches seem to have incompatibilities that bear exploration. And if a cluster of related functions are taken together in a territory about which a prior decision has been made in the light of the best average fit of territory for the cluster, it still has to be decided what the size of the territory will be. In this sense there may be an element of practical reconciliation between functionalism and regionalism. Nevertheless, arguments about the size of the region are allowable because the notion that form should follow function for all functions has been rejected.

Subsequently the implications for the future development of international society — and for the theory of functionalism — of the pressures to move beyond local sectoralism, towards regional management and co-ordination, are considered. Local sectoralism in the sense of participation in international arrangements with proximate states is the first stage, and in many ways it is a practice which is being strengthened in the 1980s. Common management, however, is a different matter, and in most parts of the world, with the exception of the European Community, it is more remote. There is, however, a very good case for examining at this time the nature of the pressures which may encourage it.

There are three different dimensions of regional space, and distinct arguments about its unavoidability are suggested by each dimension. These will now be tackled in turn. They are: area (the region exists as a plane, or surface, more usually in international relations referred to as territory); contiguity (the area may be fragmented or unitary, its parts immediately proximate to each other or remote); and size (each has a given extent, and there may be arguments about whether the region should be larger or smaller, or local, intermediate or global). It should be noted that these dimensions though related, are analytically distinct: size may vary, the tasks may be organized according to a functional need, rather than within an area; and an area may be regarded for some purposes as a unit, though its parts are distinct and widely dispersed.

It should be stressed that economic. and administrative/technical criteria are the focus of this discussion. While political, cultural and identitive considerations are relevant when deciding upon the claim to independence of administrative regions, particularly, of course, in the form of states, nevertheless the appearance of 'mini-states', and of other states which lacked the assets which make for viability, suggests that economic and administrative or technical criteria have been unduly ignored. Such factors have not always been allowed to prevail. Indeed, until the period after the Second World War it was felt necessary by the great powers to be careful to balance political and cultural pressures against technical and practical considerations in permitting the creation of new states. For instance, at the time of the settlements after the First World War such notions as national self-determination were balanced against others such as defensibility and economic viability.

The following discussion rests upon an idealized view of a process of the rational planning, management and execution of projects and programmes, which has been deduced from the practice of some international institutions and governments, and from various proposals about how to improve matters when this was needed. It affects the behaviour of all those concerned with developing and executing policy, including national representatives at the intergovernmental level, and administrators in international and national bureaucracies. it is a prescription about the way in which diplomacy with regard to these matters should be structured. The stages of the process may be observed in the making and implementation of a wide range of policies, such as EEC Regulations and the Force Plan in NATO. It is, however, also essentially the way of working which is recommended in the various major proposals for reforming the economic and social organization of the United Nations in, for instance, General Assembly Resolutions 32/197,[1] the Jackson Report of 1969,[2] the Bertand Report of 1985[3] and the 1986 proposals for strengthening international control of UN spending.

It is important to stress that although this process may be easier to understand if it is related to ways of creating something new, such as the promotion of economic development, it is nevertheless a process which applies equally to the general organization of economic and social actions. It is also not akin to any political ideology, be it of the right or the left, though its detailed implementation may vary with the ideological context. It also remains as necessary for the management of developed states as it is for the development of those which are less fortunate. In practice it is, of course. continuous and contains numerous 'feed-back' loops, though it is described here as if it were sequential. As will become evident in the following arguments, it is in denying that such a process is necessary that the chief weakness of sectoral approaches, such as functionalism, lies.

The first phase is one in which the tasks are identified, the scale of resources evaluated, research into technical aspects carried out, and a mandate agreed for the appropriate organization. A crucial part of this phase should be that of reconciling the scale of resources allocated with the needs identified, a process which typically involves negotiation, and the 'confrontation of policies' of the providers and the recipients: if successful, an agreed programme is the outcome. A second stage is the 'operational': technical assistance may be called for, the details of projects specified, and the actual implementation of the programme begun. The third phase now begins and involves supervising and relating achievement at any moment to the goal which is to be obtained so that necessary adjustments in management or resources can be made: the impact of the operation is studied, reports of progress are delivered to those with overall responsibility, and the immediate tasks are altered in the light of experience to serve the overall purpose. It is this phase of the process which has seemed by observers such as Bertrand to be a major source of the ineffectiveness of the United Nations' economic and social arrangements. The sectoral arrangements have been pursued by too narrowly based organizations without much regard on a day-to-day basis for any general purpose.

The process of rationally planning and executing a programme — hereafter referred to as the rational process — can be described without any necessary reference to regional space in any of its dimensions. The next step in the argument is, therefore, to establish such links. In the first place the necessity for the dimension of area is to be discussed.

A single sector can be subjected to the rational process only if it is regarded as an end in itself, and is not related to the need to achieve an integrated programme in an area about which a prior decision has been made. This is a crucial point in functionalism: the area is to be determined by the dimensions of the particular task. The possibility is therefore raised that the integrated character of the various needs of individual human beings will be at odds with the requirement that each individual task should be tackled in its own space. For some individuals these different spaces may completely overlap, but at the interstices this may not be the case. Hence two problems are likely to arise in a single sector approach. First, the third phase of the rational process is difficult to carry out satisfactorily with reference solely to intra-sector criteria: evaluation and monitoring usually require trans-sector comparisons and contextual evaluations. For example, a sectoral project which focused, say, upon providing or maintaining proper housing, has inevitably to be evaluated by reference to a wide range of other sectors of activity such as transport, communications, available employment for inhabitants, and other facilities. Similarly, an industrial policy can only be effective if considered in the context of policies such as transport, training and housing. Very few functions are not dependent upon a wide range of others for their successful implementation, and it follows that the individual function cannot be monitored in a satisfactory way in isolation. The explanation of this is probably a more superficial manifestation of the integrated character of individual human needs, that no function is an end in itself.

Second, however, the fact that new tasks continually appear makes it essential to obtain the effective co-ordination of the work of existing organizations in order to succeed with the new purpose. It is not possible to start with, as it were, a clear administrative slate. Rather it is in the nature of things that what has to be done is to alter and build upon existing arrangements. Once again, therefore, the tendency is for a number of functions to be dealt with together rather than separately, those that reflect the functions of the earlier organizations and those which have more recently become evident. In the United Nations system, for instance, there are a large number of examples of new tasks appearing which had simply not been anticipated when the Specialized Agencies were established. Existing administrations dealing with identified problems were forced to deal with each other in order to tackle new problems which overlapped their various spheres of competence. Hence the Funds and Programmes were set up which were intended to cover, however imperfectly, some of the functional gaps between the Specialized Agencies. This explains in large part the creation of UNDP, UNFPA, and UNICEF, UNFPA, for instance, needed to work with UNESCO, WHO and the World Bank in developing a number of population control programmes after the mid-1970s when the goal of population control was widely accepted.[4] In other words, once again there were considerable pressures towards establishing integrated pro-grammes, rather than dealing with individual sectors, which derived from the fact that it was necessary to have co-ordination.

What is striking though is that both effective co-ordination and the satisfaction of the range of integrated needs of individual human beings are more likely to be attained if a prior decision has been taken about the appropriate determinate space; that is that some notion of a single area in which these things are to be done together is needed, as distinct from trying to find that space which would be best for the individual function. The felt-need sectors cannot provide trans-sectoral evaluative criteria precisely because they do not necessarily overlap. The lack of a natural coextensive-ness amongst sectors, seen as a virtue of functionalism , which is discussed further below, in fact becomes a major difficulty in the way of effectively implementing integrated programmes. The question always has to be put of precisely where this or that programme is to be, or has been, achieved. A programme has to be about a specific territory. Similarly, any notion of co-ordination demands a clear spatial reference: it is impossible to evaluate the extent to which there has been or has not been effective co-ordination without referring to a particular space.

If the above argument is accepted by the sectoralist, significant progress in the defence of regionalism has already been made. But the determined sectoralist might argue further that the territory within which functions are organized does not have to be contiguous: the argument about the necessity of space can be accepted without conceding that regionalism as defined in this study is necessary.

Significant costs do, however, arise if the territory is not contiguous and there are three ways in which these are produced. First, effective administ-ration and decision-making is dependent upon what has been called 'regimes' by Krasner[5] and others. These include sets of norms, principles and values, which are frequently unstated, but which guide and facilitate decision-making. They constitute rules of thumb, a tool-box of established practices, which are generally accepted among those involved in a regime; their existence helps to maintain co-operation between members by, for instance, allowing decisions about new problems in the areas in which they have already emerged to be made more quickly than would otherwise have been the case, and by encouraging actors to accept short-term costs in order to increase their chances of long-term benefit. They exist in addition to, and apart from, the formal stated laws and regulations of a society. There is, of course, a lot more to regimes than this, but it is only necessary here to suggest that they are a useful, and probably essential adjunct of effective decision-making, not only among but also within states.

Large communities of people having similar norms, principles and values are more likely to emerge in a continuous territory than in areas that are remote from each other. The regime may be rooted in compatible cultural values: it is not necessarily an aspect of socio-psychological community, but it is stronger if this is the case. If a territory is also contiguous and the people within it are therefore proximate, time and opportunity for the growth of such values are more likely to be available. It is itself a reflection of the unfashionable character of regionalism that this point has not been made in the literature on regimes. Conversely, dispersal is likely, over time, sooner or later, to lead to a weakening of common culture, and beyond that to the erosion of regimes. One reason for this is that despite modern technology, communication over long distances remains more difficult and slower than over shorter distances. In illustration of this point it is only necessary to think of the Commonwealth, where despite a surprising durability, regimes have nevertheless been weakened, compared with the European Community, where they have been strengthened. A British observer might be tempted to assert that the cultures of say, New Zealand, Australia and Britain had remained similar. But the point is that they have steadily become less so, and those of Britain and her European neighbours have moved closer together. A crucial reason for this is that the level of transactions with Europe in comparison with the old Commonwealth has greatly increased.

It is striking that it is not simply a matter of deciding to do something and creating a regime, but rather that a regime appears over a period of time as a result of the pursuit of common activities; as a consequence, however, the common activities are sustained. In the European Communities the increasing level of integration supported the gradual consolidation of regimes; practical co-operation in turn encouraged the development of an underpinning of common values. Whilst it would be foolish to assert that regimes always arrive in regions, it is, nevertheless, the case that once a significant range of common practice and a supporting array of regimes have appeared, it is more likely that these will survive and expand in a continuous territory than in a dispersed one. The attempts by the larger local states to establish themselves as regional powers may, of course, also be part of a process of consolidating regimes at the regional level. In the parlance of regime theory they may be seen as regional hegemons.

A second advantage of contiguity is that it avoids a wide range of transaction costs which arise if the territory is dispersed. Communication systems are in this case likely to be more expensive, despite the reduction in costs which have resulted from more advanced technology; indeed the significance of this development as a factor which would reduce significantly the advantages of proximity was overestimated by many in the 1960s. But non-contiguity is also likely to increase the costs deriving from greater uncertainty about political and economic circumstances; and the movement of goods and people is also likely to incur financial penalties and to run into a greater range of physical barriers.

Third, contiguity is desirable because it facilitates the internalization of the market: it is easier to introduce a single market and the necessary supporting arrangements in adjacent territories and to encourage business enterprises to conduct their activities in those territories in ways which are similar to those within the participating domestic economies. For instance, the problems in creating and managing arrangements for a liberal capital market or a monetary union among non-adjacent territories are much greater than where such territories are contiguous. If a common market is to survive and develop such arrangements are, however, necessary.

For a number of reasons, therefore, the attempt to meet the major welfare needs of individuals should not be exclusively through narrowly defined sectoral activities, but more through integrated programmes located on a particular and contiguous space. At this stage, however, a crucial question has not yet been addressed: whether from the technical point of view a judgement can be made about the appropriate dimensions of that territory. A first reaction might be to say that the larger the territory, the better, and that the best integrated programme, the one in which the maximum effectiveness would be reached, would be at the global level when every function, no doubt with the aid of giant computers, could be related to every other function. But obviously the technical and administrative problems involved in carrying out global integrated programmes would be over-whelming, and cross-sector monitoring at that level would be daunting. A second reaction should be perhaps to distinguish between the research and planning, and resource-gathering phase on the one hand, and the operatio-nal and monitoring phase on the other. It cannot be denied that there are indeed global issues and a real need for research into the problems of 'spaceship' earth such as those of the Club of Rome.[6] These are in the first category. But when it comes to the operational side, as Bertrand has pointed out, there are stronger reasons for moving from the global to some other lower level.[7] Very little has been written, however, about the question of how the optimum scale of that lower level might be judged. This is not to say that if it could be done it would overwhelm the more obvious considerations such as identitive, political or security factors; but it would enter into the argument as a normative element and exert a continuing pressure.

That this question is not a trivial one may be indicated by the fact that the size of the units itself has important implications for the integration of international society, which are distinct from political and economic considerations. This is because the global integration of a smaller number of larger developed territories is more difficult than that of a larger number of smaller territories, as larger territories can be the territorial base for larger integrated programmes which are necessarily more encompassing than smaller ones. They involve a larger number of sectors which administrators attempt to manage in relation to each other. Conversely, smaller territories can encompass a more limited number of sectors within the integrated

programmes which they contain and they therefore form a varying proportion of the areas of the various functions which extend beyond their
territory. The latter form a part of a less differentiated cobweb than the
former. The conclusion that it is easier for smaller territories to become
more involved in a group of sectors at a larger level follows because for them
it is a question of altering the stress within a functional boundary with the
outside world which is to some degree blurred, whereas for the larger areas
integration involves deciding to relocate a more sharply defined frontier.

What technical considerations might be reasonably taken into account
when making a judgement about whether the size of a particular region is
appropriate? This question is put at this stage in the argument not in order
to demonstrate that this or that size is best in Africa, Europe or elsewhere,
but rather to list arguments which seem to be relevant. At this stage the
arguments focus upon what happens within the region rather than upon
relations between the region and the outside world which are considered
later. The point should perhaps be repeated that arguments about size arise
only after the necessity of area and contiguity has been accepted.

There are three kinds of criteria: administrative, economic and functional,
which will be discussed briefly. A judgement about the most appropriate
size of the territory follows from the observation that larger territories
generally require larger administrations for given sectors or integrated
programmes, which are more remote from their operation, whilst smaller
territories require smaller administrations, which tend to be more
immediately involved. This remark may appear to be somewhat banal but it
nevertheless sums up a sentiment that often drives movements for regional
devolution within countries, and may equally sustain an interest in larger
regions: on the one hand people may be more closely involved and the
administration more responsive to their needs, and on the other the
administration may have greater capacity and reflect larger interests. Yet
large administrations are more likely to be inflexible and slow to adjust in
response to changes in local circumstances. They are more likely to be
subject to bureaucratic politics, that is, more given to organizational
survival and expansion rather than to the setting-up and efficient conduct of
operations. They may, however, have the benefit of more sophisticated
research programmes, and be more capable of developing a well-informed
expert overview of particular problems at a higher level. Local administrations on the other hand may be too small to generate or respond to
advanced research, and they may operate on a scale which is too small for
the effective management of an integrated programme.

Small size may also be associated with inefficiency where there is a
duplication of administrative provision in the same sector in adjacent areas
and an inability to co-ordinate at that level among sectors. The ideal level of
administration and the ideal scale of territory are therefore, self-evidently,
big enough to play a useful role in development programmes and research,
even though the activities of several administrations which perform
satisfactorily in these respects may need to be co-ordinated by another
administration at a higher level; adequate for the management of integrated

programmes, but small enough to be responsive to changes in local circumstances; big enough for the efficient use of available resources, but small enough not to waste them in excessive bureaucratization. The list may obviously be extended and each criterion may be the subject of debate.

Economic criteria also give general indications of optimum size. One complication in this context is, however, that economic criteria may be concerned with an infrastructure, which can be defined in a wider sense as including not only tangibles, such as transport facilities and power-stations, but also the range of regulations and laws about economic conduct; or they may be concerned with performance, which is more a matter of the energy, skills and attitudes of the people who inhabit that infrastructure. A regional space which is the right size to create an adequate infrastructure is no guarantee of an adequate performance.

Two kinds of economic criteria affect judgements about the minimum size of the regional space. There are, first, productivity criteria which concern the price and the range of goods produced. Within the region the market for domestically produced goods should be big enough to allow production at the unit price which approximates that in other regions. The range of such goods, both consumer and capital, should be reasonably comprehensive in terms of the standards of a modernized economy. Finally, the variety of locational and geographical circumstances in the space should be sufficient to permit a wide range of specialization. These are some of the conditions which are assumed in the theory of economic integration developed by Meade, Viner et al.[8] What they mean in basic terms is that the region should be big enough, rich enough and varied enough to provide for an adequate standard of living for its inhabitants without undue dependence on outsiders. This is not, however, to reject interdependence but rather to point to the need to place some limit upon the vulnerability to the actions of the other states which it creates.[9] This is a crude political fact based on economic criteria which could shape a judgement about whether a particular region had an appropriate size.

A second kind of economic criterion of size may be called a performance criterion. There are certain activities which, for technical reasons and/or for reasons of social convention, are not performed adequately if a facility is below a certain size. Again the need for a certain level of performance indicates a need for a certain scale of territory. Sometimes this may be a fairly straightforward matter, as with transport systems: it is obviously unsatisfactory if a railway network is confined within a minute territory, and desirable to integrate it with other modes of transport in a large one. Sometimes, however, the scale of territory is indicated more by the requirement, based on values and conventions, that a particular standard of performance is mandatory, as is the case with regard to, say, health provision: the problem of finding the resources to pay for this may be eased if the size of a territory is increased. Again the notion stands out that there can be a scale of territory which is optimal for this purpose. Indeed experience suggests that a wide range of provision is sustained in the long term only be a level of finance which can be generated in an intermediate region. Advanced research, in medicine and other matters, simply cannot be afforded within 'small' state finance; it needs sustenance from larger economic units which can exist only if they can operate within a larger space.

Of course it is possible for a unit in a smaller territory to obtain special assistance from outsiders, or to be larger than could be financed solely from that small territory because in practice it provided for and was supported by a larger functionally specific region. But in both of these cases the support will be perceived by insiders as being less reliable than if the support base were internalized. In justification of this view is the less secure legal underpinning of external support, and its relative insulation from domestic political instruction. This was a persuasive argument in favour of the EEC in the sense that it was argued that research in general could be supported more fully and at a more advanced level in the larger market. It might be argued that there are multinational companies which can afford such provision and that these are often global in scope. On the other hand they have established themselves in reasonable numbers in the Community precisely because of the size of that market compared with others around it. They would have been far less enthusiastic about this if the dominant markets were still national ones. Again the unreliable character of support from beyond the region was indicated in the late 1980s by the increasing anxiety of companies to be within the frontiers of the Community as the deadline for completing the market by 1992 drew nearer.

The third criterion by which the size of the region might be judged is indeed the functionalist one, but it should be stressed that this is only one of the three kinds of criteria. There are problems which have a specific geographical extent, though not as many as Mitrany assumed, and there is a case for tackling them in that area. For example, soil erosion in the Tennessee Valley had a clear geographical extent, as does the requirement of disease control amongst plants or animals — or people — and there are various industrial activities such as coal and steel production which can be more effectively organized on the basis of the distribution of their raw materials or sources of power, as with aluminium smelting, or of skilled labour. This was one of the reasons for Mitrany's support of the European Coal and Steel Community.[10] But, it should be repeated that the functional imperative is only of the indicators of appropriate space. This argument and its implications for functionalism are considered further later.

These then, are the main arguments against sectoralism: they generally imply a parallel argument in favour of regionalism. The costs of sectoralism are one of the explanations of the growth of regional organizations, as it indicates the source of a tendency in decision-making about technical matters in modern times which cannot be disputed. There has been a continuing, if spasmodic, concern with finding the appropriate area within which to attempt the solution of particular problems, which has frequently led to participation in regional organization; the first three explanations related to this. However, at the same time there has been the realization that it is impossible to detach one problem from a group of other related problems, so that if the first is to be solved in a particular area so must all the others: they are functionally linked. A natural inclination on the part of decision-makers to deal with single issues is therefore constantly frustrated. It turns out that problems are all too often bigger than they seem, and a start cannot be made without risking the generation of pressures towards the expansion of the functional territory. This stresses the importance of the element of process as an explanation of the growth of local sectoralism; one regional organization tends to lead to another. But it also suggests a further pressure towards regionalism in the sense defined earlier: a tendency towards the contiguity of functional boundaries beyond the state.

The anti-sectoralist argument was, therefore, not only part of an explanation of the development of regional organization: it also implied a prediction about the future development of regionalism which is explored further in the next section.

Nye has argued that local sectoralism would be extended but implied that this would not alter the international system in any significant way.[11] The prediction ventured here is different. It is that functional regions will emerge increasingly clearly in particular territories over the next few decades and that these will more frequently act together in dealings with other states. (Evidence in support of this view is in chapter 11 above.) It is not suggested that there will be any necessary merging of sovereignties or that this process will be fuelled by the appearance of regional nationalisms. Pan-Africanism, for instance, is unlikely to become a significant force, and it is difficult to detect anything analogous in Asia. Neither will the creation of these regions be the result of a conscious act of political creativity by decision-makers; there will be no outbreak of political federalism. Rather the emergence of more distinct regions will be the result of attempts to solve practical problems within and to achieve security against military attack and economic domination by outsiders.

The example of the European Communities was one reason for supposing that this would be the way of the future. In the 1980s, and especially since 1984, it became increasingly evident that there had come a point when it was increasingly difficult for member states, such as Britain, which wished to place firm limits upon the pace of increasing integration, to resist the process.[12] Viewed from the perspective of the British government the argument was pursued on the following lines: in order that the British economy should continue to grow, it was essential to be in the common market: the completion of the common market would increase the scale of benefits for the British economy; therefore there was a need to accept arrangements which would make it possible for British companies to act in the market in general as if it were the domestic market, such as those which were included in the Single European Act of 1986; these in turn made it necessary to introduce legislation on such practical matters as the specifications of goods and the simplification of the documentation required for trade between the member countries. But it also set up pressures for going beyond these immediate measures to the harmonization of the levels of taxation on goods and services, and, indeed, to the establishment of a common monetary system leading to the setting-up of a European Central Bank.

There were, in other words, a series of practical further measures which were seen as necessarily arising from having reached a particular scale in the scope of integration. What seemed to have happened was a version of what the neo-functionalists had called 'spill-over', with the significant difference that in this new form the expansive logic applied directly only to the scope rather than to both the scope and the level of integration. It placed states in the position of having to face major pressures to go forward in order to keep what they had, and indeed of having to go further forward then they really wanted to go in order to obtain a perceived benefit, in this case a Europe without frontiers[13]: this was a formidable pressure to expand the scope of integration. It derived from having reached a kind of critical mass of previous co-operative measures. A qualitative change had taken place in the pressures towards their future extension.

There was, however, a further force that was conducive to the strengthening of the regional arrangements with which the British had to deal. That was the realization, probably deliberately enhanced by the French, that a collection of states from the inner core could move ahead of them in achieving a more extensive integration unless they were careful to stay with the process. They could not opt out lest they be relegated to what in the terminology of the Communities would be described as the second tier of a two-tier system. The only course of action which was acceptable on both economic and political grounds was, therefore, to remain party to negotiations about further integration, even though this could be at the risk of having to make unwelcome concessions. The dynamic of integration within the region therefore included not only a perceived need to take steps to obtain specific benefits, but also a political element: a reluctance to be placed on the sidelines in the emerging system.

This argument may be put in terms which make it applicable to regions in general as follows: that as the scope of integration is increased, the chances of that scope being further extended are enhanced by the fear of any one partner that, unless they accept this, a more progressive coalition of their partners could emerge. This integrative dynamic therefore contains elements both of economic self-interest and of political fear. Its underlying condition is probably the appearance in the state of the widespread conviction that the benefits arising from integration are real and important, and that the costs of even partial exclusion would be considerable, resulting not only in economic disadvantage but also in political enfeeblement. This, it should be stressed, does not imply the kind of progressive fusion of sovereignties that was foreseen by the neo-functionalist, but rather the emergence of a what could be called a symbiotic relationship between the state and the region: the well-being of each is seen as being necessary for the sustenance of the other. If the trend towards increased participation in regional organizations discussed above continues, the judgement that they generate significant benefits must become a valid one in a number of regions outside Europe, and the emergence of a modified 'spill-over' in these other areas is, therefore, to be expected.

These are incentives towards the strengthening of regional arrangements which were contained within the area. But there were also pressures in that same direction which derived from relationships between that area and international society. Some of these were contingent. They depended on assumptions about likely developments in that society: that there would be continuing turbulence in the international economic system in the sense that liberal trade arrangements at the global level would remain under threat, and pressures towards protectionism and special trade deals — the new mercantilism — would remain; and that the superpowers would tend, as they seemed to be doing in the late 1980s, to be less activist in their preparedness to intervene militarily outside their own areas, and, indeed, would become indifferent towards, or supportive of, the playing of a greater role by other states in the latter's own locality. Given these assumptions, the prediction ventured is that there would be a tendency among the various emerging regions to equalize upwards — not that they would all become equal but that there would be pressures from international society which pushed in that direction. The pattern of relations with the outside world would enhance the regions' internal consolidation and tend to increase the size of the smaller towards that of the larger units in the system. In practice, of course, this meant once again a tendency to emulate the dimensions of the European Communities and the United States.

The history of the European Communities suggests that as the scope of integration increased so did the tendency to increase membership. The three stages of expansion, in 1973, 1981 and 1986, all suggested that governments sought to join because they thought that members were completing the phase of negative integration — removing barriers on exchanges between them — and going beyond that to positive integration, namely the setting in place of new common arrangements. In all cases the evidence of political commitment to unification in the states seeking membership was ambiguous. There was little enthusiasm for joining a political union, though there was an anxiety not to be marginalized either economically or politically. On the other hand, had the scope of integration remained at a low level there was little evidence to suggest that the British and the others would have been much worried about joining or that the Scandinavian countries, Switzerland, and others, would have been so anxious to join the same economic space, whilst stopping short for reasons of their own from full membership. So it seemed probable that increasing scope amongst the core of original members set up pressures towards expansion.

The question arises, however, of when the expansion might be expected to stop. The general answer to this question must be that this happens when in the judgement of members the costs of further expansion are seen as being likely to exceed the benefits of not doing so. On the one hand the costs in terms of the drain upon the resources of the regional organizations are likely to increase with expansion, because the core states are likely to be richer than later applicants, and because the latter are likely to seek the help of the former with their economic development.

Founding members — core states — have in practice been richer than later candidates for admission, but according to Karl Deutsch this is also probable for theoretical reasons.[14] On the other hand the case for further enlargement, from the point of view of existing members, in order to enhance economic security — to provide for economic defensive needs, which were discussed earlier — is likely to become weaker as size increases.

This goal is an incentive towards the creation of regional organizations, but it is also an incentive towards increasing their membership until the size has reached a point at whcih members together are more capable of withstanding turbulence in a relatively less managed international economy — their vulnerability has been lessened. The net increment in the effectiveness with which these defensive economic needs are met is likely to become smaller as the size is increased until a point is reached at which costs incurred outweigh any further benefits. At this point prospective members are likely to receive a cool response, especially if, like Turkey in the case of the European Communities, their accession threatens to impose serious burdens upon the resources of the region.

Equalization is therefore driven by the perception by governments that it is in their interest to reduce vulnerability and, beyond that, to equalize the degree of mutual sensitivity.[15] It is not denied that other considerations may impede this process in the short and medium term. But nevertheless it must be regarded as a constant in the international economic system. It should also be stressed again that it has not been assumed that states involved in this process are being required to sacrifice their sovereignty. Indeed, precisely the opposite is the case. The symbiotic relationship between the region and the member states encourages governments to see the strengthening of the region as a way of enhancing their own sovereignty. The only important caveat in this context is that as scope expands, it is inevitable that perceptions of what is necessary in that sovereignty should also change.

It is also necessary to look at the way in which regionalization is related to international coalitions, alliances and spheres of influence. The experience of the European Communities suggests that the emergence of the region changes the dynamics of the alliance of which it is a part and the idea of a sphere of influence in which regional states were previously subordinate is weakened. This is because economic interests and military strategic interests are on a continuum: as governments acquire a wider range of common economic interests it is likely that incentives towards creating a common defence also increase. Hence in the late 1970s the idea that the members of the European Communities should strengthen their common defensive arrangements was more frequently proposed and discussed than had earlier been the case. One idea which had become current in the mid-1980s was that the West European Union should be reactivated, but there were other proposals for moving the Community itself from a civil power to a military one.[16] This again was a logical outcome of the expansion of the scope of integration; it was probable that any region would be more likely to seek a stronger common defence as its range of common economic interests expanded.

In the Third World regionalization would necessarily only appear at the expense of the grand coalition of the Group of 77 which had solidified around a consensus about anti-colonialism and support for the New International Economic Order. In the late 1970s and 1980s there was, however, evidence to suggest that this consensus was under pressure. Peterson concluded:

it is possible that in the 1990s politics in the [General] Assembly will return to conditions prevalent between 1955 and 1964 when *ad hoc* coalitions controlled proceedings and decisions on different issues . . . the tendency to link as many issues as possible by insisting on the need for 'new international orders' of similar characteristics across them would also decrease.[17]

She added:

the next few years are likely to see the third world coalition limp along, trying to bury disagreements by keeping them out of the Assembly or taking very vague general positions . . . once discussion gets beyond generalities to specifics, intra-third world divisions surface [as in] comprehensive North-South negotiations, the law of the sea, or UN restructuring.[18]

The implication of Peterson's remarks was that as the larger coalition came under threat it would become more likely that smaller coalitions would emerge in time among contiguous territories in response to the various pressures towards regionalization. The attempts to preserve the fiction of Third World harmony, which had earlier obstructed such developments, would be abandoned.

In the major alliance of the Western developed world, NATO, the dominant power, the United States began in the 1980s to push more vigorously the idea that the junior partners, the Europeans, should, given their greater economic prosperity, contribute more to their own defence within the alliance. There should be a more equitable burden-sharing.[19] At the same time, therefore, there appeared at this particular stage in the development of regional integration in Western Europe incentives from within and from without to emerge as a regional military power. Of course the US government and some commentators had seen such a prospect not as damaging the NATO alliance but rather as a way of persuading the Europeans to play a more active role within it. It is, however, difficult to see how encouraging Europeans to pay more to the defence budget would do any such thing: they would be more likely to be encouraged to consolidate their own distinctive arrangements and pursue more actively their own personal interests. NATO may survive but with a greater tendency towards bifurcation and the idea of an American sphere of influence extending over the Atlantic would look clearly less credible.

In other parts of the world these pressures towards the adding of a military dimension to regional economic integration are more remote and may take different forms. However, the conclusion that the organization of military defence is likely to follow close behind that of economic defence, wherever there is regionalization, is hard to resist. The developments within regions in the late 1980s therefore seem to justify the conclusion that the kind of multi-bloc world discussed by Masters in the 1960s could yet emerge.[20] This is another dimension of the process of equalization upwards.

The argument has moved from an attempt to show that local sectoralism would evolve into regionalism in the sense of an increasing participation in co-extensive regional arrangements, to an argument which suggested that international society, for reasons which related to what happened within the regions and also to what happened between them and the outside world, would become dominated by a small number of regional blocs. As the argument was developed so the time span in which their validity might be demonstrated was increased. Nevertheless it seemed to me that pressures towards regionalization were inherent in international society and that grounds for doubt arose only with regard to the time span in which they might be expected to succeed.[21] In other words they would lead to the transformation of international society.

A number of conclusions about the development of international organization and society may be deduced from the preceding discussion. There is, first, a point to be made about the reform of global international institutions which derives from the evidence of emerging local sectoralism. This is that discussion of the reform of the major controlling intergovernmental committees of states now needs to pay much more attention to the development of regional representation. In the Security Council this already seemed to be emerging in that in the 1980s there was a tendency to elect more frequently the various major regional leaders to the temporary positions. Conversely it was much less likely that states which were too minor to be able to bring any real diplomatic assets to the role would be elected. This was the emerging practice. It might be argued, however, that such a practice, which could only strengthen the global institutions, should be formalized. Certainly any scheme for the reform of international institutions now needed to take account of this and Bertrand was surely correct to do so.[22]

A number of points about the implications of the preceding discussion for the approach to international organization called functionalism also need to be made. The question must be asked of whether it would be possible to produce a modified version of functionalism, so that as a version of sectoralism it would nevertheless be compatible with the notion that regional space was necessary. Could it in some sense be softened, as with the other two major alternatives, nationalism and globalism, so that it could be reconciled with regionalization? (See chapter 11 above.)

Such a reconciliation begins with the observation that there always was in functionalism a certain discontinuity between its premises and the way in which the arguments were developed by Mitrany. This discontinuity has been sharpened by the use of the word 'cobweb' to describe the kind of world which the functionalists allegedly wished to create and, indeed, predicted.[23] The problem with the analogy of the cobweb, however, was that it implied the discounting of the relative discontinuities and concentrations of international transactions in international society: states would be progressively subsumed in a seamless web. There is, however, something misleading about the analogy which might be revealed in a brief examination of what a spider's web actually looks like. It is not, in fact, a continuous seam but rather has a whole series of discontinuities. There are clusters of denser webbing which are linked together with weaker and sparser threads, and, of course, at the centre of each cluster sits in his or her own territory the individual spider. The cobweb is, therefore, a highly differentiated system with subunits, highly territorial, easily identified. It is necessary only to recall the evidence about the increasing number of regional organizations in the world to draw the conclusion that the spider's web is about as misleading an analogy of what the world is in fact like, or what it is turning into, as is that of the billiards balls.

As with the cobweb a closer examination of functionalism reveals a degree of differentiation which is often ignored. The point is often missed that Mitrany did not intend the state to disappear: instead, like Gulliver in the land of the Lilliputians, it was to be tied with a myriad of functional ties to other states in the system. But it was also unclear what the functions of the state were to be. In the early days of the functionalist process it could be a political umbrella for the new international institutions, and it could also be a kind of residual category of functions in which 'form' had not yet followed 'function'. At various points in the functionalist writings it was also implied that the state could have a role as custodian of cultural values: Mitrany was anxious that it would not be understood that he was advocating the abandonment of cultural diversity, and seemed to think that different culturally defined groups could prosper in the new functionalist world.[24] So functionalism also admitted at various points a compromise with sectoralism: at the beginning of the process, as a residual category and with regard to cultural values.

However, a further kind of compromise was implied in the early arguments derived from the experience of the Tennessee Valley Authority (TVA), which was, according to Mitrany, the exemplar of the functionalist approach.[25] This was that the area of the Valley was chosen, not because it was the result of a happy coincidence of a number of applications of the rule that 'form should follow function', but rather of the judgement that it was necessary to choose a single area in which to base an integrated programme of social, economic and ecological activities. In this case the functionalist imperative was decisive only in the sense that there was an overriding need to tackle the problem of soil erosion in that particular valley, but, beyond that, sectoralism in Mitrany's arguments, and in the practice of the

Authority was largely ignored. The deriving of the analogy of the undifferentiated cobweb from this experience was, therefore, unfortunate. Rather it supported the argument that the choice of that territory which was most appropriate to the integrated programme must take priority over 'form follows function' if the primary task was to be achieved: the cobweb had to be differentiated. The example of the Tennessee Valley Authority illustrated the pressures in favour of regionalism rather than the virtues of sectoralism.

Where does this leave the doctrine that 'form follows function'? As was suggested earlier this is one — but only one — of the considerations which affects and should affect the choice of a particular size of regional space. As is implied by the example of the TVA, the size which is ideal for the attainment of one functional goal may need to be adjusted to suit the integrated programme. Ideally, therefore, it is a question of balancing the costs of not following the doctrine in the particular instance against the benefits which this produces for the integrated programme.

These modifications to functionalism reinforce a view about the pattern of development of international society in the long term which was episodic rather than evolutionary. Three stages are indicated. The first was the loose bipolar world of the period from the 1950s until the late 1960s. Second was a period of increasing regionalization emerging from an enhanced local sectoralism such as was postulated above for the late 1980s and 1990s. In this period the ratio of interactions and organizations in international society in general declined in comparison with that at the regional level. The world would become increasingly differentiated, as regional interactions became more intense. A third stage would be reached when a small number of multi-bloc systems had emerged which were perceived as being of roughly similar levels of development and, putting the matter in very general terms, of power. There had been equalization upwards.

At this third stage the links between the blocs were likely to increase in comparison with those at the regional level: the cobweb would become less differentiated. The functionlist argument could also be interpreted as being applicable at the global level only when this stage was reached. As Inis Claude pointed out in his excellent critique of functionalism, the approach seemed to be irrelevant in a world in which a large number of states were underdeveloped[26]: there was not much upon which to base transnational functional activities. It was a paradox that a period of modernization, of development and, therefore, of the consolidation of the state, had to precede the functionlist epoch: states had to be stengthened in order to be transcended.

The points could now be added. First the creation of multi-bloc regionally based systems had the advantage of helping with development and with the creation of the hooks upon which the myriad ties of the Lilliputian analogy could be anchored. Second, it also had the very considerable advantage, as the experience of the European Communities suggested, of allowing individual states to be strengthened at the same time as the region as a whole had an increasing propensity to act as a single unit in relations with the outside world — the sovereignty of the individual states did not appear to be threatened despite the fact that they increasingly seemed to be a single actor in the eyes of the outside world. Third, the regionalization process, through equalization upwards, would also counter the problem that global sectoral arrangements were frequently seen as benefiting the bigger and richer states more than the smaller, poorer ones.

There were, therefore, a number of reasons for supposing that in the third phase the cobweb was more likely to become less differentiated at the global level. This would also be a reflection of the modified functionalism outlined above — an appropriate compromise between sectoralism and regionalism. Yet there was also in this, of course, an intimation of a fourth phase which could appear in the distant future, one in which out of the relative inefficiences of inter-group sectorialism arose new pressures towards the creation of an increasing range of global integrated programmes.

There is, of course, a further vitally important question which will be dealt with all too briefly in this chapter: would a world dominated by a relatively small number of regions be a stable and orderly one? I agree with the conclusions reached by Masters that it probably would be orderly, and it is not proposed to repeat Masters' argument here. It might be added, however, that the dynamics of the new regionalism suggest that the new groups would not be expansionist or highly active in their external policy. Again the experience of the European Communities is relevant, which was that a considerable proportion of governments' total available diplomatic energy was expended in managing the regional system of which they were members; there would be little inclination to seek actively new possessions in the external environment.

Mancur Olson developed a number of further arguments on similar lines which reinforced Masters' conclusions.[27] He reasoned that a larger number of smaller groups, such as lobbies, professional associations, and trade unions, were more likely to seek to acquire a greater share of a particular pie for themselves, whilst a smaller number of larger units, which he labelled 'encompassing organizations' were more likely to make common cause in increasing the size of the pie. These arguments seem to have a number of important implications for co-operation between states, even though there are obvious differences between international society and domestic society.

On the one hand, as regionalization must mean that there were fewer units in the international system, they would be more easily persuaded both of the 'pay-offs' from co-operation and of the need to participate in international arrangements in order to obtain them. This naturally assumes that global sectoralism is perceived as being capable of producing signficant benefits. As with 'encompassing organizations', the governing systems of the larger units would be more likely to judge that co-operation would increase the size of the pie, and that their positive involvement was necessary for this to happen. On the other hand, there would by definition be a reduction in the number of smaller units, which may be seen as the equivalent of Olson's special interests and collusions, and, following his reasoning, there would therefore also be a reduction in the weight of the pressures directed primarily towards the redistribution of wealth, as, for example, through the radical reordering of international society, rather than towards its creation, and of the numbers of 'free-riders' in the system. Olson's thesis, therefore, also suggests that an international society dominated by a smaller number of regional blocs is likely to be an orderly place.

However, these are very much arguments about the longer term. There is now evidence to show that in the 1980s regional organization, for a number of reasons, had continued to grow at an impressive rate in Africa and Asia. This in itself was a significant development. But there were also grounds for supposing that this would be beyond local sectoralism and would evolve on the pattern of the European Communities into a number of regional blocs in which there was an increasing tendency to expand the scope of integration whilst at the same time maintaining a symbiotic relationship between the state and the collectivity. A crucial part of the argument at this point was that the sectoral approach produced, for technical reasons, a number of costs which could be overcome by a greater measure of co-ordination in integrated programmes. These costs were the source of a continuing underlying pressure towards expanding the scope of integration, and hitherto they have been rather neglected in the academic literature about regional integration. All this had important implications for functionalism and the future of international society.

There was, however, another aspect to the argument. This was that the relative unpopularity of regionalism in the literature had been overtaken by events. The time had come to re-examine the empirical and normative aspects of the subject, which had been impeded in the mid-1970s by a sense of what was fashionable among the community of scholars.

Notes

1. 32/197 is contained in UN GA Official Records: Thirty-second Session, Supplement No. 45 (A.32/45) September–December 1977, at pp. 121–7.
2. R.G.A. Jackson, *A Study of the Capacity of the United Nations Development System* UN Doc. DP/5 1969, Geneva, 1969.
3. Parts of the Bertrand Report are included in Paul Taylor and A.J.R. Groom (eds), *International Institutions at Work* London, Pinter Publishers, 1988.
4. Jason L. Finkle and Barbara B. Crane, 'Ideology and politics at Mexico City: the United States at the 1984 International Conference on Population', *Population and Development Review* Vol. 11, March 1985, No. 1.
5. Stephen D. Krasner (ed.), *International Regimes* Ithaca, Cornell University Press, 1983; see also his *structural Conflict: the Third World against global liberalism*, Berkeley, University of California Press, 1985.
6. See Donella Meadows *et al.*, *The Limits to Growth*, New York, New American Library, 1972; and Mihajlo Mesarovic and Edouard Pestel, *Mankind at the Turning Point*, New York, Dutton, 1974.
7. See note 3.
8. For a discussion of their work and a bibliography, see Peter Robson, *The Economics of International Integration*, London, Allen & Unwin, 1980.

9. The terms 'vulnerability' and 'sensitivity' are used here in the special sense developed by Robert O. Keohane and Joseph S. Nye in their *Power and Interdependence*, Boston, Little, Brown, 1977.

10. David Mitrany, 'The functional approach in historical perspective', *International Affairs*, Vol. 47, No. 3, 1971.

11. Joseph S. Nye, 'Regional Institutions', In Cyril E. Black and Richard A. Falk, *The Structure of the International Environment*, which is Vol. IV of their *The Future of the International Legal Order*, Princeton, Princeton University Press, 1972; reproduced in Richard A. Falk and Saul H. Mendlovitz (eds), *Regional Politics and World Order*, San Francisco, W.H. Freeman, 1973.

12. Paul Taylor, 'The new dynamics of EC integration in the 1980s', in Juliet Lodge (ed.), *The European Community and the Challenge of the Future*, London, Pinter Publishers, 1989.

13. 'Europe without frontiers' was the popular description of the proposal to complete the liberalization of the common market in the European Community by 1992.

14. Karl W. Deutsch *et al.*, *Political Community and the North Atlantic Area*, Princeton, NJ, Princeton University Press, 1957.

15. See note 9 above.

16. Hedley Bull, 'Civilian power Europe: a contradiction in terms?', in Loukas Tsoukalis, *The European Community: Past, Present and Future*, Oxford, Basil Blackwell, 1983, pp. 149–64; Bernard Burrows and Geoffrey Edwards, *The Defence of Western Europe*, London, Butterworth, 1982.

17. M.J. Peterson, *The General Assembly in World Politics*, Boston, Allen & Unwin, 1986, p. 204.

18. Ibid., p. 257.

19. David Calleo, *Beyond American Hegemony: the future of the Western Alliance*, Brighton, Wheatsheaf Books, 1987; and Andrew J. Pierre (ed.), *A Widening Atlantic? domestic change and foreign policy*, New York, Council on Foreign Relations, 1986.

20. Roger Masters, 'A multi-bloc model of the international system', *American Political Science Review*, Vol. 55, No. 4, December 1961, pp. 780–98.

21. See note 11 above.

22. See note 3 above.

23. A.J.R. Groom, 'Functionalism and world society', in A.J.R. Groom and Paul Taylor (eds), *Functionalism: theory and practice in international relations*, London, University of London Press, 1975.

24. David Mitrany, *The Functional Theory of Politics*, Martin Robertson, London, 1975.

25. David Mitrany, *A Working Peace System*, Chicago, Quadrangle Books, 1966, pp. 157–8.

26. I.L. Claude, *Swords into Plowshares*, New York, Randon House, 1971.

27. Mancur Olson, *The Rise and Decline of Nations*, New Haven and London, Yale University Press, 1982.

Selected reading

The Bertrand Report: contained in Paul Taylor and A.J.R. Groom (eds), *International Institutions at Work*, London, Pinter Publishers, 1988.

Kothari, Rajni, *Footsteps into the future: diagnosis of the present world and a design for an alternative*, New York, The Free Press, 1974.

Masters, Roger, 'A multi-bloc model of the international system', *American Political Science Review*, Vol. 55, No. 4, December 1961.

Taylor, Paul, 'The new dynamics of EC integration in the 1980s', in Juliet Lodge (ed.), *The European Community and the challenge of the future*, London, Pinter Publishers, 1989.

Yalem, Ronald, *Regionalism and World Order*, Public Affairs Press, Washington, DC, 1965.

17 Transactions, networks and systems
Peter Willetts

The term 'international organizations' is usually taken to refer to the institutional structures of intergovernmental organizations (IGOs). In more modern writing, since the beginning of the 1970s, some writers would also use it to cover the institutions of international non-governmental organizations (INGOs). This chapter will explore the idea of a much wider usage of 'international organization' (without the 's'), to cover any regular structure of interactions, whether or not it is formally institutionalized. Such a concept may be used within each of the four competing paradigms for the study of international relations: the Realist, Functionalist, Structuralist and Global Politics paradigms.[1] The general concept of international organizations is not favoured by most Realists, but transactions, networks or systems are — in different forms — central to each of the other three paradigms.

The Realist approach to international organization

While the Realist emphasis on sovereign 'states' pursuing 'power' within a condition of international anarchy is not usually seen to be compatible with the idea of an international system exercising control over the actions of states, there is also a Realist tradition of studying international order, in which the international system does have a structure and states are subject to external constraints.[2] In its weakest form, the concept of international society is used. A recent book explained the concept as follows:

By an international society we mean a group of states . . . which not merely form a system, in the sense that the behaviour of each is a necessary factor in the calculations of the others, but also have established by dialogue and consent common rules and institutions for the conduct of their relations, and recognise their common interest in maintaining these arrangements.[3]

Such a concept of international society encompasses intergovernmental institutions, international law, the procedures and the practice of diplomacy and the extent to which a common global morality has developed. It is still state-centric (neglecting or denying the role of non-governmental actors, even though they are involved extensively in IGOs, in international law, in diplomacy and in the development of global morality) and it is still compatible with power-theory, by emphasizing the rational consent of states to their participation in international society.

The concept of a regime, which was outlined in chapter 14 by Roger Tooze, is accepted by some Realists. it has more theoretical impact than does the concept of international society. The norms and procedures of regimes impose significant constraints on governments within the relevant issue-area; the structure of a regime does not necessarily correspond to the overall structure of 'the international system'; and most regimes include some transnational corporations (TNCs) and/or non-governmental organizations (NGOs) as major participants. (This chapter will follow the UN practice of using TNC to describe organizations whose activities are primarily commercial and NGO to describe non-profit-making private associations, including the industry-wide lobbies for commercial organizations.) For some writers, including the current author, these features of regimes make them *one* of the phenomena which invalidate the claim by Realists that they understand world politics; for others, regime theory provides a significant, but not critical, modification of Realism; while for some Realists the importance of regimes must be denied, because they believe that the effects of regimes in the real world have been exaggerated.[4]

Lastly, the concept of a balance of power has varying interpretations among Realists. In a loose form it just indicates a process of interaction by which rivalries between states are played out. In Kaplan's formal model, which reflects historians' views of the nineteenth-century international system, the balance of power depended upon a great fluidity in the choices of alliances made by states.[5] But for Waltz the emphasis is on a highly structured system, which dominates the choices of individual state actors.[6] It is important to acknowledge that the concept of a structured global system is not incompatible with state-centric power-theory. Nevertheless, with the exception of Waltz and some more recent writers, the concept of a system has usually been adopted by those who wish to challenge Realism.

Karl Deutsch was the first writer from within the Realist tradition to give consideration to non-state international exchanges, in what became known as the analysis of transactions. His starting point in *Nationalism and Social Communication* was that 'cultures produce, select and channel information'.[7] Therefore, study of the patterns of communication will reveal the fundamental political structures: 'A larger group of persons linked by such complementary habits and facilities of communication we may call a people.'[8] But Deutsch shows himself still to be following the logic of the Realist tradition in the argument that a people become a nationality when they seek power; they become a nation when they acquire some power; and they become a nation-state when they take control of a state organization.[9] (Other writers have not followed Deutsch in his distinction between a people, a nationality and a nation and just use the one word, nation, to describe the three situations.) While most Realists take for granted the existence of contemporary states, Deutsch asked important questions about the assimilation of different peoples into a single people and about the differentiation of one people into two or more separate peoples, through changes in communication patterns. His challenge would have been much more revolutionary, if he had taken the next logical step and asked how much the peoples of the modern world now actually match the current boundaries of states. We will return to the question later, with the consideration of multi-nation states and multi-state nations.

In *Political Community and the North Atlantic Area*, Deutsch and his team of researchers went on from the analysis of the formation of nations within individual countries to the analysis of the integration process across country boundaries.[10] He was concerned with the development of 'security communities', defined as groups of people with institutions, practices and a sense of community, such that social problems will be resolved without the use of physical force.[11] It is interesting that writing in the 1950s Deutsch's group focused more on the historical cases of integration, which brought together diverse territories into the current countries of Europe. Now, such a work would have to address itself to the fact that the whole of Western Europe, with a total of 22 separate countries (excluding Greece, Turkey and Cyprus), has become a single security community. In addition the theory must deal with the paradox that in Africa, while few countries are security communities internally, the continent as a whole (excluding perhaps Morocco, Libya, Somalia and South Africa) has become a security community for relations between the countries.[12]

Indeed, on a world-wide basis, war between governments has become so morally unacceptable, so irrelevant to most contemporary problems and, when it is used, so ineffective as a policy instrument that the evolution of a global security-community within a few decades from now does not seem fanciful. War is still a common phenomenon, but largely through groups which feel oppressed within their own country, fighting, sometimes with external support, against their government. (After the ferocity of the 1980-8 Iran–Iraq war, such an assessment may seem too optimistic. But even in this case one may note that neither side formally declared a legal state of war, each limited its actions against the other's cities and against merchant shipping, neither received direct military support from its allies and each government had to contend with the Kurdish nation and other minority groups.) Change has been so fast that just three decades ago Deutsch did not apply his concept of a security community to the North Atlantic area as a whole, whereas now we take it for granted that inter-governmental war in this region has become obsolete. Arend Lijphart has argued that consideration of such developments presents a fundamental challenge to Realism, because theorizing about pluralistic security communities 'disputes the axiomatic character of the relationship between anarchy and war'.[13] Again the implications of Deutsch's work are more profound than its explicit content.

One important line of research to develop from Deutsch's emphasis on communications was 'transactions analysis'. As computers became available to United States academics in the 1960s, vast arrays of statistics for all countries could be processed. Data was analysed on the international movement of mail, tourists, students, migrants, books, news, phone calls and air flights. These variables measured inter-society contacts, in which the data reflected the aggregation of decisions taken by thousands, or millions, of individual people. Further data, on diplomatic exchanges, treaties, shared memberships in intergovernmental organizations, technical assistance, official aid and cultural exchanges, measured intergovernmental contacts, which reflected the decisions of small numbers of political leaders. In addition, data on the attributes of countries, such as their internal economic, social and political structures, did not cover transactions, but gave measures of the similarity of different countries. This research school reached its culmination in the studies by Russett and by Rummel, both of whom used factor analysis to identify clusters of variables, which correlated with each other, and clusters of countries, which could be seen as more integrated regions.[14]

Despite the continuing theoretical value of Deutsch's emphasis on communications, the transactions research of the 1950s and the 1960s failed to live up to the promises it appeared to offer. Firstly, most of the data was only available to give each country's gross exchanges with all the other countries in the world, rather than exhanges between pairs of countries. Thus the data was inappropriate for the study of integration, because the fact that two countries may relate in idential ways to the world as a whole is no evidence that they relate to each other at all. While this point seems obvious, we need to remember it when reading the work of Russett and of Rummel. Secondly, the data was aggregated within each country, so that we cannot tell within the overall pattern whether key economic, social or political groups have different levels of transactions from the average for the country as a whole. Thirdly, there were few good time-series, so the data could not capture the dynamic nature of the communications approach to integration. Finally, neither the theory nor the methodology readily copes with the fact that transaction patterns may vary substantially from one type of exchange to another. Thus, British people have their main tourist links with Western Europe; their migration, church and student exchanges with Commonwealth countries; and their plays, films and pop music shared with the United States — with whom are the British integrated? Yet again the next step, of conceptualizing the world as a multitude of networks, had to be made later by other writers.

While Deutsch never fully broke with the Realist approach, and in particular continued to use its language of 'states' and 'power', his work laid the foundations for two research schools which did make the break. Deutsch's work on integration fed into the Neo-Functionalists study of integration in Western European institutions and Deutsch's work on transactions fed into the study of the transnational relations of TNCs and NGOs within the Global Politics paradigm. The communications approach to nationalism is rarely referred to now, but should still be regarded as one of the foundations for theory-building.[15]

A more typical Realist reponse to all the literature on non-governmental transactions is to admit the existence of the economic, social, cultural and information flows across country boundaries, but to deny their importance. The core of the global system is seen as the 'high politics' of diplomacy and security among 'states', while other relationships are dismissed as 'low politics'. the distinction appears to imply a dubious normative proposition, that low politics transactions should be of less concern, and two false empirical propositions: that governments are not involved in low politics and that governments can prevent these transactions occurring when they object to them. This chapter will argue: (1) that governments are involved in networks of transactions with non-governmental actors on all issues: (2) that governments do have an impact upon most international interactions; but (3) governments are also constrained by their interactions. In other words, the high-politics/low-politics distinction does not exist in the real world. The TNC, NGO, INGO, governmental and IGO interactions take place within separate systems of international organization for each political issue. Before this position is argued, we will briefly consider the Functionalist and Structuralist approaches to transactions.

The Functionalist approach to international organization

The Functionalist paradigm has provided an explicit attack upon Realist concerns, with David Mitrany being the first major writer to develop this approach. His ideas are examined in more detail in Paul Taylor's chapter, but will be presented in brief outline here. Mitrany from the early years of this century reacted against the spread of intolerant nationalism, fascism and communism, with the idea that the existence of the state encouraged unscrupulous politicians to develop ideologies in order to seize power. When ordinary people were freed from ideology, they would realize that states were becoming obsolete. Certain tasks or *functions* have to be performed to improve the common welfare in a modern society. The appropriate structures for each task will not be territorially based governments, but organizations of individuals involved in the particular function.

Mitrany saw this both as a prescriptive analysis, the world *ought* to develop this way, and as an explanatory analysis, the world *is* empirically changing this way. The significance for the study of international relations is that many functions cannot be handled within single countries. Some functions, such as air travel, are intrinsically transnational. Other functions — a classic example would be the final elimination of smallpox by the World Health Organization in 1980 — can be handled on a local basis, but are much more efficiently and effectively tackled by an appropriate regional or global organization.

Thus Mitrany's emphasis in the field of international organization was on the development of many specialized, economic and social institutions. These might be international NGOs or, if governments are involved, they should include the specialist welfare and technical ministries, rather than the foreign ministries. Mitrany's ideal was that international organizations would not be based on geographical regions, unless that was appropriate for their task, nor should they be 'political'. Contemporary Functionalists have decried the 'politicization' of United Nations specialized agencies, by the introduction of disputes about general North–South issues, apartheid and the Palestinian question.[16] Mitrany did not pay attention to the UN or general regional intergovernmental organizations. After welcoming the formation of the European Coal and Steel Community, he became antagonistic towards the European Community and the federalist aspirations associated with it.

Burton with his ideas of World Society is sufficiently similar to Mitrany to be classified as being within the Functionalist paradigm. He too is a strong polemicist against the state and asserts the moral superiority of voluntary co-operation of networks of individuals operating across country boundaries. His work is more abstract than Mitrany's. Burton is concerned with any type of network, whether or not it is institutionalized. He is also concerned with any type of transaction, though there is a presumption that most will be for functional reasons. Burton's famous metaphor is of cobwebs of interactions:

there are so many direct communications, or systems, that a world map which represented them would look like a mass of cobwebs superimposed on one another, strands converging at some points more than others and being concentrated between some points more than between others. The boundaries of states would be hidden from view.[17]

The state is seen as a non-legitimate institution because it uses coercive relationships, but it is also on the decline as legitimized relationships come to predominate in world society. Burton went further than Mitrany in developing a theory of conflict and conflict resolution. This is an extension of Functionlism, because his fundamental assumption is that misperceptions of reality prevent the parties to conflicts from perceiving their common interests. Conflicts may be resolved by their conversion from 'zero-sum games' to 'positive-sum games'.[18] Like Mitrany, Burton does not expect the UN or other intergovernmental institutions to be relevant to conflict resolution.

The United Nations is in some respects a closed club of state authorities seeking to preserve themselves, even, if necessary, against the interest of many peoples. . . . We cannot assume that an international institution comprising governments reflects the interest of world society.[19]

The interesting point to note is that Mitrany and Burton have an analytical approach that in some senses is a mirror image of the Realists. The image is identical in that both paradigms characterize 'states' as being involved in power relationships and both see economic, social, cultural and information flows as occurring in networks, which are not inter-state. Each paradigm acknowledges the other paradigm in the high-politics/low-politics distinction. Where the Realists and the Functionalists differ is in the assertion as to which type of politics is typical of the modern world. The two paradigms are equally deficient in failing to consider the relationships between governmental and non-governmental organizations. Both are

dismissive of intergovernmental organizations. Each tends to see governments as relying on coercion and NGOs as engaging in legitimized,
voluntary action: neither is much concerned with how governmental
relations may be legitimized nor how patterns of conflict including the use
of coercion may arise in non-governmental relations. Given the lack of
attention paid to the whole United Nations system and the regional
intergovernmental organizations, Functionalists cannot be seen as making a
contribution to the study of the politics of decision-making in international
institutions. Indeed it is built into the paradigm that this is not their
concern. Functionalists are focused on international organization, in the
broad sense of networks of co-operative interactions, but not in the specific
sense of political conflict over policy within institutional structures.

As we have already mentioned, Deutsch's work on integration led on to a
research school which focused on the process of integration within Western
European institutions. Because this school emphasized the economic and
social realm rather than the traditional concern with security and military
alliances and because it considered the transnational relations of the
relevant social groups, it was seen as a form of Functionalism. However, the
new writers also gave a central role to governments in their analyses and this
made them different from Mitrany's Functionalism. There was also a shift
in emphasis from NGOs, which often may been seen as working for the
general interest within society, to TNCs working for their own private
interests. The new research school came to be known as Neo-Functionalism.
Again, this is covered in more detail in chapter 10 of this book, by R. J.
Harrison.

Ernst Haas produced the most impressive Neo-Functionalist work: in
Beyond the Nation-State, he made a careful critique of Functionalism,
suggested major modifications to the theory and applied his approach to a
case-study of the International Labour Organisation.[20] Haas denied the
separability of high and low politics and downgraded the Utopian rationality of believing that welfare issues automatically produce co-operation
for the common good. Integration is the result of conscious decisions by
political actors that they want to pursue common goals, or perhaps just
compatible goals. Institutions may develop increased authority and
legitimacy for co-operation and individual actors may come to learn that it
benefits them. Then, when it is realized that the original goals cannot be met
within the original institutional mandate, the task may be expanded and the
mandate extended. Haas stressed how political decisions produce
'unintended consequences' and coined the term 'spill-over' to describe the
haphazard progress of integration.

During the 1960s a major research school developed from Haas's work
and it predominantly concentrated on integration in the European Communities. After President de Gaulle's veto on British membership and his
refusal to adopt supranational, majority voting, which brought into question the inevitability of integration in the EEC, this specialization served to
weaken the research school's appeal. Neo-Functionalism seemed to assume
steady incremental progress, even though Haas had allowed for the

possibility of disintegration.[21] The criticisms of Neo-Functionalism are similar to those of Functionalism. Social and economic groups, in particular circumstances, may come to feel that their interests lie in opposing integration. A theory which is based on processes of political communication is inadequate if it ignores the barriers of language and differing political cultures. Non-economic connections between domestic and foreign political groups can affect the political outcomes. (The East African Community, which in many areas had achieved greater integration than the EEC, was destroyed by the connections between Ugandan domestic politics, Tanzanian politics and the EAC institutions.) Finally, the integration process may be affected significantly by events in the wider international environment.[22]

Neither Functionalism nor Neo-Functionalism is now a major research school. While articles are still produced from within the paradigm, neither has more than a small number of adherents.[23] Functionalism does not survive the charge that it is more prescriptive than analytical and seems to have little relevance to most issues, because it gives inadequate attention to governments and intergovernmental relations. Neo-Functionalism became vulnerable to the complex ebbs and flows buffeting the flagship of integration in Western Europe. If it is restricted to pluralist democracies and to their regional economic institutions, then Neo-Functionalism may appear not to be generally applicable to the study of all IGOs and INGOs. However, the Functionalists have performed a valuable service in drawing attention to the complex, overlapping networks of economic and social NGOs. Similarly, the Neo-Functionalists should encourage us to ask about the activities of TNCs and NGOs in *all* IGOs, Both the Functionalists and the Neo-Functionalists are concerned with important aspects of international organization, which the Realists have ignored.

The Structuralist approach to international organization

The Marxists analyse each country in terms of the class structure of its society, which is based upon the underlying economic relationships. This provides an impressive paradigm covering economics, sociology, politics and even aspects of psychology. Lenin extended it to the international domain with his theory of imperialism and in the 1960s Neo-Marxists elaborated ideas of neo-colonialism to explain co-operation between Western élites and the élites of newly-independent former colonies. Modern dependency theorists and World Systems writers may not share all the Marxists' assumptions, but they are still within the same paradigm when they deal with North–South global relations. The label, Structuralists, is used in this chapter, because they all emphasize the impact upon politics of the economic structure of the capitalist system.[24]

The Realists concept of the state, as a collective entity encompassing both government and society is disaggregated by the Structuralists. They use the term 'state', with a different meaning, to cover government in its broadest sense of the executive, the legislature, the administration, the judiciary, the police and the armed forces. The importance for theory is that Realists believe there is a common national interest, whereas Structuralists see a conflict of interest between state and society.

Within the Structuralist paradigm there is a debate between those who see the capitalists of the Northern industrialized countries as preventing any development in the countries of the South and others who think that Southern capitalists may at times succeed in producing their own centres of development. There are also differences between those who see *economic* relationships as dominating all relationships and others who would accept an independent effect from global hierarchical *political* structures.[25] Galtung goes the furthest in identifying separate structures, and so is a Structuralist without being a Marxist. He distinguishes five types of imperialism involving 'Centre and Periphery nations' and centre and periphery groups within each country: namely economic, political, military, communication and cultural imperialism.[26]

All Structuralists of the type discussed above emphasize patterns of economic flows, whereby resources are drawn from peasants and workers to the benefit of capitalists, and from the countries of the South to the countries of the North. The flows are not necessarily through centralized institutions: markets are seen as systems, which dominate the individual actors as much as any centralized institution could do. Although there are some uses of systems ideas within both the Realist and the Functionalist paradigms, the distinctive feature of these Structuralists is the insistence that there is a single global capitalist system which dominates the activities of all its members. The Structuralists tend to ignore international institutions (except for occasional attacks on conditionality imposed on loans from the International Monetary Fund), but their concept of a global system is a strong example of the more general idea of international organization.

For Structuralists, states play their part in the global system, by helping to sustain it in the interest of the dominant social classes. Unlike the Realists and the Functionalists, the Structuralists do cover both governments and non-governmental groups, and the relationships between them. In principle they could cover both formal institutions and non-formal structures, like markets. Finally, they cover both conflict (between classes) and co-operation (within classes).

Despite these advantages, the Structuralists have an incomplete paradigm for the study of international relations, partly because Marxists and others whom they have influenced have given relatively little attention to the discipline and are still primarily concerned with what happens within individual countries. While transnational companies (TNCs) and the debt crisis have been covered, other aspects of the globalization of capitalism — the changing role of the IMF, the oil crises, the food crises and the revolutions in banking, capital markets, foreign exchange dealings and commodity markets — have not been subject to detailed analysis to define the nature of the global structures. Even if these deficiencies were remedied, the orthodox Marxist rejection of an *autonomous* political realm, covering nationalism, religious beliefs, gender politics and ideologies, means that a

Marxist-derived paradigm cannot readily be used for non-economic global networks. It is difficult to imagine a Structuralist theoretical analysis of INGOs (such as Amnesty International or the International Planned Parenthood Federation), or of regional intergovernmental organizations (such as the Non-Aligned Movement or the Islamic Conferenece).[27]

Transnationalism, interdependence and international organization

There is some confusion on how to classify the joint work of two authors, Robert Keohane and Joseph Nye. Some writers see their work as being within the Functionalist paradigm, while others correctly see it as the basis of a fourth approach, which we may call the Global Politics paradigm.[28] In their first book together, *Transnational Relations and World Politics*, Keohane and Nye edited a collection of essays on the general phenomenon of TNCs, NGOs and INGOs and some case studies of particular TNCs/NGOs and particular issue-areas. In their second book, *Power and Interdependence*, they considered the complexities of relations between the United States and Canada and between the United States and Australia. (Although they do not acknowledge the fact, this is a direct inheritance from Deutsch of the study of political and economic transactions in security communities.) The Interdependence book also gives detailed studies of the politics of the use of the oceans and of international monetary relations.[29]

Part of the reason for the confusion about Keohane and Nye is that the styles of their two books are not compatible. Both books are firmly set in a theoretical framework and can be used to challenge the Realist paradigm. The work on transnationalism explicitly concludes that Realism must be replaced by a 'world politics' paradigm. On the other hand, the second book is much less ambitious. Complex interdependence is only offered as an alternative on the basis that the nature of the issue being studied determines whether it provides better understanding than Realism does. The challenge would have been much greater if interdependence had been offered as another concept, alongside transnationalism, in the enterprise of building the world politics paradigm to replace Realism for the study of *all* issues.

Because the word 'international' is consciously or subconsciously used by very many writers to mean 'inter-state', the word 'transnational' is used to emphasise exchanges across country boundaries which are not under the control of the government. Similarly, the word 'interdependence' contrasts with the Realists' insistence on the independence of 'states'. Three conditions are specified for 'complex interdependence' to exist: that multiple channels connect societies; there is no single hierarchy of issues, so security concerns do not predominate; and the use of military force is not an available option.[30]

The multiple-channels condition provides the link between transnational contacts and interdependence: the spread of transnationalism increases the number of communication channels between societies. But Keohane and Nye also pointed to another basis for multiple channels, that is increased international activity by different government bureaucracies, without co-ordination by the foreign ministries. This they called transgovernmental relations. The assertion of transnational relations is the denial that governments are the only actors and the assertion of transgovernmental relations is the denial that governments are coherent actors.

The concept of transgovernmental relations opens up a totally new basis for theorizing about intergovernmental organizations. This Keohane and Nye did in a less well-known article in the journal, *World Politics*, which is as important as their two books. Few passages in international relations textbooks could better the following description of IGOs:

One of the important but seldom-noted roles of international organisations in world politics is to provide the arena for sub-units of [different] governments to turn potential or tacit coalitions into explicit coalitions characterized by direct communication among the partners. In this particular bit of political alchemy, the organization provides physical proximity, an agenda of issues on which interaction is to take place, and an aura of legitimacy. Informal discussions occur naturally in meetings of international organisations, and it is difficult given the milieu, for other sub-units of one's own government to object to these contacts.[31]

The result may be that coalitions of ministers from different governments responsible for one particular subject form against their colleagues in the same governments but responsible for other subjects: for example, the European Community regularly witnesses battles between all the agricultural ministers and all the finance ministers. In the sub-discipline of foreign policy analysis, there is a literature on the bureaucratic politics of rivalry between government departments within individual countries.[32] The concept of transgovernmental relations integrates domestic and international politics, by linking domestic bureaucratic politics and the politics of intergovernmental organizations. This strikes at the heart of the state-centric approach by simultaneously denying the coherence of the state and asserting the irrelevance of state boundaries.

In their first book, Keohane and Nye unambiguously reject the adequacy of the state-centric approach, but in their second book they are much more cautious. Realism and complex interdependence are presented as ideal types, which may or may not apply in particular situations. In the Interdependence book, they offer four models of how issues may be decided. If Realist assumptions apply, then the overall distribution of power will decide political outcomes or economic rationality may decide issues which do not have political significance. Alternatively, under conditions of complex interdependence, the distribution of resources which are specific to the immediate issue will make an issue-structural model appropriate, or the political processes within IGOs and regimes will correspond to an international organization model, 'in the broad sense of networks, norms and institutions'.[33]

Keohane and Nye have not offered anything near a complete paradigm. They have concentrated more on the actors in the global system than on the processes of interaction;[34] they are not rigorous in their approach to theory;[35] and they have portrayed transnationalism and interdependence as applying mainly to economic issues, when they could have been presented as useful concepts for the analysis of all types of international issues.[36] Despite these criticisms, transnationalism, transgovernmental relations and interdependence remain core concepts for building the Global Politics paradigm.

A synthesis of the challenge to Realism from economic issues

Transactions analysis, Functionalism, Neo-Functionalism, Marxist-derived Structuralism, transnationalism and interdependence have several important points in common. All are moving beyond analysis of 'power' relations between supposedly coherent 'states'. All are concerned with groups within each country, which are not continuously subject to centralized governmental control. All wish to explain international interactions which are only marginally affected, at the most, by traditional diplomacy, prestige and security. All are doing this because of the desire to include the economic issues of international relations within their analysis.

One way Realism can survive the attack from this vast literature is to define economic questions as being 'low politics', secondary concerns, which do not affect the more important 'high politics' of security. Yet, since the oil crisis of 1973–4, this position has not been tenable. The change of perspective was symbolized by the appearance of the arch-proponent of *Realpolitik*, Henry Kissinger, at the UN Special Session in 1974 on development questions and his speech calling for recognition of interdependence.[37] In practice governments devote much of their time to economic questions; for many developing countries the debt crisis is the greatest threat to their security; and the seven major Western leaders hold regular multilateral summits on economic questions, but not on 'political' questions.

An alternative defence of Realism lies in accepting concepts of economic power and economic security, in addition to traditional concepts of military power and military security. Some writers go as far as making a significant modification to Realism, by arguing that the structure of economic power may vary from one 'issue-area' to another. For one critic, Richard Ashley, the concern with economic issues was sufficiently distinctive among modern Realist writers, such as Robert Gilpin and Stephen Krasner, that he regarded this as a basis for calling them Neo-Realists.[38] In reply Gilpin accepted that Morgenthau, Herz and Kissinger were not concerned with economic questions, but argued that earlier Realist writers, notably E.H. Carr, laid great stress on economic power and economic variables. However, Gilpin still appears to make economics a subsidiary domain:

the international political system provides the necessary framework for economic activities. The international economy is not regarded as an autonomous sphere . . . Although economic forces are real and have a profound effect on the distribution of wealth and power in the world, they always work in the context of the political struggle.[39]

This quotation also suggests that Gilpin is denying that the global system can be seen as containing separate issue-areas.

Once it is accepted that economic issues are significant, then the challenge to the state-centric assumptions of Realism (and Neo-Realism), from the literature on transactions, networks and systems, become important. Transactions analysis tends to emphasize the volume of connections between individuals and groups within each country and those in other countries. Functionalist networks point to the regularity and institutionalization of contacts that may occur between NGOs on a particular issue. Structuralist views of capitalism, along with writing on interdependence and transgovernmental perspectives on intergovernmental organizations all move towards the stronger concept of *systems*, in which the independence of individual countries is ruled out for two reasons. Firstly, countries are seen as being open to penetration from the global system and secondly the ability of any one country, *on its own*, to affect the system is minimal. Many political decisions affecting outcomes within individual countries and virtually all political decisions affecting outcomes in more than one country are the product of exchanges at the level of the global system.

In terms of answering the question, 'who are the actors in the global system?', all the alternatives to Realism can be accepted as offering contributions, which are not inherently incompatible with each other, but are all incompatible with the core Realist assumption of the coherent 'state'. Information and material transactions are generated by the communications of individual people; technical and professional groups co-operate to perform their welfare tasks; capitalist companies and private financial institutions (TNCs) pursue their narrow economic interests; non-profit-making NGOs seek to promote their political values; government ministries each have their own separate economic and political goals; IGO secretariats seek to strengthen the status and authority of their bureaucracies; and IGO plenary bodies and committees have procedures and norms, which make them distinct subsystems within the global system.

One may generalize this by saying that whether they are governmental or non-governmental, and whether they are single country, multi-country, regional or global, the actors are organized groups. This generalization carries the presumption that the transactions of individual people can be ignored for the analysis of global systems and their impact can be accounted for by the groups through which the transactions pass, such as telephone companies, tourist operators or non-commercial NGOs. Occasionally it is wrong to ignore the impact of individuals, as when a young German, Mathias Rust, in May 1987 flew a light aircraft from Helsinki to land in Red Square next to the Kremlin, with the result that the Commander-in-Chief of the Air Defence Forces in the Soviet Union was dismissed and one can assume air forces in several countries reviewed their radar systems. Analytically one can handle such events as being external inputs to the inter-group system, similar to natural disasters, which do not have to be explained by the model of the system.

The Global Politics approach to international organizations

A group-based approach to the analysis of politics within countries is usually known as pluralism and this label has sometimes been applied at the international level. Pluralism has been criticized for presumptions that on all issues there are many competing groups, that changes in policy are only incremental, that governments do little more than hold the ring and that the results are for the common good: in other words that political systems are like 'perfect markets' in economics, establishing a pluralist political equilibrium. These presumptions would not be shared by all the various approaches which emphasize economic actors in international relations. Functionalists emphasize co-operation and the common good, while Structuralists emphasize conflict and exploitation. Functionalists downplay the role of governments and economic Structuralists usually consider governments to be the agents of economic groups, while transnationalism and interdependence puts governments on an equal footing with other groups.[40] Whatever one's view of the role of governments in world politics, there is no precise equivalent at the global level to the pluralist image of a country's government ensuring fair play between the competing groups. It is possible to have a group-based approach to international relations without holding the assumptions associated with the pluralist equilibrium model. Partly for this reason and partly to emphasize the idea of complex systems, with participants from many countries, the term Global Politics is preferable to pluralism as a label for the fourth paradigm.

Rosenau has been one of the most innovative and prolific writers in this paradigm. He actually wrote about both transnationalism and interdependence before Keohane and Nye, yet has not been so widely quoted as they have.[41] Rosenau tends to lay less emphasis on the need for theorists to change their paradigm than on his assertion that the real world of international relations is currently changing from a state-centric to a multicentric system. He applies the concepts of transnationalism and interdependence to all aspects of world politics, rather than restricting them to economic relations. His work is permeated with a sense of dynamic and turbulent change. In particular he draws attention to the new issues, such as environmental pollution, which neither academic theorists nor government practitioners used to think were of concern in international relations. As far back as the mid-1960s he used the concept of issue-areas to suggest that political systems vary in their structure from issue to issue.[42] Rosenau also asks questions about the degree of political authority possessed by governments and the processes of aggregation of support by political actors. He has offered the building blocks for an alternative theoretical approach, but Rosenau's work has been less influential than it might have been, because his ideas on world politics have never been presented in an integrated conceptual framework.

The logical extension of Deutsch's transaction analysis, with the disaggregation of states into a myriad of groups, each relating to the wider world, is reached with Alger's work on the foreign relations of United States residents in the city of Columbus, Ohio. Alger brings together the possibilities of involvement in NGOs or in government, at the city, the provincial, the federal or the international (INGO/IGO) level, to suggest thirteen potential routes to international participation for the individual.[43] This is valuable in pointing to an integration of the politics of transnational groups, government bureaucracies, INGOs and IGOs.

If the focus of interactions is not the Realist's struggle for power, nor the Functionalists' pursuit of welfare, nor the Structuralists' clash of economic interests, what is the basis of group relations? Richard Mansbach and John Vasquez provide the answer in their book, *In Search of Theory*, which offers an issue-based paradigm.[44] An issue may be defined as consisting of contention among actors over a set of related questions, concerning the allocation of economic resources or support for non-material values. This generalized formulation is compatible with any organized group being considered as a political actor. In addition their work raises questions which the other three paradigms are not easily able to ask, such as 'Why are new groups formed to take political action?' and 'How do issues get put on the political agenda?'

International systems and issue-areas

The idea of systems, consisting of groups contending over issues, allows us to incorporate a concept, which we mentioned as being used in both the interdependence and the Neo-Realist literature. The term issue-area is used to assert that the pattern of international organization varies from issue to issue. In other words there is not a single international system, but a separate system for each issue. The implied assumptions behind this are (1) that there is no overarching issue encompassing all the main issues as variations on the central theme, and (2) that power is not fungible: there is no single resource, which may be used to gain influence on all issues. (To the extent that they share these assumptions, Neo-Realists are abandoning Realist axioms.) Groups will be active on an issue only if it is salient to them and different resources will be relevant to influencing outcomes. Table 17.1 illustrates the diverse groups which have become actors in two global systems, covering two different issue-areas.

Consideration of just these two issue-areas is enough to show departures from the pluralist equilibrium model. Although each system has several hundred actors, one system is relatively homogeneous, with finance dominated by bankers and those who share their values, while the other system shows much more diversity, with the pollution issue showing a real clash between commercial and conservation interests. In the financial system, the dominance of private banks, central banks, finance ministries and the IMF over development ministries, NGOs, UNCTAD and the UN is too marked

Table 17.1 The principal actors in two different global systems

	International Finance	Marine Pollution
Government Bureaucracies	Central banks, finance and development ministries	Environment, transport and energy ministries
TNCs	Commercial banks	Shipping, nuclear energy, oil and chemical companies
NGOs	Development NGOs, e.g. Oxfam, Care	Environmental NGOs, e.g. Friends of the Earth, Greenpeace
INGOs	ICDA, ICVA	WWFI, ICRP
Iquangos	Group of Thirty, IIF	IUCN, ICS, OCIMF, IPIECA
IGOs	IMF, Paris Club, World Bank, G7, UNCTAD, UN	IMO, IOPCF, UNEP, IAEA

INGO Abbreviations
ICDA: International Coalition for Development Action; ICRP: International Commission on Radiological Protection; ICVA: International Council of Voluntary Agencies; WWFI: World Wide Fund for Nature International.

*Iquango Abbreviations**
ICS: International Chamber of Shipping; IIF: Institute of International Finance; IPIECA: International Petroleum Industry Environmental Conservation Association; IUCN: International Union for Conservation of Nature and Natural Resources; OCIMF: Oil Companies International Marine Forum.

IGO Abbreviations
IAEA: International Atomic Energy Agency; IMF: International Monetary Fund; IMO: International Maritime Organization; IOPCF: International Oil Pollution Compensation Fund; G7: Group of Seven, meeting as finance ministers or as heads of government; UNCTAD: United Nations Conference on Trade and Development; UNEP: United Nations Environment Programme.

*For the definition of an iquango, see the section 'Regimes and international institutions' p. 274, below.

to be described as an equilibrium. The marine pollution system might more reasonably be seen as an equilibrium. Changes are not incremental: in the financial system, the collapse of the Bretton Woods regime in 1971–3 and the impact of the Mexican debt crisis in 1982 were large scale, dramatic, unexpected and sudden; in the marine pollution system, responses to the 1967 *Torrey Canyon* disaster took several years to have their full effect, but there were nevertheless major changes in the structure of the system by the mid-1970s. In neither system can governments be seen as neutral arbiters of the conflicting interests in the global society: in both cases most countries would have more than one government ministry involved, taking different positions on the issue. In the marine pollution issue-area, it could be argued that effective pollution control without all the costs being borne by commercial interests is slowly being achieved to the common good. However, in the international financial system, it is difficult to imagine an argument that the common good is being achieved either within or between countries. The fact that neither issue-area corresponds to the pluralist equilibrium model does not prevent us from seeing both as systems of contention among diverse types of groups.

So far, with the Global Politics approach, we have moved from loose ideas of international organization as regular patterns of transactions or networks of interactions to the stronger concept of systems. The discussion has made it obvious that concepts of transnationalism and transgovernmental relations are included. The concept of interdependence is also included and not just because it must, by definition, focus on a higher level of analysis than the single political actor. Everyday use of the term may refer to no more than high numbers of connections between groups in different countries, as in transactions analysis. But there is debate about the concept because its derivation from the word 'dependence' implies that mutually-dependent actors are significantly constrained: interdependence is the denial of independence.[45] If the concept is to make any contribution to theory-building, it must mean more than the loose idea of connectedness, which has no impact on theory and is compatible with all the four paradigms. The stronger meaning of mutual dependence gives the term interdependence a theoretical value and makes it virtually synonymous with the term system.[46]

The hold of traditional Realist language is so strong that, except when we explicitly say otherwise, 'international system' tends to be used to mean 'inter-state system'. Similarly, interdependence is normally taken to mean mutual dependence between countries. Yet, the concepts of transnationalism and transgovernmental relations imply a denial that countries should be used as units of analysis. How does interdependence fit into a group theory of issues? The answer must be that it is the groups, which we take to be the political actors, which are mutually dependent. The break with Realism is seen to be complete, when we assert that government bureaucracies, TNCs, NGOs, INGOs and IGOs are interdependent.[47] This integration of the governmental and the non-governmental worlds is also incompatible with the Functionalists (because they separate the two worlds) and with the Structuralists (because they assume dependence rather than interdependence).

Given the centrality of government, authority and power in Realist thinking, the traditional assumption is that the only alternative to international anarchy is some supranational system of centralized global authority. One advantage of the Functionlist concept of networks is that it points to the idea of order which is not based on a hierarchical system. The stronger concept of systems can also be used to refer to regular patterns of interactions which constrain the actors and hence are not anarchic, but also can be non-hierarchical. For example, in the global system concerned with the Middle East political issue of the status of the Israeli government and the Palestinian nation, while various actors differ greatly in the resources at their disposal, there are no dominant actors and it is a non-hierarchical system. We may also note that this is also a good example of a system displaying high levels of conflict: interdependence does not necessarily promote co-operation.

The idea of a global system is not unique to the Global Politics paradigm. But it is a new development in modern writing to move from conceptualizing a single system to multiple distinct systems, one for each issue-area. For most Realists who use the system concept, there is only one international system which is structured by the overall distribution of power capabilities. For the economic Structuralists, there is one global system of capitalism, structured by the control of capital. (Both these approaches are rather curious applications of systems: although both would be seen by their advocates as focusing on systemic relations, the determining factors in their view of systemic structure are the attributes of their elements, that is their power or their capital respectively. Yet structure is supposed to be a systemic property, not a property of its elements.[48]) What then provides the structure to issue-based systems? The essential requirements for contention to occur, for support to be mobilized, for conflict or co-operation to be expressed is the existence of channels of communication between the political actors.

Communications structures of issue-systems

An emphasis on communications brings us right back to the first challenge made to Realism in the 1950s by Karl Deutsch, when he produced a communications-based theory of nationalism. At the beginning of this chapter it was argued that Deutsch did not push this challenge to its logical conclusion. His political-sociological concept of the nation is different from the legal concept of the state and therefore it should be possible to ask what is the match between the two. The Realist assumes the match is perfect or nearly perfect:

in a world of scarce resources and conflict over the distribution of those resources, human beings confront one another ultimately as members of groups . . . loyalty to the tribe for most of us ranks above all loyalties other than that of the family. In the modern world, we have given the name 'nation-state' to these competing tribes and the name 'nationalism' to this form of loyalty.[49]

The empirical reality is that the Realist's most fundamental axiom is false: nation-states do not exist. A nation is a group of people who share a common identity and have loyalties to each other. A state is an abstract legal concept to cover the control by a government of its citizens within a defined geographical boundary. Nowhere in the world do these two phenomena match: nowhere do virtually all the people of one nation live within the boundaries of a single state, without the presence of groups from other nations. The handful of states, such as Somalia and Portugal, which are nearly homogenous in their national compositon have their nation spread across more than one state.[50] All other states are multinational, with very many of them experiencing serious conflict between the nations residing within the boundary of the state. Nations are too amorphous to be considered as elements in our issue-systems, but nationalism does lead to the formation of cultural, economic, professional, party-political and guerrilla groups, which become political actors. These groups are not necessarily in accord with governments. National groups and government bureaucracies are different types of actors, which cannot be merged under the heading 'nation-states'.

Deutsch extended his ideas of political communication to pluralistic security communities which extend across the boundaries of nations and countries. Such patterns of high levels of transactions and a wider sense of common identity depend upon the existence of multiple communication channels. One feature of the modern world is the rapidly increasing density and speed of operation of world communication channels: radio, TV, the telephone system and airlines have become global in just the last thirty to forty years. These are fundamental structures, along with the older roads, shipping, railway and telegraph systems, which both respond to and help to create the pluralistic security communities. They are also structures which underlie issue-systems.

In as much as Deutsch is correct in seeing increased levels of communication leading to shared identity in security communities, the globalization of communication structures in recent times is fundamental to the development of a global security community in which the use of force is rapidly losing legitimacy and efficacy. We must be cautious in not adopting a simplistic 'enlightened' view that communication automatically promotes understanding and hence mutual sympathy, but clearly communities cannot begin to identify with each other if they have no contact at all.

To speak of global communication structures is not to assume that communication is equally easy between any two points on the globe. However, all points are now reachable instantly by radio and by some, direct or indirect, travel-route with unprecedented speeds. One hundred years ago travel between two remote points within the United States took as long as travel between two remote points anywhere on the globe does now. It is even more important that we do not all have equal access to communications. Economic resources are needed to dispatch materials, information or people. Information communications are crucial to political contention and use of the correct language is essential to effective information communication. The language distributions of the world are one of the fundamental features of communications structures which differentiate people's access to them. English dominates air, shipping, radio, TV and press agency communications systems. French also allows more narrow access to the global systems. Spanish and Arabic are major regional languages. Russian has a more limited regional usage in Eastern Europe. All other languages are of very limited utility in global politics.[51] One or more of these five languages are used as the official languages, with English and French as the predominant working languages, of all IGOs and INGOs and can therefore be seen as one of the structural characteristics of international organizations.

Groups which feel the need to interact with relatively high frequency create their own organizational structures which are designed to enhance communication capabilities. The diplomatic system is an organizational structure to promote communication between foreign ministries and it even has its own physically-distinct communication channels. The formal institutions of INGOs and the informal information networks are designed to promote NGO communications. One of the major advantages TNCs possess over their single-country commercial rivals is their superior ability to communicate material resources, information and finance around the globe.

Regimes and international institutions

A system of issue-contention can be a system of patterned conflict in which communications between the main parties are distorted or misperceived and threats are made more often than rewards are offered. In contrast to this, regimes and institutions are systems in which co-operative behaviour is more likely to occur than conflict behaviour. Regimes are defined as 'sets of implicit or explicit principles, norms, rules and decision-making procedures around which actors' expectations converge in a given area of international relations'.[52] To the extent that values are shared the intensity of conflict will be reduced and by definition this will be extensive in regimes. The contention is usually over finding common methods to solve common problems rather than achieving victory over an opponent. The Neo-Realists' assumption that regimes are dominated by governments need not be shared. (International sports, with the norm that 'sport should be kept free from politics', operate within a regime in which governments are actors of secondary importance compared to the international federations and the International Olympic Committee.) As the decision-making procedures define the patterns of political communication, they should be seen as one of the fundamental structures of co-operative issue-systems. A regime need not have a centralized decision-making procedure. The regime for international diplomacy, governed by the Vienna conventions, is completely decentralized, but is nevertheless highly structured.

We have seen that the Realists and the Functionalists both acknowledge the existence of intergovernmental organizations (IGOs) and international non-governmental organizations (INGOs), but assess their significance differently. As the Global Politics approach has no prior theoretical commitment to assuming that either government bureaucracies or NGOs are the groups which will come together at the global level, the possibility should be entertained that groups of both types could jointly form a hybrid IGO/INGO. Only cursory reflection is required to establish that many of the organizations that are conventionally classified as IGOs or as INGOs are not pure examples of their type. In the study of the politics of individual countries the concept of 'quangos', quasi non-governmental organizations, is widely recognized. We should also recognize the concept of iquangos, international quasi non-governmental organizations.

An 'iquango' may be defined as an international organization which includes in its *membership both* government departments and/or other governmental institutions *and* single-country, non-governmental organizations and/or multi-country, international non-governmental organizations. This restrictive definition, emphasizing joint membership, is necessary because almost all IGOs give NGOs and INGOs some form of official consultative or observer status and many INGOs have some governments which give them support, particularly funding for special projects. Therefore an iquango cannot be defined loosely as an organization in which both NGOs and governments participate. The tight definition applies only when both are full members with equal rights to participation in decision-making, including the right to vote on resolutions and on other formal decisions.

This tight definition is of theoretical impact because it breaches the distinction between high and low politics and the assumption that only 'states' are recognized as having any status in international law. 'States', which are supposedly equal in their 'sovereign' status and superior to other 'non-state' entities are, when they join iquangos, actually according not just recognition but also legal equality to NGOs and INGOs. The Realist view that 'the international system consists of states' is offered an unavoidable and an unanswerable challenge by the existence and the activities of iquangos. The challenge cannot be avoided by separating the world into a high politics of governments and a low politics of NGOs. The challenge cannot be answered by asserting that governments alone have the ultimate authority over NGOs, as the Realists would argue in the case of intergovermental organizations such as the UN. Iquangos are unambiguously phenomena which can only be described by the concepts of transnationalism, transgovernmentalism and interdependence.

Table 17.2 gives some examples of organizations along a seven-point spectrum from the pure IGO, which accords no formal status to NGOs, to the pure INGO, which maintains financial independence from governments. It is striking how few pure IGOs or pure INGOs can readily be brought to mind. The great majority of IGOs accord, to at least a small number of NGOs, formal rights of participation, such as circulating documents or taking part in debates. Similarly, many of the major NGOs receive some direct funding from governments and/or receive special tax privileges

Table 17.2   Classification of international organizations

IGOs Intergovernmental Organizations

Type		Example
1)	Only government members Limited informal NGO links	North Atlantic Treaty Organization
2)	Only government members Extensive formal NGO links	United Nations

Iquangos International Quasi Non-Governmental Organizations

Type		Example
3)	Government and NGO members Governments dominant status	International Labour Organization
4)	Government and NGO members The two with equal status	International Red Cross
5)	Government and NGO members NGOs dominant status	International Council for Bird Preservation

INGOs International Non-Governmental Organizations

Type		Example
6)	Only NGO members Government funding welcomed	International Planned Parenthood Federation
7)	Only NGO members Government funding not routinely accepted	Amnesty International

Note: Throughout the table 'NGO' can mean NGOs and/or INGOs.

through obtaining charitable status in many countries.

Within the iquango category one may distinguish organizations established by intergovernmental treaties, in which the membership technically consists of 'states'. The NGOs therefore participate by courtesy of their governments. On the other hand there are organizations which behave like INGOs and have the majority of their membership from the NGO world, yet also admit specialist government bureaucracies as members. Thus, most observers would regard the International Labour Organisation as an IGO and the International Council for Bird Preservation as an INGO. In reality both the ILO and the ICBP are hybrid organizations in the fullest possible sense that both governments and private bodies are involved, independently, in their authoritative decision-making.

For some of the iquangos there is no way that either NGOs or governments can be regarded as dominant members. For example the International Red Cross has a complex structure, with three NGO components — the ICRC, the League and over 130 National Societies — and over 150 governments, together forming the International Conference, which is 'the supreme deliberative body for the Movement'.[53] Governments in theory could dominate as they have more members. In practice, a conflict of all National Societies against all governments is unlikely to occur; there is an obligation to seek consensus before moving to a majority vote; and governments are supposed to avoid 'controversies of a political, racial, religious or ideological nature'.[54] In the case of the International Union for the Conservation of Nature and Natural Resources, the balance is guaranteed by providing for the two categories of voting members, (A) 'states' and government agencies and (B) NGOs and INGOs, each being required to give majority approval for a motion to be carried.[55]

International institutions, whether they are INGOs, iquangos or IGOs, do not constitute the global system for any issue-area. They are elements in the systems, which always include governments, TNCs and NGOs. While institutions will be treated as elements when we are considering issue-systems as a whole, if we are interested in the politics of the institutions themselves, they can be analysed as subsystems of the wider issue-systems.[56] The institutions are involved both in conflict systems and in co-operative regimes. Their importance lies in being major focal points for aggregating support. In conflict, actors strive to maximize support for resolutions against their opponents, with the UN frequently being used for this purpose. In regimes, they usually, but not always, provide the decision-making forum. The international financial system is a regime which has the IMF as its focus for decision-making and the marine pollution regime has the IMO as its prime focus. One of the most valuable developments in the writing on international organizations is that textbooks have appeared in the 1980s, which cover both INGOs and IGOs and treat them as systems, in which a diverse range of actors, not just 'states', seek to mobilize support.[57]

International institutions are important communication centres and as such are major structures within global political systems. The UN is the most important as the General Assembly and the UN's specialized conferences are attended by representatives from virtually all governments, from TNCs (not directly but via industrial and commercial INGOs), from NGOs, INGOs, iquangos and other IGOs. The smaller and the more specialized institutions may only come into play as communication structures when they hold meetings of their plenary organs or their main committees. But the larger institutions and those with a broader scope become permanent centres, with diplomatic missions and NGO, INGO, iquango and IGO representatives permanently stationed at their headquarters. Thus, contrary to Realist logic, the UN headquarters in New York has a larger diplomatic corps and more representatives from other groups than does either Washington or Moscow. If structures are seen in traditional 'power' terms or in economic terms, then international organizations may not seem to be of much significance, but focusing on political communication gives a central role to international organizations.

Conclusion

We now have a general approach which gives meaning to the wider concept of international organization. It consists of regular patterns of interactions between interdependent sets of government bureaucracies, TNCs, NGOs, INGOs, iquangos and IGOs, utilizing differential abilities to gain access to communications structures, in order to pursue contention over an issue. The actors, the structures and the interactions form distinct systems for each issue-area. Within these general patterns regimes fit in as issue-systems which display more co-operative behaviour than conflict behaviour. International institutions have special significance as centres of political communication. Thus, along with the physical and information systems of communication run on a commercial basis, INGOs, iquangos and IGOs are fundamental structures in political systems. As such they may also be the focal point for decision-making in regimes. International organization in general and international institutions in particular have been neglected or underplayed in much theorizing about international relations. They have a central place in a Global Politics paradigm, based on contention among groups within issue-systems.

Notes and references

1. The paradigms are classified on the following basis: Realists and Neo-Realists study states engaging in the struggle for power; Functionalists study socio-economic groups seeking to maximize welfare; Structuralists study classes pursuing their economic interests; and Global Politics researchers study political actors mobilizing support in contention over issues. Several writers use this classification of the paradigms, but the latter two labels are not standard and not all acknowledge the Functionalists as a separate category. Structuralists is used as a term to group traditional Marxists, Neo-Marxists, dependency theorists and the World Systems writers in the United States. For a full exposition of this classification see Peter Willetts, *Issues in World Politics*, London, Edward Elgar Publishing, forthcoming, chapter 1.

2. The author does not accept the usefulness either of the concept of the state or of the concept of power. Both concepts hinder understanding by aggregating a very diverse range of distinct phenomena. They will only be used in this chapter in the context of explaining the ideas of other writers who use these concepts.

3. H. Bull and A. Watson (eds), *The Expansion of International Society*, Oxford, Clarendon Press, 1984, p. 1.

4. For a discussion of the theoretical significance of regimes, see the first and last sections of S.D. Krasner (ed.), *International Regimes*, Ithaca, Cornell University Press, 1983.

5. M.A. Kaplan, *System and Process in International Politics*, New York, John Wiley and Sons, 1957, pp. 22–36.

6. K.N. Waltz, *Theory of World Politics*, Reading, Mass., Addison-Wesley, 1979.

7. K.W. Deutsch, *Nationalism and Social Communication. An Enquiry into the Foundations of Nationality*, Cambridge, Mass., MIT Press, 1953, quote from p. 92.

8. Ibid., p. 96.

9. Ibid., pp. 104–5.

10. K.W. Deutsch et al., *Political Community and the North Atlantic Area*, New York, Greenwood Press, reprinted 1969 from a 1957 original publication.

11. Ibid. p. 5.

12. Africa forms a double challenge to Deutsch's theorizing, firstly in the need to explain the paradox of an inter-state security community without intra-state peaceful relations, and secondly that the presumed essential requirement of 'compatibility of major values' has not been met and 'mutual responsiveness' is

present but not at a high level. See op. cit., pp. 123–33.

13. A. Lijphart, 'Karl W. Deutsch and the New Paradigm in International Relations', pp. 233–51 of R.L. Merritt and B.M. Russett (eds), *From National Development to Global Community*. Essays in Honor of Karl W. Deutsch, London, George Allen & Unwin, 1981, quote from p. 236.

14. B.M. Russett, *International Regions and the International System. A Study in Political Ecology*, Westport, Conn., Greenwood Press, 1975, from a 1967 original publication. R.J. Rummell *et al.*, *The Dimensions of Nations*, Beverly Hills, Calif., Sage Publications, 1972. Deutsch's own earlier work on transactions was scattered in a variety of journals. The main articles have now been brought together in K.W. Deutsch, *Tides Among Nations*, New York, The Free Press, 1979.

15. Arend Lijphart puts this position more forcefully in calling Deutsch 'one of the leading "revolutionaries" ' in the creation of 'the [sic] new paradigm' (op. cit., p. 233). Three important modifications of Lijphart's position need to be made. Firstly, Deutsch's challenge to Realism was implicit rather than explicit. Secondly, the methodological challenge from behaviouralism did not necessarily produce a theoretical challenge. Lastly, three new paradigms rather than a single new paradigm now offer alternatives to Realism.

16. The charge of 'politicization' by Western governments against the UN specialized agencies is in reality more of a mask for deploring the decline in Western bloc influence in the organizations. In earlier years, the Western governments themselves introduced 'extraneous' Cold War questions.

17. J.W. Burton, *World Society*, Cambridge, Cambridge University Press, 1972, p. 43. Burton's similarity to Mitrany is most evident in 'The Zonal-Functional System', chapter 9 of his *Global Conflict. The Domestic Sources of International Crisis*, Brighton: Wheatsheaf Books, 1984. Burton also argued in the 1960s that international agreements had 'taken politics out of international commercial relations' and so regionalism and functionalism 'might provide a surer foundation of peaceful international relations' than the United Nations could. (This argument differs from Mitrany in being optimistic about *intergovernmental* co-operation through regionalism and functionalism.) See 'Regionalism, Functionalism and the United Natons', in M. Waters (ed.), *The United Nations. International Organisation and Administration*, New York, Macmillan, 1967, pp. 57–68: quotes from p. 67.

18. Burton, *World Society*, chapter 10; and J.W. Burton, *Deviance, Terrorism and War. The Process of Solving Unsolved Social and Political Problems*, Oxford, Martin Robertson, 1979, Chapter 5.

19. Burton, *World Society*, p. 117. See also Burton's inability to move beyond Realist perceptions of the UN, in *Global Conflict*, chapter 8, and in the article in Waters, op. cit.

20. E.B. Haas, Beyond the Nation-State. *Functionalism and International Organisation*, Stanford, Calif., Stanford University Press, 1964. For the clarity of its exposition, its breadth of scholarship, its theoretical sophistication, the quality of its empirical work and its originality, this could be considered one of the best books ever written on international relations. This is not to say that the whole work should stand unchallenged two and a half decades later.

21. Ibid., p. 80.

22. For a Realist review of Neo-Functionalism, which develops several of these criticisms, see N. Heathcote, 'Neo-Functionalist Theories of Regional Integration', in A.J.R. Groom and P. Taylor (eds), *Functionalism. Theory and*

Practice in International Relations, London, University of London press, 1975, pp. 38–52. Heathcote's criticism, that the 'power politics' aspects of de Gaulle's actions showed Neo-Functionalism to be overtaken by the pattern of events, has itself been overtaken by events. The reappearance of majority voting, the formation of the EMS, the 1992 harmonization proposals and the co-ordination of foreign policy have gone further than she thought was possible in a grouping of 'sovereign states'.

23. It is interesting to note that in a recent book written in honour of John Burton, with the exception of Dennis Sandole, the contributors wish to move beyond the theoretical limitations imposed by Burton's Functionalist approach to 'World Society'. For example, the chapter by Chris Mitchell argues the case for replacing Burton's Functionalism with a Global Politics approach (but Mitchell does not put his argument in these terms). A.J.R. Groom is a prolific writer on intergovernmental organizations, while Burton just ignores them as part of the obsolete, inter-state system. Christopher Hill criticizes Burton for thinking that an emphasis on Functionalism and problem-solving can replace the need for World Society to have some structure of government. Michael Banks avoids the problem of choosing between Functionalism and the Global Politics paradigm, hence suggesting that a wider range of writers share Burton's assumptions, when they do not. See M. Banks (ed.), *Conflict in World Society. A new perspective on international relations*, Brighton, Harvester Press, 1984).

24. For the range of economic Structuralist writing, see the following collections of readings: R.I. Rhodes (ed.), *Imperialism and Underdevelopment: a reader*, New York, Monthly Review Press, 1970; R. Owen and B. Sutcliffe (eds), *Studies in the theory of imperialism*, London; Longman Group, 1972); M. Smith, R. Little and M. Shackleton (eds), *Perspectives on World Politics*, London, Croom Helm for the Open University, 1981, Section 3, 'The Politics of Dominance and Dependence'.
The most prolific writers among the modern dependency theorists, whose works should be consulted, include Samir Amin and André Gunder Frank. The World Systems ideas are found in the work of Immanuel Wallerstein and the series of books he has edited.

25. For the assertion that 'there are not one but two sets of conflicting relationships: (1) the economic core *regions* in relation to the economic peripheral regions; (2) the dominant *states* in relation to the dominated states', see T.R. Hopkins, I. Wallerstein *et al.*, *World Systems Analysis. Theory and Methodology*, Beverly Hills, Sage, Explorations in the World Economy, Vol. 1, 1982), p. 58 (emphasis in the original). It is not clear why the word 'regions' is used here to cover what appears to be a class analysis.

26. J. Galtung, 'A Structural Theory of Imperialism', *Journal of Peace Research*, Vol. 8, No. 2, 1971, pp. 81–94.

27. One may find historical, descriptive studies in which Structuralist language is used. There may also be quite detailed *ex post facto* explanations of change within individual countries. But formal theoretical generalizations, such as Frank's 'satellites experience their greatest economic development . . . when their ties to their metropolis are weakest' (Rhodes, op. cit., p. 10, also Smith *et al.*, op. cit., p. 296), are unusual in the dependency literature and are not made at all about international organization.

28. Clive Archer puts Functionalists, Neo-Functionalists, Transactionalists and Interdependence as subheadings, under his main heading 'Revisionist Views'. Michael Banks covers Keohane and Nye together with Mitrany and Burton in

his category of the Pluralist Paradigm. The Open University reader includes two extracts from Keohane and Nye among their twelve readings for 'The Politics of Interdependence and Transnational Relations', but omits the Functionalists. James Rosenau similarly distinguishes a 'multicentric' approach, without mentioning the Functionalists. C. Archer, *International Organizations,* London, George Allen & Unwin, 1983, pp. 82–102. M. Banks, 'The Inter-Paradigm Debate', in M. Light and A.J.R. Groom (eds), *International Relations. A Handbook of Current Theory,* London, Frances Pinter, 1985), p. 16. M. Smith *et al.,* op. cit., for the Open University. J.N. Rosenau's introduction to R. Maghroori and B. Ramberg (eds), *Globalism Versus Realism: International Relations' Third Debate,* Boulder, Westview Press, 1982.

Undoubtedly one reason for confusion on how to classify Keohane and Nye stems from the lack of rigour or consistency in their theoretical work. Joseph Nye moved into transnationalism and interdependence after being one of the leading Neo-Functionalists in the 1960s. On the other hand, Robert Keohane moved in the 1980s to become a leading Neo-Realist.

29. R.O. Keohane and J.S. Nye (eds), *Transnational Relations and World Politics,* Cambridge Mass., Harvard University Press, 1972.
R.O. Keohane and J.S. Nye, *Power and Interdependence. World Politics in Transition,* Boston, Little, Brown, 1977. It is not clear why these two authors should be so much better known than their predecessors who used the same concepts. One may guess that it is the value of book-length studies of single concepts, the attraction of mixing theory with detailed case-studies, their appearance at a time when people were open to such ideas and the impact of making the paradigm challenge explicit.

30. R.O. Keohane and J.S. Nye, *Power and Interdependence,* pp. 24–9.

31. R.O. Keohane and J.S. Nye, 'Transgovernmental Relations and International Organizations', *World Politics,* Vol. XXVII, 1974, pp. 39–62.

32. M.H. Halperin *et al., Bureaucratic Politics and Foreign Policy,* Washington DC, The Brookings Institution, 1974.

33. R.O. Keohane and J.S. Nye, *Power and Interdependence,* chapter 3, quote from p. 55.

34. Keohane and Nye recognize this criticism themselves in a review of their book, ten years after it was first published: R.O. Keohane and J.S. Nye, '*Power and Interdependence* Revisited', *International Organization,* Autumn 1987, Vol. 41 No. 4, pp. 725–53.

35. For example in *Power and Interdependence,* note the lack of a precise definition of interdependence, the ambiguity surrounding the concept of sensitivity and confusion on the level of analysis question. Interdependence is a systems-level concept, while sensitivity and vulnerability are actor-level concepts, but the authors sloppily refer to 'sensitivity interdependence' and 'vulnerability interdependence'.

36. For the extension of transnationalism to non-economic groups, see P. Willetts (ed.), *Pressure Groups in the Global System. The Transnational Relations of Issue-Orientated Non-Governmental Organizations,* London: Frances Pinter, 1982; and, for the extension of interdependence to non-economic issues, see P. Willetts, 'The Politics of Global Issues: Cognitive Actor Dependence and Issue Linkage', in R.J.B. Jones and P. Willetts (eds), *Interdependence on Trial. Studies in the Theory and Reality of Contemporary Interdependence,* (London: Frances Pinter, 1984).

37. *United Nations General Assembly Official Records,* Sixth Special Session,

2214th plenary meeting 15 April 1974. See also the quotes from Kissinger's speeches given by Keohane and Nye, in *Power and Interdependence*, pp. 3 and 26.

38. R.K. Ashley, 'The Poverty of neorealism', International Organization, Spring 1984, Vol. 38, No. 2, pp. 226-86. Ashley believes that within Neo-Realism 'structuralism, statism, utilitarianism [characterised by its individualist and rationalist premises], and positivism are bound together in machine-like, self-enclosing unity' (p. 237, the phrase in brackets being from p. 243). He charges that Neo-Realism denies history as process, denies the significance of practice, does not comprehend the social construction of power and ignores politics as a creative critical enterprise (pp. 258-60).

39. R.G. Gilpin, 'The richness of the tradition of political realism', *International Organization*, Spring 1984, Vol. 38, No. 2, pp. 287-304, quote from p. 295.

40. While Keohane and Nye's work on transnationalism puts private groups on an equal footing with governments, their work on interdependence has not completely broken with the state-centric approach: see P. Willetts, 'Interdependence: New Wine in Old Bottles', in J.N. Rosenau and H. Trompe, *Interdependence and Conflict in World Politics*, Aldershot, Gower Group, 1989.

41. Rosenau preceded Keohane and Nye in writing about transnational relations, with J.N. Rosenau (ed.), *Linkage Politics: Essays on the Convergence of National and International Systems*, New York, The Free Press, 1969. He also preceded them in writing about interdependence, with 'Capabilities and Control in an Interdependent World', in *International Security*, Vol. 1, 1976, pp. 32-49. Rosenau's innovative theoretical work in the 1970s became more accessible with the reprinting of his articles in J.N. Rosenau, *The Study of Global Interdependence: Essays on the Transnationalization of World Affairs*, London, Frances Pinter, and New York, Nichols Publishing, 1980.

42. J.N. Rosenau, 'Pre-Theories and Theories of Foreign Policy', in R.B. Farrell (ed.), *Approaches to Comparative and International Politics*, Evanston, Illinois, Northwestern University Press, 1966, pp. 27-92.

43. C. F. Alger, 'Foreign Policies of US Publics', *International Studies Quarterly*, Vol. 21, No. 2, 1977, pp. 277-318. C. F. Alger and D. C. Hoovler, *You and Your Community in the World*, Colombus, Ohio, Consortium for International Studies Education, 1978.

44. R. Mansbach and J. Vasquez, *In Search of Theory: A New Paradigm for World Politics*, New York, Columbia University Press, 1981.

45. The difference between interdependence as connectedness and interdependence as imposing significant constraints seems to be one of the main bases of Keohane and Nye's distinction between sensitivity and vulnerability (*Power and Interdependence*, pp. 11-17). For a more detailed discussion of the definition and theoretical impact of the concept, see Willetts, 'The Politics of Global Issues', and Willetts, 'Interdependence: New Wine in Old Bottles', both cited above.

46. All political systems must consist of interdependent sets of actors. It is an essential feature of the systems concept that no one element can determine outcomes affecting the system as a whole, which is another way of saying that each element (actor) is dependent upon one or more other element(s). Whether the reverse is true, that all interdependent sets of actors are systems, is subject to one's concept of holism. This question is beyond the scope of the current discussion.

47. For a more extended discussion of the argument that interdependence loses

much of its theoretical impact unless the concept of the state is completely abandoned and replaced by private groups and government bureaucracies, see Willetts, 'Interdependence: New Wine in Old Bottles', in J.N. Rosenau and H. Trompe, op. cit.

48. This is one of the most forceful and most effective of the criticisms made by Ashley of Neo-Realism. See Ashley, 'The Poverty of Neo-Realism', pp. 254–7.

49. Gilpin, op. cit., p. 290.

50. The Germans and the Somalis are clearly multi-state nations. The Danes, despite the Faroes and Greenland, and the Norwegians, despite the minorities of Lapps and Finns, dominate their home countries, but also have large communities in the United States. The Portuguese similarly dominate Portugal, but have large overseas communities in the former territories of their empire. No other nations control 'states' in which there are not significant minority communities.

51. It might appear that the logic of the previous criticism of Realism and Structuralism applies here: attributes of elements cannot define a systems structure. While language capacity is an important attribute of political actors, it is also an attribute of the structures themselves. The news agencies AP, UPI and Reuters are global structures working just in English. Ship and airliner captains must be able to speak English and those dealing with travellers usually are competent in English. Radio and TV systems may work in local languages on a local basis, but the major global systems operate in English.

52. This is the common definition accepted by the writers in S. Krasner, *International Regimes*.

53. Statutes of the International Red Cross and Red Crescent Movement, *International Review of the Red Cross*, January–February 1987, Articles 1 and 8, quote from Article 8.

54. Ibid., Article 11. It could be argued that this balance was overthrown when the South African government, but not the South African National Society, was expelled from the International Red Cross.

55. *Statutes and Regulations*, Gland, Switzerland, IUCN, 1985, Article II (1), (17) and (18).

56. For a consideration of IGOs as systems themselves, see P. Willetts, 'The United Nations as a Political System', in P. Taylor and A.J.R. Groom, *International Institutions at Work*, London, Pinter Publishers, 1988.

57. H.K. Jacobson, *Networks of Interdependence. International Organizations and the Global Political System*, New York, Alfred A. Knof, 1979.

J. Kaufman, *United Nations Decision Making*, Alphen aan den Rijn, Sijthoff and Noordhoff, 1980.

W.J. Feld and R.S. Jordan, *International Organizations. A Comparative Approach*, New York, Praeger, 1983.

M.J. Peterson, *The General Assembly in World Politics*, Boston, Allen & Unwin, 1986.

L.S. Finkelstein (ed.), *Politics in the United Nations System,* (Durham, NC, Duke University Press, 1988.

Kaufman is excellent on how governmental delegations work, but is deficient in concentrating almost exclusively on them. For example, he even manages to do a case study on 'The Question of Torture' without mentioning Amnesty International's involvement.

Peterson is the most traditional in his choice of chapter topics and supports the classic Realist view of the UN in pp. 4–5 of his Introduction, but the subsequent pages then implicitly contradict this theoretical position.

There are also now some valuable issue-based studies. See K. Suter, *An International Law of Guerrilla Warfare. The Global Politics of Law Making*, London, Frances Pinter, 1984. A. Chetley, *The Politics of Baby Foods. Successful challenges to an international marketing strategy*, London, Frances Pinter, 1986. K. Kirisci, *The PLO and World Politics. A Study of the Mobilization of Support for the Palestinian Cause*, London, Frances Pinter, 1986. C. Jönsson, *International Aviation and the Politics of Regime Change*, London, Frances Pinter, 1987.

Selected reading

Burton, J.W., *World Society*, Cambridge, Cambridge University Press, 1972.

Hopkins, T.R., I. Wallerstein *et al.*, *World Systems Analysis: theory and methodology*, Beverly Hills, Sage, 1982.

Maghroori, R. and B. Ramberg (eds), *Globalism versus Realism: International Relations' Third Debate*, Boulder, Colo., Westview Press, 1982.

Merritt, R.L. and B.M. Russett (eds), *From National Development to Global Community: Essays in Honor of Karl W. Deutsch*, London, Allen & Unwin, 1981.

Willetts, P. (ed.), *Pressure Groups in the Global System: the Transnational Relations of Issue-Orientated Non-Governmental Organizations*, London, Frances Pinter, 1982.

Index

(Page numbers in italics indicate an article by the author indicated.)